THE BOOK

Other Baseball Books from Potomac Books, Inc.

The Rocket: Baseball Legend Roger Clemens,
Joseph Janczak

Home Run: The Definitive History of Baseball's Ultimate Weapon,
David Vincent

Deadball Stars of the American League,
The Society for American Baseball Research, Edited by David Jones

*Burying the Black Sox: How Baseball's Cover-up of the
1919 World Series Almost Succeeded,*
Gene Carney

Forging Genius: The Making of Casey Stengel,
Steven Goldman

*You Never Forget Your First:
Ballplayers Recall Their Big League Debuts,*
Josh Lewin

THE BOOK
PLAYING THE PERCENTAGES IN BASEBALL

TOM M. TANGO
MITCHEL G. LICHTMAN
ANDREW E. DOLPHIN

Potomac Books, Inc.
Washington, D.C.

Library of Congress Cataloging-in-Publication Data

Tango, Tom M.
  The book : playing the percentages in baseball / Tom M. Tango, Mitchel G. Lichtman, Andrew E. Dolphin.—1st ed.
    p.   cm.
  Includes index.
  ISBN-13: 978-1-59797-129-4 (alk. paper)
    1. Baseball—Statistics.   I. Lichtman, Mitchel G.   II. Dolphin, Andrew E.   III. Title.   IV. Title: Playing the percentages in baseball.

GV877.T36   2007
796.357—dc22

                                                              2007012634

Printed in the United States of America on acid-free paper that meets the American National Standards Institute Z39-48 Standard.

Potomac Books, Inc.
22841 Quicksilver Drive
Dulles, Virginia 20166

First Edition

10   9   8   7   6   5   4   3   2   1

CONTENTS

LIST OF TABLES

FOREWORD

By Pete Palmer

Back in the 1960s, when I started my baseball analysis work, there was virtually no source of play-by-play data of any kind. The data I used which ended up in *The Hidden Game of Baseball* in the 1980s was obtained from the play-by-play accounts of thirty-five World Series games from 1956 to 1960 in the annual Sporting News Baseball Guides. George Lindsey gathered play-by-play data from over 300 games in 1958 and 1959 and published several articles in the *Journal of Operations Research* in the early 1960s analyzing game strategy. Earnshaw Cook's work in the mid-1960s involved strategy and palyer evaluation and was based on simulations. Eldon and Harlan Mills commissioned the Elias Sports Bureau to produce computerized play-by-play data for 1969 and 1970 which was used for their Player Win Average calculations, a new player evaluation method. They did not tackle strategy. Unfortunately, they were ahead of their time, and their work did not catch on.

Now there are a great many play-by-play databases that are available to everyone. The whole process was kicked off by Bill James, because he had trouble getting data for his annual *Baseball Abstracts* in the late 1970s. Bill's multitude of readers were encouraged to team up to gather and share data by scoring games at the ballpark or from radio and TV game broadcasts. This developed into Project Scoresheet in 1984.

Gary Gillette has kept the effort going until this day, first with Project Scoresheet through 1990, then with his Baseball Workshop through

1996, and now with 24–7 Baseball. Meanwhile, Dave Smith (who had helped tremendously with the last few years of Project Scoresheet) got into the act with Retrosheet in 1989. Retrosheet started to collect pre-1984 games and now has posted almost every game back to 1960 on its website at www.retrosheet.org. Gary provided 1984–1990 games to Retrosheet from the Project's files after its demise, as well as making available raw game stats for 1991–1998, which were the basis for the Retrosheet game logs. Dave later obtained 1991–1992 play-by-plays from STATS Inc. Retrosheet recently has also been publishing current seasons, which are now available back to 2000.

So now between Dave and Gary and the hundreds of volunteers who have contributed to Project Scoresheet and Retrosheet, we have over 45 years of games available for analysis. Dave is busy collecting games back to 1900 (and earlier), and already has hundreds of games from almost every season in the past century.

This vast source of data has permitted very detailed analysis of strategy, which Tom, Mitchel, and Andy have used to its fullest. Their analysis of the sacrifice bunt, stolen base, intentional walk, and pitchout are more thorough than any I have seen. Construction of the lineup, including platooning, and the use of starting and relief pitchers provide some fascinating results as well. There are no simple answers to the questions of strategy, but the information presented herein would be helpful for anyone actually charged with making strategic decisions, as well as being interesting to the average fan who likes to delve into these matters.

PREFACE

The biggest player on the field makes the slow walk from the on-deck circle to the batter's box. The left fielder shouts out something, and the pitcher turns around. Four fingers. The left fielder, who also happens to be the coach of the team, is holding out four fingers. Half of the players on the fielding team have their mouths agape, and the other half nod approvingly. There's a man on second base and one out, after all. The inning ends with three runs scoring, including the batter who was intentionally walked.

The left fielder/coach strides into the dugout, content he did the right thing. Then it starts.

"Why did you want me to walk him?"

"I was playing the percentages. He was their best hitter, by far, we had first base open, and one out."

"But . . . ," the reply starts.

"It's what *The Book* says." Well, that ends that debate, and just about every debate on this topic, ever. Once you call out the words *The Book*, that's it. It's gospel.

I was only the second baseman, and 19 years old at the time. What did I know? Apparently, the preachers of *The Book* were taught in the same manner that teenagers learn all about sex education. *The Book*, whether baseball or sex, is handed down generation to generation through the wisdom and experience of those more learned. It doesn't matter if any of these preachers knew anything about the topic. As long as they can claim one success somewhere, that was enough. *The Book*, the unwritten rules created by generation after generation of baseball followers, was gospel. The preachers did not have to quantify and qualify their reasonings, unlike every other multi-million-dollar corporation in the world.

What you are about to read is an attempt to quantify or qualify the ideal strategies in baseball. Each chapter will tackle a particular topic, and ask several very specific questions. We will use empirical data from recent MLB seasons to answer them. While we will not always have all the answers, we will at least have enough answers to make the followers better equipped to answer their own specific questions.

The unwritten Book is about to be written.

CHAPTER 1 – TOOLSHED

If you've ever read Tom Clancy or Stephen King, you know that they sometimes go into very specific technical and psychological details. You could easily skip those paragraphs and not miss a beat with the whole book. But, by reading those details, you gain an extra level of appreciation.

There are several major tools that we will be using throughout this book. In this chapter, we will introduce and describe them as completely as possible, as well as explain how they all relate to each other. Since these tools are used in some shape or form throughout the book, we find it more convenient for us (and perhaps more palatable for you) to dump/explore them here.

As with the King and Clancy novels, feel free to skip this chapter in its entirety if the technical presentation does not appeal to you.

Base/Out States

Everything about baseball (for that matter, everything about anything) is about context. All actions, events, data, and information are meaningless without context. And we don't mean meaningless in some theoretical sense, but in an actual, practical sense. Consider these words that you are reading right now. The primary context is the English language. You can expand that context to include the subject matter, baseball. Without understanding English and baseball, the words on this page and throughout the book would be gibberish to the reader.

So how do you describe baseball? For starters, a baseball game consists of nine (or more) innings, each of which is more or less equivalent in terms of what can happen. So we can think of the inning as the fundamental building block of the game. What contexts do we find within an inning? The most important is that you have three outs per inning. The second-most important is that you have three bases at which players can rest between batters on the way to scoring by touching a fourth base (home plate), and that each base will either be occupied or open. So combining these two contexts, you can have one out and men on first and second, two outs and a man on third, or any other combination of number of outs and occupied bases. The total number of potential combinations that you can have is exactly 24.

We refer to these 24 combinations as *base/out states*. These give us the context with which we can understand the events that unfold during an inning.

The inning always starts with the same initial base/out state: bases empty and no outs. The inning always ends when a team accumulates three outs. We can think of this as a 25th base/out state, though it differs from the other 24 because nothing can happen once this three-out state is reached.

From the start of the inning to the end of the inning, you will transition from base/out state to base/out state as the events unfold—hits, outs, baserunning, and so on. Along the way, you can pile up runs until you reach that final state (end of inning).

Run Expectancy

On average, when a team starts an inning, it will score about .555 runs before the inning ends. We know this because, from 1999 through 2002, major league teams scored an average of just under five runs per nine innings, or .555 runs per inning. We also know that a team beginning an inning is in a base/out state of bases empty with no outs. Therefore, that particular base/out state is worth .555 runs. Just by being in that base/out state, the hitting team has an expectation of scoring .555 runs to the end of the inning.

Technical note: We excluded from this analysis any home halves of the ninth or later innings, and any other partial innings. The reason is one of context. Once the home team has won the game, the inning ends immediately instead of continuing to the normal three-out state. So it's fairly obvious that we cannot include the partial innings, since they were abruptly ended. However, we also cannot include the home halves that did go to three outs. If the home team was batting in the ninth and didn't tie or win, we know they didn't score a lot of runs, while the fact that the inning ended without three outs means that runs were scored. And we can't include those halves of the ninth innings where the batting team went to three outs but didn't score a lot of runs, but exclude those halves in which the team didn't get to three outs and did score a lot of runs. The best thing to do is to exclude this situation altogether. The overall impact is tiny, in any case. However, it is more technically correct.

Back to the topic at hand. What happens when the leadoff batter reaches first base? The average number of runs scored from the moment the batter reaches first base with no outs to the end of the inning is about 0.953 runs.

How do we know that? In this case, it requires a little more work. From 1999 through 2002, teams had a man on first with no outs 44,552 times. And teams in that state scored a total of 42,432 runs until the end of the inning. So the average number of runs scored by a team in this particular base/out state is 42,432 divided by 44,552, or .953.

Now, we just had a transition from bases empty and no outs, to man on first and no outs. The run value for the starting base/out state is .555 runs. The run value for the next base/out state is .953. So by making this transition, the expected number of runs increased by .398 runs. The *trigger* for the change in states was the event itself. So, the event that causes the base/out state to go from bases empty and no outs, to man on first and no outs is worth .398 runs. It doesn't matter if it was a single, walk, hit batter, or error. It was worth .398 runs. (Again, all of this is based on major league averages; we will discuss the effects of high- or low-scoring environments later.)

Using the type of calculation we used to determine the .953 above, we can go through the 24 base/out states and figure out the average number of runs scored from each. Here are these numbers, which we refer to as *run expectancies* (or *RE*). (See Table 1.)

Table 1.   Run Expectancy, By The 24 Base/Out States, 1999–2002

1B	2B	3B	0 Outs	1 Out	2 Outs
--	--	--	0.555	0.297	0.117
1B	--	--	0.953	0.573	0.251
--	2B	--	1.189	0.725	0.344
--	--	3B	1.482	0.983	0.387
1B	2B	--	1.573	0.971	0.466
1B	--	3B	1.904	1.243	0.538
--	2B	3B	2.052	1.467	0.634
1B	2B	3B	2.417	1.650	0.815

Pete Palmer produced a similar chart, but based on a different run environment, in his classic book, *The Hidden Game of Baseball*, which we recommend you pick up at your local library or favorite online store.

Do you want to know how many runs scored, on average, with men on second and third and one out? 1.467. Would you prefer to have a man on first and no outs, or a man on second and one out? From this table, it's an easy answer. Remember, though, that these are runs scored in typical situations—average hitters, average pitching, average fielders, etc. And while more runs generally means more wins, it isn't always the case. We'll discuss these caveats later.

Run Values

While we will use base/out states, transitions, and run expectancies as the basis for most of our analysis, we don't always have easy access to initial and final base/out states for all of a player's plate appearances during the course of a season. Instead, we know the total number of appearances, and what happened in those appearances—how many singles, doubles, etc., the player had.

To convert this sort of information into a player's run value, what we need to do is determine the average number of runs created by each type of event (single, double, etc.). This also has the advantage of giving us a more context-neutral value of a player—in other words, a player is valued based on his own performance, rather than whether or not his teammates managed to get on base and set the table for him. (See Table 2.)

Table 2.   Runs To End Of Inning, By Event

Event		N	Runs to End of Inning	Average Runs
Home Run	HR	21026	40838	1.942
Triple	3B	3644	5887	1.616
Double	2B	34121	44728	1.311
Error	RBOE	7323	8286	1.132
Interference	INT	60	65	1.083
Sac Bunt	SAC	7878	8121	1.031
Passed Ball	PB	1176	1206	1.026
Single	1B	110538	113308	1.025
Wild Pitch	WP	5358	5357	1.000
Hit by Pitch	HBP	6559	6354	0.969
Balk	BK	624	592	0.949
Non-intentional Walk	NIBB	60572	51432	0.849
Intentional Walk	IBB	4626	3910	0.845
Stolen Base	SB	10597	8388	0.792
Defensive Indifference	DI	418	217	0.519
Bunt	BUNT	2892	1392	0.481
Pickoff	PK	2269	944	0.416
Out (on Batted Ball)	OUT	345580	82787	0.240
Strikeout	K	120275	24909	0.207
Caught Stealing	CS	3741	614	0.164

These are all the types of events in baseball, along with how often they occurred and how many runs were scored from the instant before that event occurred to the end of the inning. For example, there were 21,026 HR in the years in our data. From the time the HR was hit, to the end of the inning, 40,838 runs scored, for an average of 1.942 runs scored by team per HR hit by player. Now, go to the bottom of the chart. Once an out is recorded on a hit ball, you can expect to score .240 runs to the end of the inning.

Look more closely at the chart, and specifically at the Sac Bunt, with an average of 1.031 runs, and the regular Bunt (.481 runs). How is that possible? A sac bunt is almost always followed by an out, while a regular bunt will often get the batter on base. So, how is it possible that a team will score more runs to the end of the inning, starting with a sac bunt, rather than starting with a regular bunt? The reason is the context. With a regular bunt, you usually have the bases empty. On the other hand, the sac bunt, by definition, requires at least one runner on base. The starting base/out state already has a higher run expectancy when the sac bunt is called, than when a regular bunt is executed. An important note is that we've defined the sac bunt here as a bunt with a sacrifice situation in effect (man on base, and less than two outs). A regular bunt is all other situations. A quick glance at the run expectancy table shows that base/out states we define as sac bunt situations have higher run values than base/out states we define as regular bunt situations, and therefore it follows that the number of runs expected *following* the sac bunt attempt is also higher.

So, to account for the contexts in which events happen, let's add another column to the table, which will show the average starting run expectancy of each event type. (See Table 3.)

The overall starting RE is .546, averaged over all event types. Look at the HR, 3B, 2B, 1B, NIBB (non-intentional walk), and Out: they all have a starting RE of between .52 and .56. This implies that these events occur rather randomly across the 24 base/out states. Now, let's go back to our bunts. The starting RE for the regular bunt is .409, which implies that the bunt is attempted when the run potential is lower than normal (late in the inning, or no men on base). But, the starting RE of the sac bunt is 1.058, which is the highest of any event. In this case, the sac bunt is attempted when the run potential is much higher than normal (early in the inning and with men on base).

Table 3.   Runs To End Of Inning, By Event (Part 2)

Event	N	Runs to End of Inning	Average	Starting RE
Home Run	21026	40838	1.942	0.533
Triple	3644	5887	1.616	0.553
Double	34121	44728	1.311	0.547
Error	7323	8286	1.132	0.586
Interference	60	65	1.083	0.655
Sac Bunt	7878	8121	1.031	1.058
Passed Ball	1176	1206	1.026	0.741
Single	110538	113308	1.025	0.551
Wild Pitch	5358	5357	1.000	0.716
Hit by Pitch	6559	6354	0.969	0.584
Balk	624	592	0.949	0.712
Non-intentional Walk	60572	51432	0.849	0.520
Intentional Walk	4626	3910	0.845	0.743
Stolen Base	10597	8388	0.792	0.597
Defensive Indifference	418	217	0.519	0.456
Bunt	2892	1392	0.481	0.409
Pickoff	2269	944	0.416	0.672
Out	345580	82787	0.240	0.538
Strikeout	120275	24909	0.207	0.517
Caught Stealing	3741	614	0.164	0.620

Compare the regular walk to the intentional walk: the number of runs scored from the point either walk was issued is .85 runs for either type of walk. But, isn't the point of the IBB to face a batter of lesser quality (or set up the double play). Shouldn't there be fewer runs scored to the end of the inning? Again, we have the same situation: the starting run expectancy for the regular walk was .520 (slightly below the random .546, implying that regular walks are issued slightly more often with two outs or with no men on base) but was a whopping .743 for the IBB.

Since we realize that the IBB is issued usually with two outs, there are not only runners in scoring position, but the runs to end of inning leads us to believe that we also have worse batters coming up to bat.

Thus, it is not only important to look at how many runs the team scores from the moment the event happens, but to also look at how many runs the team was expected to score based on the base/out context when the event occurred.

Let's add yet another column to our table: the run value of the event, which equals the difference between the runs to the end of the inning and the starting RE. (See Table 4.)

Table 4.   Runs To End Of Inning, By Event (Part 3)

Event	N	Runs to End of Inning	Average	Starting RE	Run Value
Home Run	21026	40838	1.942	0.533	1.409
Triple	3644	5887	1.616	0.553	1.063
Double	34121	44728	1.311	0.547	0.764
Error	7323	8286	1.132	0.586	0.546
Single	110538	113308	1.025	0.551	0.474
Interference	60	65	1.083	0.655	0.429
Hit by Pitch	6559	6354	0.969	0.584	0.385
Non-intentional Walk	60572	51432	0.849	0.520	0.330
Passed Ball	1176	1206	1.026	0.741	0.285
Wild Pitch	5358	5357	1.000	0.716	0.284
Balk	624	592	0.949	0.712	0.237
Stolen Base	10597	8388	0.792	0.597	0.195
Intentional Walk	4626	3910	0.845	0.743	0.102
Bunt	2892	1392	0.481	0.409	0.072
Defensive Indifference	418	217	0.519	0.456	0.063
Sac Bunt	7878	8121	1.031	1.058	-0.027
Pickoff	2269	944	0.416	0.672	-0.256
Out	345580	82787	0.240	0.538	-0.299
Strikeout	120275	24909	0.207	0.517	-0.310
Caught Stealing	3741	614	0.164	0.620	-0.456

The table has been re-sorted based on the *run value* column. The average HR adds about 1.41 runs to the inning, relative to how the average player would perform. The average *out* subtracts .30 runs relative to average.

Come again? Negative runs? How is that possible? Let's try to make a distinction between total absolute runs, and runs relative to some fixed scale. The run values presented above are the run values relative to the average player. As we see above in the *out* line, in this typical situation, the average team will score .538 runs to the end of the inning. However, in the situations when an out does occur, the average team will score .240 runs to the end of the inning (as we discussed from the earlier chart). That's .240 total and absolute runs. But, that's a far cry from what was expected before the out was recorded. Before the out, we expected the average team to score almost .54 runs. The player who got the out dropped the run expectancy for the inning by .30 runs. That's what we are talking about here. This is the cost of the out.

Run Values by State/Transition

Just for fun, let's break down the line for the HR, in the last table presented, into the 24 base/out states from which the HR occurred. Here is how those 21,026 HR break down. (See Table 5.) In the table, we use *REOI* as an abbreviation for *runs to end of inning*.

These are the value-added runs that a HR creates from each of the 24 base/out states, from 1999 through 2002. To read the first line: there were 5,518 home runs hit with the bases empty and no outs. From the moment that batter stepped to the plate to the end of the inning, 8,779 runs scored. That gives you an average of 1.591 runs scored to the end of the inning following a HR with the bases empty and no outs (and including the run that was scored by the HR). We've already established from the first RE chart that the average team, with an average batter, will score 0.555 runs in that situation. The difference is 1.036 runs.

Table 5.   Runs To End Of Inning, By Base/Out State, For HR

1B	2B	3B	outs	HR	REOI	Avg REOI	Start RE	Run Value
--	--	--	0	5518	8779	1.591	0.555	1.036
--	--	--	1	3498	4528	1.294	0.297	0.997
--	--	--	2	3023	3382	1.119	0.117	1.002
1B	--	--	0	1195	3137	2.625	0.953	1.672
1B	--	--	1	1401	3213	2.293	0.573	1.721
1B	--	--	2	1394	2957	2.121	0.251	1.870
--	2B	--	0	292	728	2.493	1.189	1.304
--	2B	--	1	535	1243	2.323	0.725	1.599
--	2B	--	2	661	1395	2.110	0.344	1.766
--	--	3B	0	42	106	2.524	1.482	1.042
--	--	3B	1	193	440	2.280	0.983	1.296
--	--	3B	2	273	583	2.136	0.387	1.748
1B	2B	--	0	305	1042	3.416	1.573	1.844
1B	2B	--	1	544	1826	3.357	0.971	2.385
1B	2B	--	2	588	1831	3.114	0.466	2.648
1B	--	3B	0	120	426	3.550	1.904	1.646
1B	--	3B	1	230	760	3.304	1.243	2.062
1B	--	3B	2	312	981	3.144	0.538	2.607
--	2B	3B	0	59	210	3.559	2.052	1.508
--	2B	3B	1	133	438	3.293	1.467	1.826
--	2B	3B	2	155	491	3.168	0.634	2.534
1B	2B	3B	0	78	354	4.538	2.417	2.122
1B	2B	3B	1	230	969	4.213	1.650	2.563
1B	2B	3B	2	247	1019	4.126	0.815	3.311

Wait a minute! 1.036? Why is it not exactly one run? Didn't the HR leave us in the same state (bases empty, no outs) that we began in, with the addition of one run? We have to remember what we are looking at here. We are looking at a sample of performances of one group of players (teams with guys who hit HR with the bases empty and no outs), and we are comparing them to the different sample of performance of a different group of players (all teams). There's nothing to say that the first group is exactly the same as the second. And, they aren't. As you can see, even with over 5,000 home runs, the random differences between these two samples cause errors of a few hundredths of a run in our calculations.

Check out the situation with a runner on third and no outs. The run value of the HR here is 1.042 runs, which is virtually the same value as with no one on base. But notice that this happened only 42 times. This is a very small sample size, and we clearly cannot put much faith in conclusions drawn from 42 instances.

What would be a better way to figure out the run value of the HR? Instead of figuring out how many runs are scored to the end of the inning, let's compare the run values of the starting and ending states, and award the difference between those values to the event that caused the transition, in this case the HR. And, of course, any runs that actually scored during the event need to be added in as well.

Let's again use the home run as our example. Start the inning with the base/out state of bases empty, no outs, and have the trigger be a home run. So the starting run value is the run expectancy of the bases empty, no out state: .555 runs. What's the ending base/out state? Bases empty, no outs, with a run having scored. The ending run value is thus the run expectancy of the bases empty, no out state, plus one for the run that scored. The total ending run value is 1.555 runs. The difference between the ending run value (1.555) and the starting run value (.555) is exactly one run. We should have been able to figure that out by ourselves anyway.

How about if the bases were loaded with two outs? In that case, we expected an average of .815 runs to score to the end of the inning. After the HR, we get four runs scored, plus you are now at an ending state of bases empty, two outs, which has a run value of .117 runs. So the total ending run value is 4.117, compared with the starting run value of .815. The difference in run values between the two states is 3.302 runs, and this value is assigned to the event (the HR) that triggered the change of states.

We are guessing there are at least a couple of doubters there. Why is a grand slam not worth exactly four runs? Because we expected some of these runners to score with an average batter. Specifically, we expected

.815 runs to score. The extra value provided by the HR, above and beyond what an average batter would have provided, was 3.302. OK, then, why give the whole credit to the HR? We aren't. Having three guys on base with two outs is worth .815 runs. That's the credit we are giving to the events that left us in this situation.

Table 6.   Run Value Of HR, By Base/Out State

1B	2B	3B	Outs	HR	Original	Starting RE	Ending RE	Run Value
--	--	--	0	5518	1.036	0.555	1.555	1.000
--	--	--	1	3498	0.997	0.297	1.297	1.000
--	--	--	2	3023	1.002	0.117	1.117	1.000
1B	--	--	0	1195	1.672	0.953	2.555	1.602
1B	--	--	1	1401	1.721	0.573	2.297	1.725
1B	--	--	2	1394	1.870	0.251	2.117	1.865
--	2B	--	0	292	1.304	1.189	2.555	1.367
--	2B	--	1	535	1.599	0.725	2.297	1.573
--	2B	--	2	661	1.766	0.344	2.117	1.772
--	--	3B	0	42	1.042	1.482	2.555	1.073
--	--	3B	1	193	1.296	0.983	2.297	1.314
--	--	3B	2	273	1.748	0.387	2.117	1.729
1B	2B	--	0	305	1.844	1.573	3.555	1.983
1B	2B	--	1	544	2.385	0.971	3.297	2.326
1B	2B	--	2	588	2.648	0.466	3.117	2.651
1B	--	3B	0	120	1.646	1.904	3.555	1.651
1B	--	3B	1	230	2.062	1.243	3.297	2.054
1B	--	3B	2	312	2.607	0.538	3.117	2.579
--	2B	3B	0	59	1.508	2.052	3.555	1.504
--	2B	3B	1	133	1.826	1.467	3.297	1.830
--	2B	3B	2	155	2.534	0.634	3.117	2.483
1B	2B	3B	0	78	2.122	2.417	4.555	2.139
1B	2B	3B	1	230	2.563	1.650	4.297	2.647
1B	2B	3B	2	247	3.311	0.815	4.117	3.302

Any change in state is given to the event that causes the change in state. The average batter, seeing three guys on base with two outs, will have an added value of *exactly* zero runs. Zero; not more, and not less.

The average batter is not worth nothing, but he's worth nothing more or less than . . . average. Sometimes, four runs will score. Many times the batter will make the third out. Overall, the number of runs he adds by his hits and walks will be exactly offset by the potential runs his third out prevents from scoring. In this case, when he hits a HR, he has added 3.302 runs above what an average batter would have produced.

To figure out the overall run value of the average HR, you take the weighted average of the run values for each of the 24 states. Here is Table 5, but modified to follow the state/transition process we just discussed. (See Table 6.) The *original* column gives the run values from our earlier table (the one with the bases empty and a no out HR being worth 1.036 runs).

Table 7.   Run Values By Event

Event	Run Value
Home Run	1.397
Triple	1.070
Double	0.776
Error	0.508
Single	0.475
Interference	0.392
Hit by Pitch	0.352
Non-intentional Walk	0.323
Passed Ball	0.269
Wild Pitch	0.266
Balk	0.264
Intentional Walk	0.179
Stolen Base	0.175
Defensive Indifference	0.120
Bunt	0.042
Sac Bunt	-0.096
Pickoff	-0.281
Out	-0.299
Strikeout	-0.301
Caught Stealing	-0.467

That makes a lot more sense. The run value of the HR with the bases empty (with any number of outs) is exactly one run. If you take the weighted average of all the above run values for the HR, the average run value for the HR is 1.397 runs.

Repeating this process for all events, here are the average run values. (See Table 7.) Anyone who has read *The Hidden Game* is not surprised at all with the numbers in the table. Some of these situational-dependent events (sac bunt, stolen base, intentional walk) deserve their own chapters, in which we'll give them in-depth analyses.

Weighted On Base Average or wOBA

On-base percentage is a great statistic because it tells you something important, and in a clear language: at what rate did this player reach base? It doesn't tell you how far he reached base (second base? third? home?), but only whether he did or did not.

Slugging percentage is another great statistic because it tells you something important, and in a clear language: how many bases did the batter gain for himself per at-bat? It doesn't consider walks as either a positive or negative event (it simply strips them away as if they don't exist). It also tries to establish the importance of the single and HR by weighting the HR four times as much as the single.

We have one statistic that is deficient in one area, and another one that is deficient in another. Why not simply combine them as: OBP plus that is deficient in another. Why not simply combine them as OBP plus SLG and call it this new-age statistic named OPS? Might this statistic see.

From the preceding section we know the run values of each event. For example, we know that the run value of the HR is 1.4 runs above average, and 1.7 runs above the run value of the out. In rate measures, like OBP, the value of the out in the numerator is zero. If we recast the run values of the most common events relative to the out (rather than relative to the result of an average plate appearance), we get the following:

HR 1.70, 3B 1.37, 2B 1.08, 1B 0.77, NIBB 0.62.

Those numbers are the values of each of our events (again, relative to an out, which now has a value of zero). If we apply these weights to the statistics of a league-average hitter, and divide by plate appearances, we end up with a rate of almost .300. This is a fairly convenient number for an average, but we can do better. Since we like OBP as a measure of a batter's effectiveness, let's scale our new statistic so that the resulting values are similar to OBP values. It turns out that, if we add 15% to this .300 figure, we get the league-average OBP. Therefore, we will add 15% to the weights of each event and define our new statistic as follows:

$$wOBA = \frac{.72 \times NIBB + .75 \times HBP + .90 \times 1B + .92 \times RBOE + 1.24 \times 2B + 1.56 \times 3B + 1.95 \times HR}{PA}$$

Note: Depending on the specific analysis, the PA term (plate appearances) may exclude bunts, IBB, and a few of the more obscure plays.

Do we really need another statistic? Yes, we do. Instead of trying to take two statistics (OBP, SLG) and combine and correct their flaws in the hopes of getting one number, we prefer to start from scratch. Furthermore, by recasting the number onto the OBP scale, it makes it much easier for the reader to get a grasp on the number. wOBA is weighted on-base average (we call it an average rather than a percentage). When you look at wOBA numbers throughout the book, just think OBP, and you'll be fine. In other words, an average hitter is around .340 or so, a great hitter is .400 or higher, and a poor hitter would be under .300.

If you are a little more experienced with run values, you might have figured out the following:

$$\text{Run value per PA above average} = \frac{wOBA \text{ for player} - wOBA \text{ for league}}{1.15}$$

So the run value chart, which we presented in the previous section, and the wOBA statistic defined in this section are directly related.

OPS Interlude

And, for you OPS lovers, you will note that $(OBP \times 2 + SLG) / 3$ is a close approximation of wOBA. The walk appears in OBP but not SLG, so that's two plus zero divided by three, or .67. The HR would be two plus four divided by three, or 2.00. The single works out to 1.00, the double at 1.33, and the triple as 1.67. All pretty close. You can't make the calculation as simple as we have because the denominator in OBP is plate appearances and the denominator in SLG is at bats. But, OPS, or even the more correct 2OPS, is not concerned with precisely representing batting contributions, but rather simply being a decent approximation. This is the last we will talk about OPS.

Markov Chains

State-to-state transitions are very powerful tools. As long as we are not concerned with how we entered the current state, then we can use a powerful mathematical technique called Markov chains.

Recall our calculation of home run values. Suppose you start with the bases empty and no outs, and a HR was hit. You have now re-entered the same state (along with piling up one run). Do we need to figure out how many runs scored to the end of the inning in only those cases where the HR was hit, and thereby establish that it was important that the second bases empty, no-out state was entered via the HR? Or, are we content that the bases empty, no-out state following the home run is the same as the bases empty, no-out state we had before the home run? For that matter, had the batter hit a triple and scored on an error (thereby re-entering the bases empty, no-outs state), shouldn't this give us the same run expectation to the end of the inning?

Markov chains use the premise that the sequence of events prior to entering any state is unimportant. All that matters is what state you are in, what potential states you can transition into, and the likelihood of each of those possible transitions. Each base/out state can lead to another and then to another until reaching the three-out state. What you end up with is a huge grid of all possibilities of state-to-state transitions. Following this process, we can determine the exact distribution of total runs scored from any base/out state to the end of the inning. (See Table 8.)

Table 8.   Scoring Distribution, By Base/Out State, For 5.0 Runs/Game

1B	2B	3B	outs	RE	0	1	2	3	4	5+
--	--	--	0	0.555	70.2%	15.7%	7.5%	3.6%	1.7%	1.3%
--	--	--	1	0.297	82.4%	10.4%	4.3%	1.8%	0.7%	0.5%
--	--	--	2	0.116	92.2%	5.3%	1.7%	0.6%	0.2%	0.1%
1B	--	--	0	0.950	55.7%	17.9%	13.2%	6.9%	3.4%	2.8%
1B	--	--	1	0.567	71.3%	12.5%	9.3%	4.0%	1.7%	1.2%
1B	--	--	2	0.244	86.5%	6.3%	5.0%	1.6%	0.5%	0.3%
--	2B	--	0	1.192	36.7%	34.2%	14.6%	7.7%	3.8%	3.1%
--	2B	--	1	0.723	58.6%	23.7%	9.9%	4.6%	1.9%	1.3%
--	2B	--	2	0.343	77.4%	15.0%	4.9%	1.8%	0.6%	0.3%
--	--	3B	0	1.445	14.1%	55.2%	15.5%	8.1%	3.9%	3.2%
--	--	3B	1	0.999	33.0%	48.2%	10.5%	4.9%	2.1%	1.4%
--	--	3B	2	0.387	73.2%	19.1%	4.8%	1.9%	0.6%	0.3%
1B	2B	--	0	1.585	35.3%	22.0%	16.2%	13.1%	7.0%	6.3%
1B	2B	--	1	0.982	56.6%	16.3%	11.1%	9.1%	4.1%	2.8%
1B	2B	--	2	0.459	76.7%	10.9%	5.6%	4.6%	1.5%	0.7%
1B	--	3B	0	1.865	12.5%	42.3%	17.6%	13.7%	7.3%	6.7%
1B	--	3B	1	1.249	33.6%	37.3%	12.4%	9.4%	4.3%	3.1%
1B	--	3B	2	0.542	70.9%	15.2%	6.5%	5.0%	1.7%	0.8%
--	2B	3B	0	2.075	13.3%	25.9%	30.1%	14.9%	8.4%	7.4%
--	2B	3B	1	1.451	30.2%	28.5%	22.4%	9.9%	5.3%	3.7%
--	2B	3B	2	0.624	72.1%	5.5%	14.7%	4.8%	2.0%	0.9%
1B	2B	3B	0	2.437	12.5%	24.9%	20.8%	15.1%	13.3%	13.5%
1B	2B	3B	1	1.671	31.8%	25.3%	15.5%	10.7%	9.7%	7.0%
1B	2B	3B	2	0.798	67.0%	9.4%	10.7%	5.7%	4.9%	2.2%

The first line reads: with the bases empty and no outs, 70.2% of the time zero runs will score to the end of the inning. If you go to the bottom of the chart, with the bases loaded and two outs, exactly one run will score 9.4% of the time from that base/out state to the end of the inning. The RE column is the average number of runs that will score. You can compare the similarity of these mathematically-derived values to the earlier empirically-based run expectancy chart. (See Table 1.)

Table 9.   Scoring Distribution, By Base/Out State, For 3.2 Runs/Game

1B	2B	3B	outs	RE	0	1	2	3	4	5+
--	--	--	0	0.356	78.5%	13.0%	5.2%	2.1%	0.8%	0.5%
--	--	--	1	0.182	88.1%	7.8%	2.7%	0.9%	0.3%	0.1%
--	--	--	2	0.066	95.2%	3.6%	0.9%	0.3%	0.1%	0.0%
1B	--	--	0	0.704	62.6%	18.1%	11.1%	4.9%	2.1%	1.3%
1B	--	--	1	0.408	76.7%	12.1%	7.1%	2.6%	1.0%	0.5%
1B	--	--	2	0.167	89.6%	5.8%	3.4%	0.9%	0.2%	0.1%
--	2B	--	0	0.936	42.7%	35.8%	12.4%	5.4%	2.2%	1.4%
--	2B	--	1	0.550	63.8%	24.0%	7.7%	2.9%	1.0%	0.5%
--	2B	--	2	0.262	80.6%	14.6%	3.4%	1.0%	0.3%	0.1%
--	--	3B	0	1.205	17.9%	59.3%	13.3%	5.7%	2.3%	1.4%
--	--	3B	1	0.825	37.9%	49.0%	8.2%	3.2%	1.1%	0.6%
--	--	3B	2	0.304	76.4%	18.7%	3.4%	1.1%	0.3%	0.1%
1B	2B	--	0	1.271	41.7%	22.8%	16.2%	11.0%	5.0%	3.4%
1B	2B	--	1	0.766	62.2%	16.2%	10.6%	7.0%	2.6%	1.4%
1B	2B	--	2	0.350	80.3%	10.4%	5.1%	3.1%	0.9%	0.3%
1B	--	3B	0	1.586	15.5%	46.1%	17.7%	11.7%	5.3%	3.7%
1B	--	3B	1	1.045	37.6%	38.7%	11.9%	7.4%	2.8%	1.6%
1B	--	3B	2	0.427	74.4%	15.0%	5.9%	3.4%	0.9%	0.4%
--	2B	3B	0	1.775	17.1%	28.1%	31.8%	12.9%	6.0%	4.1%
--	2B	3B	1	1.229	35.4%	28.3%	22.8%	8.1%	3.5%	1.9%
--	2B	3B	2	0.504	76.0%	4.8%	14.2%	3.5%	1.2%	0.4%
1B	2B	3B	0	2.084	16.4%	27.4%	21.7%	14.8%	11.2%	8.5%
1B	2B	3B	1	1.400	37.2%	25.3%	15.6%	10.3%	7.5%	4.1%
1B	2B	3B	2	0.631	72.6%	7.5%	10.2%	5.2%	3.4%	1.2%

You might be wondering why we are going through all this effort. Didn't we already show the expected number of runs to be scored from each state? The power of Markov chains is that now you can start tweaking your inputs. For example, instead of the average pitcher, you can input Mariano Rivera and get a chart that tells you how often Rivera gives up two or more runs with a man on second and one out. Here's that chart. (See Table 9.)

To be more precise, this chart shows the run distribution of a pitcher or team that averages 3.2 runs per nine innings. We saw in the previous chart that a pitcher or team averaging five runs per nine innings would be scoreless 70.2% of all innings, when starting with the bases empty and no outs. The corresponding figure for the 3.2 runs per nine innings pitcher would be 78.5%.

Win Expectancy

Now that we know the run distribution for any single inning at each base/out state, we can expand that run distribution to two, three, or even nine innings. Not only that, we can do this for both teams. At this point, we've got the run distribution from any point in the game to the end of the game for each team. Once you know that, you then simply apply basic probability theory, and you end up with a win expectancy matrix. That is, for any game state (half-inning, score difference, base, out), we can establish the probability of winning the game.

You can further expand this idea to also include the count, the opponent, the park, and your teammates. Context. Establish the exact context, and we can tell you the exact win probability. This book is not big enough to handle all the possible permutations of context. (Actually, no book is big enough to handle all possible permutations.) We will limit publishing the charts for two teams that are exactly average major league teams. On the following nine pages, you will find those long-sought-after charts. (See Table 10.) Note that the score difference and win percentages are always from the viewpoint of the home team.

Table 10.   Win Expectancy, By Game State

Inning: 1, Top

1B	2B	3B	Out	-4	-3	-2	-1	Tie	1	2	3	4
--	--	--	0	0.182	0.246	0.322	0.409	0.500	---	---	---	---
--	--	--	1	0.194	0.261	0.341	0.430	0.524	---	---	---	---
--	--	--	2	0.202	0.272	0.354	0.445	0.540	---	---	---	---
1B	--	--	0	0.165	0.224	0.296	0.377	0.466	---	---	---	---
1B	--	--	1	0.181	0.245	0.322	0.408	0.500	---	---	---	---
1B	--	--	2	0.196	0.264	0.345	0.434	0.529	---	---	---	---
--	2B	--	0	0.152	0.208	0.276	0.356	0.444	---	---	---	---
--	2B	--	1	0.173	0.235	0.309	0.394	0.485	---	---	---	---
--	2B	--	2	0.191	0.257	0.337	0.425	0.519	---	---	---	---
--	--	3B	0	0.139	0.191	0.256	0.333	0.420	---	---	---	---
--	--	3B	1	0.158	0.216	0.286	0.369	0.459	---	---	---	---
--	--	3B	2	0.188	0.254	0.333	0.421	0.515	---	---	---	---
1B	2B	--	0	0.139	0.191	0.255	0.329	0.413	---	---	---	---
1B	2B	--	1	0.164	0.223	0.294	0.375	0.464	---	---	---	---
1B	2B	--	2	0.186	0.251	0.329	0.417	0.509	---	---	---	---
1B	--	3B	0	0.125	0.172	0.232	0.305	0.386	---	---	---	---
1B	--	3B	1	0.150	0.205	0.272	0.351	0.439	---	---	---	---
1B	--	3B	2	0.182	0.246	0.323	0.409	0.502	---	---	---	---
--	2B	3B	0	0.116	0.162	0.219	0.288	0.368	---	---	---	---
--	2B	3B	1	0.141	0.194	0.259	0.335	0.421	---	---	---	---
--	2B	3B	2	0.179	0.242	0.318	0.403	0.494	---	---	---	---
1B	2B	3B	0	0.108	0.149	0.203	0.268	0.343	---	---	---	---
1B	2B	3B	1	0.136	0.186	0.249	0.323	0.405	---	---	---	---
1B	2B	3B	2	0.173	0.234	0.307	0.390	0.480	---	---	---	---

Inning: 1, Bottom

1B	2B	3B	Out	-4	-3	-2	-1	Tie	1	2	3	4
--	--	--	0	0.208	0.279	0.363	0.455	0.551	0.644	0.727	0.799	0.856
--	--	--	1	0.189	0.257	0.339	0.430	0.528	0.623	0.711	0.785	0.846
--	--	--	2	0.175	0.242	0.322	0.413	0.512	0.609	0.698	0.776	0.838
1B	--	--	0	0.239	0.314	0.399	0.491	0.585	0.673	0.752	0.818	0.870
1B	--	--	1	0.209	0.281	0.364	0.456	0.552	0.644	0.728	0.799	0.856
1B	--	--	2	0.185	0.253	0.334	0.426	0.523	0.619	0.707	0.782	0.843
--	2B	--	0	0.256	0.334	0.422	0.515	0.608	0.694	0.770	0.832	0.881
--	2B	--	1	0.220	0.294	0.378	0.471	0.567	0.658	0.740	0.808	0.863
--	2B	--	2	0.192	0.261	0.343	0.435	0.533	0.628	0.715	0.789	0.848
--	--	3B	0	0.273	0.354	0.445	0.540	0.632	0.716	0.789	0.848	0.893
--	--	3B	1	0.239	0.316	0.404	0.498	0.594	0.683	0.761	0.826	0.877
--	--	3B	2	0.194	0.264	0.347	0.440	0.537	0.632	0.718	0.791	0.850
1B	2B	--	0	0.290	0.370	0.458	0.549	0.637	0.719	0.789	0.847	0.892
1B	2B	--	1	0.242	0.317	0.403	0.494	0.587	0.675	0.753	0.819	0.871
1B	2B	--	2	0.201	0.272	0.354	0.446	0.542	0.636	0.721	0.793	0.852
1B	--	3B	0	0.310	0.393	0.484	0.576	0.664	0.743	0.810	0.863	0.905
1B	--	3B	1	0.260	0.339	0.427	0.520	0.613	0.698	0.773	0.835	0.883
1B	--	3B	2	0.207	0.279	0.362	0.454	0.550	0.643	0.727	0.798	0.855
--	2B	3B	0	0.327	0.413	0.504	0.595	0.681	0.758	0.822	0.873	0.911
--	2B	3B	1	0.277	0.357	0.446	0.539	0.630	0.714	0.786	0.845	0.891
--	2B	3B	2	0.214	0.286	0.370	0.462	0.557	0.649	0.732	0.802	0.858
1B	2B	3B	0	0.360	0.446	0.535	0.623	0.704	0.776	0.835	0.883	0.919
1B	2B	3B	1	0.298	0.378	0.466	0.556	0.644	0.725	0.794	0.851	0.895
1B	2B	3B	2	0.229	0.302	0.386	0.477	0.571	0.661	0.741	0.809	0.863

Inning: 2, Top

1B	2B	3B	Out	-4	-3	-2	-1	Tie	1	2	3	4
--	--	--	0	0.167	0.232	0.311	0.402	0.500	0.599	0.690	0.769	0.833
--	--	--	1	0.179	0.247	0.329	0.424	0.525	0.625	0.715	0.790	0.851
--	--	--	2	0.187	0.258	0.343	0.440	0.542	0.642	0.731	0.805	0.864
1B	--	--	0	0.151	0.210	0.283	0.370	0.464	0.561	0.653	0.735	0.804
1B	--	--	1	0.167	0.232	0.310	0.401	0.500	0.598	0.689	0.767	0.832
1B	--	--	2	0.181	0.251	0.333	0.429	0.530	0.630	0.719	0.794	0.855
--	2B	--	0	0.138	0.194	0.264	0.347	0.440	0.537	0.631	0.716	0.789
--	2B	--	1	0.159	0.221	0.297	0.386	0.484	0.582	0.675	0.756	0.822
--	2B	--	2	0.176	0.244	0.325	0.419	0.520	0.620	0.710	0.787	0.849
--	--	3B	0	0.125	0.176	0.243	0.323	0.414	0.512	0.609	0.698	0.774
--	--	3B	1	0.144	0.201	0.274	0.360	0.456	0.555	0.650	0.735	0.806
--	--	3B	2	0.174	0.241	0.321	0.415	0.515	0.615	0.707	0.784	0.846
1B	2B	--	0	0.126	0.177	0.242	0.320	0.407	0.501	0.594	0.680	0.756
1B	2B	--	1	0.150	0.209	0.282	0.367	0.461	0.558	0.650	0.732	0.801
1B	2B	--	2	0.172	0.238	0.318	0.411	0.510	0.609	0.699	0.776	0.839
1B	--	3B	0	0.112	0.158	0.219	0.293	0.379	0.473	0.568	0.658	0.739
1B	--	3B	1	0.136	0.191	0.260	0.342	0.434	0.531	0.626	0.712	0.785
1B	--	3B	2	0.168	0.233	0.311	0.403	0.500	0.600	0.691	0.770	0.834
--	2B	3B	0	0.104	0.148	0.206	0.277	0.360	0.452	0.547	0.639	0.722
--	2B	3B	1	0.128	0.180	0.246	0.325	0.415	0.511	0.606	0.694	0.770
--	2B	3B	2	0.165	0.229	0.306	0.396	0.494	0.592	0.683	0.762	0.828
1B	2B	3B	0	0.096	0.137	0.190	0.256	0.335	0.422	0.514	0.604	0.688
1B	2B	3B	1	0.123	0.173	0.236	0.313	0.400	0.493	0.585	0.672	0.749
1B	2B	3B	2	0.158	0.220	0.295	0.383	0.479	0.576	0.666	0.746	0.813

Inning: 2, Bottom

1B	2B	3B	Out	-4	-3	-2	-1	Tie	1	2	3	4
--	--	--	0	0.193	0.266	0.352	0.451	0.554	0.654	0.742	0.814	0.871
--	--	--	1	0.173	0.242	0.326	0.425	0.529	0.633	0.725	0.801	0.862
--	--	--	2	0.159	0.226	0.309	0.406	0.512	0.617	0.713	0.792	0.855
1B	--	--	0	0.225	0.302	0.391	0.490	0.590	0.684	0.766	0.833	0.885
1B	--	--	1	0.194	0.267	0.354	0.452	0.555	0.654	0.743	0.815	0.872
1B	--	--	2	0.169	0.238	0.321	0.419	0.524	0.628	0.721	0.798	0.860
--	2B	--	0	0.242	0.323	0.415	0.515	0.614	0.706	0.785	0.848	0.896
--	2B	--	1	0.205	0.280	0.369	0.468	0.571	0.669	0.754	0.824	0.879
--	2B	--	2	0.176	0.246	0.331	0.430	0.535	0.637	0.729	0.805	0.864
--	--	3B	0	0.259	0.344	0.440	0.541	0.641	0.730	0.804	0.863	0.907
--	--	3B	1	0.224	0.303	0.396	0.497	0.600	0.695	0.776	0.842	0.891
--	--	3B	2	0.179	0.250	0.335	0.434	0.539	0.642	0.732	0.807	0.866
1B	2B	--	0	0.278	0.362	0.454	0.551	0.645	0.731	0.804	0.861	0.905
1B	2B	--	1	0.229	0.306	0.395	0.493	0.592	0.686	0.768	0.834	0.886
1B	2B	--	2	0.186	0.258	0.343	0.441	0.544	0.646	0.735	0.809	0.868
1B	--	3B	0	0.298	0.385	0.481	0.580	0.674	0.757	0.825	0.878	0.918
1B	--	3B	1	0.247	0.328	0.421	0.521	0.620	0.711	0.788	0.850	0.898
1B	--	3B	2	0.192	0.265	0.351	0.450	0.553	0.653	0.741	0.814	0.871
--	2B	3B	0	0.316	0.406	0.503	0.601	0.692	0.772	0.837	0.887	0.924
--	2B	3B	1	0.264	0.348	0.442	0.541	0.638	0.727	0.801	0.860	0.904
--	2B	3B	2	0.199	0.273	0.360	0.458	0.560	0.659	0.746	0.817	0.874
1B	2B	3B	0	0.352	0.442	0.536	0.629	0.715	0.790	0.850	0.896	0.930
1B	2B	3B	1	0.286	0.370	0.462	0.559	0.652	0.737	0.808	0.865	0.908
1B	2B	3B	2	0.215	0.290	0.377	0.474	0.575	0.671	0.755	0.824	0.879

Inning: 3, Top

1B	2B	3B	Out	-4	-3	-2	-1	Tie	1	2	3	4
--	--	--	0	0.151	0.216	0.297	0.394	0.500	0.607	0.704	0.785	0.850
--	--	--	1	0.162	0.231	0.316	0.417	0.527	0.634	0.730	0.808	0.868
--	--	--	2	0.170	0.241	0.330	0.434	0.545	0.653	0.748	0.823	0.881
1B	--	--	0	0.135	0.194	0.269	0.360	0.461	0.566	0.664	0.750	0.820
1B	--	--	1	0.151	0.215	0.296	0.393	0.500	0.606	0.702	0.784	0.849
1B	--	--	2	0.165	0.234	0.320	0.422	0.532	0.640	0.735	0.812	0.872
--	2B	--	0	0.123	0.178	0.249	0.335	0.435	0.540	0.641	0.731	0.805
--	2B	--	1	0.143	0.205	0.283	0.377	0.482	0.589	0.687	0.772	0.839
--	2B	--	2	0.159	0.227	0.311	0.412	0.521	0.629	0.725	0.805	0.866
--	--	3B	0	0.110	0.160	0.227	0.309	0.407	0.513	0.617	0.711	0.790
--	--	3B	1	0.128	0.185	0.258	0.348	0.451	0.559	0.661	0.751	0.823
--	--	3B	2	0.157	0.224	0.307	0.407	0.516	0.624	0.721	0.801	0.863
1B	2B	--	0	0.112	0.162	0.227	0.308	0.401	0.501	0.600	0.691	0.770
1B	2B	--	1	0.135	0.193	0.267	0.357	0.459	0.562	0.660	0.746	0.817
1B	2B	--	2	0.156	0.222	0.304	0.403	0.510	0.617	0.713	0.793	0.856
1B	--	3B	0	0.098	0.143	0.204	0.280	0.371	0.471	0.573	0.669	0.753
1B	--	3B	1	0.121	0.175	0.245	0.330	0.429	0.534	0.635	0.725	0.801
1B	--	3B	2	0.152	0.216	0.297	0.394	0.500	0.608	0.705	0.786	0.851
--	2B	3B	0	0.090	0.133	0.190	0.263	0.350	0.449	0.551	0.649	0.736
--	2B	3B	1	0.113	0.164	0.231	0.313	0.409	0.512	0.614	0.707	0.785
--	2B	3B	2	0.149	0.212	0.292	0.388	0.493	0.599	0.696	0.778	0.844
1B	2B	3B	0	0.083	0.122	0.175	0.242	0.324	0.417	0.515	0.611	0.700
1B	2B	3B	1	0.109	0.158	0.222	0.301	0.393	0.492	0.591	0.683	0.763
1B	2B	3B	2	0.143	0.204	0.281	0.374	0.477	0.582	0.678	0.761	0.829

Inning: 3, Bottom

1B	2B	3B	Out	-4	-3	-2	-1	Tie	1	2	3	4
--	--	--	0	0.176	0.249	0.339	0.445	0.558	0.666	0.759	0.833	0.888
--	--	--	1	0.155	0.224	0.312	0.416	0.532	0.644	0.742	0.821	0.879
--	--	--	2	0.141	0.207	0.292	0.396	0.513	0.628	0.730	0.811	0.873
1B	--	--	0	0.209	0.287	0.382	0.487	0.596	0.698	0.784	0.851	0.901
1B	--	--	1	0.177	0.250	0.341	0.446	0.559	0.667	0.760	0.834	0.888
1B	--	--	2	0.151	0.219	0.306	0.411	0.526	0.639	0.738	0.818	0.877
--	2B	--	0	0.226	0.309	0.407	0.515	0.623	0.721	0.802	0.865	0.911
--	2B	--	1	0.188	0.264	0.357	0.464	0.576	0.682	0.772	0.843	0.895
--	2B	--	2	0.158	0.228	0.317	0.422	0.537	0.649	0.746	0.824	0.882
--	--	3B	0	0.243	0.331	0.433	0.544	0.652	0.746	0.823	0.880	0.922
--	--	3B	1	0.206	0.288	0.386	0.496	0.608	0.710	0.794	0.859	0.907
--	--	3B	2	0.161	0.231	0.321	0.427	0.542	0.654	0.750	0.827	0.883
1B	2B	--	0	0.264	0.351	0.449	0.553	0.655	0.746	0.820	0.878	0.919
1B	2B	--	1	0.213	0.292	0.386	0.490	0.599	0.699	0.785	0.852	0.901
1B	2B	--	2	0.169	0.240	0.330	0.434	0.548	0.657	0.752	0.828	0.884
1B	--	3B	0	0.284	0.376	0.478	0.585	0.686	0.773	0.842	0.894	0.931
1B	--	3B	1	0.231	0.315	0.413	0.521	0.629	0.726	0.806	0.868	0.913
1B	--	3B	2	0.175	0.248	0.339	0.444	0.557	0.665	0.759	0.833	0.888
--	2B	3B	0	0.303	0.398	0.502	0.608	0.705	0.788	0.853	0.902	0.936
--	2B	3B	1	0.248	0.335	0.436	0.543	0.648	0.742	0.818	0.876	0.919
--	2B	3B	2	0.182	0.256	0.348	0.453	0.565	0.671	0.763	0.836	0.890
1B	2B	3B	0	0.341	0.436	0.537	0.637	0.729	0.805	0.866	0.910	0.942
1B	2B	3B	1	0.272	0.360	0.458	0.562	0.662	0.752	0.825	0.881	0.922
1B	2B	3B	2	0.199	0.275	0.366	0.470	0.580	0.683	0.772	0.843	0.894

Inning: 4, Top

1B	2B	3B	Out	-4	-3	-2	-1	Tie	1	2	3	4
--	--	--	0	0.133	0.196	0.280	0.383	0.500	0.617	0.721	0.805	0.868
--	--	--	1	0.143	0.210	0.299	0.407	0.529	0.647	0.749	0.828	0.886
--	--	--	2	0.151	0.221	0.313	0.425	0.549	0.668	0.768	0.844	0.899
1B	--	--	0	0.118	0.175	0.252	0.347	0.458	0.572	0.678	0.767	0.837
1B	--	--	1	0.132	0.195	0.279	0.382	0.500	0.616	0.719	0.803	0.867
1B	--	--	2	0.145	0.213	0.303	0.412	0.535	0.653	0.754	0.833	0.890
--	2B	--	0	0.106	0.159	0.230	0.321	0.429	0.544	0.653	0.747	0.823
--	2B	--	1	0.125	0.185	0.265	0.365	0.480	0.597	0.703	0.790	0.857
--	2B	--	2	0.140	0.206	0.294	0.401	0.522	0.641	0.744	0.825	0.884
--	--	3B	0	0.094	0.142	0.207	0.294	0.398	0.514	0.628	0.728	0.809
--	--	3B	1	0.111	0.165	0.240	0.334	0.446	0.564	0.676	0.769	0.842
--	--	3B	2	0.138	0.203	0.290	0.396	0.517	0.636	0.740	0.822	0.882
1B	2B	--	0	0.096	0.144	0.210	0.293	0.393	0.502	0.608	0.705	0.786
1B	2B	--	1	0.117	0.174	0.250	0.345	0.455	0.568	0.673	0.763	0.834
1B	2B	--	2	0.137	0.201	0.287	0.392	0.511	0.628	0.730	0.813	0.874
1B	--	3B	0	0.083	0.126	0.185	0.263	0.360	0.469	0.580	0.682	0.769
1B	--	3B	1	0.104	0.156	0.226	0.316	0.423	0.537	0.647	0.742	0.819
1B	--	3B	2	0.133	0.196	0.280	0.384	0.500	0.618	0.722	0.806	0.869
--	2B	3B	0	0.076	0.116	0.172	0.246	0.338	0.444	0.555	0.660	0.752
--	2B	3B	1	0.097	0.146	0.212	0.298	0.401	0.513	0.623	0.722	0.803
--	2B	3B	2	0.130	0.192	0.275	0.376	0.492	0.608	0.712	0.797	0.862
1B	2B	3B	0	0.070	0.106	0.158	0.226	0.312	0.411	0.517	0.620	0.713
1B	2B	3B	1	0.093	0.140	0.204	0.286	0.385	0.492	0.599	0.696	0.778
1B	2B	3B	2	0.125	0.185	0.264	0.363	0.476	0.590	0.692	0.779	0.846

Inning: 4, Bottom

1B	2B	3B	Out	-4	-3	-2	-1	Tie	1	2	3	4
--	--	--	0	0.156	0.228	0.323	0.437	0.563	0.682	0.780	0.854	0.906
--	--	--	1	0.134	0.202	0.293	0.405	0.534	0.659	0.763	0.842	0.898
--	--	--	2	0.120	0.184	0.271	0.383	0.514	0.642	0.751	0.833	0.892
1B	--	--	0	0.190	0.270	0.369	0.483	0.604	0.714	0.804	0.870	0.917
1B	--	--	1	0.157	0.230	0.325	0.438	0.564	0.683	0.780	0.854	0.906
1B	--	--	2	0.131	0.197	0.287	0.399	0.528	0.654	0.759	0.839	0.896
--	2B	--	0	0.207	0.292	0.397	0.514	0.634	0.739	0.822	0.884	0.926
--	2B	--	1	0.168	0.244	0.342	0.458	0.583	0.699	0.793	0.863	0.912
--	2B	--	2	0.137	0.206	0.298	0.412	0.541	0.665	0.767	0.845	0.900
--	--	3B	0	0.223	0.314	0.425	0.547	0.666	0.766	0.843	0.898	0.936
--	--	3B	1	0.185	0.268	0.373	0.494	0.619	0.728	0.815	0.879	0.923
--	--	3B	2	0.140	0.210	0.303	0.418	0.547	0.669	0.771	0.848	0.902
1B	2B	--	0	0.247	0.338	0.443	0.555	0.666	0.763	0.839	0.895	0.934
1B	2B	--	1	0.194	0.274	0.374	0.487	0.606	0.716	0.805	0.871	0.918
1B	2B	--	2	0.149	0.219	0.312	0.425	0.552	0.673	0.773	0.849	0.903
1B	--	3B	0	0.267	0.363	0.474	0.591	0.701	0.792	0.861	0.911	0.944
1B	--	3B	1	0.211	0.298	0.403	0.521	0.640	0.744	0.826	0.886	0.928
1B	--	3B	2	0.155	0.227	0.322	0.436	0.562	0.681	0.779	0.853	0.906
--	2B	3B	0	0.287	0.387	0.501	0.616	0.721	0.807	0.872	0.918	0.949
--	2B	3B	1	0.229	0.320	0.428	0.546	0.661	0.760	0.838	0.894	0.933
--	2B	3B	2	0.162	0.237	0.333	0.446	0.570	0.687	0.784	0.856	0.908
1B	2B	3B	0	0.328	0.429	0.539	0.647	0.744	0.823	0.883	0.925	0.954
1B	2B	3B	1	0.256	0.347	0.452	0.565	0.675	0.770	0.844	0.898	0.936
1B	2B	3B	2	0.180	0.257	0.353	0.464	0.586	0.699	0.792	0.862	0.912

Inning: 5, Top

1B	2B	3B	Out	-4	-3	-2	-1	Tie	1	2	3	4
--	--	--	0	0.112	0.173	0.258	0.368	0.500	0.631	0.742	0.827	0.888
--	--	--	1	0.121	0.187	0.277	0.394	0.531	0.664	0.772	0.852	0.907
--	--	--	2	0.128	0.197	0.291	0.413	0.554	0.688	0.793	0.868	0.919
1B	--	--	0	0.099	0.153	0.230	0.331	0.454	0.581	0.694	0.787	0.858
1B	--	--	1	0.112	0.173	0.257	0.368	0.498	0.629	0.740	0.825	0.887
1B	--	--	2	0.123	0.190	0.281	0.400	0.537	0.670	0.778	0.856	0.910
--	2B	--	0	0.088	0.138	0.209	0.303	0.421	0.549	0.668	0.767	0.844
--	2B	--	1	0.105	0.162	0.243	0.349	0.477	0.608	0.723	0.813	0.878
--	2B	--	2	0.119	0.183	0.272	0.388	0.524	0.657	0.767	0.848	0.905
--	--	3B	0	0.076	0.121	0.185	0.273	0.386	0.515	0.641	0.748	0.830
--	--	3B	1	0.092	0.144	0.217	0.316	0.438	0.571	0.694	0.792	0.864
--	--	3B	2	0.117	0.180	0.268	0.382	0.518	0.651	0.763	0.845	0.903
1B	2B	--	0	0.079	0.125	0.189	0.276	0.384	0.503	0.619	0.721	0.805
1B	2B	--	1	0.098	0.153	0.229	0.329	0.451	0.577	0.690	0.782	0.854
1B	2B	--	2	0.116	0.179	0.265	0.379	0.511	0.643	0.752	0.835	0.894
1B	--	3B	0	0.067	0.106	0.164	0.243	0.346	0.466	0.589	0.699	0.789
1B	--	3B	1	0.086	0.135	0.204	0.298	0.414	0.541	0.661	0.762	0.839
1B	--	3B	2	0.112	0.173	0.258	0.369	0.500	0.632	0.743	0.828	0.889
--	2B	3B	0	0.061	0.098	0.151	0.226	0.323	0.438	0.561	0.675	0.771
--	2B	3B	1	0.080	0.125	0.191	0.279	0.390	0.514	0.636	0.740	0.823
--	2B	3B	2	0.110	0.170	0.253	0.362	0.491	0.620	0.731	0.819	0.883
1B	2B	3B	0	0.056	0.089	0.138	0.207	0.296	0.404	0.519	0.630	0.729
1B	2B	3B	1	0.077	0.121	0.183	0.268	0.375	0.493	0.609	0.711	0.797
1B	2B	3B	2	0.105	0.163	0.243	0.348	0.473	0.600	0.710	0.799	0.866

Inning: 5, Bottom

1B	2B	3B	Out	-4	-3	-2	-1	Tie	1	2	3	4
--	--	--	0	0.133	0.204	0.301	0.426	0.569	0.703	0.806	0.878	0.926
--	--	--	1	0.111	0.176	0.268	0.390	0.538	0.680	0.789	0.868	0.920
--	--	--	2	0.097	0.157	0.245	0.365	0.515	0.663	0.777	0.860	0.915
1B	--	--	0	0.168	0.248	0.353	0.478	0.614	0.736	0.828	0.893	0.936
1B	--	--	1	0.134	0.206	0.304	0.428	0.570	0.704	0.806	0.878	0.926
1B	--	--	2	0.107	0.171	0.262	0.383	0.531	0.675	0.786	0.865	0.918
--	2B	--	0	0.184	0.271	0.383	0.513	0.647	0.762	0.847	0.905	0.944
--	2B	--	1	0.144	0.220	0.323	0.450	0.592	0.721	0.818	0.886	0.932
--	2B	--	2	0.114	0.180	0.274	0.398	0.545	0.686	0.794	0.870	0.922
--	--	3B	0	0.200	0.294	0.413	0.551	0.684	0.791	0.867	0.919	0.952
--	--	3B	1	0.161	0.245	0.356	0.492	0.633	0.752	0.841	0.902	0.941
--	--	3B	2	0.116	0.184	0.279	0.404	0.552	0.691	0.797	0.873	0.923
1B	2B	--	0	0.227	0.322	0.434	0.558	0.681	0.785	0.862	0.915	0.949
1B	2B	--	1	0.172	0.254	0.358	0.482	0.616	0.738	0.829	0.894	0.936
1B	2B	--	2	0.126	0.195	0.290	0.413	0.557	0.694	0.799	0.874	0.924
1B	--	3B	0	0.246	0.347	0.468	0.599	0.720	0.816	0.884	0.929	0.959
1B	--	3B	1	0.189	0.278	0.390	0.521	0.654	0.767	0.850	0.908	0.945
1B	--	3B	2	0.132	0.203	0.301	0.425	0.568	0.703	0.805	0.878	0.926
--	2B	3B	0	0.267	0.374	0.499	0.627	0.742	0.831	0.894	0.936	0.962
--	2B	3B	1	0.207	0.302	0.418	0.549	0.677	0.784	0.861	0.915	0.949
--	2B	3B	2	0.139	0.213	0.313	0.436	0.577	0.709	0.809	0.880	0.928
1B	2B	3B	0	0.313	0.421	0.540	0.658	0.764	0.845	0.903	0.941	0.966
1B	2B	3B	1	0.237	0.332	0.445	0.568	0.690	0.792	0.867	0.918	0.951
1B	2B	3B	2	0.158	0.235	0.335	0.456	0.593	0.721	0.817	0.886	0.931

Inning: 6, Top

1B	2B	3B	Out	-4	-3	-2	-1	Tie	1	2	3	4
--	--	--	0	0.089	0.146	0.230	0.348	0.500	0.651	0.769	0.854	0.911
--	--	--	1	0.097	0.158	0.249	0.375	0.534	0.690	0.802	0.879	0.929
--	--	--	2	0.103	0.167	0.263	0.394	0.560	0.717	0.825	0.896	0.941
1B	--	--	0	0.078	0.128	0.204	0.310	0.448	0.594	0.717	0.812	0.881
1B	--	--	1	0.089	0.145	0.230	0.347	0.498	0.649	0.766	0.852	0.910
1B	--	--	2	0.099	0.161	0.253	0.380	0.542	0.697	0.808	0.884	0.932
--	2B	--	0	0.069	0.114	0.182	0.280	0.410	0.557	0.689	0.793	0.868
--	2B	--	1	0.083	0.136	0.216	0.327	0.473	0.625	0.749	0.840	0.902
--	2B	--	2	0.095	0.155	0.244	0.368	0.526	0.682	0.797	0.876	0.928
--	--	3B	0	0.058	0.098	0.158	0.247	0.369	0.517	0.662	0.774	0.856
--	--	3B	1	0.071	0.118	0.189	0.291	0.427	0.582	0.719	0.820	0.889
--	--	3B	2	0.093	0.152	0.240	0.362	0.519	0.675	0.793	0.873	0.926
1B	2B	--	0	0.062	0.102	0.164	0.253	0.372	0.506	0.633	0.742	0.827
1B	2B	--	1	0.078	0.127	0.202	0.308	0.445	0.590	0.711	0.806	0.877
1B	2B	--	2	0.092	0.151	0.238	0.358	0.513	0.665	0.780	0.862	0.917
1B	--	3B	0	0.051	0.085	0.139	0.218	0.327	0.463	0.602	0.720	0.813
1B	--	3B	1	0.067	0.111	0.178	0.274	0.402	0.548	0.682	0.786	0.864
1B	--	3B	2	0.089	0.146	0.231	0.349	0.500	0.652	0.770	0.855	0.912
--	2B	3B	0	0.046	0.078	0.127	0.201	0.303	0.431	0.569	0.695	0.795
--	2B	3B	1	0.062	0.102	0.165	0.255	0.377	0.517	0.652	0.764	0.848
--	2B	3B	2	0.087	0.143	0.226	0.341	0.490	0.639	0.757	0.845	0.906
1B	2B	3B	0	0.042	0.071	0.116	0.183	0.277	0.395	0.523	0.644	0.748
1B	2B	3B	1	0.060	0.099	0.159	0.245	0.362	0.495	0.622	0.731	0.818
1B	2B	3B	2	0.084	0.137	0.217	0.328	0.471	0.617	0.733	0.823	0.888

Inning: 6, Bottom

1B	2B	3B	Out	-4	-3	-2	-1	Tie	1	2	3	4
--	--	--	0	0.107	0.174	0.273	0.408	0.578	0.735	0.839	0.906	0.947
--	--	--	1	0.086	0.145	0.236	0.366	0.543	0.712	0.824	0.897	0.942
--	--	--	2	0.073	0.126	0.210	0.336	0.517	0.695	0.813	0.891	0.938
1B	--	--	0	0.143	0.222	0.331	0.469	0.628	0.767	0.859	0.919	0.954
1B	--	--	1	0.109	0.177	0.276	0.410	0.579	0.736	0.839	0.906	0.947
1B	--	--	2	0.082	0.140	0.229	0.358	0.535	0.707	0.820	0.895	0.941
--	2B	--	0	0.158	0.245	0.363	0.511	0.667	0.794	0.876	0.929	0.961
--	2B	--	1	0.118	0.191	0.297	0.437	0.605	0.753	0.850	0.913	0.951
--	2B	--	2	0.088	0.149	0.242	0.376	0.553	0.718	0.828	0.900	0.943
--	--	3B	0	0.171	0.266	0.395	0.556	0.711	0.823	0.896	0.941	0.968
--	--	3B	1	0.133	0.215	0.331	0.487	0.654	0.785	0.872	0.926	0.959
--	--	3B	2	0.090	0.152	0.247	0.384	0.560	0.724	0.831	0.902	0.945
1B	2B	--	0	0.204	0.301	0.423	0.560	0.700	0.815	0.889	0.937	0.965
1B	2B	--	1	0.147	0.228	0.338	0.472	0.629	0.768	0.860	0.919	0.954
1B	2B	--	2	0.100	0.166	0.261	0.392	0.564	0.726	0.832	0.903	0.945
1B	--	3B	0	0.221	0.327	0.459	0.609	0.747	0.846	0.910	0.949	0.972
1B	--	3B	1	0.163	0.252	0.372	0.520	0.675	0.799	0.880	0.931	0.962
1B	--	3B	2	0.106	0.174	0.273	0.406	0.577	0.734	0.838	0.906	0.947
--	2B	3B	0	0.242	0.356	0.495	0.642	0.768	0.860	0.918	0.954	0.975
--	2B	3B	1	0.181	0.277	0.404	0.552	0.699	0.814	0.889	0.937	0.965
--	2B	3B	2	0.114	0.185	0.288	0.421	0.586	0.740	0.841	0.908	0.948
1B	2B	3B	0	0.294	0.410	0.540	0.673	0.789	0.872	0.925	0.958	0.977
1B	2B	3B	1	0.214	0.313	0.434	0.571	0.710	0.821	0.893	0.939	0.966
1B	2B	3B	2	0.134	0.209	0.312	0.443	0.603	0.751	0.849	0.912	0.950

Inning: 7, Top

1B	2B	3B	Out	-4	-3	-2	-1	Tie	1	2	3	4
--	--	--	0	0.065	0.114	0.194	0.316	0.500	0.683	0.805	0.886	0.935
--	--	--	1	0.071	0.125	0.212	0.344	0.540	0.728	0.841	0.912	0.952
--	--	--	2	0.076	0.133	0.225	0.364	0.571	0.761	0.866	0.929	0.963
1B	--	--	0	0.056	0.100	0.170	0.278	0.442	0.615	0.746	0.843	0.906
1B	--	--	1	0.065	0.114	0.194	0.316	0.498	0.680	0.801	0.884	0.934
1B	--	--	2	0.072	0.128	0.216	0.350	0.550	0.737	0.847	0.916	0.955
--	2B	--	0	0.049	0.087	0.149	0.247	0.395	0.570	0.718	0.825	0.896
--	2B	--	1	0.060	0.106	0.180	0.295	0.468	0.651	0.784	0.873	0.928
--	2B	--	2	0.069	0.122	0.207	0.336	0.529	0.718	0.837	0.910	0.952
--	--	3B	0	0.041	0.073	0.127	0.213	0.344	0.522	0.691	0.808	0.887
--	--	3B	1	0.051	0.090	0.155	0.257	0.411	0.598	0.755	0.855	0.918
--	--	3B	2	0.068	0.120	0.203	0.330	0.520	0.710	0.832	0.907	0.950
1B	2B	--	0	0.044	0.078	0.134	0.222	0.356	0.512	0.652	0.768	0.854
1B	2B	--	1	0.056	0.099	0.169	0.277	0.439	0.610	0.739	0.836	0.902
1B	2B	--	2	0.067	0.119	0.201	0.328	0.516	0.699	0.816	0.893	0.941
1B	--	3B	0	0.035	0.063	0.110	0.186	0.302	0.460	0.621	0.747	0.842
1B	--	3B	1	0.047	0.085	0.146	0.241	0.386	0.560	0.710	0.818	0.892
1B	--	3B	2	0.065	0.115	0.195	0.317	0.500	0.684	0.805	0.887	0.937
--	2B	3B	0	0.032	0.057	0.100	0.169	0.277	0.422	0.581	0.721	0.824
--	2B	3B	1	0.043	0.078	0.134	0.223	0.358	0.523	0.676	0.795	0.877
--	2B	3B	2	0.064	0.112	0.191	0.311	0.491	0.667	0.789	0.877	0.931
1B	2B	3B	0	0.029	0.052	0.091	0.154	0.252	0.385	0.529	0.662	0.772
1B	2B	3B	1	0.042	0.075	0.129	0.215	0.345	0.500	0.641	0.755	0.844
1B	2B	3B	2	0.061	0.107	0.182	0.297	0.470	0.643	0.763	0.852	0.912

Inning: 7, Bottom

1B	2B	3B	Out	-4	-3	-2	-1	Tie	1	2	3	4
--	--	--	0	0.079	0.139	0.234	0.378	0.592	0.783	0.881	0.938	0.968
--	--	--	1	0.059	0.109	0.193	0.328	0.552	0.761	0.870	0.931	0.965
--	--	--	2	0.047	0.089	0.164	0.291	0.522	0.745	0.861	0.927	0.962
1B	--	--	0	0.114	0.189	0.301	0.452	0.647	0.812	0.898	0.947	0.973
1B	--	--	1	0.080	0.142	0.239	0.381	0.593	0.783	0.882	0.938	0.968
1B	--	--	2	0.056	0.104	0.186	0.317	0.542	0.756	0.867	0.930	0.964
--	2B	--	0	0.127	0.211	0.335	0.506	0.697	0.837	0.912	0.954	0.977
--	2B	--	1	0.088	0.155	0.260	0.416	0.625	0.800	0.891	0.943	0.971
--	2B	--	2	0.060	0.111	0.199	0.340	0.564	0.768	0.873	0.933	0.966
--	--	3B	0	0.138	0.230	0.367	0.563	0.752	0.866	0.929	0.963	0.982
--	--	3B	1	0.100	0.176	0.295	0.480	0.687	0.831	0.909	0.953	0.976
--	--	3B	2	0.062	0.115	0.204	0.350	0.574	0.773	0.876	0.935	0.967
1B	2B	--	0	0.176	0.276	0.407	0.561	0.727	0.854	0.922	0.959	0.980
1B	2B	--	1	0.119	0.198	0.310	0.456	0.649	0.813	0.898	0.947	0.973
1B	2B	--	2	0.073	0.131	0.222	0.359	0.575	0.774	0.876	0.935	0.967
1B	--	3B	0	0.190	0.300	0.444	0.623	0.785	0.884	0.939	0.969	0.985
1B	--	3B	1	0.131	0.219	0.344	0.516	0.705	0.842	0.915	0.956	0.978
1B	--	3B	2	0.078	0.139	0.234	0.377	0.591	0.782	0.881	0.938	0.968
--	2B	3B	0	0.211	0.331	0.490	0.663	0.805	0.896	0.945	0.972	0.986
--	2B	3B	1	0.149	0.246	0.384	0.556	0.730	0.856	0.923	0.960	0.980
--	2B	3B	2	0.085	0.150	0.254	0.395	0.599	0.787	0.884	0.939	0.969
1B	2B	3B	0	0.270	0.395	0.540	0.693	0.822	0.905	0.950	0.974	0.987
1B	2B	3B	1	0.188	0.290	0.418	0.573	0.738	0.860	0.925	0.961	0.980
1B	2B	3B	2	0.107	0.179	0.281	0.419	0.617	0.796	0.889	0.942	0.970

Inning: 8, Top

1B	2B	3B	Out	-4	-3	-2	-1	Tie	1	2	3	4
--	--	--	0	0.040	0.078	0.146	0.265	0.500	0.734	0.854	0.923	0.960
--	--	--	1	0.044	0.086	0.161	0.291	0.550	0.791	0.894	0.948	0.975
--	--	--	2	0.048	0.092	0.172	0.310	0.587	0.833	0.920	0.963	0.983
1B	--	--	0	0.034	0.067	0.126	0.230	0.433	0.649	0.787	0.880	0.935
1B	--	--	1	0.040	0.078	0.146	0.265	0.500	0.730	0.848	0.921	0.960
1B	--	--	2	0.045	0.088	0.165	0.297	0.562	0.802	0.899	0.952	0.978
--	2B	--	0	0.029	0.057	0.109	0.199	0.372	0.591	0.761	0.865	0.927
--	2B	--	1	0.037	0.071	0.135	0.245	0.460	0.693	0.832	0.912	0.956
--	2B	--	2	0.043	0.083	0.157	0.284	0.535	0.778	0.890	0.947	0.975
--	--	3B	0	0.023	0.046	0.089	0.165	0.304	0.530	0.738	0.853	0.921
--	--	3B	1	0.030	0.059	0.112	0.207	0.384	0.625	0.808	0.900	0.950
--	--	3B	2	0.042	0.081	0.153	0.277	0.522	0.768	0.886	0.945	0.974
1B	2B	--	0	0.026	0.051	0.097	0.179	0.335	0.524	0.679	0.800	0.885
1B	2B	--	1	0.034	0.067	0.126	0.229	0.431	0.645	0.776	0.870	0.931
1B	2B	--	2	0.042	0.081	0.153	0.276	0.521	0.755	0.863	0.929	0.966
1B	--	3B	0	0.020	0.040	0.076	0.143	0.263	0.458	0.651	0.784	0.876
1B	--	3B	1	0.028	0.055	0.105	0.194	0.361	0.580	0.751	0.857	0.924
1B	--	3B	2	0.040	0.078	0.147	0.266	0.502	0.735	0.853	0.923	0.963
--	2B	3B	0	0.018	0.036	0.069	0.129	0.239	0.408	0.600	0.759	0.861
--	2B	3B	1	0.026	0.050	0.096	0.177	0.331	0.532	0.710	0.836	0.911
--	2B	3B	2	0.040	0.076	0.144	0.261	0.493	0.713	0.831	0.915	0.958
1B	2B	3B	0	0.016	0.032	0.063	0.117	0.218	0.372	0.540	0.686	0.802
1B	2B	3B	1	0.025	0.049	0.093	0.172	0.321	0.510	0.668	0.785	0.873
1B	2B	3B	2	0.038	0.073	0.137	0.249	0.470	0.685	0.803	0.885	0.938

Inning: 8, Bottom

1B	2B	3B	Out	-4	-3	-2	-1	Tie	1	2	3	4
--	--	--	0	0.050	0.096	0.180	0.324	0.614	0.861	0.935	0.971	0.987
--	--	--	1	0.032	0.065	0.133	0.258	0.565	0.845	0.928	0.967	0.985
--	--	--	2	0.022	0.047	0.100	0.209	0.528	0.834	0.922	0.965	0.984
1B	--	--	0	0.081	0.148	0.259	0.420	0.676	0.881	0.945	0.975	0.989
1B	--	--	1	0.050	0.098	0.187	0.328	0.612	0.861	0.935	0.971	0.987
1B	--	--	2	0.029	0.060	0.127	0.245	0.552	0.841	0.926	0.967	0.985
--	2B	--	0	0.090	0.166	0.291	0.493	0.741	0.901	0.954	0.979	0.991
--	2B	--	1	0.056	0.109	0.207	0.376	0.655	0.873	0.941	0.973	0.988
--	2B	--	2	0.032	0.066	0.138	0.275	0.582	0.850	0.930	0.968	0.986
--	--	3B	0	0.097	0.180	0.319	0.572	0.816	0.923	0.965	0.984	0.993
--	--	3B	1	0.063	0.125	0.236	0.463	0.740	0.898	0.953	0.979	0.991
--	--	3B	2	0.033	0.069	0.142	0.289	0.596	0.854	0.932	0.969	0.986
1B	2B	--	0	0.141	0.242	0.382	0.556	0.765	0.911	0.959	0.982	0.992
1B	2B	--	1	0.086	0.159	0.270	0.422	0.675	0.882	0.945	0.975	0.989
1B	2B	--	2	0.043	0.089	0.169	0.298	0.591	0.854	0.932	0.969	0.986
1B	--	3B	0	0.151	0.262	0.417	0.640	0.843	0.934	0.970	0.986	0.994
1B	--	3B	1	0.094	0.176	0.301	0.505	0.752	0.904	0.956	0.980	0.991
1B	--	3B	2	0.047	0.096	0.181	0.322	0.611	0.860	0.935	0.971	0.987
--	2B	3B	0	0.170	0.292	0.479	0.692	0.856	0.941	0.973	0.988	0.995
--	2B	3B	1	0.110	0.201	0.353	0.558	0.776	0.913	0.960	0.982	0.992
--	2B	3B	2	0.053	0.106	0.209	0.346	0.616	0.863	0.936	0.971	0.987
1B	2B	3B	0	0.240	0.374	0.535	0.717	0.869	0.946	0.976	0.989	0.995
1B	2B	3B	1	0.156	0.259	0.393	0.571	0.778	0.915	0.961	0.982	0.992
1B	2B	3B	2	0.077	0.141	0.239	0.374	0.637	0.870	0.939	0.973	0.988

Inning: 9, Top

1B	2B	3B	Out	-4	-3	-2	-1	Tie	1	2	3	4
--	--	--	0	0.017	0.037	0.082	0.174	0.500	0.825	0.918	0.963	0.983
--	--	--	1	0.018	0.041	0.091	0.194	0.563	0.903	0.960	0.984	0.994
--	--	--	2	0.020	0.045	0.098	0.208	0.612	0.961	0.987	0.996	0.999
1B	--	--	0	0.014	0.031	0.069	0.148	0.418	0.711	0.842	0.923	0.964
1B	--	--	1	0.017	0.037	0.082	0.174	0.502	0.819	0.909	0.962	0.984
1B	--	--	2	0.019	0.042	0.093	0.198	0.581	0.918	0.963	0.988	0.996
--	2B	--	0	0.012	0.026	0.058	0.124	0.332	0.631	0.825	0.915	0.961
--	2B	--	1	0.015	0.034	0.074	0.159	0.445	0.767	0.900	0.957	0.983
--	2B	--	2	0.018	0.040	0.088	0.188	0.541	0.884	0.960	0.986	0.995
--	--	3B	0	0.009	0.020	0.045	0.097	0.233	0.544	0.816	0.911	0.959
--	--	3B	1	0.012	0.027	0.059	0.128	0.333	0.672	0.893	0.954	0.981
--	--	3B	2	0.017	0.039	0.086	0.183	0.523	0.869	0.960	0.985	0.995
1B	2B	--	0	0.010	0.023	0.052	0.111	0.302	0.549	0.717	0.841	0.922
1B	2B	--	1	0.014	0.031	0.069	0.148	0.420	0.708	0.826	0.910	0.962
1B	2B	--	2	0.017	0.039	0.086	0.183	0.530	0.855	0.924	0.965	0.989
1B	--	3B	0	0.007	0.017	0.038	0.083	0.200	0.456	0.701	0.833	0.918
1B	--	3B	1	0.011	0.025	0.056	0.120	0.318	0.617	0.815	0.905	0.959
1B	--	3B	2	0.017	0.037	0.082	0.175	0.503	0.828	0.916	0.962	0.987
--	2B	3B	0	0.007	0.015	0.034	0.074	0.183	0.387	0.631	0.813	0.908
--	2B	3B	1	0.010	0.023	0.050	0.109	0.287	0.549	0.761	0.890	0.951
--	2B	3B	2	0.016	0.037	0.080	0.172	0.498	0.795	0.884	0.959	0.985
1B	2B	3B	0	0.006	0.014	0.031	0.067	0.168	0.355	0.559	0.718	0.839
1B	2B	3B	1	0.010	0.022	0.049	0.106	0.285	0.533	0.707	0.822	0.907
1B	2B	3B	2	0.016	0.035	0.076	0.163	0.471	0.763	0.852	0.921	0.964

Inning: 9, Bottom

1B	2B	3B	Out	-4	-3	-2	-1	Tie	1	2	3	4
--	--	--	0	0.021	0.047	0.103	0.219	0.649	---	---	---	---
--	--	--	1	0.008	0.021	0.051	0.124	0.588	---	---	---	---
--	--	--	2	0.002	0.006	0.017	0.052	0.539	---	---	---	---
1B	--	--	0	0.045	0.097	0.198	0.353	0.722	---	---	---	---
1B	--	--	1	0.020	0.049	0.116	0.225	0.644	---	---	---	---
1B	--	--	2	0.005	0.016	0.048	0.104	0.568	---	---	---	---
--	2B	--	0	0.050	0.107	0.219	0.462	0.817	---	---	---	---
--	2B	--	1	0.022	0.055	0.128	0.296	0.707	---	---	---	---
--	2B	--	2	0.006	0.018	0.052	0.151	0.613	---	---	---	---
--	--	3B	0	0.052	0.112	0.229	0.583	0.929	---	---	---	---
--	--	3B	1	0.024	0.059	0.136	0.429	0.835	---	---	---	---
--	--	3B	2	0.006	0.019	0.053	0.172	0.634	---	---	---	---
1B	2B	--	0	0.098	0.199	0.346	0.537	0.823	---	---	---	---
1B	2B	--	1	0.049	0.115	0.216	0.353	0.717	---	---	---	---
1B	2B	--	2	0.015	0.045	0.096	0.179	0.617	---	---	---	---
1B	--	3B	0	0.103	0.208	0.365	0.664	0.938	---	---	---	---
1B	--	3B	1	0.052	0.121	0.230	0.478	0.832	---	---	---	---
1B	--	3B	2	0.017	0.050	0.107	0.215	0.645	---	---	---	---
--	2B	3B	0	0.116	0.233	0.458	0.738	0.934	---	---	---	---
--	2B	3B	1	0.063	0.139	0.301	0.556	0.849	---	---	---	---
--	2B	3B	2	0.019	0.053	0.151	0.252	0.640	---	---	---	---
1B	2B	3B	0	0.201	0.343	0.523	0.751	0.938	---	---	---	---
1B	2B	3B	1	0.119	0.220	0.351	0.556	0.841	---	---	---	---
1B	2B	3B	2	0.047	0.100	0.182	0.283	0.665	---	---	---	---

Win Values of Events

We've spent a lot of time discussing the *run* values of the various events (HR is 1.4, the out is minus 0.3, etc.). However, while most events occur rather randomly across the game states, some events are specifically executed in non-random situations. They are highly dependent on the inning and score. And in any case, the true currency of baseball is neither bases nor runs; it is wins.

Let's follow a similar process for wins as we did for runs. We looked at every HR, one at a time, and determined the game state in which each occurred. Then, we looked up the win probability of that game state by consulting the win probability charts from the previous section. For the HR, the average win probability prior to the home run was .5145. We then looked at the game states following the HR. The average win probability after a HR was .6379. Therefore, the difference between the starting state and ending state is .1234 wins, which we define as the win value of an average home run.

Technical note: The astute reader will notice that when we computed the run values for the HR, we said there were 21,026 HR hit. Now, we're showing 21,734. In the earlier charts, we explained that we removed some of the innings, because of their bias. This problem no longer exists when computing *win* values.

We can repeat this process for all events. As expected, the most valuable event is the HR. Let us present the complete win chart, along with each event's run value that we showed earlier. (See Table 11.) We'll also add another column called Runs/Win, and it is simply the Runs column divided by the Wins column.

The Runs/Win column shows you how many runs it takes to add a win. The more runs it takes, the more frequently this event takes place in unimportant situations. The fewer runs it takes, the more important the typical situation in which the event occurs. For all the common events, the runs/win values are around 11 to 12. However, there are a few that stick out. The sacrifice bunt is only 9.9 runs per win. The effect of the sacrifice bunt is that each run has more impact than the average event. This is easy enough to understand, as the sac bunt is an elective play and managers attempt the sac bunt when one run can have a big impact on winning. Stolen bases also have a low runs-per-win ratio (9.5), and the reason is the same as the sac bunt.

Table 11.   Win Values, By Event

Event	N	Starting Wins	Ending Wins	Wins	Runs	Runs/Win
Home Run	21734	0.514	0.638	0.123	1.397	11.3
Triple	3732	0.540	0.633	0.093	1.070	11.5
Double	35141	0.521	0.587	0.066	0.776	11.7
Error	7616	0.520	0.564	0.044	0.508	11.5
Single	114832	0.514	0.556	0.042	0.475	11.3
Interference	60	0.558	0.592	0.034	0.392	11.6
Hit by Pitch	6787	0.547	0.577	0.029	0.352	12.0
Balk	649	0.568	0.597	0.028	0.264	9.3
Non-intentional Walk	63004	0.525	0.553	0.028	0.323	11.6
Passed Ball	1234	0.548	0.574	0.025	0.269	10.6
Wild Pitch	5608	0.564	0.589	0.024	0.266	10.9
Stolen Base	10908	0.583	0.602	0.018	0.175	9.5
Intentional Walk	5143	0.724	0.734	0.010	0.179	17.8
Bunt	4862	0.537	0.539	0.003	0.042	15.0
Defensive Indifference	779	0.109	0.112	0.003	0.120	44.5
Sac Bunt	6448	0.638	0.628	-0.010	-0.096	9.9
Pickoff	2294	0.607	0.583	-0.024	-0.281	11.7
Out	358019	0.512	0.486	-0.026	-0.299	11.4
Strikeout	125876	0.506	0.479	-0.027	-0.301	11.0
Caught Stealing	3800	0.608	0.565	-0.043	-0.467	10.8

On the flip side, you have the defensive indifference play. As you can see by this chart, the win probability for this event changes very little (.003 wins) relative to its run impact (.120). With a 44.5 runs per win value, you can see it takes a great deal of runs to generate an extra win. The intentional walk also has the win impact of its runs reduced. While the run value of the IBB is almost identical to the run value of the SB, its win value is worth half as much. This is because managers issue the IBB when it won't impact the game as much.

USEFUL DEFINITIONS

In addition to our baseball analysis tools, like wOBA and RE, there are several mathematical tools that we will be using throughout the book. Some of you will already know these things, others may find the following few sections informative, and as always, those who wish to skip ahead to the next chapter are welcome to do so.

Average: the expected value of some statistic. For example, if a coin flip is assigned the value of zero for heads (which it gets half the time) and one for tails (which it gets the other half), the average value is 1/2. We will use the symbol $\bar{x}$ to denote the average value of a variable x.

Standard Deviation: the typical difference between the average value and a measured value. Since the coin flip is either zero or one and the average is 1/2, the standard deviation will be 1/2. In normal statistics (i.e., a bell curve), values fall within one standard deviation of the average about two-thirds (precisely, 68%) of the time and within two standard deviations 95% of the time. We will use the symbol $\sigma(x)$ to denote the standard deviation of a variable x, or occasionally simply σ. In plain English, we will refer to standard deviation as "typical variations," or similar terms.

Variance: the square of the standard deviation. We don't use the variance very often, since the standard deviation is what is interesting, but it is mathematically important since it is what is calculated.

Uncertainty: the accuracy with which a number is given, or more precisely the standard deviation of our measurement of a value. For example, if we report that a number is 2±1, this means there is a 68% certainty that the value we are measuring is between 1 and 3.

Regression: a technique used to estimate a player's true skill based on his performance and one's knowledge of the player-to-player variations in that skill.

Random Fluctuations

One of the running themes in this book is that, very frequently, fans and analysts make too much from too little. Specifically, a small number of plate appearances will be used to identify a particular tendency, such as a player's ability to hit in high-pressure situations, against a particular opposing pitcher, and so on. The problem is that OBP or wOBA values are unreliable in a small number of appearances, due to the very large amount of random fluctuation inherent in such small samples.

Consider the following illustration. If you roll a die and get a one, you won't jump to the conclusion that the die is loaded and only comes up ones. Likewise, if you roll the die five times and roll a one or two four of those five times, you chalk it up to luck of the random draw since the odds of a die being loaded are quite small. However, if a batter is 4-for-5 lifetime against a particular pitcher, broadcasters will often mention this as if it has some bearing on the upcoming at-bat.

In order to better discern what is real and what is just random luck, we need to know the exact amount of expected random fluctuation. For example, if a player's wOBA is .450 and the random fluctuation (i.e., the standard deviation expected from random variations) is .001, then we will believe that the player is a legitimate .450 hitter. However, if the random fluctuation is .250, then we can infer very little from that .450.

Here are two tables. One gives the expected random fluctuations in OBP for an average hitter as a function of number of plate appearances. (See Table 12.) We also list the ranges inside of which we would expect 68% and 95% of average players to have measured OBP. In other words, if you took 1,000 hitters, all of whom are legitimate .330 (OBP) hitters, around 680 should have OBP between .181 and .479 after ten appearances, while 950 should have OBP between .033 and .627. After 100 plate appearances, the ranges decrease to .283–.377 and .236–.424. (Details on how this is calculated are given in the appendix.)

Table 12.   Random Variations For Players With An OBP Skill Of .330

Number of PA	Random Variation (one standard deviation)	68% of players will have measured OBP between...	95% of players will have measured OBP between...
10	.149	.181 and .479	.033 and .627
20	.105	.225 and .435	.120 and .540
50	.066	.264 and .396	.197 and .463
100	.047	.283 and .377	.236 and .424
200	.033	.297 and .363	.264 and .396
500	.021	.309 and .351	.288 and .372
1000	.015	.315 and .345	.300 and .360

The effects of random variations are probably surprisingly large to you. One might expect that after 100 plate appearances, averages have significant meaning. Yet only two-thirds of players will have an OBP within 67 points of their true skill level. Even among starting pitchers who faced 1,000 batters (generally more than one season), one in twenty will have an "OBP against" more than 30 points away from his true skill level—a difference of nearly a full run in ERA.

Next is a table with the same data, but computed for random variations in wOBA. (See Table 13.) These random variations are larger than those in OBP by about 7%.

We wish to emphasize that random variation is inevitable in baseball. In other words, if a large number of .330 hitters have 100 plate appearances each, the standard deviation in their measured OBP values will be .047. If the hitters are not all identical, the standard deviation will be even greater. Likewise, even the most consistent hitter imaginable can only assure us that his OBP *skill* will remain the same. In any set of, say, 100 plate appearances, his *measured* OBP will inevitably fluctuate with a standard deviation of .047. That's the best a player can do; it is, of course, possible that an inconsistent player (one whose OBP skill varies), if there is such a batter, will have his OBP fluctuate more than what is expected from randomness alone. Interestingly, because of this random fluctuation inherent in all samples of performance, the truly consistent hitter could easily have more inconsistent measured results, especially in a relatively small number of plate appearances, than the truly inconsistent hitter! In other words, the consistency of a hitter's measured OBP (or any other offensive metric), even over the course of a season or two, is not going to tell us a whole lot about his true consistency (whether or not his OBP skill really is around the same at all times, at least as compared to the average player).

Table 13.   Random Variations For Players With wOBA Skill Of .330 And Average Profile

Number of PA	Random Variation (one standard deviation)	68% of players will have measured wOBA between...	95% of players will have measured wOBA between...
10	.159	.171 and .489	.011 and .649
20	.113	.217 and .443	.105 and .555
50	.071	.259 and .401	.187 and .473
100	.050	.280 and .380	.229 and .431
200	.036	.294 and .366	.259 and .401
500	.023	.307 and .353	.285 and .375
1000	.016	.314 and .346	.398 and .362

Regression Toward The Mean

One of the most important uses of statistics in baseball is estimating a player's true talent level (or equivalently, his expected future performance) based on his past performance and whatever other knowledge one has. The lazy approach is merely to expect that his future performance will equal his past performance, but one can do significantly better.

For example, there were 162 players who posted a wOBA of .370 or better for a full season between 2000 and 2003, and had at least 400 plate appearances in the .370 season and the following season. For their .370 season, these players had an average wOBA of .406; in the next season they averaged merely .391. What happened? Did these players all get worse? No. On average the players were legitimate .391 hitters (which is still very good, mind you) who also got a bit lucky in that first season.

In other words, there are two factors that influence performance. One is how good a player really is; the other is how lucky (or unlucky) he has been. If we are trying to predict future performance, his luck is expected to balance out, while his skills should remain intact (aside from age, injury, etc.). Thus, estimating true talent or skill is essentially the same as making a projection.

So how exactly do we estimate this? For starters, if a player has yet to play, then you would assume he is a fairly average player (since you have nothing else to go on). The certainty of how close to average he is depends on how much variation there is between good and bad players. For example, prior to flipping a coin, you are pretty certain that the odds of getting heads is very close to 50%.

As the player accumulates plate appearances (or whatever performances you are hoping to measure), you gradually adjust your estimate of his true skill level from being average toward whatever his performances indicate. For example, if he consistently outperforms the average, you will begin to realize that he is a good player. The rate at which your estimate of his abilities changes depends on how much variation you believe there is in a particular skill. Going back to the coin flips, for example, it would take quite a few coin flips and a significant deviation from 50-50 to convince you that the coin was biased because you know that this is not very likely.

Mathematically, the simplest way to accomplish this is by adding some fixed number of "average" performances to a player's actual performance. For example, if we want to estimate a player's likely wOBA next season, we need to add approximately 220 average plate appearances to his totals. Back to our sample of hitters who hit .370 or better, we find that adding 220 appearances with a wOBA of .370 (the average for hitters with consecutive 400-PA seasons) to 450 plate appearances with a wOBA of .406 (their actual average performance) produces an expected wOBA of .394 the following season. You may recall that the actual wOBA next season was .391, which is in agreement with what we should have expected. (In the appendix, we explain how we arrive at the number 220.)

The effect of regression is that a player's talent estimate is closer to average than to his measured wOBA if he has fewer than 220 plate appearances, while it is closer to his measured wOBA than to average with more than 220. So the number 220 can also be considered the break-even point at which his measured wOBA becomes reasonably reliable. Note that the number 220 is valid only for regressing batter wOBA; for regressing other player skills (such as pitcher wOBA), one uses a different number.

We note that when we say we are regressing "toward the mean," we mean the mean of similar players, and not necessarily the mean of all major leaguers. In other words, the "mean" that we are using is the level we would expect this player to perform in the absence of any performance record. So, we want to regress toward the best possible initial guess of the player's skill. (Recall that in the previous example, we regressed to the average wOBA of batters with consecutive 400-PA seasons rather than the league average.)

For a more extreme example, consider the problem of estimating hitting skills of pitchers. It is plainly wrong to expect that a pitcher's OBP or wOBA will be around .340 before his first major league at-bat, right? Rather, we should expect that his performance would be something like that of other pitchers, and thus we would regress his performance toward that of an average pitcher. Furthermore, if one had evidence that left-handed pitchers hit better than right-handed pitchers, or that tall pitchers hit better than short ones, we could use regression further to improve our initial guess.

The Book Says:

When estimating a player's true talent level or projecting future performance, one needs to adjust his past performance toward the mean performance of *similar* (not *all*) players. The simplest approach is to add a specific number of average performances to his performance record.

CHAPTER 2 – WHEN YOU'RE HOT, YOU'RE HOT

BATTER STREAKS

Many of us are aware of how much stock baseball announcers, commentators, fans, managers, coaches, and players put in the significance of a player or team being *hot* or *cold*. It is nearly impossible to watch or listen to a game without the commentator at some point remarking that, "So-and-so has been red-hot or ice-cold," referring to the fact that said player has recently had a very good or very bad spate of performance.

While there is no doubt that players and teams go through short, and even long, periods of time when their performance is well above or below their norm, the question that this chapter examines is, "Is there any predictive value to these hot and cold streaks?" Another way to couch this question is, "Are hot and cold streaks solely a result of normal, random fluctuation, or are they due to a combination of random fluctuation *and* a temporary change in a player's ability?"

It is unlikely that fans, commentators, baseball pundits, and the like, are infatuated with hot and cold streaks simply for the sake of pointing out what has already happened. To mention that, "So-and-so has hit over .400 in his last five or ten games," with no implication that this has anything to do with how we expect him to hit in the near future would be banal. The fact is that when most people talk about hot and cold streaks, they generally believe that these streaks do, in fact, have predictive value—that a player (or team) who has been hot is expected to hit better than his norm in the near future, and that a player who has been cold will continue to be cold, at least for some finite period of time. This belief is evidenced by several things that occur in baseball:

- Managers will sometimes bench regular players who have been cold, or start reserve or part-time players who have recently been hot.
- Managers will often rearrange their batting orders depending upon who is hot and who is cold.
- Opposing managers will occasionally pitch around or even intentionally walk hot players and pitch "right at" cold players.
- Managers will sometimes play *small ball* when their offenses have been cold, and eschew such an approach when their hitting has been hot. How often have we heard an announcer say, "So-and-so (team) is sacrificing in the first or second inning because they have had trouble scoring runs lately?" The clear implication is that because the team has been cold (hitting-wise) in the past few games or weeks, they are likely to score fewer runs than normal in the current game.
- Finally, fans and sports handicappers regularly assess the current strength of a team depending, at least in part, upon whether its players, as a whole, have been hot or cold in the recent past.

This chapter looks at what happens exactly one game immediately following a five-game hot or cold streak, as well as what happens over a five-game period immediately following that same hot or cold streak. If the fans, commentators, and pundits are right, players, as a group, should hit significantly better than their own normal level of performance for some period of time following a hot streak, and significantly worse following a cold streak. While it might be difficult to predict how long this effect would last, either our one-game or our five-game snapshot (or both) should capture this effect, if in fact it does exist.

At this point you might be thinking, *you are looking at a one- or five-game period after a streak has been identified, therefore the streak may be over*. Remember, however, that in real life we are always looking at a point in time subsequent to a streak—the streak is always in the past. While we may have no idea whether the streak is over or not, our (actually, *their*) hypothesis is that there is still *something* left to the streak, at least for some period of time in the near future. Let's see if this is true, and if so, to what extent.

The data used in this chapter encompass all major league play from 2000 to 2003. We've used our computer to go through the play-by-play data one game at a time and keep a running five-game total of every player's stats during each of the four seasons of play. Each player had up to 158 possible five-game streaks per season, starting with the fifth game of each year. In other words, if a player played in the first five games of the season, he completed his first potential five-game streak after the fifth game. After the sixth game, he completed his second possible five-game streak, games two through six. If a player played in his team's games 1, 2, 5, 6, and 7 (missing games 3 and 4), then *his* first possible streak starts after game seven (*his* fifth game). Also, a player's *last* five games in a season are never counted, as there is no subsequent time period to examine.

Next, we culled all those five-game periods in which a player was either hot or cold. Any given player could have more than one five-game period selected. In fact, many players, especially the very good and very bad ones, had several five-game hot or cold periods in the same season, as well as in multiple seasons. Also, some players were included in the hot as well as the cold group (they were hot in one five-game period and cold in another). In addition, because some five-game periods have games in common (e.g., for some players, games 1–5 is one period, games 2–6 is another period, etc.), if a player had a hot or cold five-game period, it was likely that he had additional overlapping five-game hot or cold periods.

What were the criteria for being hot or cold over any five-game period? We used wOBA to measure a player's offensive performance. Remember that wOBA accurately reflects a player's contribution to his team's offense, and is directly related to runs per plate appearance (see the *Toolshed* chapter).

Getting back to the selection criteria for identifying and culling a hot or cold five-game period, we chose a wOBA above which a player's component stats (single, double, walk, etc.) from that five-game hot period went into the *hot bucket*, and a wOBA below which a player's component stats from that five-game cold period went into the *cold bucket*. In addition, a player must have had at least twenty PA in the five-game period in order to *qualify* for a bucket. The hot and cold wOBA thresholds were chosen such that around 5% of all five-game periods with at least twenty PA went into the hot group, 5% into the cold group, and 90% into neither group. The exact minimum and maximum wOBA for hot and cold periods varied from year to year, but a typical minimum five-game wOBA to qualify for admission into the hot group was .525, and a typical maximum five-game wOBA to qualify for the cold group was .195.

We chose to use absolute wOBA maximums and minimums for the group selection criteria rather than a wOBA relative to a player's normal wOBA for the following reason: we wanted to mimic real life as much as possible. We don't normally identify a hot or cold streak by how well a player has performed relative to his norm. A hot or cold streak is usually defined by whether a player has been hitting well or not, relative to a more or less average player. For example, if Rey Ordonez has a batting average of .290 over a five-game period, we normally don't call that a hot streak, even though .290 is significantly higher than his typical average. Similarly, if Bonds is 8 for his last 25 (.320), we probably don't call that a cold streak, even though .320 is less than *his* typical batting average, at least during the years of our study.

Once the hot and cold five-game periods were selected, we looked at the hitting results for each player: one game immediately following the hot or cold streak, and during the five games immediately following the streak. In order to determine whether or not the hot and cold streaks had any predictive value, we compared each bucket's collective wOBA one game after the streak, and then again during the five games following the streak, with their expected or normal wOBA. Each group's expected wOBA was simply the average of every player's wOBA over the three seasons surrounding (one year before and one year after) and including the year of the streak, weighted by each player's total number of PA in the group.

For example, let's say that in 2001 Barry Bonds had five hot streaks and a total of 95 PA in the five games following each of those streaks (a total of twenty-five post-streak games), Steve Finley had three hot streaks and 63 post-streak PA, and Alex Rodriguez had four hot streaks and 89 post-streak PA, and that those were the only players and streaks in the hot bucket. Here is how we would compute the expected wOBA for this particular group or bucket:

We would look up Bonds's wOBA for 2000, 2001, and 2002 combined. We would then do the same for Finley and A-Rod. Finally, we would average all three players' three-year wOBA weighted by the number of post-streak (either one- or five-game) PA each player has. This number is the expected wOBA for all the players in this particular bucket.

Let's now look at the real players and the real streaks. Remember, all of the data in this study is from the 2000–2003 seasons, AL and NL combined. In the streak and post-streak data, all home games at Coors Field as well as the road stats for all Rockies' players were excluded, as Coors Field has an abnormal impact on hitting stats both at home and on the road (on the road, the so-called "Rockies hangover effect"). None of the stats has been adjusted for park effects, nor for the quality of the opponent. In case you were wondering, the average temperature during the hot streaks and the post-hot streak periods was slightly higher than during the cold streaks and the post-cold streak periods, although no adjustments were made for temperature, per se. An adjustment was made, however, for the month in which the streak and post-streak periods occurred, in order to somewhat control for game-time temperature.

Again, the expected wOBA for the post-streak periods, both one and five games, were computed by averaging each of the players' (in the hot or cold buckets) three-year wOBA, weighted by their number of post-streak PA. In other words, the expected wOBA of all the players in the hot or cold bucket is what we would expect them to collectively hit (their *normal* rate), based on their three-year wOBA, and not withstanding any hot or cold streak. The reason that the expected wOBA of the players in the hot bucket is 30 points higher than that of the players in the cold bucket, is that the former, as a group, are better hitters than the latter; better hitters are more apt to have one or more hot streaks, and poorer hitters are more apt to have one or more cold streaks.

Table 14.   Batting Performance In Game, After 5-Game Hot Or Cold Streaks

Hot Streaks	
Number of distinct players with one or more 5-game hot streaks	543
Total number of streaks	6,408
Total PA during the streak	141,259
Avg. wOBA during the streak	0.587
Expected wOBA 1 game after the streak	0.365
Actual wOBA 1 game after the streak (27,477 PA)	0.369
Expected wOBA during the 5 games post-streak	0.365
Actual wOBA during the 5 games post-streak (135,167 PA)	0.369
Actual wOBA *on* the fifth game after the streak (26,950 PA)	0.374

Cold Streaks	
Number of distinct players with one or more 5-game cold streaks	633
Total number of streaks	6,489
Total PA during the streak	139,252
Avg. wOBA during the streak	0.151
Expected wOBA 1 game after the streak	0.336
Actual wOBA 1 game after the streak (26,619 PA)	0.330
Expected wOBA during the 5 games post-streak	0.337
Actual wOBA during the 5 games post-streak (132,207 PA)	0.332
Actual wOBA *on* the fifth game after the streak (26,395 PA)	0.332

As you can see from these charts, hot and cold players hit around five points in wOBA better or worse than their norm, respectively, immediately following their five-game streaks. (See Table 14.) While that is a statistically significant difference (in 130,000 PA or so), we don't know about you, but five points of wOBA doesn't exactly send chills down our collective spines. On second thought, we'll leave it up to you to decide how important or worthwhile five points of wOBA is.

Just for the heck of it, what if we extended the number of games constituting a streak to seven (maybe a five-game streak is not enough to have a whole lot of predictive value), and then looked at the three games immediately following the streak? (See Table 15.)

Table 15.   Batting Performance In 3 Games, After 7-Game Hot Or Cold Streaks

Hot Streaks (7-game)	
Number of distinct players with one or more hot streaks	486
Total number of streaks	6,303
Total PA during the streak	193,905
Avg. wOBA during the streak	0.553
Expected wOBA during the 3 games post-streak	0.369
Actual wOBA during the 3 games post-streak (80,262 PA)	0.373

Cold Streaks (7-game)	
Number of distinct players with one or more cold streaks	614
Total number of streaks	7,508
Total PA during the streak	225,565
Avg. wOBA during the streak	0.186
Expected wOBA during the 3 games post-streak	0.336
Actual wOBA during the 3 games post-streak (92,441 PA)	0.328

Again, some slight predictive value—four points for the hot hitters and eight points for the cold ones.

What about hitters who were extremely hot? Here is a list of the ten players who had the hottest seven-game streaks in 2003, along with their three-game post-hot streak wOBA, and their expected (three-year) wOBA. (See Table 16.)

For some reason (or perhaps for no reason at all), these torrid players collectively hit 29 points *below* their expected wOBA in the three games subsequent to their seven-game hot streaks. In fact, nine of them hit worse than their expected wOBA following a hot streak and only one of them hit better.

What about players who had very cold seven-game streaks in 2003? (See Table 17.) For the players who had the coldest streaks in 2003, as a group, their frigid ways did not continue either. Six of the ten players did hit less than their expected wOBA in the three games following their cold streaks, however, three of the ten players were on fire after being ice-cold for seven straight games. The most glaring examples of continued coldness were Al Martin and Jason Larue, weak hitters overall. Both remained anemic for at least three games following a week of offensive futility. Keep in mind that when looking at only ten player streaks (around 140 PA), there is a large amount of random fluctuation when measuring wOBA.

Table 16.   The 10 *Hottest* Streak Hitters In 2003

Player	wOBA during 7-game hot streak	Expected wOBA	wOBA during the 3 games post-streak
Marcus Giles	.693	.354	.249
Vinny Castilla	.694	.309	.234
Barry Bonds	.695	.452	.375
Magglio Ordonez	.697	.377	.867
Albert Pujols	.707	.411	.293
Troy Glaus	.711	.339	.260
Miguel Tejada	.719	.360	.259
Manny Ramirez	.726	.378	.234
Shea Hillenbrand	.732	.351	.289
Jason Giambi	.742	.373	.347
All Players	.712	.370	.341

Looking at all of this data (five- and seven-game hot and cold streaks for all players), there *is* evidence that a hot or cold streak has some predictive value. However, what little predictive value there may be is so small as to be relatively unimportant, in our opinion. In fact, the small differences we see between expected and actual wOBA after five- and seven-game hot and cold streaks could be explained either in part or in whole by weather and park effects. In a previous study we did, looking at seven-game hot and cold streaks from 1998 to 2001, and adjusting all the data for park, weather, and opponent (opposing pitcher) effects, we found *no difference* between expected and actual wOBA, for both the one game and during the seven games immediately following a seven-game streak.

What about injuries? Do players on cold streaks tend to be less healthy than players on hot streaks? When we looked at the average time spent on the disabled list (DL) for players in both the hot and cold groups, we found no difference. Both hot and cold players spent an average of 12.7 games on the DL during the year of the streak. Since we just looked at DL data, we have not eliminated the possibility that players on a cold streak are suffering from some nagging injury and/or players on a hot streak are unusually healthy.

Table 17.   The 10 *Coldest* Streak Hitters In 2003

Player	wOBA during cold streak	Expected wOBA	wOBA during the 3 games post-streak
Luis Castillo	.060	.352	.536
Nick Johnson	.068	.356	.596
Lee Stevens	.075	.302	.223
John Jaha	.076	.314	.669
Pat Mears	.078	.302	.243
Frank Catalanotto	.078	.371	.385
Mike Kinkade	.078	.365	.360
Jason Larue	.081	.305	.000
Rafael Furcal	.082	.275	.164
Al Martin	.084	.302	.060
All Players	.076	.324	.324

The Book Says:

Knowing that a hitter has been in or is in the midst of a hot or cold streak has little predictive value. Always assume that a player will hit at his projected norm (adjusted for the park, weather, and pitcher he is facing), regardless of how he has performed in the very recent past. A player's recent history may be used as a tiebreaker.

Also keep in mind that we are *not* saying that scouts, managers, or coaches are unable to recognize a (presumably small) subset of hot and cold players who are truly on or off-kilter enough for their streaks to have some significantly large (larger than we see in the entire group) predictive value. We are merely looking at and commenting on all hot and cold streaks (as defined by our study) in general.

PITCHER STREAKS

We've just looked at hitter hot and cold streaks and found that they had some small (and in our opinion, relatively unimportant) predictive value. What about pitchers? Intuitively, it would seem that pitchers are more likely to have legitimate periods when they are healthy (or not), their mechanics are exceptional (or not), or they are simply *locked in* (again, or not), and that such physical and mental characteristics, and corresponding performance, are apt to last for some short, or even long, periods of time. Curiously, you don't as often hear announcers or fans referring to pitchers as being hot or cold, as you do with hitters. Perhaps that is simply because pitchers don't play every day. In any case, we are optimistic that streakiness among pitchers may have some significant predictive value, contrary to what we found among batters (where hot and cold streaks had some minor predictive value). Let's see if that optimism comes to fruition.

Our methodology for analyzing hot and cold streaks among pitchers was similar to that of batters. We looked at all pitcher performances from 2000 to 2003 and analyzed starters and relievers separately. We categorized a pitcher hot streak as four performances in a row where a pitcher had a combined opponent wOBA of less than a certain threshold amount (around .240 for starters and .175 for relievers). A cold streak was four consecutive performances above a certain threshold of opponent wOBA (around .425 for starters and .455 for relievers). About 15% of all four-appearance blocks were put into either the hot or cold buckets. As with the batter streaks, a pitcher could be in both the hot and cold buckets in any given year or years and could have several four-game streaks in one or both buckets. Also, as with the batters, pitcher streaks tended to overlap and the better pitchers were more likely to be in the hot bucket and the poorer ones in the cold bucket. In fact, the average three-year opponent wOBA of all the starting pitchers in the hot bucket, weighted by the number of batters they faced in the appearance immediately following the four-game streak, was .312. In the cold bucket, it was .346. So the average starter in the cold bucket was 34 points in opponent wOBA worse than the average starter in the hot bucket. That's a large difference—over one run in ERA (after converting opponent wOBA into expected ERA). In order to see whether a hot or cold streak had any predictive value, we looked at each hot or cold pitcher's very next performance after the four-appearance streak. We compared the collective opponent wOBA of that one-game post-streak performance to all the hot or cold pitchers' normal, or three-year, opponent wOBA.

As with the batters, all games in Coors field, as well as Rockies' players' road data, were removed from the database. Once again, wOBA was not adjusted for park effects, nor for the quality of the opponent, but was adjusted for the month of the season (league-average wOBA is slightly higher in June and slightly lower in September).

Here are the results. (See Table 18.) *Expected opponent wOBA,* in the table, is a pitcher's three-year overall opponent wOBA before, during, and after the year of the streak—just like with the batters. wERA is opponent wOBA converted into an ERA (we won't go into the details of the conversion, but it is relatively straightforward).

As you can see from these charts, our optimism did not go unrewarded. The hot pitchers—those who had at least four consecutive starts where their combined performance was exceptional—pitched 11 points in wOBA better than expected in their very next start. That corresponds to around .3 runs in expected ERA. That is enough to turn an otherwise average pitcher into a good one and a good pitcher into a near-great one. After a cold streak, pitchers continued to pitch somewhat worse than their norm—to the tune of around six points in opponent wOBA, or .22 runs in expected ERA, a less significant difference. In fact, in 18,000 total batters faced (TBF) or so, a difference of 11 wOBA points is right around 3 standard deviations from the mean and 6 points is 1.6 standard deviations from the mean.

Table 18.   Starting Pitcher Performance In Game, After 4-Game Hot Or Cold Streaks

Starting Pitcher 4-game Hot Streaks	
Number of distinct pitchers with one or more hot streaks	183
Total number of streaks	681
Total TBF during streak	73,915
Avg. opponent wOBA during the streak	0.217
Avg. wERA during the streak	2.00
Expected opponent wOBA 1 game after the streak	0.310
Expected wERA 1 game after the streak	3.82
Actual opponent wOBA 1 game after the streak (18,265 TBF)	0.299
Actual wERA 1 game after the streak	3.51

Starting Pitcher 4-game Cold Streaks	
Number of distinct pitchers with one or more cold streaks	266
Total number of streaks	851
Total TBF during streak	76,538
Avg. opponent wOBA during the streak	0.453
Avg. wERA during the streak	9.98
Expected opponent wOBA 1 game after the streak	0.348
Expected wERA 1 game after the streak	5.06
Actual opponent wOBA 1 game after the streak (17,658 TBF)	0.354
Actual wERA 1 game after the streak	5.28

Let's look at the same data for relief pitchers, again using four appearances as the length of our streaks. (See Table 19.)

With relievers, the hot group also continued their above-the-norm pitching. The cold relievers pitched at almost exactly their expected level after a four-game cold streak. *Technical note*: We expect all of the hot and cold pitchers to regress a negligible amount toward the league-average, as all pitchers in each respective bucket were by definition (because they are a selective sample) slightly lucky or unlucky in the year of the streak (because of the streak), and hence in their three-year overall baseline performance.

Table 19.   Relief Pitcher Performance In Game, After 4-Game Hot Or Cold Streaks

Relief Pitcher 4-game Hot Streaks	
Number of distinct pitchers with one or more hot streaks	478
Total number of streaks	3730
Total TBF during streak	54,179
Avg. opponent wOBA during the streak	0.102
Avg. wERA during the streak	2.15
Expected opponent wOBA 1 game after the streak	0.309
Expected wERA 1 game after the streak	3.79
Actual opponent wOBA 1 game after the streak (16,288 TBF)	0.299
Actual wERA 1 game after the streak	3.51
Relief Pitcher 4-game Cold Streaks	
Number of distinct pitchers with one or more cold streaks	504
Total number of streaks	2929
Total TBF during streak	54,884
Avg. opponent wOBA during the streak	0.547
Avg. wERA during the streak	16.26
Expected opponent wOBA 1 game after the streak	0.333
Expected wERA 1 game after the streak	4.53
Actual opponent wOBA 1 game after the streak (13,958 TBF)	0.332
Actual wERA 1 game after the streak	4.5

What if we change the number of consecutive games constituting a streak? As we might expect, after only a one-game hot or cold streak, starters performed at almost exactly their three-year norms, .326 expected and .324 actual for the hot pitchers, .341 expected and .341 actual for the cold pitchers. So one good or bad game for a starter does not a streak make. Relievers, on the other hand, show a similar, but not quite as marked, pattern after a one-game streak as they do after a four-game streak. The hot ones pitch seven points better than their norm, and the cold ones actually pitch four points *better* than their norm. While the seven-point difference for the hot relievers is statistically significant, the four-point reverse difference for the cold relievers is not.

How about seven-game streaks? Are they more significant in terms of their predictive value? For starting pitchers, seven-game streaks are almost exactly like (have the same predictive value as) four-game streaks. Hot starters continue to pitch well, .299 expected and .289 actual, and cold pitchers perform a little worse than expected, .353 and .355. For relievers, after a seven-game hot or cold streak, the hot pitchers pitch exactly as expected, and the cold ones pitch three points worse than their norms. We are at a loss to explain why four-game hot streaks have some predictive value for relievers, while seven-game hot streaks do not. As always, we are at the mercy of the vagaries of random fluctuation associated with finite sample sizes. Even in 15,000 TBF or so, differences of four or five wOBA points are not statistically significant.

If hot and cold pitcher streaks do, in fact, have some predictive value, how long do they last? We also looked at the next four appearances (as opposed to only one game) combined after a hot and cold streak. Hot starters remained hot for at least four more games. The expected opponent wOBA for the hot starting pitchers with at least four subsequent appearances was .311, and their actual opponent wOBA over those four post-hot streak games was .299, a difference of 12 points. For the cold starting pitchers, their four-game post-cold streak performance was right at their expected level—.345 to .345. For relievers, there was only a slight (not significant) continuation in hotness during the entire four games after a hot streak—.308 expected and .305 actual. For the cold relievers, there was no continued coldness, as expected (since there was no continued cold pitching *one* day after the streak).

How about in the sixth game *only*, after the identified hot or cold block (i.e., six games removed from the identified streak)? The hot starting pitchers still had some residual hotness—.310 expected and .304 actual, a marginally significant difference. The cold starters again pitched exactly at their expected norm. For relievers, any residual hotness or coldness was gone after six games. In fact, the cold relievers pitched eight points better than expected in the sixth game after the end of the streak. That also may be a sample size fluke, as eight points is only marginally significant in that many TBF.

What about injuries? Do the cold pitchers tend to be injured and are the hot ones especially healthy? As with the batters, for each group of pitchers, hot and cold, we looked at the average number of days, per pitcher, spent on the disabled list (DL) in the year of the streak. For starting pitchers, the cold ones spent a few more days on the DL than the hot ones—15.9 days to 12.4. For comparison, the average pitcher spent 15.9 days on the DL per year. (For some reason, pitchers who went into neither the hot nor the cold buckets averaged 17.6 days on the DL.) So the hot starting pitchers appeared to be especially healthy and the cold ones were about as healthy as an average pitcher. For relievers, the cold ones spent 11.6 days on the shelf, and the hot ones, 11.7—an insignificant difference. The average reliever spent 12.5 days per year on the DL.

It appears that one of the reasons for the predictive value of hot and cold pitching is the health of the pitchers, at least for starters. Pitchers who have spent more time on the DL in any given year are more likely to have a four-game cold streak and pitchers who have spent less time (by an average of four days) on the DL tend to have more four-game hot streaks. The presumption is that the former are less healthy than the latter. How much of a factor does health play in the predictive value of pitcher hot and cold streaks? Unfortunately, we have no idea.

If we look at only those starting pitchers who were red-hot or ice-cold over a four-game performance span, here is what we get: for the 53 hottest starters from 2000 to 2003, their opponent wOBA during their four-game hot streak was .183. Their expected performance was .297, and they pitched at a .288 clip in their very next game. For the 89 coldest starters during that same time period, their opponents had a .502 wOBA over their four-game cold streak, their expected opponent wOBA was .354, and their actual performance in that fifth appearance was .353. So we basically get the same results with the red-hot and ice-cold starters as we do with the regular hot and cold starters: a slight continuation of their hotness or coldness in the next game—more for the hot pitchers than for the cold ones. Interestingly, there was no difference in average time spent on the DL between the red-hot and the ice-cold starters. Both groups averaged a little over 11 days per year on the shelf. Red-hot and ice-cold relievers had a similar profile: the hot ones were .310 expected and .300 actual following their streaks, and the cold ones were .334 expected and .334 actual. The ice-cold relievers also did not spend more time on the DL than the red-hot ones. The suggestion here is that if a pitcher is healthy, a cold streak has little if any predictive value.

Keep in mind that there may be some selection bias in terms of which pitchers get to continue pitching after four consecutive poor performances. If managers relegate some starters to the bullpen or send some pitchers to the minor leagues after several poor outings, which they no doubt do, we may be missing out on a certain percentage of pitchers who are having some genuine mental or physical infirmity such that they are in fact more likely to continue pitching poorly if given the chance to do so.

The Book Says:

If a pitcher has pitched exceptionally well for four consecutive appearances or so, we can expect him to continue to pitch better than his norm for at least one more appearance. If a pitcher has pitched poorly for several appearances in a row, if he is otherwise physically and mentally fit, we can expect him to continue to pitch at his usual (long-term) level of performance.

CHAPTER 3 – MANO A MANO

BATTER/PITCHER CONFRONTATIONS

There's been a proliferation of batter/pitcher confrontation results presented in the daily paper in an ongoing effort to provide the fans with seemingly relevant and important information. 16 for 38, 7 for 9, 0 for 3. What does it all mean? Aren't some of these cases just too small a sample to draw any kind of conclusions whatsoever?

Let's look at all batter/pitcher confrontations from 1999–2002. We'll exclude any PA with position players as pitchers, pitchers as batters, bunts, and IBB. We're going to split up the data into two sets, to determine if performances in past years can predict performances in a subsequent season. The 1999–2001 confrontations will be the *before*, and the 2002 confrontations will be the *after*. We'll ensure that the same confrontation pairs exist in both the *before* and *after* groups. This gives us 20,208 confrontation pairs: from the three PA confrontations between Brent Abernathy and Rolando Arrojo (two before, and one after), to the eleven before PA and three after PA of Todd Zeile and Masato Yoshii, and the 20,206 pairs in-between.

Let's concentrate on those confrontations with at least seventeen before PA and nine after PA. This reduces our data set to exactly three hundred pairs. This sample will be much more manageable, as well as being presumably more relevant. After all, not many people will argue that the two times that Abernathy/Arroyo faced each other would be predictive of the third time they faced each other. With our three hundred confrontation pairs, we get an average of twenty-two before PA and eleven after PA.

So, if a batter has faced a particular pitcher twenty-two times in the past, how predictive are the results of those twenty-two PA? In other words, do they tell us anything about how he is going to do the next time he faces that same pitcher? Let's see.

In terms of performance, the biggest mismatch was between Luis Gonzalez and Andy Ashby. How incredible was it? In eighteen PA, Gonzo had four HR, one triple, two doubles, two singles, one walk, and struck out once. That's an OBP of .556, and a SLG of 1.471! Even Barry Bonds would be jealous of numbers like that. Most people would say that Gonzo *owns* Ashby.

How about the flip-side? Let's take a look at Mike Mussina and Jason Varitek. One single, one walk, and seventeen outs (of which nine were strikeouts). We don't think we need to figure out Varitek's OBP and SLG.

So, we've got some really lopsided confrontations here. But, how significant are they? How much attention should we pay to these batter/pitcher confrontations? Are hitters who have shown a tendency to *own* pitchers (and vice versa) exhibiting some real trait? Is the identity of a pitcher crucial to a batter's performance (and vice versa)?

If this was real, if from 1999–2001, Luis Gonzalez really has Andy Ashby figured out, if Mike Mussina knows how to pitch to Jason Varitek, then we would expect these lopsided confrontations to continue at least somewhat in 2002, right?

Luis Gonzalez

Here is how Luis Gonzalez did in 1999 to 2001 against all pitchers that met the thresholds mentioned above. Gonzalez was a .418 (wOBA) hitter against all pitchers from 1999–2002. His performance against Rueter, Ortiz, Schmidt, and Neagle, while very good, is not out of line with his overall performance level. But, his performance against Andy Ashby really stands out here.

Pitcher	PA	1B	2B	3B	HR	NIBB	HBP	RBOE	SO	wOBA
Andy Ashby	18	2	2	1	4	1	0	0	1	0.798
Kirk Rueter	24	2	1	1	2	3	0	1	3	0.483
Russ Ortiz	25	7	2	0	0	2	1	0	3	0.439
Jason Schmidt	18	2	2	0	1	2	0	0	2	0.426
Denny Neagle	18	4	2	0	0	2	0	0	3	0.418

Let's check in to see how Gonzo did against these same pitchers in 2002:

Pitcher	1999–2001 PA	wOBA	2002 PA	wOBA
Andy Ashby	18	0.798	12	0.300
Kirk Rueter	24	0.483	12	0.298
Russ Ortiz	25	0.439	14	0.334
Jason Schmidt	18	0.426	15	0.384
Denny Neagle	18	0.418	9	0.463

That's quite a reversal of fortune. Luis Gonzalez, against the one guy he owned in the previous eighteen PA, the one guy that he took to the cleaners more often than any other pitcher he's faced, the one pitcher that any hitter has taken advantage of more than any other pitcher in baseball, crumbled in his sight for the next twelve PA.

Is Gonzalez/Ashby an exception here, or are they the rule? Or, are confrontation pairs simply insignificant? We know we have three hundred pairs of confrontations to choose from. We'll sort them based on the *before* wOBA performance levels. Let's look at the top 10%, the thirty pairs of confrontations whereby the hitters owned their pitchers.

Giles and Fullmer

Here's the #2 pair on the list: Brian Giles and Elmer Dessens.

When	PA	1B	2B	3B	HR	NIBB	HBP	RBOE	SO	wOBA
Before	20	6	3	1	2	1	0	0	0	0.765
After	10	1	1	0	0	0	0	0	4	0.214

This one is even more damaging. Brian Giles is a better overall hitter than Gonzalez. And his before performance against Dessens was almost as good. And yet, look what happens during the ten times he faces him in 2002. A single, a double, and four strikeouts. Let's keep a tally here. We are now 0 for 2.

How about #3? Brad Fullmer and Freddy Garcia. Fullmer is a pretty good hitter, and Garcia is a pretty good pitcher. Let's see if Fullmer really had Garcia figured out.

When	PA	1B	2B	3B	HR	NIBB	HBP	RBOE	SO	wOBA
Before	17	1	4	0	3	0	0	0	1	0.689
After	12	1	1	0	0	1	0	0	0	0.238

0 for 3.

Tejada, Sheff, Bernie, Colbrunn

Let's take a look at the before numbers of the #4 through #7 pairs:
- Miguel Tejada and Jamie Moyer
- Gary Sheffield and Pedro Astacio
- Bernie Williams and Sidney Ponson
- Greg Colbrunn and Kirk Rueter

When	PA	1B	2B	3B	HR	NIBB	HBP	RBOE	SO	wOBA
Before	18	4	2	1	1	2	0	1	0	0.664
Before	24	8	3	0	1	3	1	0	3	0.658
Before	23	2	2	1	2	6	0	1	1	0.651
Before	24	6	2	0	3	1	0	1	5	0.640

Plenty of great performances in there. These hitters all owned these pitchers, right? Surely, two or three of them would continue to own them? You decide:

When	PA	1B	2B	3B	HR	NIBB	HBP	RBOE	SO	wOBA
After	20	3	1	0	0	0	0	0	3	0.197
After	9	0	0	0	0	1	1	0	0	0.163
After	12	2	0	0	0	0	0	0	3	0.150
After	10	2	0	0	0	0	0	0	1	0.180

These are the worst performances yet. We are now 0 for 7. We selected the seven most lopsided batter/pitcher performances from 1999–2001, and in each instance, not only did the hitters stop owning these pitchers, but the pitchers completely turned the tables around, and they started owning the hitters. Surely, this can't be the norm?

All Thirty Batters Owning Pitchers

Here are the thirty pairs of most-lopsided performances from 1999–2001, with their before and after numbers. (See Table 20.)

We count ten for the batters, thirteen for the pitchers, and seven even matches. Overall, these thirty confrontation pairs produced an overall wOBA of .349, which is just a shade over the league-average.

If this skill existed, if certain batters have figured out certain pitchers, surely we would have found at least *some* of them in this group. We have thirty hitters with a fabulous hitting record against thirty pitchers. And yet, given the chance to prove this skill in subsequent confrontations, they fail miserably. As a group, they hit pretty much what we expected them to hit, without considering the identity of the opposing pitcher.

Table 20. **Batter/Pitcher Performance In Season Following Batter Owning Pitcher**

Batter	Pitcher	1999–2001 PA	wOBA	2002 PA	wOBA	Who owns whom (2002)
Luis Gonzalez	Andy Ashby	18	0.798	12	0.300	Pitcher
Brian Giles	Elmer Dessens	20	0.765	10	0.214	Pitcher
Brad Fullmer	Freddy Garcia	17	0.689	12	0.238	Pitcher
Miguel Tejada	Jamie Moyer	18	0.664	20	0.197	Pitcher
Gary Sheffield	Pedro Astacio	24	0.658	9	0.163	Pitcher
Bernie Williams	Sidney Ponson	23	0.651	12	0.150	Pitcher
Greg Colbrunn	Kirk Rueter	24	0.640	10	0.180	Pitcher
Mike Redmond	Tom Glavine	26	0.634	9	0.300	Pitcher
Vladimir Guerrero	Randy Wolf	18	0.606	9	0.517	Batter
Edgar Martinez	Tim Hudson	24	0.593	11	0.234	Pitcher
Jeff Bagwell	Ryan Dempster	17	0.589	10	0.433	Batter
Shawn Green	Livan Hernandez	26	0.585	12	0.210	Pitcher
Steve Finley	Russ Ortiz	20	0.583	12	0.328	
Carlos Delgado	Jeff Weaver	18	0.559	12	0.627	Batter
Todd Helton	Livan Hernandez	24	0.558	13	0.578	Batter
Garret Anderson	Barry Zito	20	0.552	15	0.441	Batter
Rafael Palmeiro	Scott Schoeneweis	19	0.546	16	0.524	Batter
Barry Bonds	Mike Hampton	20	0.546	10	0.342	
Paul Konerko	Jeff Suppan	24	0.546	14	0.461	Batter
Jeff Bagwell	Darryl Kile	22	0.544	12	0.447	Batter
Bernie Williams	Scott Erickson	17	0.536	10	0.343	
Brian Giles	Jimmy Haynes	17	0.536	13	0.249	Pitcher
Brian Jordan	Mike Hampton	17	0.535	10	0.286	Pitcher
Mike Lieberthal	Tom Glavine	21	0.529	15	0.493	Batter
Jacque Jones	Jeff Suppan	21	0.529	18	0.477	Batter
Orlando Cabrera	Kevin Millwood	18	0.528	11	0.147	Pitcher
Carlos Delgado	Jason Johnson	21	0.521	9	0.354	
Adrian Beltre	Livan Hernandez	24	0.518	11	0.371	
Doug Glanville	Al Leiter	27	0.517	12	0.310	
Chipper Jones	Al Leiter	32	0.513	12	0.345	

The Pitchers

What about the flip-side—pitchers who *own* certain batters? Here is everyone whom Mike Mussina faced in 1999 to 2001, once again meeting the above-mentioned threshold (minimum of seventeen PA, with the usual exceptions):

Batter	PA	1B	2B	3B	HR	NIBB	HBP	RBOE	SO	wOBA
Jason Varitek	19	1	0	0	0	1	0	0	9	0.085
Ben Grieve	18	2	0	0	0	1	0	0	6	0.140
Trot Nixon	31	1	2	0	0	2	0	0	12	0.155
Jose Cruz Jr.	19	3	0	0	0	1	0	0	7	0.180
Jose Offerman	35	6	1	0	0	2	0	0	13	0.231
Manny Ramirez	24	2	1	1	0	1	0	1	6	0.260
Carlos Delgado	26	2	2	0	1	1	0	0	8	0.267
Brian Daubach	27	2	3	0	1	1	0	0	14	0.303
Johnny Damon	21	4	1	0	1	1	0	0	3	0.358
Rey Sanchez	19	4	2	0	0	0	0	1	0	0.368

Mike Mussina actually owned four different hitters: Varitek, Grieve, Nixon, and Cruz. He also had excellent performances against Offerman, Ramirez, and Delgado. For some reason, he had the toughest time against Sanchez, normally a very weak hitter. Here's how Mussina did against each of these batters in 2002:

Batter	1999–2001 PA	1999–2001 wOBA	2002 PA	2002 wOBA
Jason Varitek	19	0.085	9	0.100
Ben Grieve	18	0.140	9	0.378
Trot Nixon	31	0.155	17	0.328
Jose Cruz Jr.	19	0.180	9	0.182
Jose Offerman	35	0.231	11	0.082
Manny Ramirez	24	0.260	13	0.261
Carlos Delgado	26	0.267	9	0.297
Brian Daubach	27	0.303	18	0.188
Johnny Damon	21	0.358	21	0.197
Rey Sanchez	19	0.368	13	0.277

He continued his mastery of Varitek, but was lost with the next hitter, Grieve. With the rest of the hitters, sometimes the *before* and *after* performances were consistent, and other times they were not.

Table 21.   Batter/Pitcher Performance In Season Following Pitcher Owning Batter

Batter	Pitcher	1999–2001 PA wOBA		2002 PA wOBA		Who owns whom (2002)
Jason Varitek	Mike Mussina	19	0.085	9	0.100	Pitcher
Luis Castillo	Greg Maddux	29	0.125	11	0.195	Pitcher
Ben Grieve	Mike Mussina	18	0.140	9	0.378	
David Justice	Jamie Moyer	19	0.142	18	0.180	Pitcher
Edgardo Alfonzo	Randy Wolf	24	0.150	13	0.307	
Trot Nixon	Mike Mussina	31	0.155	17	0.328	
Carlos Delgado	Mike Stanton	17	0.159	10	0.252	Pitcher
Bob Abreu	Tom Glavine	29	0.161	11	0.407	Batter
Jorge Posada	Pedro Martinez	30	0.162	12	0.368	
Rey Ordonez	Tom Glavine	22	0.164	11	0.413	Batter
Cristian Guzman	Jeff Suppan	22	0.164	15	0.241	Pitcher
Troy Glaus	Freddy Garcia	27	0.166	12	0.345	
Jose Vidro	A.J. Burnett	18	0.169	12	0.210	Pitcher
Mike Lowell	Kevin Millwood	18	0.172	12	0.463	Batter
Darin Erstad	Freddy Garcia	29	0.174	10	0.643	Batter
Doug Glanville	Tom Glavine	33	0.175	14	0.384	
Ryan Klesko	Livan Hernandez	17	0.176	10	0.428	Batter
Jose Cruz Jr.	Mike Mussina	19	0.180	9	0.182	Pitcher
Derrek Lee	Greg Maddux	24	0.182	16	0.336	
Richie Sexson	Wade Miller	25	0.187	12	0.416	Batter
Preston Wilson	Al Leiter	22	0.188	11	0.532	Batter
Jermaine Dye	Jamie Moyer	18	0.190	9	0.100	Pitcher
Adrian Beltre	Kirk Rueter	18	0.190	10	0.360	
Adrian Beltre	Randy Johnson	25	0.194	16	0.356	
Adam Kennedy	Freddy Garcia	17	0.198	12	0.357	
Mike Sweeney	Brad Radke	19	0.198	13	0.480	Batter
Joe Randa	Jon Garland	17	0.201	10	0.214	Pitcher
Andruw Jones	Tony Jr. Armas	22	0.203	14	0.306	
Edgardo Alfonzo	Tom Glavine	26	0.205	13	0.523	Batter
Jim Thome	Jeff Suppan	20	0.207	10	0.481	Batter

All Thirty Pitchers Owning Batters

Let's do the same thing we did for the hitters; this time, we'll look at the thirty confrontation pairs where the pitchers dominated. (See Table 21.)

That's nine wins for the pitchers, and ten for the batters, with nine draws. Overall? A .343 wOBA. League-average. Once again, the identity of the opponent was irrelevant. These pitchers didn't own these hitters. If they did, we would have expected something; alas, we found nothing.

Summary

Here are the combined 2002 performances of the batters who owned the pitchers (from 1999–2001) and the pitchers who owned the batters (again, from 1999–2001). (See Table 22.)

Table 22.   Batter/Pitcher Performance In Season Following Lopsided Performances

Who owned whom From 1999–2001	In 2002 PA	1B	2B	3B	HR	NIBB	HBP	RBOE	SO	wOBA
Batters owned pitchers	361	50	22	1	9	38	7	2	41	0.349
Pitchers owned batters	361	58	21	2	8	30	2	4	69	0.343

Coincidentally, both groups had 361 PA in 2002. And, look what happened. The batters, the guys who hit like Barry Bonds, ended up with nine HR. The pitchers, the guys who pitched like Sandy Koufax, gave up eight HR. In exactly the same number of PA. The singles, doubles, triples, and walks, all were virtually identical. The strikeout difference really stands out. But overall, their performances were almost identical.

If batters really had their pitchers figured out, and if pitchers really had their batters figured out, we wouldn't have expected this. We would have expected to see their Bonds-like and Koufax-like performances continue, at least somewhat, in 2002. We didn't.

Why? Because having twenty to thirty PA against an opponent is a drop in the bucket, and it tells you almost nothing about what to expect. The player has a long history, say 1,500 PA, against the rest of the league. Any way you slice it, you can't equate, or even compare, twenty-five PA against one opponent to 1,500 PA against the rest of the league. Contrast that with the typical manager or commentator who says something like, ". . . four or five times at bat is meaningless, but once you have fifteen or twenty . . ." Well, once again, they are wrong. When a particular batter has faced a particular pitcher two hundred or three hundred times, come back and we'll talk. Maybe.

> *The Book* Says:
>
> Knowing a player will face a particular opponent, and given the choice between that player's 1,500 PA over the past three years against the rest of the league, or twenty-five PA against that particular opponent, look at the 1,500 PA.

COMPARABLES

OK, so you buy the dangers of small sample sizes. But, surely there must be something there for larger samples? How can we increase our sample sizes, given the fact that batters only face a particular pitcher five or ten times a year? What if we look at similar pitchers?

We like to look at certain "classes" or "types" of pitchers. You know the kind: Jamie Moyer
- is a lefthander.
- Batters have no problem making contact with his pitches,
- he has an excellent command of the strike zone, and

- he is fairly neutral with respect to the frequency of balls hit in the air or on the ground.

A couple of years ago, Bill James talked about the same kind of idea when discussing the "Robin Roberts Family of Pitchers" concept. Family. That's a great word, and is both more descriptive and less technical than "class" or "type." We'll use that term, but so as not to steal Bill's thunder, we'll use the Italian word for family: *famiglia*.

So, if Jamie Moyer is the *capo di famiglia*, who are the other members of this *famiglia*? Who exhibits similar traits to Moyer? Remember, even in all *famiglias*, there are some members who are less effective than others. We aren't looking for players of the same quality, but only pitchers who pitch in a similar fashion. Of course, if you've got excellent command of the strike zone, like Moyer, that goes a long way toward establishing effectiveness.

La Famiglia Moyer

Welcome to *la famiglia* Moyer: Mark Buehrle, Mark Redman, Glendon Rusch, Boomer Wells. Each of these pitchers exhibits the above traits to varying degrees.

Each of these pitchers is also a *capo* of his own *famiglia*. Mark Buehrle is *capo* of a *famiglia* consisting of: Moyer, Redman, Wells, Rusch, as well as Odaliz Perez and Mike Sirotka. Buehrle is just slightly different enough from Moyer that Perez and Sirotka make the cut for his *famiglia*, but not for Moyer.

Some pitchers have no *famiglia*. They are so unique, that no one compares. Greg Maddux for one. No one is even close to him. Pedro. How about Randy Johnson? Even though he doesn't look anything like him, Billy Wagner is a somewhat decent comp to RJ. Both pitchers are lefties who have superb control of the strike zone, and hitters can barely make contact with their pitches. However, one is a starter and the other is a reliever.

Note: if other pieces of data were more widely available, like percentage of curve balls thrown, average speed of fastball, arm angle, or release point, whether they tend to pitch up or down in the zone, or in or out, we would have used those as well. As it stands, we think we have very good sets of comps.

So, if you have a batter who has faced Jamie Moyer, but your sample size is small, you can also look at how that batter did against the rest of *la famiglia* Moyer. And we could do this for all *famiglias*. Let's see what happens.

Edgar Martinez against *La Famiglia* Adams

Edgar Martinez owns the Adams family. What is *la famiglia* Adams, and who is in it? Terry Adams is a righty who has very good control of the strike zone, is an extreme groundball pitcher, and is fairly neutral in terms of the frequency in which batters make contact. So, that's *la famiglia* Adams, with Terry Adams as the *capo*. And who belongs to this *famiglia*? Jason Grimsley, Roy Halladay, Tim Hudson, Jose Jimenez, Jay Powell, Lou Pote, and Mike Timlin.

Here's how Edgar did against *la famiglia* Adams from 1999–2001:

Pitcher	PA	1B	2B	3B	HR	NIBB	HBP	RBOE	SO	wOBA
Terry Adams	1	1	0	0	0	0	0	0	0	0.900
Jason Grimsley	7	0	2	0	0	0	2	0	0	0.569
Roy Halladay	12	4	0	0	1	1	0	0	3	0.523
Tim Hudson	24	8	0	0	1	6	1	0	1	0.593
Lou Pote	7	2	0	0	0	0	1	0	0	0.364
Famiglia Adams	51	15	2	0	2	7	4	0	4	0.547

He really had his way with all these pitchers. You might be tempted to think that Edgar has a special ability to take advantage of groundball righties with good command of the strike zone. After all, we just looked for pitchers who look like that, and we found them. Not only that, but Edgar loved hitting against these pitchers. Now, how did he do in 2002 against these same pitchers? Does Edgar Martinez particularly like these kinds of pitchers, or was it just good fortune, a random variation in a relatively small sample of performance (51 PA)? Well, it looks like he might like them to some degree:

Pitcher	1999–2001 PA	wOBA	2002 PA	wOBA
Terry Adams	1	0.900	0	
Jason Grimsley	7	0.569	2	0.620
Roy Halladay	12	0.523	4	0.765
Tim Hudson	24	0.593	11	0.234
Jose Jimenez	0		1	0.000
Lou Pote	7	0.364	2	0.975
Jay Powell	0		4	0.180
Famiglia Adams	51	0.547	24	0.398

The overall wOBA is .398. That doesn't compare to the .547 in the *before* group, but it's still pretty good, right? Not so fast! Edgar is a great hitter *overall*. Against the league, in 1999–2002, he was .424! So, we expected him to perform at least as good as against the rest of the league, and really somewhat better. He didn't get there.

Let's look for all confrontation pairs with at least fifty PA in the before group, and twenty PA in the after group. Here's how the top (highest *before* wOBA) twenty-five hitter/pitcher *famiglia* did. (See Table 23.)

Looks like a similar pattern to earlier: almost random. Some hitters performed better and others worse. Overall, a wOBA of .368, which is actually quite good. But, look at some of the names in this group: Edgar, Berkman, Edmonds, Vlad, Delgado, A-Rod, Nomar, Chipper, Sosa, Kent. Overall, these hitters had a wOBA of .390. So, they actually performed *worse* than expected.

Table 23.   Batter/Pitcher Performance In Season Following Batter Owning Famiglia

| Batter | Famiglia | 1999–2001 | | 2002 | | 1999–2002 |
		PA	wOBA	PA	wOBA	Batter v League
Edgar Martinez	Terry Adams	55	0.560	24	0.398	0.424
Lance Berkman	Curt Leskanic	50	0.548	25	0.330	0.422
Garret Anderson	Mark Buehrle	71	0.535	28	0.344	0.356
Jim Edmonds	Javier Vazquez	69	0.534	22	0.471	0.414
Paul Konerko	Brad Radke	72	0.515	22	0.341	0.376
Geoff Jenkins	Javier Vazquez	68	0.514	24	0.307	0.378
Mike Cameron	Tom Glavine	61	0.514	24	0.528	0.362
Vladimir Guerrero	Mike Magnante	53	0.513	20	0.393	0.422
Todd Zeile	Mike Magnante	55	0.511	27	0.273	0.355
Derrek Lee	Javier Vazquez	78	0.510	31	0.397	0.365
Carlos Delgado	Rick Helling	52	0.507	21	0.360	0.423
Roberto Alomar	Jeff Fassero	53	0.503	21	0.256	0.380
Shannon Stewart	Rick Helling	51	0.503	22	0.312	0.374
Mark Grudzielanek	Kenny Rogers	67	0.502	21	0.522	0.332
Alex Rodriguez	Jeff Fassero	57	0.501	26	0.262	0.430
Mike Sweeney	Brad Radke	72	0.495	22	0.625	0.405
Nomar Garciaparra	Mark Buehrle	52	0.495	22	0.436	0.417
Chipper Jones	Al Leiter	73	0.490	23	0.329	0.432
Jose Cruz Jr.	Rheal Cormier	68	0.485	24	0.271	0.351
Rafael Palmeiro	Omar Olivares	96	0.478	21	0.306	0.411
Paul Konerko	Mike Trombley	61	0.477	22	0.495	0.376
Sammy Sosa	Javier Vazquez	64	0.473	27	0.211	0.443
Jeff Kent	Kenny Rogers	64	0.471	22	0.455	0.405
Kevin Millar	Javier Vazquez	59	0.470	28	0.346	0.382
Michael Tucker	Brad Radke	52	0.466	25	0.320	0.341

Tony Batista against *La Famiglia* Cormier

Rheal Cormier is the *capo* of: Graeme Lloyd, Mark Mulder, Odaliz Perez, Andy Pettitte, Kenny Rogers, J.C. Romero, Mike Sirotka. There's that Mike Sirotka again (we saw him as a comp to Moyer). *La famiglia*

Cormier is a group of lefties with very good command of the strike zone; hitters have it somewhat easy in making contact with their pitches; and they are groundball pitchers.

How did Tony Batista do against *la famiglia* Cormier from 1999–2001?

Pitcher	PA	1B	2B	3B	HR	NIBB	HBP	RBOE	SO	wOBA
Rheal Cormier	6	2	0	0	0	0	0	1	1	0.453
Graeme Lloyd	1	0	0	0	0	0	0	0	0	0.000
Mark Mulder	15	2	0	0	0	0	0	0	4	0.120
Odaliz Perez	5	0	0	0	0	0	0	0	1	0.000
Andy Pettitte	13	1	0	0	0	1	0	0	2	0.125
Kenny Rogers	9	1	0	0	0	0	0	0	4	0.100
J.C. Romero	2	0	0	0	0	0	0	0	0	0.000
Mike Sirotka	12	0	0	0	0	2	0	0	3	0.120
Famiglia Cormier	63	6	0	0	0	3	0	1	15	0.135

Not good. Not good at all. Heck, downright terrible. Even though he held his own against the *capo*, he was completely under the spell of the rest of *la famiglia*. Batista's performance against *la famiglia* Cormier was by far the worst performance any batter had against any *famiglia* of pitchers. In 2002, against these same pitchers, Batista again didn't perform very well.

Pitcher	1999–2001 PA	wOBA	2002 PA	wOBA
Rheal Cormier	6	0.453	1	0.900
Graeme Lloyd	1	0.000	0	
Mark Mulder	15	0.120	9	0.238
Odaliz Perez	5	0.000	3	0.000
Andy Pettitte	13	0.125	8	0.225
Kenny Rogers	9	0.100	5	0.330
J.C. Romero	2	0.000	1	0.900
Mike Sirotka	12	0.120	0	
Famiglia Cormier	63	0.135	24	0.274

La famiglia Cormier certainly had some decent success against Batista, who is a league-average hitter. The success was nowhere near the 1999–2001 performance, but very good nonetheless. Mulder, Pettitte, and Perez stand out as pitchers who were able to dominate Batista.

Are we on to something here? Let's look at the next one: #2 is Cristian Guzman against *la famiglia* Cormier (again). In 1999–2001 they were .193, and .214 in 2002. Hmmm, those Cormier pitchers seem to be doing pretty well.

Here are the top fourteen (lowest *before* wOBA) performances. (See Table 24.) Unfortunately, we couldn't find any more and maintain a *they really owned them* threshold.

Table 24.   Batter/Pitcher Performance In Season Following Famiglia Owning Batter

		1999–2001		2002		1999–2002
Batter	**Famiglia**	**PA**	**wOBA**	**PA**	**wOBA**	**Batter v League**
Tony Batista	Rheal Cormier	63	0.135	27	0.274	0.342
Cristian Guzman	Rheal Cormier	65	0.193	21	0.214	0.304
Doug Glanville	Tom Glavine	55	0.200	21	0.376	0.319
Torii Hunter	Odaliz Perez	56	0.209	29	0.364	0.344
Michael Barrett	Kenny Rogers	51	0.228	20	0.324	0.314
Jose Cruz Jr.	Joe Beimel	50	0.229	20	0.421	0.351
Joe Randa	Rick Helling	50	0.233	20	0.249	0.346
Neifi Perez	Omar Olivares	67	0.236	21	0.359	0.302
Bob Abreu	Kenny Rogers	57	0.236	24	0.395	0.414
Benito Santiago	Joe Beimel	59	0.245	20	0.215	0.320
Terrence Long	Glendon Rusch	54	0.245	38	0.280	0.327
Richie Sexson	Mike Trombley	51	0.246	29	0.278	0.374
Garret Anderson	Bob Wickman	58	0.248	21	0.424	0.356
Cliff Floyd	Javier Vazquez	85	0.249	27	0.557	0.399

As a group, these hitters faced these groups of pitchers and performed at a level of .338 in 2002. A shade under league-average, and a shade under their own overall average. Sigh. We wish we could tell you that we'd find something, but we can't. And the reason is always the same: small sample size. We looked for confrontations with an average of sixty PA, and that was still not enough.

You see, we're not saying that it doesn't matter which pitcher is facing which hitter. It most certainly matters. Every person is different, and there's no reason to think that two overall equally talented pitchers, but talented for different reasons, will necessarily have the same success level against the same hitter. However, you can't tell by looking at the numbers from twenty-five or sixty PA. There is simply too much noise masking the truth under those numbers. You can't say Edgar owns *la famiglia* Cormier, or that Mussina owns Varitek because, *well, look at the numbers*. The numbers don't support your statement, because of the small sample sizes. For you to say that a certain hitter owns a certain pitcher, you have to go beyond the numbers. You have to look at the very specific traits of these players. We'll look at a few traits soon, but as noted earlier, there are many different kinds of traits to consider. When looking at batter/pitcher confrontations, scouting information becomes a critical component to the analysis.

The Book Says:

Sixty highly-targeted PA are still not enough evidence to overwhelm the knowledge contained in 1,500 random PA.

PROFILES

We all know that, as a general rule, hitters perform better against opposite-handed pitchers. How about some of the other characteristics we've talked about so far, like strike zone judgment, contact rates, and groundball/flyball tendencies? Certainly we can buy the small sample size issues, but at the same time, there must be some effect along these lines. Let's find out how much of an effect.

Profile #1: Handedness

We're going to limit our study to all pitchers and batters who, from 1999–2002, had at least 800 PA (after the usual exclusions of IBB, bunts, and any position player acting, literally, like a pitcher). As usual, these numbers represent the wOBA of the actual *mano-a-mano* confrontation. (See Table 25.)

Table 25.   Batter/Pitcher Performances, By Handedness

Batter Hand	Pitcher Hand		Hitter's Platoon Advantage
	Left	Right	
Left	0.339	0.364	0.025
Right	0.358	0.344	0.014
Switch	0.336	0.346	N/A
Pitcher's Platoon Advantage	0.019	0.020	

The first thing we notice is that the platoon advantage is real (we realize that is not earth-shattering news to most of you). A lefty batter hit .339 against all lefties he faced in this pool, whereas he hit .364 against the righties. So, the lefty batter has a 25-point platoon advantage. A righty batter has only a 14-point advantage. That's a 39-point swing. Now, why would that be? One thought is that a righty batter faces many more righties from the time he's a teenager and throughout the big leagues, than a lefty batter faces a lefty. Certainly sounds right, until . . .

Look at how switch hitters do. They prefer to hit righties! There are a couple of thoughts as to the reason for the existence of a switch hitter. You have players who are equally adept at both sides, and have hit that way all of their lives. Or, they are original righties who decided to learn to hit from the left side in order to take advantage of the preponderance of right-handed pitchers. If you are a lefty batter, you already have the platoon advantage most of the time, so why bother learning to hit right-handed?

So, if switch hitters would have a difference in performance, you would expect them, as original righties, to hit lefties better. That is, hitting on your comfortable right side against a lefty pitcher should result in a better performance than hitting on your new left side against a righty pitcher. But, it doesn't happen.

What if instead, something else is happening. What if there are just too many righties in MLB? Righties have a job in MLB because they get the platoon advantage far more than lefties. So, if you have two pitchers, one lefty, one righty, and they are equals pound-for-pound, you'd rather have the righty. This righty will have the platoon advantage far more often than this lefty pitcher simply because there are far more righty batters than lefties.

By the way, this chart shows the number of batters and pitchers by handedness. (See Table 26.)

Table 26. Number Of Regular Players, By Handedness

Batter	Count		Pitcher	Count
Left	109		Left	74
Right	183		Right	240
Switch	48			

So, a righty pitcher will find an easier time than a lefty. But, what if there are too many righty pitchers (or not enough lefty pitchers)? Just for fun, let's take out the 34 worst righty pitchers. So, instead of having 24% LHP (74 out of 314), we'll now have 26% LHP. Doesn't sound like a big change, but look what happens. (See Table 27.)

These are the actual performance numbers, with those pitchers re-moved. The lefty batter and righty batter advantage is now the same. Exactly the same. The lefty and righty pitcher platoon advantage are also now exactly the same (though they were quite close to begin with anyway). Righty against righty? .339. Lefty against lefty? .339. Righty against lefty? .358. The other way? .358. Could it be that the reason that lefty hitters enjoy such a platoon advantage is simply because there are too many righty pitchers (or not enough lefties) to hit against?

Table 27.   Batter/Pitcher Performances, By Handedness (What-If Scenario, Part 1)

| | Pitcher Hand | | |
Batter Hand	Left	Right	Hitter's Platoon Advantage
Left	0.339	0.358	0.019
Right	0.358	0.339	0.019
Switch	0.336	0.342	N/A
Pitcher's Platoon Advantage	0.019	0.019	

Overall, the swing in platoon advantage is around 38 points. So, if you have a hitter who has a true talent level of .340, then you would consider him to be about .350 with the platoon advantage, and .330 without the advantage. It's quite a difference those 20 points. If you had another hitter, a .355 hitter, but who is opposite-handed to that .340 hitter, his splits would be .365 and .345. In this case, if the .340 hitter has the platoon advantage, you would need to play him over the .355 hitter without the platoon advantage.

Switch hitters on the other hand still enjoy the same split. That's a little disturbing. After all, we removed all the bad righties. So, their average should have gone down. Switch hitters might have many conflicting things going on that we're not getting a good handle on them. Plus there are only 48 of them. Small sample.

Take it to a more extreme. Let's get crazy and remove all the below average righty pitchers. We're going to remove 149 righty pitchers from the league. Now we have 45% of the pitchers being lefties. What do you expect will happen to the above numbers? Well, with all the bad righties gone (and all the good righties remaining), the wOBA for all three groups of hitters should go down against righties, correct? (See Table 28.)

Table 28.   Batter/Pitcher Performances, By Handedness (What-If Scenario, Part 2)

| Batter Hand | Pitcher Hand | | Hitter's Platoon Advantage |
	Left	Right	
Left	0.339	0.339	0.000
Right	0.358	0.316	0.042
Switch	0.336	0.320	N/A
Pitcher's Platoon Advantage	0.019	0.023	

Look at the lefty batters now. No platoon advantage. None. And righty batters? Now they have a 42-point advantage. Switch hitters also drop substantially. Actually, they all drop about 20 points by removing all the bad righty pitchers.

So, what happened? Well, lefty batters face all lefty pitchers, good or bad. But, they only face good righties. That's why they have no (apparent) platoon advantage. In fact, they do have an advantage. Lefties hit righty pitchers 23 points better than righty hitters do.

Table 29.   Batter/Pitcher PA Breakdown, By Handedness

| Batter Hand | Pitcher Hand | | Batter Splits |
	Left	Right	
Left	6.4%	26.0%	32.3%
Right	13.3%	40.4%	53.7%
Switch	3.3%	10.7%	14.0%
Pitcher Splits	22.9%	77.1%	100.0%

Do teams actually take advantage of the platoon effect? Well, we know they do. They talk about it all the time. (One look at the number of lefties that Randy Johnson has faced will tell you that.) Here are the numbers. (See Table 29.)

When a lefty is on the mound, a lefty is at bat about one-fourth of the time (6.4 / 22.9 = 28%). When a righty is on the mound, a lefty or switch hitter is at bat almost half the time (26.0 + 10.7 / 77.1 = 48%). So, there is a definite pattern being applied. But is it enough? Even though there is a huge swing, should there be even more lefty batters brought into the game with a righty on the mound? We'll look at that specific question in a later chapter, when we look at platoon strategies.

The Book Says:

The platoon advantage based on handedness is real. There is a 40-point swing in platoon effect.

Profile #2: Groundballs and Flyballs

Is there a platoon advantage based on the tendency of the pitcher and batter to hit the ball on the ground or in the air? Here are the face-to-face confrontation performance numbers. (See Table 30.)

Table 30.   Batter/Pitcher Performances, By Groundball/Flyball Tendencies

Batter Tendency	Pitcher Tendency		
	FB	Neutral	GB
FB	0.364	0.376	0.374
Neutral	0.347	0.350	0.344
GB	0.335	0.337	0.313

Now, we have a situation similar to our handedness profile. But it is much clearer here. Flyball hitters perform better than groundball hitters against all groups of pitchers. Why? Because they *are* better hitters. As a general rule, your power hitter is your best hitter, and power hitters are flyball hitters. Pitchers don't have the same level of split, because pitchers have other ways of getting a batter out: principally, not letting them make contact. In other words, lots of good pitchers are flyball pitchers and lots of good pitchers are groundball pitchers (although groundball pitchers do tend to be a little better than flyball pitchers). The same is true of bad pitchers.

What do the above numbers tell us? A FB hitter is 29 points better than a GB hitter against a FB pitcher (.364 v .335). However, he is 61 points better than a GB hitter is against a GB pitcher (.374 v .313). The advantage here? You want the FB hitter against the GB pitcher. GB pitchers own GB hitters.

Looking at this from the other perspective, a FB pitcher is ten points better than a GB pitcher against FB hitters (.364 v .374). But, against GB hitters, it's the GB pitcher who is 22 points better than the FB pitcher (.313 v .335). FB pitchers own FB hitters.

Overall, the swing advantage is 32 points (61 to 29, or 22 one way to 10 the other way). This is not as big as the handedness platoon advantage, but it is still rather large. Do MLB teams know about this? Here is the breakdown of times at bat, based on taking advantage of the GB/FB tendency. (See Table 31.)

Table 31. Batter/Pitcher PA Breakdown, By Groundball/Flyball Tendencies

Batter Tendency	Pitcher Tendency			Batter Splits
	FB	Neutral	GB	
FB	2.2%	12.0%	2.8%	17.0%
Neutral	9.0%	50.6%	11.4%	71.0%
GB	1.5%	8.6%	1.9%	12.0%
Pitcher Splits	12.7%	71.2%	16.1%	100.0%

Anyway, with a GB pitcher, we said we wanted as few GB hitters as possible, since GB pitchers eat them up. With a GB pitcher on the mound, 12% of the hitters are GB hitters (1.9 / 16.1). With a FB pitcher on the mound, 12% of the hitters are GB hitters (1.5 / 12.7). We won't bore you with the rest of the splits as they all show the same thing.

Managers are not making use of this platoon advantage!

The Book Says:

The *platoon* advantage based on tendency to hit or allow a ball to hit the ground or the air is real. Same-type tendencies mimic those of handedness (e.g., groundball pitchers prefer groundball hitters). It cannot be leveraged as much as handedness since most pitchers and batters are near neutral (in FB/GB ratio), whereas that is not true for standard (handedness) platoon ratios.

Profile #3: Controlling The Strike Zone

Is there a platoon effect with respect to controlling the strike zone? (See Table 32.)

Table 32.   Batter/Pitcher Performances, By K/BB Tendencies

Batter Tendency	Pitcher Tendency		
	High BB/K	Neutral	High K/BB
High BB/K	0.406	0.383	0.341
Neutral	0.374	0.351	0.312
High K/BB	0.360	0.325	0.300

When a batter faces a pitcher who has poor control (high BB/K), the batter with great strike zone judgment (high BB/K) performs 46 points better than the batter with poor strike zone judgment (high K/BB). That was .406 to .360. How about when these same batters face the pitcher with great control? The batter with the better strike zone judgment has a 41-point advantage (.341 to .300).

In short, no platoon effect.

The same applies from the pitcher's perspective. With a batter who has great strike zone judgment, the pitcher with better control has a 65-point advantage (.341 to .406). With a batter with poor strike zone judgment, the pitcher with better control has a 60-point advantage (.360 to .300).

Again, no platoon effect.

Profile #4: Making Contact With The Pitch

How about with respect to making contact with the pitch? (See Table 33.)

Table 33.   Batter/Pitcher Performances, By Contact Tendencies

Batter Tendency	Pitcher Tendency		
	High Contact	Neutral	Low Contact
High Contact	0.359	0.340	0.312
Neutral	0.365	0.349	0.325
Low Contact	0.383	0.375	0.335

Another interesting tidbit: a batter who *doesn't* put the ball in play a lot is in general a better hitter than a batter who puts the ball in play. These hitters tend to have a lot of walks. A pitcher who doesn't let the batter put the ball in play, is also better than a pitcher who allows batters to put the ball in play. These pitchers probably have a lot of strikeouts. These are just general rules of course. You'd have to look at each specific player to establish his exact level of ability.

Anyway, what do we have here? When facing pitchers who allow the ball to be put in play (think pitchers like Brad Radke), batters who put the ball in play a lot are 25 points worse than the opposite batters (.359 to .383). When facing pitchers the opposite of the Radke-type (think Randy Johnson), batters who put the ball in play are 23 points worse than the opposite batters (.312 to .335).

No platoon effect.

We won't bore you with looking at it from the other perspective. Same thing. No platoon effect.

The Book Says:

There is no platoon effect with respect to how well a player can control the strike zone, or make contact with the ball.

Profile #5: Good Hitting Meets Good Pitching

This is one that we hear all the time: good pitching beats good hitting. First of all, what does that even mean? If you are a good pitcher, don't you beat everyone? After all, that is the reason you are a good pitcher to begin with. If you only beat the bad hitters, then you are a bad pitcher.

Presumably, of course, they are talking about having an extra advantage, like a platoon advantage. That is, when a good pitcher faces a good hitter, the good pitcher has an extra advantage. Is that true? This is easy enough to check, so let's find out. Let's concentrate on good pitchers, and how they perform against good and bad hitters. (See Table 34.)

Table 34.   Batter Performances, By Quality, Against Good Pitchers
(Part 1)

Batters	vs Good Pitchers	vs All Pitchers	Difference
Bad	0.260	0.304	0.044
Average	0.296	0.348	0.052
Good	0.358	0.417	0.059

Good hitters really take a beating don't they? Bad hitters lose 44 points on their performance, but good hitters lose 59 points. Maybe good pitching really does eat up good hitting. Or maybe not.

Up until now, we have been looking at differences. Why? Because that's a lot easier to grasp. We've gotten away with it because the starting point for the comparisons was always close enough. Until now.

In this case, the bad hitters are starting off at a .304 level, while the good hitters are at a .417 level. At this point, we have to leave the ease of using differences, and go with the more accurate way: percentage change. So, we'll repeat the last column, but this time, it'll be the percentage change. We'll label this column the Pull Rate. The Pull Rate is how much the player's overall performance level was pulled down to the pitcher's performance level. (See Table 35.)

Table 35.   Batter Performances, By Quality, Against Good Pitchers
(Part 2)

Batters	vs Good Pitchers	vs All Pitchers	Pull Rate
Bad	0.260	0.304	14.5%
Average	0.296	0.348	15.0%
Good	0.358	0.417	14.0%

Good pitchers have the exact same effect on all groups of hitters. Bad hitters, good hitters, average hitters. It doesn't matter. Good pitchers pulled down the performance level of all these hitters by 14 to 15%.

How about bad pitchers? (See Table 36.)

Table 36.   Batter Performances, By Quality, Against Bad Pitchers

Batters	vs Bad Pitchers	vs All Pitchers	Pull Rate
Bad	0.332	0.304	9.1%
Average	0.381	0.349	9.4%
Good	0.457	0.416	9.7%

Any questions?

What it comes down to is the same thing. A .300 pitcher against a .400 hitter will result in exactly the same performance level as a .400 pitcher against a .300 hitter. Good pitchers will pull down any kind of hitter to the pitcher's performance level, as much as a good hitter will pull up any kind of pitcher to the hitter's performance level.

The Book Says:

There is no platoon effect with respect to the quality of the pitcher or hitter. Good pitching beats good hitting as much as good hitting beats good pitching.

CHAPTER 4 – JORDAN, WOODS, . . . SPIEZIO?

CLUTCH HITTING

The concept of "clutch" is so central to our understanding of sports that it needs little in the way of introduction. Simply put, a clutch player is one who performs better when the game is on the line. The usual criterion for recognizing "clutchness" is something along the lines of, "If your life depended on a jump shot/putt/hit being made, whom would you want to attempt it?" For most people, the answers would be Michael Jordan and Tiger Woods—but what about baseball? If you're a manager, whom do you want at the plate in the ninth inning with two outs and you're down by a run? Or if you're up by a run and the other team is batting in the ninth, whom do you want on the mound? Is there any way to answer these questions objectively? Let's take a look.

The most obvious way is to look at a player's history—compare his wOBA in high-pressure situations to his overall wOBA, and chalk up any difference to the player's ability to come through in the clutch. That much is straightforward, but what exactly constitutes a high-pressure situation? Obviously there is no concrete definition, but as long as we divide plate appearances into two groups, such that one set is mostly low-pressure and the other is mostly high-pressure, we're fine. We'll define a high-pressure situation as one in which runs are needed in the very near future but the game is not yet out of hand: i.e., any plate appearance in the eighth inning or later in which the batting team is trailing by one, two, or three runs. Again, there really is no perfect definition of a "clutch" or high-pressure situation, but this will do just fine for our analysis. All other PA will be classified as "non-clutch."

Looking at all players with at least 100 high-pressure plate appearances between 2000 and 2004, we find that the best clutch hitter in our sample was Scott Spiezio, with a clutch wOBA of .416 and a non-clutch wOBA of .329. In other words, Spiezio is pretty much an average offensive player overall, but when the game is on the line, he seems to turn into one of the game's top players. That's saying something, right? Of course, one might expect that Spiezio would be getting some more attention (Scott who?) if this transformation could be counted on in the future. Well, maybe Spiezio is a statistical fluke. What about some other elite clutch performers? Aramis Ramirez is second-best with a clutch/non-clutch differential of .079, followed by Bret Boone (.075), and J. T. Snow (.067). And how about Derek Jeter, who is widely regarded as one of the game's great clutch hitters? His improvement is a mere .022. Perhaps something else is going on.

One of the pervasive themes of this book is the danger of inferring too much from too little by underestimating the influence of randomness. In the case of clutch hitting, clutch plate appearances, according to our definition of "clutchness," typically account for 7% of a player's total, which means that a regular player will see approximately 30 clutch situations over the course of a full season. Perhaps what we're actually seeing is just random variation caused by the small number of clutch plate appearances. Recalling the *Toolshed* chapter, we expect that the typical random fluctuations (for the mathematicians, one standard deviation) to be around .050 in wOBA after 100 plate appearances, meaning that 16% of players in our sample will have clutch wOBA more than 50 points higher than their true clutch wOBA due to randomness alone.

As you have already seen a few times in this book, the quickest way to examine this is to determine whether or not a player's history of clutch performance is useful in predicting his future clutch performance. For example, in 2005, would a manager have had any reason to expect Spiezio's .416 clutch wOBA to continue, and thus make decisions accordingly? Or put differently, if you're managing a team, how important is it to your decision-making process that a player has done well in the clutch in the past?

To answer this, we have to examine consecutive seasons in which a player had 25 or more clutch plate appearances, and pick players based on how well they hit in the clutch in the first of those two seasons. (Technically, we should have looked at clutch minus non-clutch wOBA, but this would not have affected our findings.) The best clutch season from 2000 through 2003 belongs to Magglio Ordonez, whose 2002 clutch wOBA was a phenomenal .675. This was followed by a clutch wOBA of .368 in 2003—lower than his non-clutch wOBA of .396 in 2003. Even accounting for the fact that average players tend to hit slightly worse in clutch situations, his 2003 clutch hitting was sub-par. Of course, that's just one player; how about the top-ten list? (See Table 37.)

Table 37.   The 10 *Best* Clutch Seasons, 2000–2003

Player	Clutch wOBA	Non-clutch wOBA next season	Clutch wOBA next season
Magglio Ordonez, 2002	.675	.403	.368
Mike Piazza, 2000	.658	.422	.303
Bret Boone, 2001	.619	.348	.429
Alex Rodriguez, 2003	.610	.398	.339
Bernie Williams, 2000	.606	.402	.419
Eric Karros, 2000	.589	.313	.210
Manny Ramirez, 2002	.592	.430	.410
Brian Giles, 2000	.581	.424	.422
Tino Martinez, 2000	.579	.363	.333
Ben Grieve, 2000	.569	.348	.320
Average	.607	.385	.355

Well, that's something, isn't it? The ten best clutch seasons from 2000 through 2003 were followed by seasons in which the players hit 33 points *worse* in clutch wOBA than in non-clutch wOBA! To be fair, we need to account for the fact that clutch situations generally bring the best pitchers to the mound; indeed the whole sample of major leaguers had wOBA that were 8% worse in clutch situations than in non-clutch situations over this period (meaning that we expect our .385 non-clutch hitters to hit .354 in clutch). So our all-star clutch performers were only one point of wOBA better than we would have expected—*in other words, they performed almost exactly how we would have expected based on their overall wOBA alone.*

Looking at this differently, we see that five of the ten players followed up their great clutch seasons by hitting well in the clutch the next year—"well" being defined as a clutch wOBA better than non-clutch wOBA minus 8%. And, of course, the other five hit poorly in the clutch the next year. So again, we don't see any evidence of a correlation between hitting well in the clutch one season and the next. This finding is nothing new; previous attempts to study this topic have likewise found little or no correlation between clutch performance one season and the next.

As an aside, we have to confess that our decision to rank players by clutch wOBA rather than by clutch minus non-clutch wOBA was intentional. The ten best clutch seasons accounted for six all-star appearances, five silver slugger awards, as well as A-Rod's MVP and Hank Aaron awards in 2003. So it seems that what we're measuring as "clutch wOBA" is, in fact, important in the eyes of the fans and media. As it should be—a player's performance when the game is on the line is more important than other situations. We think this point is key. While we haven't yet figured out whether or not clutch performance can be predicted (or even if it has any meaning aside from sheer luck), it's clear that clutch performance does happen—i.e., because of the small number of plate appearances in high-pressure situations, some player is bound to hit well in those while another is bound to hit poorly.

So, to clarify this distinction, we will refer to "clutch performance" as the player's actual performance in clutch situations, and "clutch skill" as the player's ability to perform better in the clutch. The difference between these two is solely attributable to luck.

Anyway, back to the topic at hand—trying to statistically identify clutch performers. How about the chokers? (See Table 38.)

Table 38.   The 10 *Worst* Clutch Seasons, 2000–2003

Player	Clutch wOBA	Non-clutch wOBA next season	Clutch wOBA next season
Jeff Conine, 2001	.116	.328	.319
John Vander Wal, 2000	.135	.351	.423
Omar Vizquel, 2001	.137	.340	.252
D'Angelo Jimenez, 2002	.137	.343	.375
Juan Encarnacion, 2001	.139	.347	.264
Marlon Anderson, 2002	.141	.312	.309
Jose Hernandez, 2001	.148	.353	.535
Doug Glanville, 2001	.150	.295	.218
Brad Ausmus, 2002	.150	.282	.330
Jack Wilson, 2003	.150	.354	.303
Average	.140	.331	.333

Once again, we see that our marquee case on the list (Jeff Conine), followed his dismal clutch season with one in which he reversed his trend—in this case, hitting almost as well in the clutch in 2002 as he did in non-clutch situations (rather than the MLB average 8% drop-off). Once again, this doesn't bode well for our attempt to identify clutch (or choke) players, does it?

The whole list is no more helpful in our attempt to identify clutch players. As a group, the chokers followed up their bad seasons with ones in which they had an average wOBA of .333 in the clutch, compared with the .305 that would have been expected based upon their non-clutch wOBA. Of these ten players, only four had worse-than-expected clutch performances in the subsequent season, while the other six were better than expected. So once again, it doesn't seem as though clutch perform-ance in one season translates into clutch performance the next.

The astute reader might have noticed that our clutch hitters one sea-son actually did worse in the clutch the following season (compared with their overall performance) than did the chokers. Are we sweeping something under the rug by ignoring this apparent anti-correlation? The answer is no—not because of any attempt to rationalize this away, but rather because of randomness. The typical amount of randomness in one player's clutch wOBA for a single season is around .095, so the randomness for a sample of ten players is approximately .030. Given that our discrepancies were .001 and .028, this falls well within the range of what might be expected from chance alone.

Unfortunately, this points to a fundamental problem in trying to identify clutch skills. Since a player's wOBA is expected to vary randomly (up or down) by nearly 100 points in the 30 or so clutch plate appearances he sees in a season (or for that matter, any set of 30 plate appearances), clutch skills could vary tremendously from player to player and not be easy to measure. Clearly we're going to have to work a lot harder.

The Book Says:

Expect a player's performance in an upcoming clutch at-bat to be much more like his overall performance than his past clutch performances.

So far, we've figured out that a player's clutch hitting over the course of a season, or even over several seasons, is mostly determined by luck. This shouldn't be much of a surprise, given the small number of clutch plate appearances a player will have in any one season. In 25 plate appearances, a player with a true wOBA skill of .330 has only a 68% likelihood of hitting between .230 and .430—as well as a 16% chance of hitting worse than .230 and a 16% chance of hitting better than .430, *by chance alone*. Such variation is significantly more than anything we would expect to see due to talent. In other words, *the fact that clutch hitting is primarily random doesn't disprove the presence of a significant clutch hitting skill*. But it does mean that we will need to adopt more sensitive statistical techniques to identify such a skill, something noted by Bill James in his commentary "Underestimating the Fog."

We also need to use more data to combat the large random errors present in small samples such as these. So instead of using only the

2000–2004 data, we'll be supplementing it with all major league games from 1960 through 1992. We'll also be a little more careful in the selection of data, as the test we're using here requires that the two sets of data (clutch and non-clutch plate appearances) be as similar as possible except for the difference we're testing. For starters, we'll need to eliminate plate appearances in which the pitcher was left-handed. Not that we have anything against lefties, but since managers try to exploit favorable lefty-righty matchups late in games (especially in situations we are defining as "clutch"), we don't want to be confusing platoon hitting skills with clutch hitting skills.

Because we are trying to discern whether or not the difference between a player's clutch performance and his non-clutch performance is *totally* (as opposed to mostly) random, we will use as sensitive a statistical test as is possible. As you may recall from the *Toolshed* chapter, OBP is less affected by random fluctuation than is wOBA, so we will use that instead. Actually, we will use a slight modification of OBP, in which intentional walks are ignored, while players who reached base on an error are credited with successful plate appearances (due to the occasional ambiguities between errors and hits). Still, this is close enough to regular OBP that we will call it OBP for the sake of simplicity.

Lifetime OBP in clutch and non-clutch situations (for the years our data cover, of course) were computed for all players in our data set. We have also calculated the quality of opposing pitchers faced, and adjusted the lifetime OBP accordingly. To qualify for the final list, a player needed at least 100 clutch plate appearances and 400 non-clutch plate appearances.

Overall, 848 batters met the minimum number of clutch and non-clutch plate appearances during the years in our sample. On average, each batter had approximately 2,450 plate appearances in non-clutch situations and 200 in clutch situations. Comparing their clutch and non-clutch performances, we find that the differences are indeed *mostly* explained by randomness. However, because of the sensitivity of this test, we can report that the differences are not *solely* due to randomness—in other words, there is another factor that influences how well a player performs under pressure compared with ordinary plate appearances. We believe this factor is the elusive "clutch skill" that we have been searching for. (For the record, this result holds true regardless of the precise way we have defined clutch situations.)

It is tempting to dismiss the significance of this result. After all, most of us intuitively believe that different people react to pressure differently, and that this will cause some players to perform better when under pressure while others will perform worse. The fact that we're able to confirm this belief (after quite a bit of work) is hardly newsworthy, right? Actually, the presence of a clutch hitting skill has been a controversial topic in the field of sabermetrics for quite some time, as previous studies were not able to detect any such skill. The difference between our analysis and earlier work on this topic is our use of more rigorous statistical tests; previous work generally looked at year-to-year correlations, which we saw above, and (as James surmised), lacked the sensitivity to provide any firm answer. (In the appendix we give an illustration of why this sort of test is far superior to year-to-year correlation tests.)

Of course, we need to know more than whether or not a clutch skill exists. How much effect does it have, and how does one estimate a player's clutch skill? We find that the standard deviation of player clutch skills is eight points of OBP. In other words, about two-thirds of batters facing a clutch situation will be expected to perform within eight points of OBP of their usual performance level. Remember we are talking about true "clutch skill" level now and not the random fluctuation we see in all samples of performance. *Technical note*: We note that there is always an uncertainty when making these types of measurements. So we cannot state with certainty that the typical amount of "clutch skill" is *exactly* eight points of OBP; we can merely state that there is a 68% probability that it is between 3 and 12 points.

This isn't much, is it? For comparison, the standard deviation of the overall OBP skills for these 848 players was 28 points. (A player's "OBP skill" is defined here as the true probability of him getting on base; the actual OBP values will show greater variation due to randomness.) In other words, the difference between a good batter and an average batter is three to four times that of the difference between a good clutch player and an average clutch player. So when in doubt, use your better batters. That's still not to say that an eight-point standard deviation in true clutch skill among players is inconsequential. Actually, we'll leave it up to the reader to determine for him or herself how consequential that is.

The Book Says:

Batters perform slightly differently when under pressure. About one in six players increases his inherent "OBP skill" by eight points or more in high-pressure situations; a comparable number of players decreases it by eight points or more.

Clutch wOBA

For the purpose of establishing the presence (or absence) of a clutch skill, we used plain OBP because its yes/no design makes it less susceptible to random fluctuation. However, as has been emphasized throughout this book, wOBA is the statistic of significance since it translates directly into run production. Making the same calculations to measure player-to-player variations in clutch wOBA skill, we find that the inherent spread in clutch wOBA values is slightly smaller than that in OBP: six points. (Again, the details on calculating population variations can be found in the appendix.)

Estimating Clutch Skills

Rules of thumb, such as the one in the preceding box, are useful. But if you really want to play the percentages (and chances are you do if you're reading this book), you want to know how to estimate a player's clutch abilities so that you can make the best decisions possible. Doing this involves a technique called *regression toward the mean*, which is also explained in the appendix. We give an example here. (If you don't want to wade through the math, feel free to skip the next two paragraphs.)

Suppose that a player has a clutch wOBA of .400 in 100 clutch at-bats, and a non-clutch wOBA of .300 in 1,000 non-clutch at-bats. The uncertainty of the player's clutch wOBA equals the random variation from 100 clutch at-bats, which equals approximately .053. The uncertainty of his non-clutch wOBA is .015. Thus, based on his performance alone, we estimate a clutch skill of +.100, with an uncertainty of .055 (calculated by taking the square root of the sum of the squares of the uncertainties).

Of course, since we know that the typical amount of clutch skill is .006, it is extraordinarily unlikely that any player has a clutch hitting skill of +.100 in wOBA. To correct for this, we perform a weighted average, in which both the player's measured clutch skill (+.100 ± .055) and the distribution of ballplayer clutch skills (.000 ± .006) are weighted by the inverse of the uncertainty squared. In this case, we estimate that the player's clutch skill is +.001. In other words, if he is truly a .309 wOBA hitter (the combination of his clutch and non-clutch wOBA), we expect him to be hitting .310 in clutch situations in the future. To summarize these two paragraphs, if a player has hit 100 points (in wOBA) higher in the clutch than in the non-clutch, in around three full seasons of play, we expect him to hit only around one point higher (than his overall expected wOBA) in the clutch in the future.

Like we said, this isn't a big difference. And even if you understood the preceding two paragraphs, it's highly unlikely that you would actually want to go through all of that work just to adjust your expectations of player performances by a couple points of wOBA. Surely there must be a simpler way. If you are willing to make a couple of approximations, there is indeed a shortcut using regression. Assuming that the player's wOBA values are not too far from league averages, and assuming that most of a player's at-bats come in non-clutch situations, the estimated clutch skill equals his actual wOBA difference times the number of clutch at-bats, divided by the number of clutch at-bats plus

7,600. Plugging our example batter into this equation, we estimate his clutch wOBA to equal .100 times 100 divided by 7,700, or .001. Much simpler, don't you think?

Likewise, for a player with 200 clutch plate appearances but the same clutch and non-clutch wOBA as above (.400 and .300), we estimate the clutch skill to equal .100 times 200 divided by 7,800, or .003. Clearly one would need an enormous number of clutch plate appearances to ever measure a large clutch skill—a good thing, given that the actual variation in player clutch skills is rather small. Even a player with 7,600 appearances in clutch situations (this would require over *200 seasons* in the majors) would still have his clutch performance divided by two when estimating his true clutch skill.

Using the procedure described above, we've estimated the clutch wOBA skill of all major leaguers from 2000–2004. (See Tables 39 and 40.) These two tables list the players with the best and worst clutch skill estimates, along with their actual wOBA in clutch and non-clutch situations (again ignoring plate appearances while facing left-handed pitchers).

The knowledge that a certain player will probably increase his wOBA by .001 in a clutch situation is hardly cause to put him into the lineup, or pinch-hit him in place of an overall better hitter. Case in point is Hank Aaron, who registered as the second-biggest choker in our full (1960–1992, 2000–2004) data set. Of course, Aaron's overall wOBA was so high that we'd rather have Aaron than any of the ten best true clutch hitters in that group.

Obviously what we really want is a list of players ordered by expected clutch wOBA—in other words, who will do *well* in the clutch, not who will do better in the clutch than he does overall. We have one element of clutch wOBA, namely the difference between clutch wOBA and overall wOBA, which we have been calling clutch wOBA skill. Now we just need a way of estimating overall wOBA. As you might expect, estimating a player's overall ability isn't simply a matter of looking at his career OBP or wOBA. Rather, the same sort of correction for the distribution of player OBP/wOBA skills must be made that we made to calculate the player's most likely clutch skill. Doing this, we finish this section by listing the players in our data set whom we would most and least want to see at the plate in a pressure-packed situation — without taking into consideration platoon factors, such as the handedness or groundball/flyball tendencies of the pitcher. (See Tables 41 and 42.)

Table 39.   The 10 *Best* Clutch Skills, 2000–2004

Player	Clutch wOBA	non-Clutch wOBA	Estimated Clutch wOBA skill
Bret Boone	.458	.349	.0018
Scott Spiezio	.424	.331	.0013
Jacque Jones	.431	.362	.0012
Marlon Anderson	.389	.308	.0012
Alex S. Gonzalez	.365	.307	.0012
Brian Roberts	.441	.324	.0011
Trot Nixon	.488	.395	.0011
Brent Mayne	.396	.310	.0011
Cesar Izturis	.360	.279	.0010
Tino Martinez	.412	.349	.0010

Table 40.   The 10 *Worst* Clutch Skills, 2000–2004

Player	Clutch wOBA	non-Clutch wOBA	Estimated Clutch wOBA skill
Frank Thomas	.230	.407	−.0019
Doug Glanville	.160	.302	−.0017
Tony Clark	.172	.354	−.0014
David Eckstein	.198	.328	−.0013
Brady Clark	.150	.368	−.0013
Jeff Cirillo	.213	.345	−.0013
Carlos Beltran	.271	.376	−.0012
Terrence Long	.233	.338	−.0012
Royce Clayton	.214	.309	−.0011
Edgardo Alfonzo	.284	.366	−.0011

Table 41.   The 10 *Best* Clutch Hitters, 2000–2004 (Minimum 1500 PA)

Player	Expected Clutch wOBA	Clutch wOBA Skill
Barry Bonds	.493	-.0001
Todd Helton	.447	-.0010
Jim Thome	.427	.0005
Carlos Delgado	.424	-.0002
Jason Giambi	.423	.0007
Lance Berkman	.421	-.0001
Brian Giles	.420	.0008
Jim Edmonds	.418	.0000
Albert Pujols	.417	-.0001
Bobby Abreu	.410	.0008

Table 42.   The 10 *Worst* Clutch Hitters, 2000–2004 (Minimum 1500 PA)

Player	Expected Clutch wOBA	Clutch wOBA Skill
Neifi Perez	.284	-.0004
Brad Ausmus	.286	-.0001
Mike Matheny	.287	.0005
Alex S. Gonzalez	.288	-.0000
Rey Sanchez	.290	.0002
Doug Glanville	.293	-.0017
Jack Wilson	.299	-.0005
Royce Clayton	.300	-.0011
Alex Cora	.301	.0000
Marquis Grissom	.305	.0003

It probably comes as no surprise at this point that the players in these lists are also the ten best and worst overall hitters: the normalizing factor of 7,600 clutch plate appearances is simply too large to *ever* predict a specific player to have a significant clutch hitting skill. Put differently, the fact that one of three players performs at least .006 better or worse in the clutch doesn't mean that we can tell which players have this skill, even when looking at several seasons' worth of data.

Again, the "expected clutch wOBA" values are the players' overall wOBA skill plus their clutch wOBA skill. Given the small estimated clutch wOBA skills, the best and worst clutch hitters are basically the same as the best and worst overall hitters.

The Book Says:

For all practical purposes, a player can be expected to hit equally well in the clutch as he would be expected to do in an ordinary situation.

Clutch Pitching

So far we've looked only at batters. What about pitchers? Do they show a change in performance in the clutch as well? You would probably think so. After all, that's much of the rationale behind the designation of *closers*—pitchers who presumably have some sort of innate ability to perform when everything is on the line. Furthermore, pitching has a more obvious mental component, as evidenced by pitchers who have great stuff but are ineffective (and vice versa).

Rather than boring you with several pages detailing our study of clutch pitching, we'll go straight to the results. We've duplicated our clutch hitting analysis for pitchers, with the additional restriction that we're considering only plate appearances involving relievers. This allows us to sidestep the problem that a particular pitcher will inherently pitch differently when starting than he will in relief (as we detail in our chapter on starting pitchers), as well as problems caused by fatigue (since starters pitching in cluth situations will, by definition, be pitching very late in the game).

Running our clutch performance analysis, there are 430 relievers who saw 100 clutch plate appearances and 200 non-clutch plate appearances. (We reduced the minimum number of non-clutch plate appearances in order to increase our sample size.) From these players, we find no evidence that relievers perform any differently in pressure situations (a 1–3 run lead in the eighth inning or later) than they do otherwise. Putting this into numbers, we can be reasonably confident (84%, or one standard deviation, for those statistically inclined) that any change in OBP for relievers is no more than .003 in clutch situations, and likely zero.

The importance of eliminating starters from this study is exemplified by what would have happened had we not made this exclusion—we would have incorrectly concluded that a clutch pitching effect exists that is even larger (.009) in OBP, .011 in wOBA) than the clutch hitting effect. Of course, we're really measuring the effects of starters pitching tired in the eighth and ninth innings, pitchers pitching differently as starters and relievers, and a variety of things other than clutch pitching.

While our findings on clutch hitting generally confirm most people's suspicions (although perhaps you expected clutch hitting skills to be a more significant factor), our results regarding pitchers is probably somewhat of a surprise. After all, much of the justification for having a *designated closer* is based upon the belief that some pitchers have a special ability to handle pressure better than others. This simply doesn't appear to be the case.

The Book Says:

Pitchers perform no differently in high-pressure situations than they do otherwise. It is advisable to give the role of closer to your best overall reliever, not necessarily the pitcher with a history of clutch performance.

Playing to the Score

Before wrapping up this chapter, it is worth examining whether or not players (hitters and pitchers) have the ability to change their performance in a few other special situations. First we'll address the theory that certain players perform better in close games (not just late and close, which we've defined as "clutch") than they do during blowouts. With the machinery and large data already set in place, all we have to do is eliminate the inning requirement from our clutch definition to search for such an ability. For this test, we'll define "close" as situations in which the game is tied or the pitcher's team is leading by one or two runs, since these run differences create the highest leverage. Since we're now considering all innings, we can use our entire data sample as well—no need to eliminate plate appearances featuring starting (or relief) pitching, left-handed pitchers or batters, etc.

Using this criterion (*close* and *not close*) to divide the situations, we find rather conclusively that neither pitchers nor batters show any tendency to perform differently in situations in which one or two runs would make a difference. Given the much larger number of plate appearances, we can be reasonably confident that the inherent change in OBP skill is no more than .004, and likely zero for both pitchers and batters.

The Book Says:

Neither pitchers nor batters demonstrate any ability to play to the score.

Pinch Hitting

Another situation in which one might expect players to perform differently is when pinch hitting. For players with significant numbers of at-bats as starters and pinch hitters, do they perform differently? If so, do these differences vary from player to player, or do all players show similar changes in performance?

Against right-handed relief pitchers, batters posted an average OBP of .337 and wOBA of .334 from 2000–2004 when starting, numbers that plummeted to .313 and .300 when pinch hitting, after accounting for quality of opposing pitching. This is quite a surprise. When a pinch hitter is brought in, it is because the manager thinks this is a situation in which the batter should perform relatively *well*. As such, you might expect that pinch hitters would, if anything, perform better than expected when pinch hitting, not worse. Our best explanation for this phenomenon is that a player coming off the bench simply isn't as prepared (mentally or physically) to hit as one who has been playing the entire game.

This might lead one to believe that some players are more "disciplined" pinch hitters, and thus don't suffer from this overall performance decline, while others perform much worse. We don't find any evidence of this. Even using our full (1960–1992 and 2000–2004) data sample, there is no evidence that some players are any more or less susceptible to this loss of effectiveness. Quantitatively, our upper limit on any player-to-player variation is about 15 points of OBP or wOBA, meaning that we are very confident that few (if any) players will perform as well as pinch hitters as they do as starters. Thus a player's past pinch hitting performance is unimportant, especially given the small sample sizes; one should be concerned with a batter's overall stats rather than those "as a pinch hitter." In other words, we find no evidence that there is any such thing as a "good pinch hitter" (think Lenny Harris or Manny Mota)—only good and bad *hitters*.

Another explanation for this dramatic difference in pinch hitter performance might be that pinch hitters are used in non-average situations. For example, we find that pinch hitters preferentially hit with one or two outs and at least one man on base. Such situations account for 38% of plate appearances by starting position players, compared with 44% of pinch hit appearances. While this is a significant difference, shifting 6% of plate appearances to those when getting a hit is more critical should hardly result in the dramatic performance drop-off we are seeing. Indeed, if we make this comparison for one base/out state at a time (i.e., one out, man on second), we find that pinch hitters are still much less effective. Likewise, we find that pinch hitters are used frequently in the ninth inning, as you would expect. Nevertheless, restricting our analysis to ninth-inning plate appearances leaves our results unchanged. Thus, we are forced to conclude that the game situation is not the reason for the drop-off in pinch hitter performance.

Looking at the typical stats of players in pinch hitting and starting roles, the primary difference we see is that players seem to be a lot pickier when pinch hitting. From 2000 through 2004, players with at least 50 appearances as a pinch hitter and 100 as a starter facing right-handed relievers, struck out 18.5% of the time and walked 8.5% of the time when starting, rates that jumped to 23.8% and 9.3% when pinch hitting. Every statistical category related to making contact—home run rate, batting average on balls in play, extra-base hits—was shifted in favor of the pitcher during pinch-hit at-bats. So our best guess is that there is something about spending two hours sitting on the bench that hinders a player's ability to make good contact with a pitch, and that knowing this, a pinch hitter will attempt to work the count in order to draw a walk or get a more hittable pitch on a hitter's count. (Incidentally, this finding refutes the notion that pinch hitters generally swing early and don't work the count.)

We also find that players are less effective when used as designated hitters, suffering about half the performance penalty incurred when pinch hitting. Interestingly, the DH penalty does vary significantly from player to player, indicating that the time between at-bats is something that some players are able to withstand and others are not. (Or, perhaps we're simply seeing the effect of slightly injured players being used as designated hitters. Our data do not allow a more detailed study of this, so we will not examine this question further.)

The Book Says:

A player is significantly less effective as a pinch hitter than he is as a starter. All players show a comparable decline in effectiveness; in other words, there is no such thing as a pinch hitting specialist. Therefore, a pinch hitter would have to be significantly better than the player he is hitting for in order to make the substitution worthwhile.

The Book Also Says:

Players also lose effectiveness when being used as a designated hitter; the DH penalty is about half that of the PH penalty. This does vary significantly from player to player—some players hit as well as a DH as they do otherwise, while others perform as badly as they would as pinch hitters.

Pitching from the Stretch

Notions of clutch hitting, playing to the score, or pinch hitting specialists defy a physical explanation—either one must believe that players don't always play their best, or that we are measuring some sort of intestinal fortitude. So let's close this chapter with something that may be easier to interpret in terms of what we can actually see. When the bases are empty, a pitcher (at least if he is a starter) generally uses a windup. In a potential steal situation (a runner on first with second empty, or a runner on second with third empty), he pitches from the stretch. We'll throw out other situations with men on base, as we're less certain of whether or not the pitcher was pitching from the stretch. Additionally, since relievers frequently throw from the stretch in all situations, we'll ignore their plate appearances. Do we see any effect of this on performance, and is such an effect constant, or does it vary from pitcher to pitcher?

The first question is simple to answer. In our 1960–1992 and 2000–2004 data sample, the mean wOBA was .312 from the windup and .317 from the stretch—a change of .005 in the batter's favor when pitching from the stretch. Of course, these situations are also ones in which defensive positioning is often different, such as the first baseman playing close to the bag to hold the runner. Could it just be that we're seeing the effect of this? Indeed, we find that batters reach base more frequently on balls hit into play in "stretch" situations than in "windup" situations, something that is most likely attributable to defensive positioning. However, we also see changes in the rates of strikeouts, walks, and home runs, so clearly the pitcher/batter matchup is also different in these situations, regardless of how the defense is positioned.

At any rate, our primary interest is whether or not some pitchers suffer more than others when pitching in stretch situations. As you can guess, this is a very similar sort of test to that which we've used to look for performance changes in clutch situations or close games; all we need to do is use "men on base" and "bases empty" as our criteria for dividing the data sample. Doing so produces a very clear result—the "stretch penalty" for pitchers varies by roughly .008 in OBP and .005 in wOBA from player to player.

Using the same regression technique we used to estimate clutch hitting skills, we have estimated each pitcher's stretch wOBA "skill" (stretch minus bases empty performance), as well as his overall wOBA skill. For example, Hideo Nomo performed 76 points of wOBA *better* in the stretch than in bases empty situations, giving him a measured (sample, not "real") wOBA stretch penalty of -.076. For this calculation, we regress by averaging his actual performance with a whopping 14,000 "stretch" plate appearances at an average penalty (of .005). So averaging Nomo's actual 656 stretch plate appearances with the 14,000 average ones, one estimates his inherent stretch penalty to be .0014. Doing it the more complicated way, we get .0012, so our simple estimate is close enough.

Table 43.   The 10 *Best* Stretch Pitchers, 2000–2004

Player	Measured Stretch wOBA Penalty	Estimated Stretch wOBA Skill	Overall wOBA Skill
Hideo Nomo	-.076	.0012	.332
Doug Davis	-.056	.0013	.333
Steve Trachsel	-.061	.0016	.342
Tom Glavine	-.022	.0020	.321
John Lackey	-.084	.0021	.322
Pedro Martinez	-.033	.0022	.275
Bartolo Colon	-.026	.0025	.310
Derrick May	-.054	.0027	.348
Kazuhisa Ishii	-.040	.0028	.337
Mark Buehrle	-.017	.0029	.319

Table 44.   The 10 *Worst* Stretch Pitchers, 2000–2004

Player	Measured Stretch wOBA Penalty	Estimated Stretch wOBA Skill	Overall wOBA Skill
Mark Mulder	.051	.0076	.314
Jamie Moyer	.055	.0076	.301
Kenny Rogers	.042	.0074	.344
Glendon Rusch	.050	.0072	.331
Eric Milton	.050	.0072	.320
Jimmy Anderson	.055	.0068	.343
Mark Redman	.044	.0068	.327
Brad Radke	.055	.0067	.318
Mike Mussina	.049	.0065	.309
Brad Penny	.056	.0063	.310

The pitchers with the ten lowest and highest stretch wOBA skills are listed here. (See Tables 43 and 44.) We find two things of note in these tables. First, the estimated stretch wOBA penalties are always much closer to the league average (.005) than they are to the player's actual performance. This should be no surprise; after all we are mixing something like 14,000 league-average plate appearances in. However, even with this much regression toward the mean, we find greater variety in estimated stretch wOBA skill than we did in estimated clutch skills; this is because pitchers are in stretch situations far more than batters are in clutch situations.

We did the same test on batters. Do all batters improve by the same amount when the pitcher is throwing from the stretch? One would likely think so. After all, our pitcher analysis can be readily explained by the fact that pitchers are using two different throwing motions for these two situations, and it's certainly plausible (and probably expected) that different pitchers have different levels of effectiveness for those two motions. But for batters, we have no similarly obvious reason to expect such a change. Indeed, we find no strong evidence for the presence of a "stretch hitting" skill, although the statistical uncertainty is such that an inherent variation of as much as five points of OBP is possible.

The Book Says:

Pitchers show inherent abilities to perform slightly differently with the bases empty than when throwing from the stretch. Any similar variation in batter performance is small, if it exists at all. And of course, overall, pitchers pitch worse from the stretch than they do from the windup. How much of that is due to the position of the fielders, how much is due to the pitcher's approach, and how much is due to the inherent nature of the different motions, is difficult to ascertain.

SUMMARY

In this chapter, we have examined how well players perform in a variety of special situations, compared with how well they would be expected to perform in general. There are three main questions we have addressed. First, are there player-to-player differences in situational performance? For example, is there such thing as a pinch hitting specialist? Or do some pitchers play to the score? Or do some hitters elevate their skills under pressure? (The answers are no, no, and yes.)

Second, how much variation is there in situational performance? In the case of clutch hitting, not much. The vast majority (95%) of batters should be expected to hit within 12 points of their overall wOBA. Pitcher-to-pitcher variations in pitching from the stretch are smaller still.

The third and most pertinent question is, how can we estimate a player's ability in a specific situation? In the case of clutch hitting, for example, we know that the player-to-player variation is relatively small, but we would like to make *some* use of the data. This is done with regression, in which the player's situational performance is padded by some number of attempts with league-average situational performance. In the case of clutch hitting, one pads the player's measured clutch performance with 7,600 league-average plate appearances. Given that the typical player faces some 30 clutch plate appearances per season, it would take a very long time for his actual deviation from typical clutch performance to be a significant predictor of future clutch performance. Thus for all practical purposes, we can presume that all players perform as well in the clutch as they do overall.

Our other positive finding was stretch pitching. There we regress a player's stretch performance by padding it with 14,000 league-average plate appearances. While pitchers face many more stretch situations in a season than hitters face "clutch" situations, it still takes a long time for the player's actual performance to have much predictive value.

In short, measuring situational performance is very difficult. Unless the player-to-player variation is quite large or the situation is a common one, it requires several seasons or even several decades for players to distinguish themselves as being especially capable of performing in special situations. In most cases, we can simply ignore a player's past *situational* performance, in terms of having any significant predictive value, and focus on his past *overall* performance.

CHAPTER 5 – BATTING (DIS)ORDER

One of the running themes throughout this book is context. To understand the impact of your possible choices, you have to understand the environment in which you are working. Context. Whenever you are trying to figure out what to do, take a step back, and ask yourself, "What's the context?" Context, context, context. We can't repeat it enough.

In this chapter, we'll turn our attention to the batting order and how to construct an optimal lineup. What does conventional wisdom say about this? Some managers or fans think you want a fast guy at the top of the order, without too much regard for how often he gets on base; others think that OBP is the most important attribute for a leadoff hitter, and that speed is secondary. You want the #2 hitter to move the runner over into scoring position, even if it means getting an out; therefore he should be a proficient bunter with excellent bat control. Your #3 batter should be a very good hitter, maybe your best—unless you want your best hitter batting cleanup. Then, maybe set up a lefty-righty situation down the order, trying to end with your worst batters at the bottom of the lineup. There, easy, end of chapter.

But why? Why? Why must the order follow such a pattern? Let's take a step back and understand the context of the batting order.

Loop

The most important context of the batting order is that it is a continuous loop. You get to set your batting order 1 through 9, and each player takes his turn. Once the inning completes, the next batter leads off the next inning. So the term *leadoff* batter is a bit of a misnomer. He's the leadoff batter of the game, but he won't often lead off an inning.

What if the rules were set so that the batting order is restored at the start of each inning. Tim Raines would lead off the first, second, third, and all the way through to the ninth, innings. If those were the rules—if that were the context—you'd need a new strategy in place to determine the optimal lineup. One-quarter of the time, you'd end up having a 1–2–3 inning, leaving your cleanup batter on deck. In the current rules of baseball, the benefit of that huge cost is that he gets to bat in the following inning. In this fictitious league, it's the #1 hitter who will lead off the second inning. You will realize rather quickly that you can't have your best hitter in the cleanup spot if he will have 25% fewer PA than your top three hitters.

If we go back to the *real* world of baseball, we realize that you can't hide a batter. The best you can do is to defer him to the bottom of the batting order. But even batting ninth, he will eventually come up. How often will he come up? Here is how often each batter will come up during an average game, 1999–2002. (See Table 45.)

Table 45.　Number Of PA Per Game, By Batting Order

Batting Order	AL Parks	NL Parks
1	4.83	4.80
2	4.72	4.68
3	4.61	4.56
4	4.49	4.46
5	4.39	4.35
6	4.26	4.23
7	4.14	4.10
8	4.02	3.98
9	3.90	3.86

Whether playing in games in the NL parks, where the pitcher is in the batting lineup, or in the AL parks with the DH, the pattern is virtually the same: each batting spot has about .11 or .12 more plate appearances than the next one (or about 2.5%). (That .11 number is significant. If the game ended randomly, we'd expect each batting spot to make the last out equally often—1/9 of the games would end after the leadoff batter, 1/9 after the second hitter, and so on. And that would imply that the difference in the number of PA between each batting spot would be one divided by nine, or .111. We're pretty close to that figure.)

Based strictly on *this* context, you want your best hitter as the #1 hitter, since the leadoff slot obviously has more PA than any other. But, as we know, baseball is a lot more complicated than a single context.

Twenty-Four

The next important context is the base/out state you find yourself in. Walks have the most impact, relative to other events, with the bases empty. A single and a walk are identical in this case. The home run has the most impact, relative to other events, with runners on base and two outs. With no outs, the difference between a triple and a home run is not that much, simply because you have three outs to drive home the runner from third base. With two outs, the home run guarantees the batter scores. But, with the triple, you now have only a 30% chance of scoring with two outs.

So, each event will leverage each base/out state in its own way. Furthermore, each batting spot will find itself in each base/out state at different frequencies. What we want is to try to leverage the strengths of the events against the base/out states that are most conducive for them. Here is how often each batting spot comes up with men on. (See Table 46.) This chart is only for games in the AL parks.

The #1 batter has men on base only 36% of the time, both because he starts the game (with the bases empty, of course) and because he comes up after the team's worst hitters in subsequent at-bats. The cleanup hitter comes up with men on base over half the time, and he has 3.2 runners on base per game. Did you notice that the #5 batter has more men on base than the #3 hitter? Based on *this* context, you never want your best hitter as your leadoff hitter, but rather as your cleanup hitter.

Table 46.   Number Of PA, By Batting Order And Men On Base

Batting Order	PA empty	PA men on	% with men on	Number of Runners On
1	3.11	1.72	36%	2.39
2	2.63	2.09	44%	2.77
3	2.38	2.23	48%	3.00
4	2.19	2.31	51%	3.20
5	2.28	2.11	48%	3.10
6	2.29	1.97	46%	2.84
7	2.20	1.94	47%	2.74
8	2.17	1.85	46%	2.61
9	2.13	1.77	45%	2.48

Table 47.   Number Of PA, By Batting Order And Outs

Batting Order	Out 0 %	Out 1 %	Out 2 %
1	48%	26%	26%
2	33%	41%	26%
3	28%	35%	37%
4	34%	31%	35%
5	35%	33%	33%
6	33%	34%	33%
7	33%	33%	34%
8	34%	33%	33%
9	34%	33%	33%

The next context is number of outs. (See Table 47.) This chart tells us how often each batter comes up with zero, one, or two outs. Starting from the #4 spot on downwards, it is pretty stable. The leadoff hitter, as you could have guessed, comes to bat with no outs the most often, at 48%. Walks are most important with no outs, simply because you need all that extra time to try to get that runner to score; therefore we would guess from this table that we would prefer a leadoff hitter who walks a lot.

Dependency

The third important context is how each batter affects the opportunities for the following batters. All the numbers that we've shown so far are based on actual performances. Since many managers follow the same pattern in filling out their batting lineup, each batting spot is generally occupied by a particular type of player.

Some of the knocks against simulation models or Markov chains are that they do not capture all the little bits of information, and that they do not treat each person as a true individual. This is true. However, let's take it the other way. Let's construct a model where every batter is exactly the same and is exactly average. We should expect some difference to the above numbers, right? Here is a side-by-side comparison of the actual PA per game already presented, for the AL parks, and the model using all players as exactly the same and average. (See Table 48.)

Virtually no difference.

Table 48.   Number Of PA, By Batting Order (Theoretical And Actual)

Batting Order	Model PA	Actual PA
1	4.82	4.83
2	4.70	4.72
3	4.59	4.61
4	4.48	4.49
5	4.37	4.39
6	4.26	4.26
7	4.16	4.14
8	4.05	4.02
9	3.93	3.90

OK, so how about the number of men on base? Here is what the model shows in terms of how often each batting spot comes up with men on. (See Table 49.)

Table 49.   Number Of PA, By Batting Order And Men On Base
(Theoretical)

Batting Order	PA empty	PA men on	%	Runners On
1	3.01	1.80	37%	2.55
2	2.64	2.06	44%	2.78
3	2.42	2.17	47%	2.96
4	2.27	2.21	49%	3.06
5	2.34	2.03	47%	2.93
6	2.29	1.97	46%	2.79
7	2.19	1.96	47%	2.74
8	2.13	1.91	47%	2.70
9	2.08	1.85	47%	2.62

Compare this chart to the one that was based on actual data (Table 46). In this case, we do have some significant differences. There is up to a .20 runner difference between the model and reality. This is expected since, in reality, we generally have the best hitters clumped together. The leadoff hitter, in reality, sees 2.39 runners per game. The model expected 2.55. We attribute this difference to the fact that the bottom of the order, in reality, contains poor hitters. Even so, that difference is a fairly small .16 runners. On the flip side, the cleanup hitter had 3.20 runners on base in reality (more than the 3.06 expected by the model) because he is preceded by hitters who are more adept than average at getting on base.

It is important to note the meaning of the numbers from the model. Those numbers are a direct result of the primary context of the batting order: the continuous loop. Remember, we made every batter exactly the same. The reason that we get this distribution is simply that we continually cycle through the order during the game.

In reality, teams do major clumping of their best hitters together. The effect is rather muted. The manager can control getting about 5% more runners on base for his best hitters. For a HR, the run value of moving runners over is about .40 runs on average. Thus, if you can increase the number of baserunners by 5%, the run value is likewise increased 5% to .42, producing .02 extra runs per HR.

Run Values In The 24 Base/Out States

It's time to cut to the chase.

Here is a chart that shows the run value for each event, for each of the 24 base/out states. (See Table 50.) What does this monstrosity tell us? It tells us how many runs each type of event adds (or eliminates), given the base/out state. From earlier, we also know how often each batting spot finds itself in each of the 24 base/out states. The next step is simply to weight this table by those frequencies for each batting spot, and we end up with the average run values by type of event for each batting spot. (See Table 51.)

This gives us the run value of each event, by batting order. The run value of the HR for the leadoff hitter is only 1.29 runs. The run value of the walk is .35 runs, for the leadoff hitter. No surprises here. The leadoff runner sees the most no-out, bases-empty situations and thus the walk value is greater than its average and the home run value is less than its average. Moving on, we see that the run values for the events for the #5 batter are actually higher in all cases than the #4 batter! Wait a minute. This means that the better hitter should hit fifth and not fourth? As it turns out, the opportunities presented to the #5 batter are more attractive than to the #4 batter. However, the #4 batter will come to bat 2.5% more times than the #5 batter. The leadoff hitter will get 10% more PA than the #5 batter. So, we need to perform one last step before we proceed— adjust the values above for the number of plate appearances each batter is likely to see:

Table 50.   Run Values, By Event And Base/Out State

1B	2B	3B	Outs	Sngl	Dbl	Trpl	HR	NIBB	HBP	RBOE	K	Out	SB	CS
--	--	--	0	0.41	0.64	0.94	1.00	0.41	0.41	0.45	-0.27	-0.27	-	-
--	--	--	1	0.28	0.43	0.68	1.00	0.29	0.29	0.31	-0.18	-0.18	-	-
--	--	--	2	0.14	0.23	0.27	1.00	0.14	0.14	0.15	-0.12	-0.12	-	-
1B	--	--	0	0.72	1.10	1.53	1.59	0.64	0.64	0.76	-0.41	-0.49	0.24	-0.68
1B	--	--	1	0.49	0.97	1.39	1.71	0.41	0.41	0.52	-0.34	-0.38	0.17	-0.46
1B	--	--	2	0.26	0.71	1.15	1.86	0.23	0.23	0.33	-0.26	-0.26	0.09	-0.26
--	2B	--	0	0.72	0.98	1.31	1.36	0.41	0.41	0.64	-0.47	-0.37	0.31	-0.91
--	2B	--	1	0.67	0.99	1.21	1.57	0.27	0.26	0.55	-0.38	-0.37	0.25	-0.62
--	2B	--	2	0.72	1.00	1.04	1.77	0.13	0.13	0.48	-0.35	-0.35	0.07	-0.35
--	--	3B	0	0.46	0.69	1.00	1.06	0.44	0.44	0.53	-0.54	-0.37	0.11	-1.15
--	--	3B	1	0.60	0.76	1.00	1.33	0.30	0.30	0.63	-0.58	-0.26	0.33	-0.86
--	--	3B	2	0.87	0.96	0.99	1.73	0.18	0.17	0.89	-0.38	-0.39	0.73	-0.39
1B	2B	--	0	1.00	1.45	1.89	1.95	0.94	0.94	1.12	-0.63	-0.65	0.38	-0.94
1B	2B	--	1	0.93	1.57	1.98	2.31	0.72	0.72	0.88	-0.53	-0.59	0.40	-0.69
1B	2B	--	2	0.89	1.53	1.90	2.63	0.36	0.36	0.62	-0.48	-0.48	0.16	-0.46
1B	--	3B	0	0.74	1.11	1.56	1.61	0.60	0.60	0.81	-0.68	-0.56	0.14	-0.99
1B	--	3B	1	0.77	1.30	1.71	2.02	0.44	0.44	0.84	-0.73	-0.49	0.24	-0.90
1B	--	3B	2	0.96	1.44	1.82	2.56	0.29	0.29	0.96	-0.56	-0.56	0.18	-0.48
--	2B	3B	0	0.87	1.14	1.46	1.51	0.51	0.51	0.81	-0.55	-0.37	-	-
--	2B	3B	1	0.87	1.23	1.47	1.80	0.22	0.21	0.79	-0.83	-0.44	-	-
--	2B	3B	2	1.43	1.68	1.72	2.46	0.19	0.19	1.11	-0.66	-0.66	-	-
1B	2B	3B	0	1.05	1.54	1.95	2.01	1.00	1.00	1.03	-0.85	-0.73	-	-
1B	2B	3B	1	1.20	1.84	2.26	2.59	1.00	1.00	1.19	-0.86	-0.72	-	-
1B	2B	3B	2	1.47	2.11	2.54	3.27	1.00	1.00	1.36	-0.84	-0.85	-	-

Table 51.   Run Values, By Event And Batting Order

Batting Order	1B	2B	3B	HR	NIBB	HBP	RBOE	K	Out
1	0.468	0.733	1.019	1.291	0.350	0.373	0.493	-0.299	-0.298
2	0.479	0.743	1.023	1.349	0.340	0.369	0.499	-0.300	-0.301
3	0.469	0.742	1.013	1.384	0.319	0.352	0.490	-0.302	-0.300
4	0.504	0.802	1.090	1.436	0.337	0.368	0.528	-0.323	-0.319
5	0.513	0.809	1.106	1.438	0.348	0.381	0.530	-0.324	-0.323
6	0.494	0.782	1.077	1.411	0.344	0.377	0.517	-0.314	-0.314
7	0.489	0.777	1.068	1.407	0.340	0.372	0.512	-0.312	-0.312
8	0.488	0.772	1.060	1.398	0.337	0.368	0.508	-0.311	-0.309
9	0.485	0.766	1.053	1.388	0.336	0.366	0.505	-0.309	-0.308

The following table is the previous table, multiplied by the PA factor for each batting spot (+10% for the leadoff hitter, +7.5% for the #2 hitter, all the way down the line to –10% for the #9 hitter). Here it is. (See Table 52.)

Table 52.   Run Values, By Event And Batting Order (Modified By PA)

Batting Order	1B	2B	3B	HR	NIBB	HBP	RBOE	K	Out
1	0.515	0.806	1.121	1.421	0.385	0.411	0.542	-0.329	-0.328
2	0.515	0.799	1.100	1.450	0.366	0.396	0.536	-0.322	-0.324
3	0.493	0.779	1.064	1.453	0.335	0.369	0.514	-0.317	-0.315
4	0.517	0.822	1.117	1.472	0.345	0.377	0.541	-0.332	-0.327
5	0.513	0.809	1.106	1.438	0.348	0.381	0.530	-0.324	-0.323
6	0.482	0.763	1.050	1.376	0.336	0.368	0.504	-0.306	-0.306
7	0.464	0.738	1.014	1.336	0.323	0.353	0.486	-0.296	-0.296
8	0.451	0.714	0.980	1.293	0.312	0.340	0.470	-0.287	-0.286
9	0.436	0.689	0.948	1.249	0.302	0.329	0.454	-0.278	-0.277

This is it. This is the chart that we've been after. It is important to remember that the frequency of each base/out/batting slot state we used was based on the actual numbers. If we change the guidelines for assembling a batting order, the frequency rates will also change, and thus this table will change a little. We'll get into that later.

For now, let's do some comparisons. First off, let's compare the #4 and #5 hitters. The cleanup hitter has a slight advantage in almost every category, and a large advantage in the HR category (a .034 run advantage per HR). So, the hitter in the #4 slot should be better than the hitter in the #5 slot. We already knew that, though.

By the way, that .034 run advantage per HR, if we assume there's a 20 HR difference between the #4 and #5 hitter, works out to 0.7 runs gained per season. So, this is hardly a big difference. It exists, but the effect is pretty small.

What if we compare the cleanup hitter to the #2 hitter? Here, it gets interesting. The cleanup hitter has a .02 run advantage per extra-base hit (double, triple, home run), while the #2 hitter has a .02 run advantage per walk or hit batter. There is not that much of a difference. What does this mean? This means that the overall quality (as measured by wOBA) of your #2 and #4 batters should be about the same!

That's right. The advantage that the cleanup hitter has over the #2 hitter (all those runners on base) is mitigated by the 5% extra PA that the #2 hitter has. Five percent may sound small, but everything we've seen so far shows that we're dealing with small differences anyway.

When deciding between the #2 and #4 slots, if you have two batters of overall similar quality, put the guy with more extra-base hits in the #4 slot, and the guy with more walks in the #2 slot.

Let's compare the #2 and #3 hitters. The run values of each event favor the #2 hitter over the #3 hitter by .02 to .03 runs. And this is across the board, except for the HR (which is even). Likewise, the run values of the #4 hitter's events are all higher than those of the #3 hitter. This means that the #3 hitter should be worse than the #2 and #4 hitters. For most teams, the gap in talent between the hitters in the #3 and #2 slots is enormous and that talent is concentrated in the #3 slot. This is simply wrong.

How about the #3 and #5 batters? This one is also interesting. The hitter in the #5 slot gets a .02 run advantage on singles, doubles, triples, and walks, while the #3 hitter gets a .02 run advantage on the HR. The outs for the hitter in the #5 slot are more costly than those in the #3 slot. Result? The hitter in the #5 slot should be better than the hitter in the #3 slot.

That sounds weird, right? The reason is that the #3 hitter gets a lot more PA with two outs than the #5 batter. So, he has less chance to do more damage, unless that damage is done with the HR.

Again, remember that these differences are all about .02 runs per PA, at most. Over 700 PA, that's a 1.4 run difference. You can conceivably squeeze one or two runs out of each batting slot, or about 10 to 15 runs over 162 games, by optimization.

At the bottom of the order, we see that the #6 slot has lower run values than any of the top five slots. And it has more run value than the #7 slot, which has more run value than the #8 slot, which has more run value than the #9 slot. No surprises there—your four worst hitters go here in descending order.

Finally, the leadoff spot. The run value for the leadoff hitter, for each event, is closest to the #2 and #5 hitters. The biggest differences are that the run value of the HR for the leadoff hitter is the lowest among the top five spots, while the walk is the highest.

Between the #1 and #2 slots, the leadoff hitter gets the .02 run advantage on doubles, triples, and walks, while the #2 hitter gets the .03 run advantage on home runs. So, the overall quality of the hitter in the #1 slot will be around the same as the hitter in the #2 slot.

As we noted earlier, all of these rules and findings are based on the typical players found in those slots. To properly optimize the batting order, you need to construct various models, and determine the best combination.

So, what are we left with? At the moment, based only on the variables we have considered until now, we are right here:

The Book Says:

Your three best hitters should bat somewhere in the #1, #2, and #4 slots. Your fourth- and fifth-best hitters should occupy the #3 and #5 slots. The #1 and #2 slots will have players with more walks than those in the #4 and #5 slots. From slot #6 through #9, put the players in descending order of quality.

What we've presented here gives you a shortcut into figuring out the quality of hitters you want in each slot, as well as how little impact the ordering actually has. We'll now expand our context, and consider additional variables.

Strikeouts

Flip back to the chart that shows the run values by the 24 base/out states and notice the difference in run values between the strikeout and other types of outs. Concentrate on the lines when there are no outs. Actually, let's just extract the interesting part of the chart here. (See Table 53.)

With a man on first, the run value of the strikeout is .08 runs less costly than other types of outs. This makes sense, since you won't be doubled up on a strikeout. But, with a man on second or third, the run value of the strikeout is more than .10 runs more costly. Again, this makes sense, since a ground out can advance the runners on base, and an outfield flyout can also score the runner from third. With runners on first and second, the pros/cons of the strikeout and non-strikeout even out.

The runner on third and one out shows a whopping .32 run difference between a strikeout and other types of outs, in favor of the non-strikeout. The biggest difference in the chart is .39 runs with men on second and third and one out. Having a strikeout hitter here would be devastating (and similarly, a manager would love to have his strikeout pitcher here).

None of this is surprising, and it simply reaffirms what we already know. What this chart does is to precisely quantify the impact.

Table 53.   Run Values, By Event And Base/Out State (Subset Of An Earlier Chart)

1B	2B	3B	Outs	Sngl	Dbl	Trpl	HR	NIBB	HBP	RBOE	K	Out	SB	CS
--	--	--	0	0.41	0.64	0.94	1.00	0.41	0.41	0.45	-0.27	-0.27	-	-
1B	--	--	0	0.72	1.10	1.53	1.59	0.64	0.64	0.76	-0.41	-0.49	0.24	-0.68
--	2B	--	0	0.72	0.98	1.31	1.36	0.41	0.41	0.64	-0.47	-0.37	0.31	-0.91
--	--	3B	0	0.46	0.69	1.00	1.06	0.44	0.44	0.53	-0.54	-0.37	0.11	-1.15
1B	2B	--	0	1.00	1.45	1.89	1.95	0.94	0.94	1.12	-0.63	-0.65	0.38	-0.94
1B	--	3B	0	0.74	1.11	1.56	1.61	0.60	0.60	0.81	-0.68	-0.56	0.14	-0.99
--	2B	3B	0	0.87	1.14	1.46	1.51	0.51	0.51	0.81	-0.55	-0.37	-	-
1B	2B	3B	0	1.05	1.54	1.95	2.01	1.00	1.00	1.03	-0.85	-0.73	-	-
--	--	3B	1	0.60	0.76	1.00	1.33	0.30	0.30	0.63	-0.58	-0.26	0.33	-0.86
--	2B	3B	1	0.87	1.23	1.47	1.80	0.22	0.21	0.79	-0.83	-0.44	-	-

Unfortunately, when you look at the run values by batting order (Table 52), you simply won't find that big of a difference with respect to the overall impact of the strikeout. On the one hand, you have the cleanup hitter, with whom the run value of the strikeout is .005 runs more costly than other types of outs. On the other hand, the run value of the strikeout is .002 runs less costly for the #2 hitter. That's right, the #2 hitter's preferred outs are strikeouts! And the preferred outs for the cleanup hitter are "moving runners over" outs. See, the #2 hitter has too many runners on first, and that makes the double play a bit too dangerous. If he has to make an out, make it a strikeout. The cleanup hitter has more runners in scoring position, and so if he is to make an out, we don't want him to strike out.

What is the impact of these outs? Suppose the average hitter strikes out 100 times, while our hitter has 140 strikeouts. If you put him in the cleanup slot, those 40 extra strikeouts will cost the team an extra 0.2 runs over the course of a season. This number is so small as to be virtually irrelevant. If you can control when you bring in a batter or pitcher (pinch hitters or relievers), then this makes a tremendous difference. But, for someone in the starting lineup, the differences that do exist are fairly insignificant.

The Book Says:

Worry about the strikeout only if you have the opportunity to use a pinch hitter or reliever. Don't consider the strikeout, or the ability of a hitter to move runners over on outs, when constructing your starting lineup.

Basestealing

Let's go back to the *monstrosity* chart and concentrate on the last two columns, which we've completely ignored so far: SB and CS. With a runner on first and no outs, the stolen base adds .24 runs while the caught stealing costs .68 runs. If you are successful three times out of four, the stolen base makes a lot of sense. After all, 75% of the time you gain .24 runs, while 25% of the time you lose .68 runs. That's a net positive of .01 runs. In fact the break-even point is 73.6%. If you will only be safe 70% of the time, then you shouldn't steal.

With a man on first, regardless of outs, the break-even point is between 73% and 74%. With a man on second and no outs, the break-even point is 74.5%, and with one out, it's 70.8%. And, you know the old adage about never making the third out at third? A steal from second with two outs requires an 83.2% break-even rate! The old myth is a fact. The best time to steal is with runners on first and second with one out: the required success rate is only 63.4%.

Note that all these rates are also dependent on the inning/score. We'll talk about that in detail in a later chapter. For now, we are just looking at how basestealing influences the optimal batting order.

Let's compare the run values of the batting events with a runner on first or second with no outs. That is, after a successful steal, how much more valuable do all those hits become? We'll extract the necessary lines from the monstrosity chart. (See Table 54.)

Table 54.   Run Values, By Event And Base/Out State (Subset Of An Earlier Chart)

1B	2B	3B	Outs	Sngl	Dbl	Trpl	HR	NIBB	HBP	RBOE	K	Out	SB	CS
1B	--	--	0	0.72	1.10	1.53	1.59	0.64	0.64	0.76	-0.41	-0.49	0.24	-0.68
--	2B	--	0	0.72	0.98	1.31	1.36	0.41	0.41	0.64	-0.47	-0.37	0.31	-0.91
--	--	--	1	0.28	0.43	0.68	1.00	0.29	0.29	0.31	-0.18	-0.18	-	-

With a runner on first or second, the run value of the single is unchanged. However, the run values of the extra-base hits go *down*, by .12 to .23 runs. Why is that? Because a double has a chance of moving the runner from first a total of three bases, while a double with a runner on second will move him exactly two bases. The double is partly wasted with a runner in scoring position, or to be precise, its value decreases by .23 runs. Likewise, if a runner is on second, you are not getting the full benefit of the walk since the runner will not advance (but would have advanced had he been on first). A strikeout is also more costly, and since you probably took a pitch to let the runner steal, your offensive value is likely to suffer as well. So, if you are going to steal second, you need to do this in front of a slap hitter: a hitter with few extra-base hits, few walks, and few strikeouts. Does this sound like the kind of thing you want to do at the top of the order? And if you get caught stealing? Forget about it. You drastically devalue all the potential accomplishments of the hitter.

Now, what if you try to steal with one out? Here is the extract for those lines. (See Table 55.)

Table 55.   Run Values, By Event And Base/Out State (Subset Of An Earlier Chart)

1B 2B 3B Outs	Sngl	Dbl	Trpl	HR	NIBB	HBP	RBOE	K	Out	SB	CS
1B -- -- 1	0.49	0.97	1.39	1.71	0.41	0.41	0.52	-0.34	-0.38	0.17	-0.46
-- 2B -- 1	0.67	0.99	1.21	1.57	0.27	0.26	0.55	-0.38	-0.37	0.25	-0.62
-- -- -- 2	0.14	0.23	0.27	1.00	0.14	0.14	0.15	-0.12	-0.12	-	-

Here, the single becomes even more important. See, while the single will move the runner to third about one third of the time (and give him a decent chance of scoring), the single will score the runner from second two-thirds of the time. This is a huge payoff, and this is why the run value of the single is worth almost .20 runs more with a runner on second than with a runner on first. The run value of the double is unchanged, while the other positive events take a hit. Once again, we prefer to have the stolen base in front of a singles machine.

And what about with two outs? (See Table 56.)

Table 56.   Run Values, By Event And Base/Out State (Subset Of An Earlier Chart)

1B 2B 3B Outs	Sngl	Dbl	Trpl	HR	NIBB	HBP	RBOE	K	Out	SB	CS
1B -- -- 2	0.26	0.71	1.15	1.86	0.23	0.23	0.33	-0.26	-0.26	0.09	-0.26
-- 2B -- 2	0.72	1.00	1.04	1.77	0.13	0.13	0.48	-0.35	-0.35	0.07	-0.35

After a successful steal, the value of a single increases dramatically: .46 runs! Even the double gets into it, with a gain of .29 runs. The reason it's so important to get the runner into scoring position with two outs is that he really does need to score should the following batter get a hit. If the following batter advances him only to third, he doesn't have the option of scoring on a two-out fly (as would be the case with zero or one out). If you have a hitter who can get tons of singles and doubles, then that's the guy you want to steal in front of with two outs.

The Book Says:

If you need to leverage a basestealer, put him in front of a batter who hits lots of singles and doesn't strikeout much. The likelihood is that your basestealer will be batting fifth or sixth.

Baserunning

How does baserunning play into all this? A great baserunner will take the extra base about 15 percentage points more than the average baserunner. For example, if the average runner advances from first to third on a single 35% of the time, then a great baserunner will do so 50% of the time.

So let's try to use this information to further optimize the batting order. This chart shows how often a single or double is hit, with the runner on first, and no one else on base. (See Table 57.)

Table 57.   Frequency Of Singles Or Doubles, With Runner On First, By Batting Slot Of Runner

Batting Slot of Runner on 1B	AL	NL
1	23%	23%
2	22%	22%
3	22%	21%
4	21%	21%
5	21%	20%
6	21%	21%
7	22%	21%
8	21%	17%
9	23%	21%

The first line reads: when the leadoff hitter is on first base, the batter at the plate hits a single or double 23% of the time. In other words, 23% of the time, the speed of the runner on first base is on display (if that runner is the leadoff hitter). Still confused? That first line would represent someone like Juan Pierre: he's the leadoff hitter, he's managed to get to first, and 23% of the time that he's there, a single or double is hit.

How much is an extra base worth? The short answer is .25 runs. The long answer is: it depends on, yes, the context—the base/out state. For example, scoring from first on a double with no outs is not worth as much as doing so with two outs. In the first case, if you don't take the extra base, you are left with runners on second and third with no outs. This situation has a run expectancy of 2.052 runs. If you do score, the run expectancy of the situation (man on second, no outs) is 1.189 runs, plus one for the run that scored for a total run value of 2.189. The difference of .137 runs is the run value of taking the extra base on a double from first base with no outs. If there were two outs instead, the run value would be .710 runs. As you can see, the run value of the extra base will vary greatly. For our purposes, let's stick with the short answer, which is the average run value of an extra base.

Based on this chart, you want your fastest runner on first base to come from the top of the order. This is the time where he gets to leverage his speed the most. But, what's the impact here? An AL team that puts a fast runner in the worst spot, the fifth slot in the order, will take advantage of his speed 21% of the time he is on first base. If he's batting leadoff, this increases to 23% of the time that his speed can be leveraged. So, that's an extra .02 times where we can leverage his speed.

And, how often will he be on first base? About 30% of the time. A bit more for a hitter who draws a lot of walks or hits a lot of singles, a bit less otherwise. So, let's work it out. With around 4.5 PA per game, our runner will be on first base about 1.5 times. We can leverage his speed .02 times those 1.5 instances he's on first base. That's 1.5 x .02 = .03 opportunities for us to leverage his speed per game. The run value for the great baserunner is .25 runs per opportunity. The run gain is .03 x .25 = .0075 runs per game, which works out to 1.2 runs per 162 games.

How about if the player is instead on second? How often does the batter hit a single? (See Table 58.)

Table 58.   Frequency Of Singles, With Runner On Second, By
Batting Slot Of Runner

Batting Slot of Runner on 2B	AL	NL
1	21%	20%
2	20%	20%
3	20%	20%
4	19%	19%
5	20%	19%
6	20%	18%
7	20%	17%
8	20%	18%
9	20%	20%

In this case, there's not much differentiation; you don't really have the opportunity to leverage your baserunner by slotting him. This table provides further evidence of the point that was brought up with stolen bases. To leverage the speed of the runner who is in scoring position, you need to have guys who can hit singles. Extra-base hits, as wonderful as they are, don't allow you to leverage the speed of baserunners.

You will notice the differentiation in the seventh and eighth slots when the pitcher is hitting in the lineup. In this case, speed would be very much wasted, simply because the pitcher won't hit enough singles to leverage. While you can sprinkle slow runners in many slots in a DH league, you prefer to keep your slow runners batting directly in front of your pitcher.

From the last two sections, we see that there is a bit of a problem. A great baserunner is usually, but not always, a great basestealer. *The Book* says that you would prefer to steal a base, and get into scoring position, as long as you have a hitter that hits a lot of singles, but not many extra-base hits. This is the reason we want our basestealer to bat fifth or sixth. At the same time, you prefer to have your great baserunner in front of hitters that hit lots of singles, regardless of their power numbers. This is the reason we want them at the top of the order.

In other words, the benefit on one side (stolen bases) is somewhat canceling the benefit on the other side (baserunning).

The Book Says:

Try to put your good baserunners in front of good hitters, especially if those hitters are predominantly singles or doubles hitters.

The Book Also Says:

When it comes to leveraging speed: (a) you want a good hitter who puts the ball in play to move you over, and/or (b) you want to put yourself in scoring position for a hitter who would have trouble moving your over otherwise.

Staying Out Of The Double Play

Our next topic: how important is it to consider the propensity of a batter for hitting into a double play?

Let's compare the hitters in the #3 and #5 slots, as they are the two candidates that require similar quality batters. Among the top six slots, the third slot has the most double play situations (1.02 per game), and the fifth slot has the second-fewest (0.87). As you can probably guess, the leadoff hitter sees the fewest double play situations, among all batting slots.

Suppose that we have two similar hitters to put into these slots, except for their double play rates. One of the two batters hits into tons of double plays; 20% of the time a DP situation is in effect, he hits into a DP. (This would work out to about 30 DP in a season.) We're going to call this batter Rim Jice. The other, an average batter, hits into a double play 10% of the time. (We're just using round numbers to make life easier for us. We could have used 22% and 12%, etc. The important thing is that the difference between a guy who hits into tons of DP and the average is around 10 percentage points.)

The extra run value of the DP is about .35 runs. How can we figure this out ourselves? The run expectancy with a man on first and no outs is .953 runs, while with the bases empty and two outs, it is .117 runs. On the other hand, if the batter had simply grounded out, you'd be left with a man on first and one out (which is worth .573 runs). So, the DP cost you the difference between .573 and .117, or .456 runs. With one out, this calculation produces a result of .251 runs. That gives us an average of around .35 runs.

Now, we just do another math exercise.

Hitting in the #3 slot, you have 1.02 DP situations per game. Rim Jice would hit into a DP 20% of those, for a total of .204 DP per game. Meanwhile, the average hitter would hit into .087 DP in the #5 slot (10% of .87). That gives us a total of .291 double plays per game for these two hitters in these two slots.

Reversing the two, Rim Jice as a #5 hitter would face .87 DP situations, and would hit into .174 DP. The average hitter in the #3 slot would hit into .102 DP. That gives us .276 double plays per game with the batting slots switched.

The difference in double plays per game for the team is .015 (.291 minus .276). This is what we are trying to understand in terms of the impact the DP has in batting order optimization. Saving .015 double plays per game means that you are saving about 2.4 double plays per 162 games. Since each DP is worth .35 runs, this works out to a total savings of 0.85 runs.

And remember, this is with a guy who is as extreme a DP machine as you will find, in two batting slots that are just about as extreme as it gets.

This table presents the number of DP situations per game, relative to the league-average by batting order, for each league. (See Table 59.)

Table 59.   Number Of DP Situations, By Batting Order, Relative To League

Batting Order	AL	NL
1	-0.14	-0.28
2	0.09	0.06
3	0.18	0.19
4	0.04	0.10
5	0.02	0.04
6	0.03	0.04
7	-0.02	-0.01
8	-0.09	-0.06
9	-0.11	-0.09

If you want to do the quick calculation in your head, look for the two batting slots you are considering, say the three and five slots. That's a .15 PA difference per game. Multiply that by the player's DP rate relative to the league-average. In our example with Rim Jice, it was .10. And then multiply that by the run value of the DP (.35). Then multiply by the number of games (162). So, .15 x .35 x .10 x 162 = 0.85 runs.

You will note that the leadoff hitter does not face a lot of DP situation in the NL. You can thank the pitcher for that. If you have a hitter who hits into a lot of DP, but is excellent overall, and draws a lot of walks, this is an excellent candidate to put into the leadoff slot in the NL. Consider a hitter that you've identified as a potential #1 or #2 hitter. In the NL, you have a difference of .34 DP situations per game. If this hitter is like Rim Jice, you can save .034 DP per game by having him in the leadoff slot. This works out to saving 5.5 DP per 162 games, or nearly two runs! We put the two runs as an exclamation, because this is a big deal relative to the other findings we have in *lineup optimization*. In isolation, it is of course a tiny gain.

The Book Says:

The propensity to ground into, or avoid, double plays is an important consideration for players at the extreme double play levels. It is also an important consideration for leadoff hitters in the NL.

Swapping Places

If you remember, we started the chapter by explaining that the frequency rates of the various base/out states for each lineup spot was based on actual data. If we start rearranging the pieces, the frequency rates will also change. How much will this change what we've learned? Let's create some player performance lines, and run them through our Markov model. (See Table 60.)

Table 60.   Optimal Batting Order, For A Sample Team

Optimal Order	BA	OBP	SLG	wOBA
1	0.273	0.439	0.439	0.407
2	0.298	0.390	0.529	0.405
3	0.275	0.326	0.466	0.352
4	0.298	0.362	0.578	0.407
5	0.260	0.364	0.396	0.351
6	0.250	0.316	0.402	0.326
7	0.242	0.307	0.389	0.316
8	0.234	0.298	0.377	0.307
9	0.227	0.290	0.366	0.298

We selected some reasonable numbers to illustrate our point. We've got three excellent hitters, each with a wOBA above .400, but each of the three has a different profile, as evidenced by their OBP and SLG. We have two good hitters, also with a different profile. And finally, we have four poor hitters, each one worse than the other.

We want our three best hitters to bat somewhere in the #1, #2, and #4 slots, and that's where we put them. The cleanup hitter gets his value in his SLG (we set him to 40 HR), the leadoff hitter leads the team in OBP (133 walks), and the #2 hitter is somewhat more balanced. The #3 and #5 hitters are the same quality, with the #3 hitter having many more HR than the #5 hitter.

So, how did they do? This batting order scored 5.448 runs per game (882.6 runs in 162 games) in our model. You would look at this batting order, and immediately think, "That's wrong. The hitter in the #3 slot should be better than the hitter in the #2 slot. Swap them." OK, so we did. And this new lineup scored 880.5 runs in 162 games, or 2.1 runs less than the other lineup.

Our run values by batting order told us we wanted the better hitter in the #2 slot. Now, our Markov model says the same thing. And, as we expected, the difference is only a couple of runs.

Pitchers In NL Parks

Now, let's put our focus squarely on games in NL parks, where the pitcher is in the lineup. Because the pitcher is so much worse than any other hitter in the lineup, this throws a huge monkey wrench in any model. Creating basic models that have the same quality hitter in every lineup spot works most of the time, since we've shown there's really very little difference between such a model and reality. But, throw a pitcher into the lineup, and the whole thing starts to blow up (as you saw by the differences between the AL and NL columns in the preceding tables).

In reality, there were 4.83 runs scored per game in NL parks (1999–2002). If we take pitchers out of the mix, the model comes out to 5.25 runs per game. (And at the other extreme, if we were to construct a lineup with nine average-hitting pitchers, it would score about one run per game according to our model.)

Going back to the model, we can insert eight equal non-pitchers (based on non-pitchers' performances in NL parks), plus one pitcher in the ninth spot, and figure out, using Markov, the expected number of runs. Such a lineup would score 4.605 runs per game. This is a far cry from the 4.83 runs scored in reality. But before we discard the model, we have to remember that the pitcher bats ninth for the first couple of times through the lineup only; after that, a pinch hitter takes his spot. Looking at the numbers, we can quantify this: the pitcher bats ninth 65% of the time, and someone else bats ninth the remaining 35%. If you take 65% of the model with the pitcher in the lineup (4.605 runs), and 35% of the model with no pitchers in the lineup (5.25 runs), this gives you . . . 4.83 runs. Thus the model agrees perfectly with reality.

OK, now that this mystery is solved, let's see if there's anything fancy we can do with the pitcher. For example, what would happen if the pitcher were the eighth batter, instead of the ninth? Let's run it through our model (where each of the non-pitchers are exactly the same), and see what it gives us: 4.582 runs.

If you remember, with the pitcher batting in the ninth spot for the whole nine-inning game, we calculated the team would score 4.605 runs. So by moving him to the eighth spot, we have given up .023 runs per game (four runs per 162 games). So, what we've done is taken a move that we know to be wrong, clearly wrong: take the worst batter, by far, on the team, and give him more times to bat. And the result was only a loss of four runs. Actually it's even less; remember that pitchers will only hit 65% of the time, and this four-run loss is when the pitcher hits through the whole game. So those four runs must be multiplied by 65%, meaning that the actual cost is just two and a half runs. This is what we are faced with when dealing with lineup optimization. Finding one of two runs with normal hitters, and four runs with clearly inferior hitters.

But, with clearly inferior hitters, there's really nothing to optimize, since we've already figured out where to put them.

So far, all we've done is moved the pitcher up one spot in the order, and filled the ninth spot with an exactly average hitter, which is what we have in all other spots. What we've tested here is simply the effect of giving the pitcher 2.5% more PA. Let's continue running this exercise, with the pitcher batting in each lineup spot, one at a time. (See Table 61.)

Table 61.   Number Of Team Runs, By Batting Slot For The Pitcher (All Other Hitters Equals)

Pitcher bats...	... and team scores this many runs
1	4.511
2	4.508
3	4.518
4	4.504
5	4.537
6	4.537
7	4.560
8	4.582
9	4.605

Moving the pitcher up from ninth to eighth to seventh to sixth removes .022 to .023 runs per game, for each slot. The three worst spots to put the pitcher in are: leadoff, second, and cleanup. But, we already knew this, right? Those are the three most important spots to put your best hitter. It stands to reason that you don't want your worst hitter there.

That never stopped Earl Weaver from batting Mark Belanger second, though. As far advanced as Weaver was in all forms of baseball strategy, he was clueless on this front. (Baseball men will surely remind us that Weaver can't hear our criticism, since his World Series rings are plugging his ears.)

Weaver has suggested that he would do such a thing when he thought that Belanger would hit better against a certain pitcher. That is, managers like to move guys from the bottom of the order into the #2 slot when they feel that there's a situation they can exploit. Here's what really happened with Belanger, and we'll leave it to the reader to decide how much foresight Weaver had. (See Table 62.)

Table 62. **Performance Of Mark Belanger, By Batting Order**

Bat Order	AVG	OBP	SLG
1st	0.235	0.304	0.302
2nd	0.231	0.306	0.289
8th	0.236	0.312	0.281
9th	0.217	0.284	0.269

So yes, Weaver was right that Belanger would hit better against certain pitchers (when he wasn't batting ninth) than others; he improved all the way from a .217 hitter to the mid .230s. But unless .235 qualified Belanger as one of the three best hitters on the team, we don't see how this justifies him batting second. So if nothing else, we will consider this book a true success if all thirty teams were to never put a below average hitter in the second spot. While the proper strategy will only gain you a few runs, why do something that is otherwise clearly wrong?

Second Leadoff Hitter Theory And The Pitcher

Now, what about the *second leadoff hitter* theory? When batting ninth, the pitcher (the worst hitter) is followed by the best hitters on the team. In terms of leveraging those great hitters, wouldn't we prefer to have a decent hitter in the ninth spot? Doesn't the pitcher hitting just simply kill, or not start, any rallies? What if instead, we move the pitcher to the eighth spot (where we know it'll cost us 2.5 runs per season), and move the eighth hitter into the ninth spot? By having such a hitter setting up the top of the order, can't these great hitters leverage this situation, so that they can gain more than 2.5 runs in the process? That is, can we trade giving the pitcher 2.5% more PA, in order to give the top of the order more runners on base, and still come out ahead? Does the second leadoff hitter theory hold water?

Once again, let's take out our Markov model. This time however, we'll put the typical actual hitter in each of the nine spots (instead of the way we've been working so far, with an average hitter one through eight, and a pitcher in the ninth). Our model says that such a lineup will score 4.835 runs. That compares favorably with the reality of 4.833 runs. (Note: in all our calculations the pitcher only hits in 65% of PA.)

Now, let's do something exciting. Let's re-run our model by swapping the players in the eighth and ninth spots. That is, let's test the second leadoff theory. This time, the model generated 4.847 runs per game! It exists! This is a gain of .012 runs per game (or two runs per season). So, the cost of having the pitcher get more PA is indeed more than balanced by having a half-way decent hitter set the table for the top of the order.

How far up can we move the pitcher? What if we let the pitcher continue to go up the chain to the seventh spot? That gives us 4.838 runs, or virtually the same as leaving the pitcher in the ninth spot. Well, that didn't help; having the pitcher hit in the seventh or ninth spot has the same impact. What this tells us is giving the pitcher's spot an extra 5% PA is balanced by having table-setters for the top of the order.

Just for fun, let's repeat this process all the way up the lineup. (See Table 63.) This chart is slightly different than the previous one. In this case, we used the actual performances of each lineup spot. So, when we say that the pitcher bats leadoff, we then move all the other batters down one spot.

Once again, the two worst spots to bat your pitcher are the #2 and #4 spots. Putting your pitcher in the #3 spot is now worse than putting him in the leadoff spot. Notice the overall impact here. Putting the pitcher in the eighth slot will have the team score 4.847 runs per game. Having the pitcher in the cleanup slot—the worst possible slot of all—will result in 4.752 runs. This difference is almost .1 runs per game, or 15 runs per season. That's as bad as it gets.

Table 63.   Number Of Team Runs, By Batting Slot For The Pitcher
(Typical Hitters In Other Slots)

Pitcher bats...	... and team scores this many runs
1	4.774
2	4.754
3	4.765
4	4.752
5	4.795
6	4.805
7	4.838
8	4.847
9	4.835

Does this also apply to the AL parks, where the difference between the eighth and ninth hitters isn't so large? The number of runs scored in AL parks, whether in reality or using the Markov model, is 5.16 runs. What happens when we swap the eighth and ninth hitters? 5.153 runs. The second leadoff hitter theory does not apply in AL parks. In order for the top of the order to leverage this situation, you need a large difference in quality between your two bottom hitters.

The Book Says:

The second leadoff hitter theory exists. You can put your pitcher in the eighth slot and gain a couple of extra runs per year.

What If You Don't Ever Let The Pitcher Hit?

We already talked about this. The model says 5.25 runs if the pitcher never hits, 4.83 if he hits 65% of the time (which is the current reality).

So, that's a loss of .42 runs by having the pitcher hit, which adds up to sixty-eight runs per season. Compared with the numbers we've been throwing around in this chapter, this is huge! Trying to optimize a realistic set of nine batters will buy us only ten or fifteen runs per season. But, trying to get all pitchers to never bat will gain us sixty-eight runs! Just to put that number in perspective, a great pitcher like Randy Johnson is worth around sixty to seventy runs, relative to an average pitcher. So preventing all pitchers from batting is the equivalent to having Randy Johnson pitching for you thirty-four times a season. And, you can do this without spending fifteen million dollars.

But, how do you do that? There's only one way to do it: pinch-hit for the pitcher every single time. Can you imagine pinch-hitting for Randy Johnson in the second inning? No, of course not. Like we said, you're going to save .42 runs per game doing that. But, having RJ as opposed to a long reliever is certainly worth a lot more than .42 runs per game. But, what about your two worst starters? These guys are certainly not .42 runs above average per game. For that matter, they are likely below-average pitchers. Why not simply remove your fourth starter for a pinch hitter, and relieve him with your fifth starter, who is then relieved by a regular reliever. This will bring you into the sixth or seventh inning. Then, you use the rest of your relievers based on the score. Two days later, you repeat the process (or swap the roles of your two traditional starters).

What you end up with is something like this:
- Day 1: Maddux
- Day 2: Smoltz
- Day 3: fourth starter, fifth starter, third-best reliever
- Day 4: Glavine
- Day 5: fifth starter, fourth starter, third-best reliever

You are now in the sixth or seventh inning in all cases. You've got your top two relievers available in all cases, if the score is close, or the fourth through sixth relievers otherwise. What you lose here (the flexibility of your third-best reliever, and two hitters lost from your bench because they pinch hit the first and second time through the order), you gain by having your pitcher never hit during the two games where runs are really needed. Since we know the gain is enormous (.42 runs), you would be hard-pressed to prove you can gain .42 runs by having that bench/bullpen flexibility.

We'll tell you one thing: other than Barry Bonds, the typical great hitter is worth about .42 more runs per game than the average player. So again, would you prefer having the bullpen/bench flexibility, or would you prefer having Alex Rodriguez come to bat four or five times a game? We're asking the same question: would you prefer the bull-pen/bench flexibility, or would you prefer not having your pitcher bat?

Same question. Same answer.

The Book Says:

Do whatever you can to prevent a below-average pitcher from coming to bat.

SUMMARY

Remember, the primary reason that we're having a hard time trying to squeeze out any runs is that the batting order is a continuous loop: everyone gets to bat. Everything in this book is about trying to squeeze out a few runs here or there. There are a lot of little pieces to optimize. A little here and a little there, and suddenly, you've managed to add 50 runs to your expectancy (the equivalent of 5 wins), just by rearranging the pieces of the puzzle! To get these five wins the "brute force" way (getting better players) would, on average, cost you ten million dollars in additional salary. This is the value of good management: if you can leverage your resources slightly better than the next guy, it gives you a true and tangible advantage.

CHAPTER 6 – LEFT, RIGHT, LEFT, RIGHT

UNDERSTANDING PLATOON EFFECTS

Coming off his remarkable 2001 season, Barry Bonds had attained a reputation for dominating right-handed pitching while being a mere mortal against lefties. Looking at wOBA numbers from 2000 and 2001, he averaged .538 against RHP and .445 against LHP. (We should note that wOBA isn't as useful when evaluating Bonds, given that he receives a large number of semi-intentional walks that get scored as unintentional.) Compared with the average platoon split of 25 points of wOBA for left-handed hitters, Bonds seemed unusually susceptible to left-handed pitching. National League rivals responded the obvious way—by loading up on lefties, especially those with previous success against Bonds.

The result? Predictably, the fraction of Bonds' plate appearances against left-handed pitchers increased. More importantly, how did this strategy work? Unfortunately for those rivals, not very well. In 2002 and 2003, Bonds averaged .579 against lefties and .523 against righties.

Interestingly, from 2000 through 2003, Bonds' wOBA vs. right-handed pitching was .531, compared with .508 against left-handed pitching—a platoon split virtually identical to the average for lefties. So which is he: the righty masher from 2000 and 2001, the lefty masher from 2002 and 2003, or a typical left-handed batter? Let's expand this question to batters as a whole. Do all left-handed (or right-handed) batters share the same platoon splits, or is there some spread in "platoon talent"? If the latter, how can a manager estimate a batter's "true" platoon split in order to take advantage of it? And of course, what about pitchers?

As usual, our primary concern is the effect of randomness when dealing with small data samples. Left-handed batters face left-handed pitchers in about one-quarter of their plate appearances, meaning that for a regular starter, we're dealing with around 150 plate appearances per season. That may seem like a lot, yet in 150 PA, a typical player's wOBA will be pushed up or down by 40 points due to randomness alone. As usual, we'll deal with this by looking for predictive power—whether or not an extreme platoon split is a sign of a non-average platoon split in the future. We'll start by examining left-handed hitters, and looking for seasons with extreme platoon splits. Of players with at least 400 plate appearances against right-handed pitching and 100 against left-handed pitching in consecutive seasons, here are the ten lefties who fared the best against southpaw opponents, and how they fared the following season. (See Table 64.)

Table 64.   The 10 *Best* Left-Handed Lefty Mashers, 2000–2003

Player	wOBA vs. LHP minus wOBA vs. RHP	Split next season
Garret Anderson, 2000	.119	-.030
Barry Bonds, 2002	.080	.016
Craig Counsell, 2001	.072	-.004
Bobby Higgins, 2001	.067	-.097
Ichiro Suzuki, 2002	.053	.050
Rafael Palmeiro, 2003	.051	-.125
Paul O'Neill, 2000	.050	-.015
Ichiro Suzuki, 2003	.050	.067
Carlos Pena, 2002	.049	-.079
Lee Stevens, 2000	.047	-.024
Average	.064	-.024

OK, so one of Bonds' lefty-mashing seasons made our list. And since it was the first of two consecutive ones, his second season also shows up as positive. But we know that his other three seasons had negative splits. The fact that Ichiro made the list twice is a good sign, as is the fact that he actually posted three seasons with positive splits (the two that got him on the list, plus the 2004 season). Overall, we see that our lefty-mashing lefties had collective splits of –.024 the following season. This is significantly higher than the average split of –.041 that we find for all left-handed hitters meeting the 400/100 criteria, which is promising. Let's push on.

Table 65.   The 10 *Best* Left-Handed Righty Mashers, 2000–2003

Player	wOBA vs. RHP minus wOBA vs. LHP	Split next season
Hank Blalock, 2003	.154	.032
Jacque Jones, 2002	.152	.054
Carlos Delgado, 2002	.148	.061
Jim Thome, 2001	.148	.133
Barry Bonds, 2000	.143	.050
Trot Nixon, 2001	.143	.072
Bobby Abreu, 2000	.142	.073
Eric Chavez, 2000	.135	.078
David Ortiz, 2003	.135	.115
Jim Thome, 2002	.133	.084
Average	.143	.075

Again Bonds makes the list, this time from his season in which he hit so poorly (relatively speaking) against left-handed pitchers. (See Table 65.) Looking over the whole list, we see that all ten lefties who hit well against righties continued to do so the following season, and all but Blalock had subsequent splits above the average of .041.

So it seems we're onto something here—both of our groups seemed to carry some of their platoon splits from one season to the next. More importantly, this result holds true as we look at more players. Taking the entire list of 170 qualifying player-seasons, we find a significant correlation between a lefty's platoon split one season and the next, implying that some of the variation in platoon splits for left-handed hitters is due to an inherent "platoon" ability. Without showing the details here, we will mention that significant results were also found for right-handed hitters, as well as for both lefty and righty pitchers (although the correlation was the weakest for right-handed hitters).

Before continuing on, we should examine the cause of platoon splits. Looking at the above lists of players, one might get the impression that power-hitting lefties tend to hit the worst against left-handed pitching, while contact-hitting lefties tend to not have very strong platoon splits. So perhaps we're getting fooled into thinking that players have unique platoon splits, when in fact we're just seeing the result of all players having a strong platoon split for home runs and a small platoon split for singles.

This theory is straightforward enough to test. Instead of measuring wOBA, we can measure platoon splits for individual outcomes. For example, what fraction of balls in play are home runs against left-handed and right-handed pitching, and does the ratio vary significantly from player to player? Once again, we find the answer to be "yes"—some players' home run rates go strongly down when facing same-handed pitching, while others are unaffected and some even seem to improve. We find the same result when examining rates of strikeouts, walks, hits on balls in play, and extra-base hits. So we can safely conclude that variations in platoon splits are real, and not merely the indirect result of particular types of players (such as power hitters) all being affected similarly.

A second, related question is what stats are most affected by platoon splits. For example, are platoon splits the result of changes in, say, home run and strikeout rates, or is it an across-the-board effect? Considering right-handed batters, we find that they perform better across the board when facing left-handed pitching: fewer strikeouts, more walks, more home runs, more hits on balls in play, and more extra-base hits. This across-the-board improvement against opposite-handed pitching is also true of left-handed batters.

So, armed with the knowledge that (a) platoon splits exist for all outcome types, and (b) player-to-player variations in these platoon splits exist for all outcome types, we will use only our two primary stats (OBP and wOBA) for the remainder of this chapter.

The Book Says:

Platoon skills vary from player to player. For example, it is incorrect to assume that all left-handed batters are equally penalized when facing left-handed pitching. This is also true of right-handed batters (to a lesser degree) as well as both left- and right-handed pitchers.

Variations in Platoon Splits

So far, we have established that players have different platoon skills—and again, by "skill" we mean a player's inherent ability to perform at a particular level rather than how well he actually performed. (For example, the fact that you may flip a coin and get "heads" twice in a row doesn't necessarily mean that you have any particular knack—or "skill"—for getting heads.)

Table 66.   Average Platoon Splits, 2000–2004

	RHB	LHB	SHB	RHP	LHP
Average OBP	.333	.349	.344	.338	.342
OBP skill variation	.041	.040	.029	.023	.025
Average OBP platoon split	.017	.019	.002 (L–R)	.025	.011
Platoon skill variation	.014	.016	.022	.021	.027
Average wOBA	.335	.349	.338	.340	.342
wOBA skill variation	.046	.045	.031	.024	.025
Average wOBA platoon split	.017	.027	.001 (L–R)	.025	.019
Platoon skill variation	.013	.018	.025	.022	.027

The next question is, just how important is it to worry about this? Is the variation in platoon skills enough to matter? Will it turn a poor hitter into a good one, or just into a marginally better (but still poor) hitter? Using the methodology we introduced in the chapter on clutch hitting, we have determined average platoon splits and the typical player-to-player variations for all types of batters and pitchers. (See Table 66.)

This table is packed with data. Let's go over it slowly. The top line shows the average OBP of each type of player—right-handed batters, left-handed batters, switch hitters, right-handed pitchers, and left-handed pitchers. We note immediately that right-handed hitters seem to be at a significant disadvantage (sixteen points of OBP and fourteen of wOBA) compared to left-handed hitters, while pitchers are more evenly balanced. As noted in our chapter on matchups, we believe that right-handed pitchers can get by with worse stuff than lefties because they usually have the platoon edge, and thus the major leagues are populated with bad righties who would otherwise get shelled if they were lefties. The presence of a lot of bad righties evens out the average OBP numbers for RHP and LHP. For hitters, lefties have the expected superior numbers because they hold the platoon advantage (when facing right-handed pitchers) more often than not.

The second line indicates the player-to-player variations in OBP skill. (For the math-inclined, these numbers are standard deviations.) For left- and right-handed hitters, this is around .040, meaning that 68% of them have true OBP that are within 40 or 41 points of the average for batters of their handedness. (We will devote a later section entirely to switch hitters.) For example, we see that an average right-handed batter has an OBP of .333, a good right-handed batter (specifically, one who is better than 84% of righties) will have a "true" OBP of .374, and a poor one (one who is better than only 16% of righties) will be at .292.

The third row gives the average OBP platoon split. Finally, the fourth row gives the player-to-player skill variations in the OBP platoon split, which is what we will discuss for the remainder of this section. (The fifth through eighth rows give identical data, but for wOBA instead of OBP.)

From this chart, we find that the average right-handed batter has a platoon split of .017 (in the sense that he hits lefties better), with a typical variation of .014. While this .014 is certainly significant, we point out that it is only about one-third of the overall player-to-player variation. In other words, a good right-handed hitter with an average platoon split is much better against lefties than an average right-handed hitter with a large platoon split (and of course, is much, much better against righties). Likewise, we see that the variation in platoon splits for left-handed hitters is significantly less than the variation in overall OBP or wOBA skill levels. This doesn't mean that we should ignore variations in platoon splits for batters, but it does indicate that it is of secondary importance.

On the flip side are pitchers, where we find variations in platoon skills that are comparable to the variations in overall skill. This is the result of two effects. First, as noted earlier, the difference between good and bad pitchers is less than the difference between good and bad hitters. The second effect is that the variation in platoon splits is much higher for pitchers than for hitters. This is somewhat understandable too, as pitchers have a wide variety of pitch types (fastballs, curves, etc.) and arm angles that can cause variations in platoon splits.

The Book Says:

Player-to-player variations in platoon splits are more important for pitchers than for hitters. In fact, a right-handed pitcher with average overall talent but a large platoon split is as good against righties as a right-handed pitcher with good overall talent and an average platoon split. (The reverse is true for lefties.) For hitters, the good hitter with an average platoon split is generally better than an average hitter with an unusually large platoon split.

We note that the measurement of *any* player-to-player variation in platoon skills for right-handed hitters is a new statistical finding. Past studies on this topic have generally been based on year-to-year correlations, which we show in the appendix to be much less accurate than the more rigorous techniques used extensively herein. (Indeed, this particular result is used to illustrate the difference between the two techniques.)

ESTIMATING HITTERS' PLATOON SKILLS

Now that we know the distributions of overall skill levels and platoon skills, we have the information necessary to calculate expected skill levels against righties and lefties. Recalling the "regression" section of the *Toolshed* chapter, we find that a right-handed hitter's platoon split is best estimated with a weighted average in which his platoon split is weighted by the number of lefties he has faced, and the league average is weighted by 2,200. In other words, a righty who has 2,200 plate appearances against left-handed pitchers will be regressed exactly halfway toward the league-average. For a lefty, the number is about 1,000 (due to the larger variation in platoon skills). In practical terms, a batter has to play for many seasons before you place too much stock in his observed platoon splits. For pitchers, the break-even points come sooner (700 for righties and 450 for lefties) and thus are more easily attainable.

Technical note: even though we refer to platoon splits in terms of the *difference* between wOBA versus left- and right-handed opponents for the sake of simplicity, our calculations are based on *ratios* between the two wOBA. For example, our default expectation is that a right-handed hitter will hit about 5% better against a left-handed pitcher than a right-handed pitcher, rather than that he will hit about 17 points better. This helps us avoid absurd results, such as that a .000 right-handed hitter hits .012 against left-handed pitchers and *negative* .005 against righties. This also correctly accounts for the fact that platoon differences are greater for better hitters (i.e., a 5% difference for a .400 hitter is 20 points, while a 5% difference for a .300 hitter is only 15 points).

These tables show the hitters with the most extreme estimated platoon splits (after correcting for population variations), considering only players with at least 200 plate appearances against righties and 100 versus lefties. (See Table 67.) The columns titled "Measured wOBA Split" indicate the players' actual platoon splits from 2000–2004. The columns titled "wOBA Platoon Skill" give our estimated platoon skills, calculated as described above—these columns are approximately what we would expect each player's platoon split to be for a future season or a future PA (in fact, any period of time in the future, not considering any changes that might occur due to injury, aging, etc.).

Table 67.   The 10 Most Extreme Platoon Splits (RHB), 2000–2004

The Largest Platoon Splits			The Smallest Platoon Splits		
Player	Measured wOBA Split	wOBA Platoon Skill	Player	Measured wOBA Split	wOBA Platoon Skill
Brian Jordan	.101	.037	Tony Batista	-.041	.003
Marquis Grissom	.082	.036	Luis Matos	-.086	.004
Edgar Renteria	.078	.036	Mike Sweeney	-.038	.007
Brad Ausmus	.078	.036	Preston Wilson	-.025	.008
Phil Nevin	.081	.034	Carlos Lee	-.025	.008
Junior Spivey	.093	.032	Craig Biggio	-.018	.009
Brandon Inge	.080	.032	Tim Salmon	-.022	.009
Eric Karros	.071	.032	Donnie Sadler	-.092	.009
Chris Truby	.129	.031	Derek Bell	-.099	.009
Jeff Conine	.061	.031	Julio Lugo	-.017	.010

As expected, these hitters were regressed most of the way from their measured platoon splits toward the average platoon split for right-handed hitters. The player on this list with the highest number of plate appearances versus left-handed hitters is Tony Batista with 826. Even with that large a number of plate appearances, he regressed about 73% of the way toward the league-average, retaining just 27% of his measured wOBA platoon split. On the other hand, Derek Bell had just 155 appearances against lefties, and thus retained only 8% of his measured wOBA platoon split.

Here are the same results for left-handed hitters. (See Table 68.) As a whole, the lefties kept a little bit more of their individual wOBA platoon splits. The player with the most appearances against left-handed pitching was Carlos Delgado, with 1,028. Consequently his estimated wOBA platoon skill is 35% based on his stats and 65% based on the league-average. David Dellucci is at the other extreme; his 132 appearances against lefties indicate that his estimated platoon skill is 12% from his stats and 88% from the league-average.

Table 68.   The 10 Most Extreme Platoon Splits (LHB), 2000–2004

The Largest Platoon Splits			The Smallest Platoon Splits		
Player	Measured wOBA Split	wOBA Platoon Skill	Player	Measured wOBA Split	wOBA Platoon Skill
Jim Thome	.103	.053	Ichiro Suzuki	-.033	.004
Brian Giles	.094	.052	Mark Grace	-.037	.012
Jacque Jones	.087	.048	Larry Walker	-.008	.016
Carlos Delgado	.084	.048	Alex Cora	-.038	.016
Bobby Abreu	.079	.048	Johnny Damon	.002	.018
Eric Chavez	.082	.047	D Mientkiewicz	.000	.018
Trot Nixon	.106	.047	Brad Wilkerson	-.008	.020
Brad Fullmer	.103	.046	Robin Ventura	-.006	.020
David Dellucci	.158	.044	Garret Anderson	.006	.020
Timo Perez	.124	.044	Nick Johnson	-.018	.021

It is probably worth noting that neither list contains a batter with a negative platoon skill—one who is actually expected to perform *better* against same-handed pitching. Instead, the platoon splits largely start at zero for the most neutral hitters and go from there in the expected direction.

Of course, as noted previously, the player-to-player variation in overall hitting skill significantly exceeds the variation in platoon skill. This indicates that what you really want is a great hitter, not necessarily one with a great platoon split. To illustrate, we've ranked batters by wOBA skill versus right-handed and left-handed pitching in these tables. (See Table 69 and Table 70.)

Table 69.   The 10 Best Right-Handed Hitters Vs. RHP/LHP,
2000–2004

Best Batters vs. RHP Player	True wOBA vs. RHP	Best Batters vs. LHP Player	True wOBA vs. LHP
Albert Pujols	.431	Manny Ramirez	.458
Manny Ramirez	.426	Albert Pujols	.452
Gary Sheffield	.420	Vladimir Guerrero	.443
Alex Rodriguez	.417	Sammy Sosa	.442
Vladimir Guerrero	.413	Gary Sheffield	.442
Sammy Sosa	.412	Alex Rodriguez	.435
Jeff Bagwell	.399	Frank Thomas	.425
Frank Thomas	.395	Jeff Bagwell	.424
Mike Sweeney	.395	Jeff Kent	.417
Jeff Kent	.392	Magglio Ordonez	.417

Table 70.   The 10 Best Left-Handed Hitters Vs. RHP/LHP,
2000–2004

Best Batters vs. RHP Player	True wOBA vs. RHP	Best Batters vs. LHP Player	True wOBA vs. LHP
Barry Bonds	.520	Barry Bonds	.477
Todd Helton	.470	Todd Helton	.430
Jason Giambi	.442	Larry Walker	.412
Carlos Delgado	.436	Jason Giambi	.404
Jim Thome	.434	Jim Edmonds	.386
Larry Walker	.433	Carlos Delgado	.383
Jim Edmonds	.431	Jim Thome	.376
Brian Giles	.427	Luis Gonzalez	.375
Luis Gonzalez	.420	Brian Giles	.371
Bobby Abreu	.418	Will Clark	.371

Doing this ranking actually requires that we make two regressions. First is for the estimate of the batter's "true" platoon split, as described above; second is the estimate of his "true" overall wOBA. (We note that one might have been tempted to merely use the batter's actual stats vs.

RHP or LHP to make this list. This turns out to be a poor approach, since his performance vs. LHP tells us something about how well he can hit RHP, and vice versa.)

In both tables, nine hitters are among the ten best both when facing right-handed pitching *and* when facing left-handed pitching. So once again, a good hitter trumps a good platoon split.

The Book Says:

A right-handed hitter needs around 2,000 appearances against left-handed pitchers before his measured platoon split can be considered reliable (in other words, using the measured platoon split is more accurate than assuming the player has an average split). From a practical standpoint, right-handers are best assumed to have average platoon skills, unless one is willing to make the calculations needed to accurately estimate a player's platoon skill. For lefties, the number is about 1,000, which means that only veteran starters have reliable platoon splits.

ESTIMATING PITCHERS' PLATOON SKILLS

We now repeat these calculations for pitchers, and show the extreme splits in these tables. (See Table 71 and Table 72.)

The difference between pitchers and hitters is striking. Tomokazu Ohka faced 844 left-handed hitters during the years in our sample, and posted a wOBA platoon split of -.032. Doing the math to compute his expected future wOBA platoon split, we find that the estimate is based 56% on his measured split and 44% on the league-average. (This result is hardly surprising, given that we noted above that platoon estimates for right-handed pitchers are half from the measured split and half from the league-average when they have faced about 700 lefties.) For comparison, Tony Batista faced a comparable number of left-handed pitchers (826), and regressed 73% of the way back toward the mean.

Table 71.   The 10 Most Extreme Platoon Splits (RHP), 2000–2004

The Largest Platoon Splits			The Smallest Platoon Splits		
Player	Measured wOBA Split	wOBA Platoon Skill	Player	Measured wOBA Split	wOBA Platoon Skill
Jon Lieber	.111	.076	Steve Trachsel	-.053	-.023
Matt Kinney	.111	.062	Kevin Tapani	-.098	-.020
Braden Looper	.103	.060	Tim Wakefield	-.033	-.011
Jose Lima	.098	.060	Hideo Nomo	-.028	-.010
Chad Bradford	.139	.059	Woody Williams	-.032	-.009
Steve Reed	.116	.057	Terry Adams	-.043	-.008
Ryan Drese	.093	.056	Roger Clemens	-.031	-.007
Elmer Dessens	.075	.055	Tomokazu Ohka	-.032	-.006
Carl Pavano	.075	.054	Jeff D'Amico	-.026	-.001
Josias Manzanillo	.142	.054	Felix Rodriguez	-.050	-.000

Table 72.   The 10 Most Extreme Platoon Splits (LHP), 2000–2004

The Largest Platoon Splits			The Smallest Platoon Splits		
Player	Measured wOBA Split	wOBA Platoon Skill	Player	Measured wOBA Split	wOBA Platoon Skill
Scott Schoeneweis	.079	.053	Jamie Moyer	-.042	-.023
Ray King	.091	.051	Denny Neagle	-.058	-.020
Aaron Fultz	.096	.050	Barry Zito	-.042	-.018
Scott Eyre	.097	.047	Mike Remlinger	-.074	-.018
Casey Fossum	.083	.047	Mike Stanton	-.063	-.017
Scott Sauerbeck	.085	.046	Wilson Alvarez	-.078	-.013
Kirk Rueter	.055	.045	John Rocker	-.109	-.011
Ricardo Rincon	.097	.045	Jimmy Anderson	-.033	-.007
Buddy Groom	.087	.045	Michael Tejera	-.060	-.006
B. J. Ryan	.080	.044	Eric Milton	-.025	-.002

Once again, we find that the variations in pitcher wOBA platoon skill estimates are quite large, compared with those of hitters. In fact, many of the lefties on this list retained most of their platoon splits; Jamie Moyer leads the list, having faced 1,213 left-handed hitters and thus regressed only 30% of the way toward the mean of .020.

All twenty pitchers listed in the lowest platoon splits show negative splits—they will be expected to perform better against opposite-handed hitters. Likewise, all of the highest platoon splits are around .05–.06, which translates into an ERA difference of well over a run.

We mentioned earlier that the larger variation in pitcher platoon splits might be expected, as some types of pitches (e.g., sliders) are more affected by the batter's handedness than others (e.g., change-ups, over-hand curves). We can test this theory now. Looking at the list of pitchers with small platoon splits, we find that about half are primarily fastball pitchers. Of the rest, we see a variety of styles that lend themselves to facing either-handed hitters, such as Wakefield's knuckler and Zito's 12-to-6 curve. Among the pitchers with large platoon splits, we find that about three quarters rely largely on a slider or a non-overhand curve. Pitchers with 3/4-arm and lower (e.g., Fossum, Bradford, and Reed) deliveries also tend to be found on the high-platoon split list. This also suggests that one can estimate pitcher platoon splits even better if one knows the type of pitches being thrown and the arm angle, and then divides pitchers accordingly, rather than merely by handedness. Unfortunately our data do not include pitch types, so we must proceed without exploiting this fact.

Moving on, we have estimated each pitcher's true wOBA against left-handed and right-handed batters, and ranked the ten best in the following tables. Because pitchers tend to perform differently in relief than they do when starting (as we'll see in later chapters), we have divided these tables further into left-handed and right-handed starters and relievers. (See Tables 73 through 76.)

Unlike hitters, we find that the lists of best pitchers change significantly depending on what side the hitter is batting from. Of the forty pitchers that we find are the most effective against right-handed hitters, only twenty make the list against lefties. The fact that not all lefties (or righties) have the same platoon split is significant, especially given the tendencies of teams to fill their bullpens according to quotas of left-handed and right-handed relievers.

Table 73.   The 10 Best Right-Handed Starters Vs. RHB/LHB, 2000–2004

Best Starters vs. RHB		Best Starters vs. LHB	
Player	True wOBA vs. RHB	Player	True wOBA vs. LHB
Pedro Martinez	.264	Pedro Martinez	.266
Jason Schmidt	.280	Curt Schilling	.303
Tim Hudson	.282	Kevin Brown	.303
Jon Lieber	.286	Jason Schmidt	.303
Kevin Brown	.287	Roger Clemens	.305
Curt Schilling	.289	Mike Mussina	.313
Freddy Garcia	.291	Roy Oswalt	.319
Greg Maddux	.291	Carlos Zambrano	.319
Brandon Webb	.294	Woody Williams	.320
Josh Beckett	.295	Tim Hudson	.322

Table 74.   The 10 Best Right-Handed Relievers Vs. RHB/LHB, 2000–2004

Best Relievers vs. RHB		Best Relievers vs. LHB	
Player	True wOBA vs. RHB	Player	True wOBA vs. LHB
Eric Gagne	.255	John Smoltz	.286
Octavio Dotel	.264	Eric Gagne	.287
Robb Nen	.267	Mariano Rivera	.291
Jason Isringhausen	.273	Robb Nen	.292
Keith Foulke	.275	Jason Isringhausen	.302
Byung-Hyun Kim	.275	Octavio Dotel	.302
John Smoltz	.276	Felix Rodriguez	.306
Francisco Rodriguez	.278	La Troy Hawkins	.306
Joe Nathan	.279	Keith Foulke	.307
Armando Benitez	.279	Scot Shields	.307

Table 75.   The 10 Best Left-Handed Starters Vs. RHB/LHB, 2000–2004

| Best Starters vs. RHB | | Best Starters vs. LHB | |
Player	True wOBA vs. RHB	Player	True wOBA vs. LHB
Randy Johnson	.283	Johan Santana	.278
Johan Santana	.296	Randy Johnson	.283
Barry Zito	.300	Al Leiter	.290
Jamie Moyer	.308	Dontrelle Willis	.297
Odalis Perez	.317	Ted Lilly	.299
Mark Mulder	.319	Odalis Perez	.300
Tom Glavine	.319	Randy Wolf	.302
Wilson Alvarez	.320	Chuck Finley	.302
Randy Wolf	.321	Mark Buehrle	.308
Oliver Perez	.321	Scott Schoeneweis	.308

Table 76.   The 10 Best Left-Handed Relievers Vs. RHB/LHB, 2000–2004

| Best Relievers vs. RHB | | Best Relievers vs. LHB | |
Player	True wOBA vs. RHB	Player	True wOBA vs. LHB
Billy Wagner	.289	Ray King	.269
Arthur Rhodes	.300	Damaso Marte	.273
Mike Remlinger	.301	Eddie Guardado	.276
Eddie Guardado	.306	Billy Wagner	.279
Damaso Marte	.307	B. J. Ryan	.279
Mike Stanton	.310	Ricardo Rincon	.280
Chris Hammond	.316	Steve Kline	.282
Ray King	.318	Arthur Rhodes	.284
Rheal Cormier	.321	Dan Plesac	.290
Brian Fuentes	.323	Kelly Wunsch	.292

The Book Says:

Pitchers' platoon splits can be reliably measured much more easily than those of right- or left-handed hitters. A right-handed pitcher's platoon split is reasonably accurate once he has around 700 plate appearances against left-handed hitters; for a lefty, the number is about 450. (As always, it's better to do the regression math than to use these rules of thumb.)

SWITCH HITTERS

There is a third class of batter that we've completely ignored until now—switch hitters. As would be expected, switch hitters have an average platoon split of near zero. Of our sample of 80 switch hitters with at least 200 plate appearances versus right-handed pitchers and 100 versus left-handers from 2000 through 2004, we find an average platoon split of .002 in OBP and .001 in wOBA, both in the sense that they hit a tiny amount better against righties.

We also find that while the player-to-player OBP and wOBA skill variations are comparable to those for right-handed and left-handed hitters (around .03), the variations in platoon skill are significantly higher. For example, while most right-handed hitters are within .013 of the average wOBA platoon split, the typical variation is .025 for switch hitters. This probably should not be a great surprise, as most switch hitters have a preference for one side or the other, unlike lefties and righties. The larger player-to-player variation in platoon skill means that the measured platoon splits are more meaningful for switch hitters than for other batters.

Running the same regressions to estimate player skills, we find that the following twenty switch hitters have the most extreme true platoon splits, or "platoon skill." (See Table 77.)

Table 77. The 10 Most Extreme Platoon Splits (SHB), 2000–2004

The Largest Platoon Splits (RHP-LHP)			The Largest Platoon Splits (LHP-RHP)		
Player	Measured wOBA Spit	wOBA Platoon Skill	Player	Measured wOBA Split	wOBA Platoon Skill
Jose Valentin	.104	.047	Bobby Kielty	.079	.032
Lance Berkman	.081	.043	Chipper Jones	.048	.024
Roberto Alomar	.062	.035	Coco Crisp	.067	.023
Carl Everett	.066	.034	Neifi Perez	.036	.021
Omar Vizquel	.048	.030	Milton Bradley	.043	.020
Orlando Hudson	.077	.029	Alex Cintron	.053	.020
Brian Roberts	.046	.025	Mark Bellhorn	.046	.019
Greg Norton	.088	.023	Chad Kreuter	.081	.017
D'Angelo Jimenez	.041	.022	Chris Magruder	.091	.016
Ramon Santiago	.071	.021	Luis Castillo	.026	.016

As with pitchers, we note that several of these players retained at least half of their measured wOBA split when we estimated their true platoon skill levels. Based on our estimate of how much to regress, a player with around 600 appearances against left-handed pitchers should regress about halfway toward the league average.

One thing that immediately jumps out is that few of these "extreme" platoon splits are really all that extreme. Only five switch hitters favor right-handed pitching more than an average lefty would, while six favor left-handed pitching more than an average righty would. Thus 69 of the 80 switch hitters are almost certainly doing themselves a favor by switch hitting, as they give themselves platoon splits that are less severe than what they would probably have if they didn't switch hit.

In fact, it seems reasonable to assume that players who switch hit probably do so because they really struggle against same-handed pitching; in other words, their platoon splits would be larger than average if they just hit from their favorite side. With this in mind, only Valentin,

Berkman, and Kielty stand out as switch hitters that might be better off sticking with their "natural" side. In fact, in recent years, Valentin has given up switch hitting entirely.

Finally, we show the ten best switch hitters against right-handed and left-handed pitching. (See Table 78.)

Table 78.   The 10 Best Switch Hitters Vs. RHP/LHP, 2000–2004

Best Batters vs. RHP		Best Batters vs. LHP	
Player	True wOBA vs. RHP	Player	True wOBA vs. LHP
Lance Berkman	.430	Chipper Jones	.424
Chipper Jones	.400	Jorge Posada	.398
Jorge Posada	.385	Bernie Williams	.388
Bernie Williams	.383	Lance Berkman	.387
Jose Vidro	.382	Mark Teixeira	.387
David Segui	.373	Jose Vidro	.385
Carl Everett	.373	Carlos Beltran	.378
Mark Teixeira	.371	Bobby Kielty	.373
Carlos Beltran	.370	Mark Bellhorn	.368
Dmitri Young	.369	Bill Mueller	.366

The Book Says:

Switch hitters have, on average, a zero platoon split, but quite a wide variety of individual platoon splits. The vast majority are probably helping themselves (or at the least, not hurting themselves) by switch hitting. A switch hitter's platoon split can be reliably measured after 600 appearances against left-handed pitching.

PINCH HITTERS

Pinch hitters are brought in for a specific situation in which platoon skills can be maximized, so one might expect that pinch hitters might have greater platoon splits than average. In other words, while a righty with a high platoon split may be a liability in the starting lineup (when facing a right-handed starter), he could be used primarily against lefties off the bench, making this a more ideal role. However, given that batters don't have a very large variety of platoon splits in the first place, it is little surprise that we find no evidence that pinch hitter platoon splits are different from overall platoon splits. From our data, we calculate platoon splits of .021 for right-handed pinch hitters and .013 for lefties, which are not statistically different from the overall platoon splits of .017 and .023.

Coupled with the fact that batters take a severe penalty of around .034 in wOBA when pinch hitting (which we showed in the chapter on clutch performance), this argues against the extensive use of pinch hitters, even when trying to leverage a platoon advantage. In fact, if you have a right-handed starter and left-handed pinch hitter of equal overall ability, the benefit one would achieve from pinch hitting (assuming the opposing pitcher is a righty) would be around .044 from the platoon advantage minus .034 from the pinch hitter penalty, for a net benefit of .010 in wOBA. Recalling the conversion from wOBA to run expectancy, pinch hitting in this situation gives your team less than a 1% chance of scoring one additional run. Put differently, one would have to make such a switch over a thousand times for it to make a one-win difference. (Of course, in high-leverage situations, this change has a greater chance of affecting the outcome.) It should go without saying that, if the two players hit from the same side, the pinch hitter would have to be substantially better.

Since pinch hitting is only useful when the pinch hitter is a better hitter than the starter, *even before the pinch hitter's platoon advantage is considered,* one should generally limit pinch hitting to cases in which the player being replaced is a very poor hitter. Pinch hitting for a pitcher is the most obvious such situation, but one can also imagine using a backup outfielder or first baseman to pinch hit for a weak-hitting catcher or shortstop.

The Book Says:

Because batters perform significantly worse when pinch hitting than when starting, bringing in a pinch hitter to face an opposite-handed pitcher is of minimal value unless the batter he is replacing is much worse.

PLATOONING STARTERS

While pinch hitting turns out to be less useful than expected, there is another situation in which a mixture of left- and right-handed players can be quite profitable: platooning. When platooning, a team gets the platoon advantage in every game, at least as long as the starting pitcher remains in the game. The only disadvantage is that you need to find two players who are willing to share playing time.

Supposing that two players in a platoon have identical overall skills, platooning would guarantee that you have the platoon advantage as long as the starter was in the game, rather than the MLB average of 46% for hitters. Since the starter will last for three trips through the batting order on average, whoever we have starting at the position in question will face starting pitching about 486 times (162×3) per season. With a platoon, we have the platoon advantage all 486 times; with just one starter we expect to have the platoon advantage in just 46% of those appearances, or a total of 224 times. Thus, platooning one position gives your team the platoon advantage an extra 262 plate appearances per season. Since the difference between having the platoon advantage or not is a wOBA increase of .044 (which translates into .038 extra runs per plate appearance), we calculate that platooning will cause the team to score about ten extra runs per season, or about one additional win. If this platoon were created on purpose, one could likely find players with unusually large platoon splits, resulting in an even greater advantage.

Note that the calculations above assume the two players are of comparable ability overall. If you have a lefty who is expected to hit .330 against lefties and .360 against righties, and a righty who is expected to hit .330 and .320, respectively, you gain absolutely nothing by platooning the two. And for the effort that went into setting up the platoon, you risk upsetting the lefty (who knows he is the better player) and tying up a roster spot. Thus, it makes little sense attempting to set up a platoon involving a player such as Eric Chavez (who is expected to hit .388 vs. RHP and .339 vs. LHP) who hits close to average against same-handed pitching (not to mention the fact that we are assuming that the platoon partners are of comparable defensive ability). Likewise, the weaker player of the platoon cannot be that bad; for example Tony Womack (.315 and .289) would be a poor platoon partner for even a sub-par righty who hits around .315 against righties and .330 or so against lefties.

The Book Says:

Platooning is an effective way of increasing a team's offensive output. A platoon featuring a lefty and righty with comparable skills (offensively and defensively) and average platoon splits will win about one extra game per season. If one or both platoon players have an unusually large platoon skill, you will gain more than a win per season.

The only disadvantage of platooning is that each platoon requires an additional roster player. Of course, since we've already determined that pinch hitting (except for pitchers) isn't all that important, setting up platoons seems to be an excellent use of the bench. As such, it would be extremely beneficial to ensure that your bench contains players who can platoon (in a starting role) with your weaker position players.

LOOGYS

Maximizing Bullpen Platoon Advantages

The overriding principle in building a bullpen is finding the right combination of relievers that will maximize your pitching performance (per dollar in salary). As we describe in the chapter on relievers, one such way of doing this is by using leverage—having a variety of relievers from excellent to poor, and *using the better pitchers when the game is on the line while reserving the poor ones for situations in which the outcome has effectively been decided.* We really can't emphasize this enough as a general, yet extremely powerful, bullpen strategy.

As you can see from this chapter, platoon splits also provide something that can be exploited to make a team more efficient. Recall that the typical wOBA difference between having the platoon advantage and not is .044, while the player-to-player variation in pitcher wOBA talent levels is only .025. *Thus even a bad left-handed pitcher will usually be as good against lefties as a good right-handed pitcher.* For example, with a left-handed hitter at the plate, you are equally well off with a righty with an overall ERA of 3.5 or a lefty with an overall ERA of 4.8 (assuming average platoon splits for both players). If your lefty has a higher platoon split, he can be even worse overall and still be equally effective against left-handed batters.

Not surprisingly, many teams have recognized this and employ left-handed relief specialists known as LOOGYs (left-handed one-out guys). The ideal LOOGY is a pitcher who is average against right-handed hitters, and very good against lefties. In other words, you want a reliever who is better than average overall, and has a larger-than-average platoon split. Mike Myers, Jesse Orosco, and Dan Plesac are some of the better relievers who fit this mold. This trio has an average regressed wOBA of .332 against righties and .301 against lefties. As expected, these pitchers faced left-handed hitters for a majority (65%) of their plate appearances, and those lefty opponents were 15 points of wOBA better than the average left-handed hitter. These pitchers were allowed to pitch against righties as well, although generally only sub-par ones (3 points of wOBA worse than average). Thus the term "LOOGY" isn't strictly correct for such pitchers; rather they are specialists brought in to face good left-handed batters and allowed to face mediocre right-handers.

A second, related set of pitchers is comprised of those who are effective *only* against left-handed hitters due to their very large platoon splits and/or the fact that they aren't very good overall. Aaron Fultz, Scott Sauerbeck, and Scott Eyre are such pitchers; they average a wOBA (again, regressed) of .299 against lefties and .346 against righties.

The biggest drawback to using LOOGYs is that the right-hander that was pulled cannot return to the game, but rather must be replaced by another (presumably less-skilled) right-hander. So if your one-out specialist faces one lefty and lowers that opponent's wOBA by the average (.044), it is quite likely that the subsequent right-handed hitters in the lineup will increase their wOBA by .01 to .02 because they are facing an inferior right-handed pitcher (and sometimes even the LOOGY himself). So the usefulness of this strategy depends on not only how good your LOOGY is in the first place (versus a LHB, as compared to the RHP he is replacing), but also on how good your next right-handed reliever is (and sometimes on how good the LOOGY is versus a RHB).

If the opposing lineup has consecutive left-handed hitters, obviously the advantage of bringing in a left-handed specialist is increased. However, in other situations one must be careful when allowing such a pitcher to stay in the game, such as to face a left-right-left (LRL) combination of hitters. While the specialist will have the platoon advantage against two of the three, you could just as easily bring him in to face only one lefty and then use a right-handed pitcher against the other two, thus also having the platoon advantage two out of three times. Thus, unless the lefty specialist is at least as good as whatever right-hander you would otherwise be using, using him against the LRL set is counterproductive. This is why it is preferable that a LOOGY be at least average against right-handed hitters. (From the other manager's point of view, this is why you should avoid having back-to-back lefties in your lineup. In fact, since exact lineup construction is never *that* important, it is rarely, if ever, correct to bat consecutive lefties in your batting order.)

If you are forced to use a pitcher who cannot pitch to righties, he should be reserved for the opponent's best left-handed hitters. This accomplishes two things. First, the wOBA impact of the platoon advantage is maximized, and second, the opposing manager is highly unlikely to pinch hit for one of his best hitters.

The Book Says:

The ideal left-handed relief specialist (LOOGY) is a pitcher who is significantly above average (wOBA of .300 or lower) against lefties and about average against righties. If a left-handed reliever is ineffective against right-handed hitters, he should only be allowed to face left-handed hitters, as much as possible.

An unorthodox solution to all of this is to have two pitchers in the game at the same time, one lefty and one righty. Depending on who is at the plate, one will be on the mound, and the other can be put in the outfield. The worst corner outfielders in the majors cost their teams around 30 runs per 162 games, which equals .185 runs per game or about .005 runs per plate appearance, assuming 39 plate appearances per game. Supposing that a pitcher moonlighting as an outfielder were twice as bad as the worst full-time outfielder in the majors, this would leave us at a penalty of around .010 runs per plate appearance.

Now let's look at the positive side of attempting this. Left- or right-handed hitters (i.e., non-switch hitters) account for 85% of all plate appearances. In the majority of these (62%), the pitcher has the platoon advantage, according to our 2000–2004 MLB data. Using this strategy, we can guarantee that the pitcher has the platoon advantage in 100% of those plate appearances. The difference (38% of these 85%) accounts for 32% of total plate appearances. Assuming that all pitchers and batters in question have average platoon splits, our two-pitcher strategy will lower the opposing hitter's wOBA by .044 in those 32% of plate appearances. That's not all. We're also forcing switch hitters to hit from their less-favorite sides, which will reduce the hitter's wOBA by an average of .012 in the 15% of plate appearances that switch hitters account for. The total effect is an average wOBA drop of .016, which saves the team an average of .014 runs per plate appearance. This is more than the presumed cost of sticking a pitcher in the outfield (.010 runs).

Several caveats should be mentioned. First, the calculations above assume an average (or close to average) set of batter handedness for the next few batters. The actual set of hitters coming up may be different. If the next three batters are LRL (or RLR), the difference between a lefty (or righty) and the proposed outfield rotation is only .013 runs per PA. If they are LSL (or RSR), the difference is even smaller—.003 runs per PA, in which case the non-pitching pitcher would have to be comparable (defensively) to a very bad everyday outfielder for this to be an effective solution. As well, we don't actually know how well a typical pitcher would perform defensively in the outfield, nor do we know how a pitcher would react to being thrown out of his regular rhythm by being sent to the outfield.

Of course, another solution to the lefty-righty relief puzzle is to acquire pitchers with minimal platoon splits. As noted earlier, these tend to be pitchers who are effective because of velocity change, a pitch that drops vertically, an over-the-top delivery in general, or a knuckleball. If you have several such pitchers on your roster, you can largely ignore pitcher platooning.

Teams tend to spend a good deal of time worrying about the need for left-handed relief specialists (indeed, we have devoted an entire section discussing this topic), but one should also be aware of the usefulness of right-handed relief specialists—pitchers who are above average (or even quite good) against right-handed hitters, but well below average against lefties. A good example would be Braden Looper, whose wOBA skill against right-handed hitters has been a solid .302, but who gets shelled to the tune of .360 when facing lefties. Pitchers like Looper can be even more useful than their left-handed counterparts, due to the greater likelihood of finding consecutive right-handed hitters in a lineup. And as many Met fans are aware, Looper should probably not be used as an exclusive closer (i.e., used regardless of the handedness of the batters coming to the plate). Even a poor overall lefty would be more effective than Looper versus a LHB.

The Book Also Says:

Keeping two pitchers in the game—one on the mound and one in the outfield—allows a team to always have the platoon advantage. Although our calculations have significant uncertainties regarding how well a pitcher can field or adjust to such a usage pattern, doing so appears to be beneficial.

Platoon Effects on Closers

For the most part, closers are exempt from considerations of pitcher handedness, as it is felt that they should always be left in the game (see the above discussion on Looper). However, as usual, we will put this assumption to the test. Specifically, of the 22 non-Rockies pitchers with at least 30 save opportunities in 2002 (we picked this year because it falls in the middle of our 2000–2004 data set), are they good enough to face both righties and lefties? For the purposes of this discussion, we define "good enough" to be an expected wOBA of .315 or better against left-handed hitting.

First, we note that two of the closers—Billy Wagner and Eddie Guardado—are actually lefties. Wagner is notable for having a platoon split of just .011, meaning that he is nearly as good against righties (.289) as he is against lefties (.279). Guardado is an average closer against righties (.306) and excellent against lefties (.276). So yes, both qualify as being sufficiently good against everyone that they should indeed remain in the game regardless of the handedness of their opponents.

We'll start with the elite lefty and righty closers—those who went to the mound with an expected wOBA of less than .300 against both lefties and righties. In addition to the lefty Wagner, we find Mariano Rivera, Robb Nen, Eric Gagne, and John Smoltz in this list. (A sixth player meeting these criteria, Arthur Rhodes, was never used as a regular closer.) Six more right-handed closers (Byung-Hyun Kim, Armando Benitez, Jason Isringhausen, Kaz Sasaki, Trevor Hoffman, and Troy Percival) fall in the "good closer" category—a closer with an expected wOBA of better than .300 against right-handed hitters and better than .315 against lefties.

So far we have accounted for 12 of our 22 regular closers. What of the others? Four (Kelvim Escobar, Jose Mesa, Juan Acevedo, and Roberto Hernandez) were sufficiently bad both ways that they should not have been closers. The final six (Danny Graves, Billy Koch, Mike DeJean, Jorge Julio, Mike Williams, and Ugueth Urbina) are the interesting cases—closers who are effective (regressed wOBA between .294 and .316) against right-handed hitters, but average or worse (.337 to .350) against left-handed hitters. Interestingly, none of the 22 closers had regressed wOBA against left-handers between .315 and .337, making it fairly straightforward to draw the line.

The problem with these six is that they are sufficiently good against righties that you don't really want to pull them since they cannot re-enter the game. On the other hand, if your best reliever can't pitch against lefties, you'd better hope that you never face Bonds, Helton, Delgado, etc., in a crucial situation. The simplest solution is to find a better closer who can pitch to lefties. There were an ample number of players meeting our "good closer" criteria who were not used as closers such that a team could have easily located one. If this were not possible, one would need to use a LOOGY when facing a dangerous left-handed hitter, even in what is normally a closer situation. Certainly with these closers, if the first or first two (or three) batters in the ninth inning were lefties, it would behoove the pitching team to bring in a lefty pitcher to start the inning and *then* the closer (when a RHB is due to bat). Likewise, if there are two outs and a lefty at the plate, it might also be advantageous to the pitching team to remove the right-handed closer and bring in a LOOGY. Whether or not a highly paid closer would "tolerate" this kind of reliever usage is beyond the scope of our analysis.

LEFT-HANDED STARTERS

The impact of left-handed starters is harder to quantify, as one isn't bringing in the starting pitcher to face a particular batter. Instead, the opposing team knows who will be starting and can set its lineup accordingly, making whatever platoon adjustments they deem necessary. So it certainly is possible that a team with too many lefty batters (and no good platoon options) would struggle against left-handed starters, but one will undoubtedly find another team that hits extremely well against lefties, so as to mitigate such an advantage over the course of 162 games.

Because the opposing lineup will be adjusted for the starting pitcher, the safest (and wisest) option for starting pitchers is to find starters with small platoon splits—righties that pitch well to left-handed hitters and vice versa—so that the opposing manager cannot significantly improve his offense by platooning.

The Book Says:

The simplest way to avoid platoon problems with your starting pitchers is to use pitchers with relatively small platoon splits.

SUMMARY

In this chapter, we have examined several aspects of the effects of handedness on performance. First and foremost, we note that the average platoon advantage is 44 points of wOBA, in the sense that an average batter (or pitcher) will be 44 points better when he has the advantage than when he doesn't, all other things being equal. Naturally, switch hitters average a roughly zero platoon spread.

This platoon advantage is not constant for all players, with pitchers and switch hitters showing the most variation. As a simple rule of thumb, regular left- and right-handed hitters, especially righties, can safely be assumed to have average platoon splits, as the player-to-player variations in platoon splits are very small. For example, if one wishes to estimate a right-handed hitter's true platoon split, one would regress his observed split by padding his actual performance with 2,200 league-average plate appearances against lefties. (Put differently, a right-hander with 2,200 plate appearances against left-handed pitching has a "true platoon skill" estimate that is based half on his measured platoon split, and half on the league-average split.) This number is "only" 1,000 for left-handed hitters.

For pitchers and switch hitters, the player-to-player variations are larger, and thus significant variations in performance can be measured based on just a few seasons' worth of statistics. It is thus possible to identify particular classes of pitchers who have smaller or larger platoon splits. Those with small platoon splits tend to be pitchers who succeed by changing speeds, throwing overhand curves or sinkers (i.e., pitches that break vertically down), or throwing knuckleballs. Pitchers that rely on sideways-breaking pitchers like a slider or slurve will generally show larger platoon splits.

The platoon advantage for pitchers is quite significant—enough to turn a bad pitcher into a good one—and thus has a significant effect on strategies. From the standpoint of managing batters, we suggest platooning as an under-used technique to increase a team's offensive productivity; a platoon consisting of equally-good hitters will win a game per season more than if one hitter started every game. On the other hand, pinch hitters tend to enter games sufficiently cold that bringing one in just to create a platoon advantage is generally not productive.

In the bullpen, left-handed relief specialists can be extremely valuable. Ideally, such a pitcher is well above average against lefties and average against righties; this permits him to be brought in to face the opponent's best left-handed hitter and remain in the game against lesser right-handers. Left-handed relief specialists who are only effective against lefties can also be valuable, but must only be allowed to face lefties. As an alternative to bringing in new relievers frequently, we suggest that teams might consider keeping two pitchers in the game at once—one pitching, and one in the outfield—and rotate according to the handedness of the hitter (or in the case of a switch hitter, his preferred side). This unorthodox strategy is especially effective when you have two pitchers who are particularly good versus same-side batters. Naturally, pitchers used predominantly in platooning roles (including right-handed relief specialists) should have large platoon splits.

For starting pitching, the safest route is to find starters with a small platoon split, as a starter with a large platoon split will be at the mercy of the make-up of the opposing batting order. The same is true of closers, as most managers prefer that the closer remain in the game regardless of the batter.

CHAPTER 7 – STARTING PITCHERS

CONTEMPT OF FAMILIARITY

Does familiarity breed contempt? As the game progresses, who has the advantage in the batter/pitcher confrontation: the batter or the pitcher? Conventional wisdom tells us that the second time (and later) through the order the batters have the advantage, as they have had time to see the pitcher's *stuff*. On the other hand, conventional wisdom also tells us that at least some pitchers need time to *get in the groove*. Let's see which, if either, of these theories is true.

Going back to the 1999–2002 data, we will look at all starting pitchers and starting batting lineups, and throw out any IBB or bunt, as well as any pitchers batting. This leaves us with 469,721 PA.

The first time through the order, the resulting wOBA was .345. What was our expectation? The pitchers in this situation had an overall wOBA of .349, the batters were .347, and the league-average for these pools of players is .344. This gives us an expectation of .353 (.349 + .347 − .344 = .352 plus a rounding error). With 163,900 PA, this 8-point advantage (an expected .353 compared to an actual wOBA of .345) for the pitcher is highly statistically significant. How about the second time through the order? The expectation is .353, and the actual performance is .354. The third time through the order shows an expectation of .354, but the actual performance was .362, or an 8-point advantage for the hitter. The progression each time through the order is eight points below expectation, followed by one point above, followed by eight points above (remember these numbers, −8, +1, +8, as we'll reference them later on in this chapter).

We're going to split up the data by each batting slot, to see if there's anything interesting or peculiar in the data. Our first step is to see if there are any advantages to hitting in any of the batting slots. (See Table 79.)

Table 79.   Batter/Pitcher Performance, By Batting Order

Batting Slot	Expected	Actual	Difference
1	0.340	0.340	0.000
2	0.342	0.340	-0.002
3	0.395	0.397	0.001
4	0.388	0.391	0.003
5	0.360	0.367	0.007
6	0.348	0.350	0.002
7	0.335	0.332	-0.003
8	0.323	0.319	-0.004
9	0.320	0.312	-0.008

Based on the hitters and pitchers involved in the leadoff slot, our expectation was a wOBA of .340, and the actual performance was a .340. So, we can say that there's no overall advantage or disadvantage to hitting leadoff. But, check out the #5 hitters. Hitters in those slots enjoy a 7-point advantage. And hitters in the bottom of the order perform worse in those slots, especially the last hitter in the lineup. Number nine hitters hit eight points below expectation. As we will see in our chapter on intentional walks, protection isn't the reason for this difference, so perhaps it relates to how much energy the pitcher had to exert facing the previous batters. In other words, the pitcher may be fatigued from facing very good #3 and #4 hitters and thus be more hittable by the #5 hitter; likewise after cruising through the #7 and #8 hitters, he can pitch well against the #9 hitter. At any rate, we need to revise our expectation for player performances by also including the batting slot the hitter finds himself in.

So, here's a chart that shows how each batting slot does each time through the order, by basing our expectations on the quality of the hitter and pitcher, as well as the batting slot effect we have just established. (See Table 80.) The numbers are the actual wOBA minus the expected wOBA. The first entry means that the leadoff hitter, the first time through the order, had an actual wOBA that was three points below expectation.

Table 80.   Batter/Pitcher Performance, By Batting Order And Time Through The Order, Relative To Expectations

	Time Through the Order		
Batting Slot	**First**	**Second**	**Third**
1	-3	-6	7
2	-13	-2	11
3	-10	6	9
4	-7	2	10
5	-14	3	11
6	-12	5	10
7	-7	5	3
8	-5	1	8
9	3	3	-8

For each batting slot #1 through #8, there is an almost steady progression in performance, each time they come up to bat. Hitters in the last batting slot actually performed worse. We're at a loss to explain this isolated case.

Now, is it that the batter is learning more than the pitcher, or is the pitcher simply getting tired as the game goes on, or some combination thereof? Another place where the numbers seem a little odd is for the leadoff and second hitter, the second time through the order. In these cases, their performances are more in-line with how hitters perform the first time up. The speculation here is that pitchers start to lose it after 10 or 11 batters. However, if pitchers really start to lose it at some point, we would expect a steady degradation in performance. And we don't see that. At most, we see pitchers hitting a wall after 10 or 11 batters. The more likely explanation is that the results for the leadoff hitter and second hitter, the second time up, are a blip, and that overall, batters are learning more than pitchers are learning.

What exactly is happening? Let's look at how our pitchers are performing each time through the order. Note that all component numbers are per 600 PA. (See Table 81.)

Table 81.   Batter/Pitcher Performance, By Time Through The Order

Time Through Order	PA	wOBA	1B	2B	3B	HR	NIBB	HBP	RBOE	SO	Other Outs
1	163,900	0.345	94	29	3	17	53	6	6	101	292
2	158,872	0.354	97	30	3	19	49	5	6	89	300
3	124,603	0.362	100	31	3	20	48	5	6	84	302
4	22,221	0.354	101	30	4	18	47	5	7	80	309

As you look at each *time through order* row, we can see modest gains in singles, doubles, and home runs, with a modest loss in walks. But the biggest change is in the strikeouts. What we have here is clear evidence that the pitchers have lost their effectiveness each time through the order. The drop in both walks and strikeouts shows that the batters are putting more balls in play. Not only are the balls in play more often, but when they are in play, the results are more positive.

The first time through the order, the batters put 73% of the balls in play. By the time they come up the fourth time against these same pitchers, that number jumps to 78%. And when the ball is not in play? The strikeout to walk ratio starts at 1.90 the first time through the order, and it works its way down to 1.70 the fourth time through.

The result is a breakdown in all facets of play. The batters make contact more often, the more they see the pitcher in a game. When they make contact, they produce more. When they don't make contact, they end up with fewer strikeouts as the game goes on. There is a definite shift in control of the strike zone.

> *The Book* Says:
>
> As the game goes on, the hitter has a progressively greater advantage over the starting pitcher.

PHYSICAL LIMITS

Let's talk about pitch count limits for a second. Each batter faces about an average of 3.75 pitches per plate appearance. So, for each time through the order, there are about 30 to 35 pitches thrown. Go through the order three times, and the pitcher has thrown about 100 pitches. That seems to be the magical level in the modern age of baseball: 27 batters, 100 pitches, three times through the order. What happens that fourth time through the order? Check out the previous chart. With over 20,000 PA, the wOBA is .354. That hardly looks like a pitcher who is tired. You might be thinking that only good pitchers throw in these cases. And you would be somewhat right. But, only good batters are left from the starting lineup as well. Let us present a different part of the previous chart. (See Table 82.)

Table 82.   Batter/Pitcher Performance And Expectation, By Time Through The Order

Time Through Order	Pitcher	Batter	Expected	Actual	PA
1	0.349	0.347	0.353	0.345	163,900
2	0.349	0.348	0.353	0.354	158,872
3	0.348	0.350	0.354	0.362	124,603
4	0.345	0.351	0.353	0.354	22,221

The fourth time through the order, the quality of pitcher is a bit better, as shown by his 1999–2002 wOBA of .345. But, the quality of batters remaining at that point in the game is also a bit better, with a .351 wOBA. The key column is the expected wOBA. Here we see that the expectation remains pretty static at .353. The actual result the fourth time through the order is an *improvement* (for the pitcher) from the third time through the order. Remember, the fourth time through the order typically means that the pitcher has thrown at least 100 pitches.

Pitch count levels may be useful for other purposes. For example, perhaps a string of high pitch count outings might have a long-term effect on a pitcher. But, on a game-by-game level? We don't think so.

The Book Says:

Don't bank on some magical pitch count level, such as 100 pitches, to tell you when a pitcher's tank level is low.

RECOVERY PERIOD

How many days does a starter need to recover? Two? Six? Three? Five? Four?

Let's take all pitchers with at least 800 PA from 1999–2002, of which at least 600 were as starters. This gives us 209 pitchers, with 16,054 starts.

Next, take each of their starts, and figure out (a) if they pitched the previous day and (b) how many batters they faced. Then, repeat this for two days prior. Then do the same thing for three days prior, four days, five, and six. These are our time slots.

If the pitcher faced at least one batter, but less than 18 batters, in any of these time slots, discard that start altogether. The reason is that we are trying to figure out how many days of rest a starter normally needs, in-between typical starts. If he didn't face at least 18 batters, it was either an aborted start, or he was a reliever in an earlier appearance.

For example, Pedro Astacio started a game on Sept 10, 2000. His previous game was a start on Sept 6, 2000. However, he only faced one batter in that game. We're excluding his Sept 10, 2000 start from consideration.

This brings us down to 14,990 starts. Still plenty to work with.

How did these pitchers do? There were 113 games where a pitcher started a game on three days rest. Their wOBA in those games was .369. Those same pitchers, when given four days rest, had a wOBA of .352. (Overall, these pitchers had a wOBA of .351.) With 2,593 PA on three days rest in our sample, this difference is 1.75 standard deviations from the mean. The worst pitcher on three days rest was Darryl Kile: .339 on four days rest, but .451 on three days rest. On the other hand, one of the best pitchers on three days rest was Greg Maddux: .221 on three days rest and .310 on four days rest. Who knows how much of these particular pitchers' results on three or four days' rest is *real* and how much is an artifact of random fluctuation? As is almost always the case, we can only make conclusions that we think are reliable based on large samples of player data.

There were 4,456 starts where a pitcher had exactly five days of rest. Their wOBA in these starts was .346. On four days of rest, the same pitchers had a wOBA of .350. While this difference seems small, with 110,937 PA, it is statistically significant, at 2.5 standard deviations from the mean.

It seems that the more the pitcher rests, the better his performance. The gain isn't much, but it seems to be there.

How about six days of rest? We have 645 games in those cases, with a wOBA of .355. Those pitchers on five days of rest had a wOBA of .346. With 15,593 PA, that is 2.1 standard deviations from the mean. It seems that too much rest is not a good thing! Interestingly, it is often said that five days rest is *too much* for a typical starter who is used to pitching on four days rest. The data seems to indicate that five days rest is fine, in fact, maybe a bit better than four, but that six days rest is indeed too much. There are some sampling issues that we have not considered, such as a pitcher's health. If a pitcher is nursing an injury, the manager might give him an extra day of rest, and we may now have a disproportionate number of somewhat-injured pitchers in the *six days of rest* category. Our cause/effect conclusions need to be taken with a grain of salt, until this issue can be resolved.

So, to maximize an individual's performance, it seems that five days of rest is the optimal point. This means pitching every six days instead of every five. The gain, on an individual basis, is 4 points of wOBA. But, if you are pitching less often, those starts need to be taken up by someone else. The team's sixth starter will have to start taking a more prominent role. This is how it's going to look. (See Table 83.)

Table 83.   Theoretical Performance, Based On Current And Optimal Rest Pattern

Starter	Current Starts	wOBA	Optimal Starts	wOBA
1	34	0.310	30	0.306
2	32	0.330	29	0.326
3	30	0.350	28	0.346
4	29	0.365	27	0.361
5	28	0.380	26	0.376
6	9	0.390	22	0.386

The first set of columns would be the typical arrangement in MLB. The #1 starter will have 34 starts, with a wOBA of .310. These numbers are not actual averages, but just a convenient illustration. The last two columns would be the optimal arrangement for each pitcher. This #1 starter would start four less games, but his wOBA will have improved by 4 points. So, across the board, we improve the performance level of all our pitchers by 4 points, since we have made each of them rest a little more. But, by decreasing the number of starts our starting five have made, we are increasing the role for our sixth starter.

The net effect? The overall team wOBA for the typical arrangement, in the above illustration, is .348. And in our optimized plan? .348. So, we have improved the performance of all our pitchers by resting them more, but at no overall gain for the team. Worse, we now have to use up our swingman, thus depleting our bullpen.

Going the other way, giving them three days of rest in hopes of not having that fifth and sixth starter to throw out there, at the cost of a worse performance for each pitcher, doesn't work either. Going through the same machinations as above, the net result is a team wOBA of .357. So much for the call to return to a four-man rotation!

The Book Says:

Pitchers perform best with five days of rest, and worst with three days of rest. To manage our entire starting rotation effectively, four days of rest seems to be the optimal point. The current MLB pattern of scheduling the starting rotation works.

GETTING TO THEM EARLY?

On a game played on Friday, September 1, 2000 at Pacific Bell Park, Kerry Wood for the Cubs and Mark Gardner for the Giants took the mound. Since Kerry Wood broke into the majors in 1999, he's been an excellent pitcher, though he had his worst year in 2000, at the age of 23. Mark Gardner was 38 years old; his year 2000 season looked just like any other year in his long journeyman career.

Here's how Gardner's night started (with play-by-play description courtesy of Retrosheet):

- CUBS 1ST: E. Young flied to center; Matthews flied to right; Sosa was called out on strikes; 0 R, 0 H, 0 E, 0 LOB.
- CUBS 2ND: Grace flied to left; Gutierrez grounded out (third to first); Reed popped to shortstop; 0 R, 0 H, 0 E, 0 LOB.
- CUBS 3RD: Gload flied to right; Huson flied to right; Wood grounded out (shortstop to first); 0 R, 0 H, 0 E, 0 LOB.

In the first three innings, Gardner retired all nine of the batters he faced. Kerry Wood on the other hand, well . . .

- GIANTS 1ST: Benard was hit by a pitch; Mueller singled [Benard to third]; Bonds singled to center [Benard scored, Mueller to second]; Kent walked [Mueller to third, Bonds to second]; Snow hit a sacrifice fly to right [Mueller scored, Bonds to third]; Burks singled to left [Bonds scored, Kent to second]; Aurilia homered [Kent scored, Burks scored]; Mirabelli lined to center; Gardner grounded out (second to first); 6 R, 4 H, 0 E, 0 LOB. Cubs 0, Giants 6.

That's as bad as it gets. What we have here are two pitchers whose days thus far were polar opposites. Gardner, the old journeyman, retiring the side in order, three times in a row. Wood, the up-and-coming star, in the midst of a mediocre year, having one of the worst performances of his major league career.

Now, a fan watching the game would be tempted to think that Gardner is *on*, and Wood is *off*. After all, it's obvious right? But, does this mean that the quality of their performance through the first nine batters is going to persist? Are these pitchers actually performing far from their normal talent level for whatever reasons (Wood has a hangover and Gardner had a nice relaxing evening), or, are they just simply having a good/bad streak of luck? If Gardner were really on, we'd expect him to at least be pretty good the rest of the way. If Wood were really off, we'd expect him to continue to struggle until the manager has had enough. Right?

As luck would have it (for us to analyze), each of their managers kept them in to face 18 more batters. Gardner pitched four more innings and gave up two runs (on four hits, three walks, two strikeouts). Nothing exciting there. That pretty much looks like a typical Mark Gardner night. What happened to the Gardner who retired nine straight batters and barely gave up a loud foul?

Wood also pitched four more innings and gave up one run (on three hits, including a solo HR, two walks, two strikeouts, and a hit batter). If anything, this performance was a hit better than Gardner's, though both pitchers performed a shade below average. But, what happened to Wood? Wasn't he off? How could he have survived facing 18 batters, giving up only a run? Is it possible that maybe, just maybe, we (or even a manager or pitching coach) can't tell if a guy is on or off based on such limited performance (9 batters)?

Of more interest to us, is this typical, or an exception? In other words, is Wood's turnaround really what happens to the typical pitcher who gets hit around to start a game? Is Gardner's change in performance typical of an average pitcher who starts a game with three perfect innings? Or, when a pitcher is hammered early, is it a sign that he is in for a rough night? Likewise, are pitchers who are perfect or near-perfect early in a game expected to be above average the rest of the way? Let's find out.

What we're going to do is look for every single starting pitcher who started a game retiring the first nine batters in a row. We found 548 such pitchers from 1999–2002. Their overall four-year wOBA was .341. Essentially, these 548 pitchers were slightly above average pitchers who started off with a great game. We'll call these pitchers the *Nifty Through Nine*. The total number of batters they faced *during* the first three innings was 4,932, of which 29% were struck out. Striking out 29% of the batters you face is something that Pedro and Randy Johnson do, not your average pitcher. On top of which, Pedro and RJ don't get the other 71% out as well. Pretty impressive, right?

What happened with the very next batter that the *Nifty Through Nine* faced? If these pitchers were really on, we'd expect them to be much better than .341. Maybe not a .000, but, perhaps something halfway between Pedro (.246) and an average pitcher? Perhaps a wOBA of .300 or so? On the other hand, if there was no such thing as *being on*, the performance should be based on the long-term talent level of our *Nifty Though Nine* pitchers and the particular hitters they are facing. In this case, the very next batter after retiring the first nine in order, is always a leadoff hitter. Considering the quality of the hitter, the pitcher, the batting slot effect, and the *second time through the order* effect, our expectation for the performance was a wOBA of .331. The average leadoff hitter actually ended up hitting .356 (wOBA) against these pitchers! If *being on* was something real, we'd certainly expect these hitters to hit below .331. These hitters actually hit *better* against pitchers who were (presumably, according to conventional wisdom) *on*. However, the next batter (#2 in the order, with an expected wOBA of .333) hit only .301. Hmmm. This result seems inconsistent with that of our leadoff hitter. As you can guess, with only 548 PA, we are at the mercy of our small sample size.

Rather than look at each batting slot, one at a time, let's total up the performance of the nine batters they faced the second time through the order. This will essentially increase our sample size by a factor of nine. In these 4,912 PA, our *Nifty Through Nine* faced hitters who performed with an actual wOBA of .329. Our expectation, if these were random confrontations, was .336. While the actual performance (.329) is 7 points below expectation, at 4,912 PA, it is only around 1 standard deviation from the mean. This difference between .329 and .336 is not significant, which means that we have so far found no evidence that pitchers who have been *on* continue to be *on*.

How about the third time through the order? At this point, we are down to 3,868 PA, and our expectation is .351. These batters, against the *Nifty Through Nine* pitchers, actually hit .345, which shows a similar level of significance as the second time through the order.

The Book Says:

You can't tell if a pitcher is *on* based solely on the results of the first nine batters he faces.

How about the flip side? Let's look for the most disastrous performances to start a game. We'll just make up a fun stat called *Hammer*. Give the pitcher one point for every double, triple, walk, hit batter, wild pitch, or passed ball. Give him two points for a home run, and half a point for a single. Take off one point for a strikeout. Add all that up. That's a pitcher's *Hammer points*. The higher the number, the more he's been *hammered*, of course. We'll select all pitchers with at least five *Hammer points*. This gives us 663 pitchers, which is in the same ballpark as the perfect pitchers. As perfect as those 548 pitchers were, these 663 pitchers were a complete disaster versus the first nine batters of the game.

Exactly how bad were our *hammered* pitchers? We have almost 6,000 PA of wretched performance, including 814 HR. Who has 814 HR in 6,000 PA? Not Aaron, Ruth, Bonds, nor Mays. No one. Couple that with 1,009 aalks to 213 strikeouts. So, not only did our hitters hit with the power of Ruth and Bonds, but they also controlled the strike zone like Wade Boggs. Overall, we get a wOBA of .701. Wow! Barry Bonds, from 1999–2002, was *merely* around .500. These 663 pitchers started off a game as bad as you can possibly imagine. They pitched as if every batter they faced were Bonds, Ruth, and Boggs, all rolled into one—and then some.

Were these pitchers *off* (for the day)? Should we expect them to continue their path of total and complete destruction? Or, was it just bad luck, and we expect them to revert to their norm in just a flash? It should be noted that these pitchers are, overall, below average pitchers, as you might expect. You just won't find great pitchers getting *hammered* that often. The wOBA of our *hammered* pitchers from 99–02 was .355, and the composite wOBA of their opponents was .343. Our expectation when they face each other the second time in the game, assuming that everyone is playing at their normal, long-term talent level, is a wOBA of .356. So, how did our *off* pitchers do the second time through the order? They were allowed to face 5,015 batters, and the wOBA of those confrontations was a whopping .375! That is 2.7 standard deviations away from the mean. The third time through the order produced a .385 performance, on 2,851 PA, which is 1.7 standard deviations from our expectation of .368 (including the effect for the third time through the order). If we look at all batters they faced after being *hammered* the first time through the order, our expectation was a wOBA of .360. Instead, in the 8,259 times they faced each other, the result was a wOBA of .378. This is 3.2 standard deviations from the mean, and is highly significant.

The Book Says:

You can indeed tell if a pitcher is *off* based solely on the results of the first nine batters he faces. Such pitchers will perform somewhat worse than their true talent levels the rest of the way.

Why is this the case? Why did we find less evidence with our *on* pitchers? Why do we find something much more easily with our *off* pitchers? One possibility is that a pitcher may be performing poorly because of some small injury. It's not bad enough to keep him from starting, but it may be bad enough that it'll affect his performance that night. Or, a pitcher can only improve so much. An MLB pitcher is already practically at the top of his game. There's only so much higher he can reach. But, the bottom of the well is indeed very deep. Or, maybe, there's something else. Could it be that perhaps a pitcher's experience can help him out? Maybe an extablished pitcher knows how to shake things off, and understands that it was luck, while an inexperienced pitcher lets it get to him?

We'll break up the pitchers into two groups: those who faced at least 800 batters from 1999–2002, and those who didn't. The second group can essentially be considered the inexperienced or washed-up pitchers. How'd they do? The established pitchers had a total of 6,888 PA, wich an expectation of .360, but an actual performance of .369. This is 1.5 standard deviations from the mean, which is moderately significant. Thee were also 1,371 PA that were given to pitchers who faced less than 800 batters from 99–02. Our expectation for these pitchers was also .360. However, the actual result of their face-to-face confrontations, after getting *hammered* the first time through the order? .427! That is 4.8 standard deviations from the mean!

The Book Says:

If a pitcher is getting *hammered* early, there is a huge carryover effect for an inexperienced pitcher. For an experienced pitcher, there may be some evidence of a carryover effect.

GET 'EM OUT OF THERE, OR GOING THROUGH A PHASE?

Imagine a situation where a pitcher has gone through the order twice over four or five innings. He's faced eighteen batters, and maybe he's given up two or three runs. He's done fairly well, but nothing sensational. He typically faces 25 to 27 batters per start, so he seems to have at least an inning, maybe two, to go.

He now faces the top of the order for the third time. The leadoff hitter gets on base. As does the #2 hitter. The #3 hitter. The cleanup hitter. The #5 hitter. All of them. Five batters, and all reached base. He's given up three runs in this inning without getting an out, and he still has two runners on base. His total number of batters faced, 23, is getting close to his usual limit. He's gotten *hammered* during the entire inning so far.

So, the manager asks the question: does he have anything left in the tank? Can he get through this inning? Is it just a phase, a string of bad luck, that just so happens to coincide with him almost reaching his limit? Or, maybe he's not that strong today, and he simply has gone beyond his limit? What does allowing five straight batters to reach base near the end of a pitcher's tank limit really mean?

Unfortunately (for us), the above situation only happened 83 times in four years. Whatever results we get won't be meaningful. Even worse, of those 83 times, managers decided to roll the dice only 43 times to let the pitcher face that sixth batter. That's a tiny sample. But, since we're here, let's go through it. Earlier, we showed that the sixth batter has a .359 wOBA the third time through the order. If this string of poor performance were indicative of a pitcher's tank being depleted, we should see a wOBA for this sixth batter higher than .359. If on the other hand, this string was just a phase the pitcher was going through, his wOBA should come in around .359. So, what happened? .451! Wow!

How about we look at all batters that these pitchers faced after that string of five straight batters reaching base? Now we have 148 batters faced. The wOBA in these cases? .331. Sigh.

What if we lower our threshold so that only the first *four* batters reached base? In this case, we have 271 pitchers who were in this situation. That certainly seems more promising for us. We have 662 batters that followed this slightly less worrisome situation. The wOBA was .372. It's a bit higher than expected, but given the small sample size, nothing alarming.

It doesn't look like we're getting anywhere. How about when the third, fourth, and fifth place hitters get on base? Those would be the 21st, 22nd, and 23rd batters that the pitcher faced. Let's see what kind of sample size we get. We find that 737 pitchers were in this situation. Actually, we're not sure that a manager would consider this a situation where the pitcher might not have anything left in the tank, since it wouldn't be that unusual for the team's three best hitters to get on base.

But, let's continue and see what happens. These pitchers ended up facing 2,163 more batters, with a wOBA of .339. Nothing. We can't find anything.

We'll try one last time. This situation resembles the *hammered* pitchers we mentioned earlier in this chapter, so we'll resurrect our *Hammer points*. We'll again go back to the first five guys in the order. Any pitcher with at least 2.5 *Hammer points* is selected. This gives us 2,457 pitchers. The risk here is that we lowered the threshold so much that we're capturing pitchers who would not be considered to be *low in the tank*. That's often the price to pay for increasing the sample size. Now we have 8,509 batters. The wOBA is .340. We're sorry, but we just can't find anything. There is no doubt that pitchers' tanks get depleted, and we're reasonably sure that the pitchers or their coaches can figure it out. We just can't figure it out based on the performance against a few batters.

The Book Says:

We can't rely on the poor results of late-game performance to establish the fatigue level of a starter. Observation of a pitcher's mechanics would be the preferred method.

STILL GOING, AND GOING, AND GOING?

How about leaving in a pitcher who's riding high? Let's look for all pitchers who went through the order a third time, and during that third time through the lineup, he got all nine batters out. This is similar to our earlier study of *Nifty Through Nine* pitchers. In this case, by the time those nine batters were put out, the pitcher will have already faced 27 batters. Typically, after 27 batters, a pitcher will call it a night. But, he's riding high, and is showing (apparently) no signs of slowing down. What's a manager to do?

Well, this has only happened 28 times. So, again, sample size *yada yada yada*. These pitchers faced a total of 62 batters after their great showing. They had a wOBA of .267! That's a superb result, but unfortunately because of the aforementioned sample size issue, meaningless. Before you think that it's only the Randy Johnson's and Pedro Martinez' who are part of this sample, the 1999–2002 overall wOBA of these pitchers was .348. Clearly the pool of pitchers who were riding high and allowed to continue pitching despite a likely high pitch count are, as a group, fairly average pitchers.

Lowering the threshold once again, let's look at all pitchers with at most negative two *Hammer points* while facing the batting order for the third time. (Remember, you get a minus one *Hammer point* for every strikeout.) In this sample, we've got 789 pitchers. After that point, they faced 2,086 batters, with a wOBA of .321. Now, it starts to get interesting. Based on the talent levels of the pitchers and batters involved, and the batter advantage later in the game, our expectation is a wOBA of .350, and our actual result is 29 points better than that! At 2,086 PA, one standard deviation is 11 points. So, at 2.6 standard deviations from the mean, we are getting significant results.

The Book Says:

If a pitcher is still getting outs late in the game, keep him in there; he may have a bit more left in the tank.

TO START OR TO RELIEVE

The average starter is better than the average reliever, pound for pound (given the same number of innings per appearance), right? Do we really need any numbers to tell us this? It should be obvious. We have five or six starters that throw 67% of the time, and we have five or six relievers that throw 33%. Certainly, a couple of those relievers throw when it counts the most, and a couple when it counts the least. But, effectively, our starting corps has more of an impact on winning than our relief corps. It stands to reason then that you put your better pitchers, on average, in the starting rotation.

We can go through each team, and we'd find this to be true. While you might have one team with an Eric Gagne or Trevor Hoffman, and so the #1 reliever is better than the #1 starter, it is more likely that the #1 reliever falls in somewhere among the top two starters. So, we think it's fair to say that baseball operates on the idea that if you have your three best pitchers, you'll probably have two of them as starters, and one of them as a reliever (sometimes it's all three as starters, and occasionally, it's two of them as relievers, and one as a starter). The same holds true for the #2 reliever, the set-up guy. He's usually not going to be as good as your #2 starter. Rather, he'd probably fall in-line somewhere alongside the #3 and #4 starters. Your #3 and #4 relievers would be worse than your #4 starters. Of your top six pitchers, four would be starters, and two would be relievers. So, on average, your top four starters are better than your top four relievers.

How much better? Just taking a guess, we'd say that the average starter should have a wOBA of .343 (five points better than the overall league-average of .348) and the average reliever should be at .358 (ten points worse). These numbers quantify what we know to be true in the preceding paragraph, right? But, what really happens in baseball? How good is our intuition? From 1999–2002, starters had a wOBA of .353 (five points *worse*), and relievers were .338 (ten points *better*).

Oh boy.

Looking at all pitchers with at least 800 PA in relief, there are twenty-four relievers with a wOBA of under .300. Rivera, Dotel, Foulke, Wagner, Nen, Hoffman, Benitez, Isringhausen, Urbina, Nelson, Remlinger, and Shuey, among others. There were only five starters in the same boat: Pedro, Derek Lowe, RJ, Zito, and Kevin Brown. That's it. After them, but above .300 (and worse than those twenty-four relievers), are Schilling, Hudson, Mussina, Oswalt, and Maddux. Are we looking at this wrong, or did we just discover that all of these relievers ought to be in the starting rotation?

Let's go back to our league totals of .353 for starters and .338 for relievers. What could cause such out-of-whack numbers? As we saw earlier, the second and third time through the order, hitters have an advantage over starters. Let's look at the wOBA of our pitchers again, but this time, let's limit it to the (at most) first nine batters they face. The relievers come in at .337 (we hardly expected much of a change), but the starters now come in at .345. This is an enormous change. Our 15-point difference is now only an 8-point difference.

What else? Our relievers face a lot more pinch hitters and bench players than do our starters (remember, we are not including any pitchers as hitters for anyone). If we discard all such PA, our relievers' wOBA goes up to .341, while our starters remain at .345. We are now down to a 4-point difference. Still, this doesn't seem to solve our problem. Even taking an average, rested starter and accounting for the quality of the batter he faces, he is worse than an average reliever.

We propose that there is a difference between how starters and relievers approach the game. It's likely that our starters are pacing themselves, even the first time through the lineup, in order to be able to last twenty-five to thirty batters. Relievers, on the other hand, have the advantage of *going all out* for an inning or so. Perhaps we can find pitchers who were used in both roles to see if the same pitcher performed differently.

Among the 314 pitchers with at least 800 PA, there were 200 who faced at least one batter both as a starter and in relief. Derek Lowe was .260 as a starter, and .309 as a reliever. He faced 896 batters as a starter, and 1,133 as a reliever. We'll take the lower PA of those two. That'll be how much we weight Lowe's performances. Dotel was .374 as a starter, and .257 as a reliever. We're going to weight Dotel at 779, since that's the lesser of his two sets of PA. Hideo Nomo had 3 PA as a reliever, and 3,174 as a starter. His weight will be an insignificant 3. We'll go through each of these 200 pitchers, and total up their weighted wOBA as a starter and reliever. The important thing to remember here is that we have the exact same pitchers with the exact same weights in both samples, so that we can answer the question, "How does a pitcher pitch in relief versus how does he pitch as a starter?"

The total of the weights is 37,837 PA. Even though we are always using the minimum of the *PA pairs*, that's a substantial total. The wOBA of these pitchers as starters is .364. These exact same pitchers had a wOBA of .337 as relievers. Finally! Something that makes sense. A starter sees a 27-point improvement in wOBA when thrust into relief. That is an enormous difference.

Let's go back once more to the league totals. We saw that the average starter had a wOBA of .353, and the average reliever had a wOBA of .338. If we took these relievers, and made them start, their wOBA would worsen by 27 points. That .338 becomes .365.

So, to put these pitchers on the same scale, our starters, as starters, have a wOBA of .353. Our relievers, but also as starters, would probably have a wOBA of .365. As a result, we can see that an average starter really is better than an average reliever. The difference is twelve points in wOBA. And this is very close to the fifteen points we guessed when we started this whole mess. (Sometimes conventional wisdom is correct, and the analysis can be wrong if it is incomplete.)

A 27-point change in wOBA is equivalent to about a 0.80 change in ERA. Next time you see a reliever with a 2.50 ERA, mentally adjust that to 3.30 to put him on a starters' scale. (At the same time, don't forget that starting pitchers that are in NL parks also get the benefit of facing the pitcher as a batter.)

> *The Book* Says:
>
> Starters have a lot going against them, as compared to relievers. They pitch a lot longer, forcing them to pace themselves. They face the same batters multiple times in a game, giving the batters an advantage. Relievers can come in and put all their efforts into a very short stint.

Dual Roles

As we've seen, we have many pitchers who see time as both starters and relievers. In some cases, as with Nomo, these are one-time types of situations, and in others, the manager is trying to find the right situation. Here is how each type of pitcher performs by role. (See Table 84.)

Table 84.   Performance Of Pitchers, As Starter And Reliever, By Role Class

Role Percent	Role Class	N	PA	wOBA Start	wOBA Relief
98%	Starter, Emergency Reliever	72	2703	0.354	0.366
89%	Starter, Spot Reliever	64	12035	0.360	0.352
66%	Swingman	22	11080	0.366	0.326
36%	Reliever, Spot Starter	25	11216	0.369	0.324
4%	Reliever, Emergency Starter	17	803	0.375	0.323

To read the chart: the first column shows the percentage of batters faced as a starter compared to the total number of batters faced as a starter plus reliever. So, the first line says that the starter with some emergency relief appearances faced an average of 98% of their batters as a starter. We have 72 such pitchers, and the total number of paired PA is 2,703. Remember, we always take the minimum of the PA as starters and as relievers. We qualified any pitcher with 95% to 99% of his PA as a starter as *Starter, Emergency Reliever.*

For these pitchers, their wOBA as starters was .354, and as relievers it was .366! This is in stark contrast to what we found for the group overall. What happened? It's most likely that these pitchers, who are full-time starters, simply do not take on the true role of the reliever. They don't pitch as if they can gas it all out. They pretty much throw as if they are still starters, even though they are technically in the relief role. And, because these were emergency situations, they might not even have been fully prepared to pitch. As well, they might just be *out of their element* when relieving, and thus don't get the normal reliever advantage.

The next line contains guys with 75% to 95% of their PA as starters, the *Starter, Spot Reliever.* These guys expect to come into the odd game as a reliever. As a result, they might be better prepared, and maybe they even throw a bit harder. The result is that these pitchers are .360 as starters and .352 as relievers.

Our next group is the *Swingmen*, guys with 50% to 75% of their PA as starters. These are guys with no real defined role, or roles that are constantly being re-evaluated. Their wOBA as starters is a very high .366, but a very good .326 as relievers. That is a huge swing: 40 points! Now, what else can be happening here? Selective sampling. The reason that they are swingmen is that their managers do not like their performance in one role, and are trying to find a role for them. In this case, it seems apparent that it's their performance as starters that is lacking. The likelihood is that these pitchers are much better than their numbers as starters are showing, but that the manager doesn't feel like waiting for the eventual turnaround. Instead, he's putting them in as relievers, until they show some better performance.

The *Reliever, Spot Starter* is showing an even bigger contrast. These are guys with 15% to 50% of their PA as starters. In addition to possibly having selective sampling issues, it's possible that these relievers are simply not prepared to pitch like starters. This may be even more apparent with the last group, guys who are *Reliever, Emergency Starter.* Their wOBA as relievers is .323. So, we know they are decent pitchers. But, as starters, albeit with only seventeen pitchers and 803 batters faced, their wOBA is an incredibly high .375: a 51-point difference! These guys may have simply not been prepared to pitch as starters, or they find it hard to change the way they pitch. Or perhaps their managers didn't like what they saw after one game, and didn't let them pitch as an emergency starter again.

We wanted to show the previous chart so that you can see that you always need to be careful when looking at data. Selective sampling is an issue throughout that chart, and you can't necessarily make the inference you want based on the data you see. When you look at the overall situations, a large portion of these problems is diminished.

Even this may not answer all of our questions. When we looked at the years 1999–2002 as a group, it forced us to place pitchers like Derek Lowe (once a pure reliever, and then a pure starter) into a swingman category. That's not a terribly accurate representation. Let's look for true swingmen, or as best we can define them. First, we'll start with our list of pitchers with at least 800 PA from 1999–2002, and take away the unrepresentative Tim Wakefield. Then, we'll select only those pitcher-years where the pitcher had between five and twenty-five starts and between ten and fifty relief appearances in a given year. Then, we'll look for those pitchers who had at least two such seasons. This gives us a list of twenty-one pitchers for a total of forty-four seasons (with Halama and Villone appearing three times, while the other nineteen pitchers have two seasons). These become our true swingmen.

Next, we'll take those forty-four pitcher-years, and see how they did as a starter and reliever in those years. As a group, our true twenty-one swingmen had a wOBA of .333 as relievers and .366 as starters. This is a difference of 33 points. With 7,000 PA as a reliever and 14,000 as a starter, this is about 3 standard deviations from the mean. Our original finding of a 27-point difference, with all the selective sampling issues that came with it, is consistent with a 33-point difference here, with the selecting sampling issue reduced (but at a cost of a smaller sample size).

The Book Says:

Selective sampling has a profound effect on interpreting the performance numbers of pitchers as starters and relievers. Be careful with any interpretation.

CHAPTER 8 – LEVERAGING RELIEVERS

The usage patterns of relief aces, along with the perceived importance of the bullpen, are continually being re-evaluated and challenged. How early to bring them in (seventh, eighth, or ninth)? Should the team be leading, tied, or slightly behind? How long should they keep pitching? These are all questions that confront and confound the manager. And, given that it's only been since the 1990s that there have been commonly accepted responses to these questions, there is probably still some doubt as to what the best answers are. For example, managers generally adopt much more aggressive strategies during the playoffs. Of course, with the season on the line, and with relievers having over three months to recover from any overuse, a manager *should* approach the playoffs in a different manner.

The Three-Run Save

The primary motivation for modern bullpen strategy (or at least, how a team's best reliever is used) is the save rule. The record books don't make distinctions between the one-run save and the three-run save, but it's rather clear that it's much easier to save a three-run game than a one-run game. Nor do contracts make this distinction. If a reliever had a saves clause, he'd love to get in those three-run games, if only to make padding his saves that much easier. As well, relievers themselves may prefer a defined role that is based on the inning, rather than the leverage of the situation. They can appreciate the fact that there may be a situation in the seventh or eighth inning that can be a turning point for the game, but their conditioning prepares them only for the ninth inning (or perhaps two outs in the eighth inning).

There is also a psychological reason for managing according to the save rule. Blowing a three-run lead in the ninth inning, while deliberately keeping your ace reliever on the bench, would be a disastrous outcome. Media, fans, even a manager's own players and upper management, will question and criticize such a move. *Win today* seems to be the motivation for the manager. We are not qualified to speak to the psychological impact. Neither, however, are most people. While we should not dismiss such claims, neither should we quickly embrace them without actually studying such claims. Most people are probably risk-averse, preferring a three-month treasury bill to a twelve-month government bond, even if you show them that in most three-month periods, the twelve-month government bond will yield higher returns. The potential for a negative return is enough for people to continue to pour money into such safe investment vehicles as the short-term treasury bills. At the same time, no one will question the manager if he lets his ace sit on the bench at a very critical moment in the game, if that moment occurs in the seventh inning. After all, an even more critical moment may come in the ninth inning. And, what happens in those times when it doesn't come? Perhaps the true motivation of the manager is *win today, but don't try to win too early in the game.*

How easy are three-run leads, and should you use your best reliever in those situations? Do you want to bring him in, and risk not having him available for the next game; or do you bring in your second- or third-best reliever, reduce your chances of winning this game, and potentially increase your chances of winning tomorrow? Here we are, in the information age, and the managers still operate almost exclusively on instincts. Instincts are valuable if you don't have all the data and time you need to make a decision. Your experience and wisdom will control your decisions when your instincts need to be kicked in. But, the three-run lead? You have plenty of time to formulate your thinking. And, there's plenty of data to assist. Let's take a look at some.

THE NINTH INNING THREE-RUN LEAD

We'll look at all games from 1999–2002 in which a reliever was brought in in the ninth inning, with a three-run lead, bases empty and no outs. This happened 1,034 times. And, how often did a team lose such a game? 31 times. 3%. A team leading in the ninth with a three-run lead will win 97% of the time.

Quick, say something. Yes, that's right. They will win 97% of the time, *if* they use relievers as they have been used from 1999–2002. And, that means bringing in your best relievers, most of the time, to hold onto such a lead. So, it's fair to say that if you split up the 1,034 games between the ace relievers and the rest, then that 97% won't hold for both groups. Right? Let's see.

The first thing we have to do is identify the ace relievers. It should be easy enough: Percival, Hoffman, Wagner, Rivera . . . But, let's try to do so in a more systematic fashion. We'll introduce a toy here. It's not something that we can prove mathematically, or that we can use as a tool to identify important aspects of the game. It's just something that tries to quantify something qualitative, while allowing for a reasonable margin for error.

Trustworthy

Which relievers have been assigned a high level of trust from their managers? Troy Percival has faced 684 batters (after exclusions of bunts and intentional walks) in the ninth inning with the game tied, or ahead by one, two, or three runs, or in the eighth inning with the game tied, or ahead by up to two runs. He's also done a little mop-up duty, by facing fifteen batters with his team behind by at least five runs. In all, he's faced 896 batters. We can quantify his usage pattern by saying that 76.3% of the batters he's faced were when the manager needed to trust him the most, and 1.7% of the batters were when the manager required almost no level of trust. That difference, 74.7%, is his trust level. Here are the top nine relievers from 1999–2002. (See Table 85.)

Table 85. Most Trustworthy Relievers

Player	Trust Level
Troy Percival	75%
John Wetteland	69%
Kazuhiro Sasaki	69%
Trevor Hoffman	68%
Robb Nen	67%
John Smoltz	67%
Mariano Rivera	66%
Jeff Shaw	61%
Billy Wagner	58%

It's a nice little toy, and gives us pretty much the names we expected. It gives you an instant sense of how a manager thought of his reliever. You could compile this historically to get a profile on the manager or reliever. You could change the definition to say "tying run on base, or at the plate," or any combination you want to reflect whatever your idea of trust is. But, we've given a very simple definition, which, for our purposes, yields results fairly consistent with our expectations. You can't ask for more from a toy.

The league-average, for 1999–2002, is 0%. If you see someone below 0%, this means he was used more often during mop-up innings than during late and close innings.

Anyway, back to the matter at hand. The above nine relievers are fairly representative of the idea of the ace reliever. They come in when it counts far more than when it doesn't. How did they do?

They came into the ninth inning with the bases empty and needing to get three outs to close the game 271 times. Their team lost 8 of those games: 8 divided by 271 is . . . 3%.

Wait a minute. We just told you that the 1,034 times tht any pitcher was brought into this situation, their team ended up losing the game 3%

of the time. But, when you have the above studs pitching, their teams also lose 3% of the time? Rivera? Yup, lost once out of 32 times: 3%. Wetteland, Sasaki, Wagner? Yup, yup, yup. Each lost once in 21, 36, and 34 tries, respectively. Hoffman and Nen? 2 for 41 and 2 for 46, respectively, which is worse than 3%. Percival was perfect in 29 tries, and Smoltz in 15 tries. Put all these studs together, and you get 3%. Just like all other pitchers.

Why nine relievers? Why not more? If we extend it to the top 31 relievers, it's 19 for 769, or 2.5%. The rest of the relievers (the set-up guys and any other reliever who found himself in the ninth inning three-run lead, bases empty, no outs situation), were 12 for 265, or 4.5%. If we use this as the definition to separate our ace relievers from other relievers, then we see that the stud closer has a .02 win advantage over the non-closer.

Table 86.   Least Trustworthy Relievers

Trust-unworthy
Alan Levine
Rich Croushore
Troy Brohawn
Scott Service
Jerry Spradlin
Matt Anderson
Kerry Ligtenberg
Guillermo Mota
Francisco Cordero
Doug Henry
David Lee
Mike Matthews
Lou Pote
Bryan Ward
John Parrish

Just for fun, what if we look at all those relievers below the 0% trust level? Those are relievers who came in more often for mop-up duty than closing duty. Surely those guys must have really hurt their team? Here are all fifteen of them. (See Table 86.)

Their trust level as a group is minus 22%. These are the fifteen guys whom the managers trusted the least, but still allowed them to come in at least once in the ninth inning with that three-run lead. As a group, they only came in twenty-five times. And, how many times do you think the manager regretted that decision? How many times would you guess? Ten times out of twenty-five, they would blow the game? Five? Four? How about *once*? That's right. Jerry Spradlin came in, and his team lost. The other twenty-four times, their teams won. One divided by twenty-five. That's 4%.

As you can see, we are talking about such a small difference here. Why is that? Why don't great relievers have much more impact than just .02 wins? Because they have a three-run lead with only three outs to go! That is such a large lead in that time frame that even a bad reliever will almost always escape with his team winning the game. As we saw, it's a difference of 97.5% for the ace reliever, and 95.5% for everyone else. Our perception, or our instincts, may make us believe that the difference was much higher. But, the actual data show how our minds can play tricks on us.

Distribution of Runs

Should we have expected this? Using our Markov model that we introduced in the *Toolshed* chapter, the average pitcher will throw a shutout inning 70% of the time. But, we've got here a three-run lead. They don't even have to throw a shutout inning, but just allow at most two runs. That happens 93.6% of the time. (Right away, we can see that a pitcher can get out of this jam, without needing any help from his hitters, almost all the time.) Or, if the pitcher allows three or more runs, just make sure his team scores enough runs to still win the game. Let's work the numbers for this last part.

If a pitcher is on the road, and he gives up four or more runs, the game is over. How often will that happen? 3.0%. If he gives up exactly three runs, which happens 3.4% of the time, the game goes to extra innings, and both teams have about a 50-50 chance at winning. So, that's 1.7% wins and 1.7% losses. Add up the losses (3.0% and 1.7%) and our pitcher on the road loses 4.7% of these three-run lead games.

When a pitcher is at home, he has the benefit of his hitters being able to bail him out, if he blows the lead. If we determine the chance of him allowing at least four more runs than his team scores, that will tell us how often the team will lose in the ninth inning. That number is 2.3%. If the pitcher allows exactly three more runs than his team scores, we're now into extra innings. This should happen a bit more than 2.7% of the time. And with the 50-50 chance at winning in extra innings, that becomes 1.4% losses. The total number of losses is 3.7% (2.3% + 1.4%).

So, assuming a team plays half its games at home and half on the road, this works out to 4.2% losses (4.7% on the road and 3.7% at home). This is in-line with what our 1999–2002 data said would happen.

But, how about the great pitcher? Those guys throw a scoreless inning 79% of the time, and not 70%. But, with a three-run lead, you don't get extra points for that. What we care about is how often their team will win the game. Going through the exact same exercise as in the preceding paragraphs, our ace road pitcher will give up four or more runs 1.3% of the time, and send the game into extra innings 2.0% of the time. With the 50-50 rule for extra innings, our total losses for our road ace is 2.3% (1.3% + 1.0%). At home, giving up at least four more runs than his team scores will happen 1.0% of the time. The game goes into extra innings 1.6% of the time. Our home losses are 1.8% (1.0% + 0.8%).

Total losses? 2.1% of the time (2.3% on the road and 1.8% at home). Our 1999–2002 data said 2.5%. Bingo.

Summary

Where are we now? We looked at actual data for three-run leads in the ninth inning, and we saw an advantage of .02 wins per game for the great reliever over the average reliever. We looked at expected scoring distributions, and we saw virtually the same advantage of .02 wins. Any way you slice it, the great reliever adds around .02 wins over your other options in the ninth inning of a three-run game. The question to ask is the following: can we give up that .02 wins now (and bring in an average reliever) and earn even more than that by having our ace reliever available and fresh for the next day's game?

Remember also that we said this three-run situation happened 1,034 times from 1999–2002. That's an average of eight to nine games per season per team. If you bring in your average reliever each time, you lose 0.4 games. If you bring in your ace reliever each time, you lose 0.2 games. That's a 0.2 win difference. Per season.

This is what we are talking about. You get a 0.2 win advantage per 162 games, by using up your ace reliever instead of an average reliever with a three-run lead in the ninth. The question is whether we can earn more by bringing him into the game in other critical, yet managerially-unpopular, situations.

The Book Says:

The three-run lead is an almost sure thing, with a 2% difference in the odds of winning between a great pitcher and an average one. Be careful in cashing in on that 2% today at the risk of losing even more tomorrow.

NINTH INNING TWO- AND ONE-RUN LEADS

How about the two-run lead? What kind of advantage are we really talking about here? Going back to our 31 ace relievers, they were in this situation 883 times, and their teams lost 43 times, or 4.9%. And the rest of the reliever pack? 36 for 400, or 9.0%. The advantage for the ace reliever in this case is .041 wins (9.0% minus 4.9%), which is double the advantage relative to the three-run lead. That is, having an ace reliever pitching with a two-run lead compared to an average reliever gives you double the win impact than having him pitch with a three-run lead. You get double the leverage comparing the two-run to the three-run lead.

And the one-run lead? 140 for 939 or 14.9%. Our ace relievers, coming in with a one-run lead in the ninth inning, will have their team lose nearly 15% of the time. And the rest of the reliever pack checks in with a 20.9% loss rate, on 93 losses over 446 opportunities. The advantage here is .060 wins, or triple the advantage relative to the three-run situation.

Is this what we had expected if we simply used the theoretical run-scoring distribution? With a two-run lead, the ace reliever will give up zero or one run 91.5% of the time, exactly two runs 5.1% of the time, and three or more (and get an outright loss on the road) 3.4% of the time. Overall, using our handy process from a little earlier, they are expected to lose 5.3% of the time. The average reliever checks in allowing zero or one run 86.2% of the time, two runs 7.4%, and three or more runs 6.4%. Overall, their teams lose 9.1% of the time. Difference? Almost 4% (9.1% minus 5.3%). And, what did we say actually happens? A nudge over 4%.

For one-run leads, the ace reliever's teams are expected to lose 13.3% of the time, while the average reliever's team will lose 19.6% of the time, for a difference of 6.3%, which is a pretty close to what really happens (6.0%). Pretty much a perfect match across the board. The expected scoring distributions work as a great way to figure out the differences between great and average relievers.

The Book Says:

In terms of leverage, for every one win you can get pitching your ace reliever with a three-run lead, you get two wins with a two-run lead, and three wins with a one-run lead.

So, this is where we are: the difference between a great and an average reliever is .02 wins with a three-run lead in the ninth, .04 wins with a two-run lead, and .06 wins with a one-run lead.

ENTER THE EIGHTH

Let's look at introducing your ace reliever in the eighth inning rather than the ninth. We've seen plenty of occasions in the recent playoffs where relievers are asked to get six outs. In fact, this was a rather typical occurrence during the regular season 25 years ago. For example, less than half of the batters Goose Gossage and Bruce Sutter faced were in the ninth inning. But, we certainly don't see this situation today. Is it simply the case that you don't get enough leverage by having your stud come in in the eighth inning? That having him come in for one game to pitch the eighth and ninth doesn't give you the same payoff as having him come in to pitch two games in the ninth? Before we can answer that, we have to know what the payoffs are.

The data is somewhat scarce here. While our ace relievers had an abundance of ninth inning appearances, there was a dearth in the eighth inning—only 100 times did they enter in the eighth ahead by one, with the bases empty and no outs. And 21 times their team lost the game. (That's 21.0% obviously.) And the rest of the relievers? 844 chances, 242 losses, for a 28.7% loss rate. So, you have a 7.7% advantage with your ace relievers compared to the other relievers.

Wait a minute. That's an almost 8% advantage, which is even higher than the ninth inning with a one-run lead. Let's remember though that this is an 8% advantage spread over two innings. On a per-inning basis, this works out to an almost 4% (.038 wins) advantage. As well, because of the small sample size, our sample result of 4% has a high uncertainty level of 2%. In these kinds of cases, seeing the sample data may be comforting, but it will be far from conclusive.

We need to resolve the small sample size issue. Is the advantage really close to .04 wins per inning? Can coming in with a one-run lead in the eighth inning and pitching two innings have the same win impact as coming in, over two games, to a two-run lead in the ninth inning?

Let's break out our expected run distribution, as this often solves the problem of small sample size. It's going to get a little hairy, and we have to keep a few considerations in mind. The first is that we are looking for runs allowed over two innings, and not one. Secondly, we also need to know whether the pitcher is coming in to the top or the bottom of the eighth, since we have to know whether his team has one more chance at bat, or two. It's going to get technical, but this is important. Here's our first important chart: the run-scoring distribution for a random inning, if scoring 5.0 runs per game, or 3.2 runs per game. (See Table 87.)

Table 87.   Distribution Of Runs Per Inning, By Quality Of Pitcher

Runs in one inning	5.0 RPG	3.2 RPG
0	70.1%	78.6%
1	16.1%	12.9%
2	7.4%	5.1%
3	3.4%	2.0%
4	1.6%	0.8%
5	0.7%	0.3%
6	0.3%	0.1%
7	0.2%	0.1%
8	0.1%	0.0%
9+	0.1%	0.0%

This is the way to read the first line: a team that scores or allows an average of 5.0 runs per game (which represents our average reliever) will score or allow no runs in 70% of their innings. For a team that scores or allows 3.2 runs per game (which represents our average ace reliever), they'll get the shutout inning almost 79% of the time. With us so far? Now, let's expand this to two consecutive innings. (See Table 88.)

What we are seeing here is even more pronounced. The great pitcher will get consecutive shutout innings 62% of the time, while the average pitcher will get consecutive shutout innings almost half the time.

Here's the first of a multi-part question: if an average pitcher comes into a game in the top of the eighth with a one-run lead, and pitches two innings, how often will his team lose the game? You lose the game if you allow at least two more runs than your team scores. The game goes to extra innings if you allow exactly one more run than your team scores. You win the game if you allow the same number of runs that your team scores, or you allow fewer runs than your team scores. This becomes a simple, but long, mathematical exercise.

Table 88. Distribution Of Runs Per Two Innings, By Quality Of Pitcher

Runs in two innings	5.0 RPG	3.2 RPG
0	49.2%	61.7%
1	22.5%	20.3%
2	13.0%	9.7%
3	7.2%	4.5%
4	3.9%	2.1%
5	2.0%	0.9%
6	1.1%	0.4%
7	0.6%	0.2%
8	0.3%	0.1%
9+	0.3%	0.1%

We'll let you do the intermediate calculations, as we've given you the process we will be following. Here are the final results for the average pitcher:

- 65.9%: Win in nine innings
- 18.8%: Lose in nine innings
- 15.3%: Extra innings

So, a loss will occur 18.8% of the time in nine innings, and 7.7% in extra innings, for a total of 26.5% of the time.

Now, how about having the ace reliever coming in to start the top of the eighth and pitch two innings? How often will his team win, lose, or tie?

- 75.7%: Win in nine innings
- 11.3%: Lose in nine innings
- 13.0%: Extra innings

The ace reliever's team will lose 17.8% of the time (11.3 + 6.5). Advantage over the average reliever? 8.7%. So, .087 of win impact spread over two innings, or .043 wins per inning.

Remember, these are the numbers when the reliever enters the top of the inning. Let's repeat this process when the reliever enters the bottom of the inning, and his team will only get to bat once. With a one-run lead and the reliever pitching in the bottom of the inning: 32.4% loss with average reliever, and 22.4% loss with ace reliever, which is a 10.0% advantage, or .050 wins per inning.

So, entering the top of the eighth with a one-run lead is worth .043 wins per inning, but entering the bottom of the eighth is worth .050 wins. This is an average of .047 wins per inning when entering the eighth with a one-run lead. If you recall, our actual data told us .038 wins per inning.

How about for the eighth inning and a two-run lead? In reality, the ace relievers lose 7 in 64, while the rest of the reliever pack loses 85 out of 717. The difference here is only .009 wins, or .005 wins per inning. (Because of the sample size, the uncertainty level here is once again a very high .02 wins.) Repeating the same process with the theoretical model, and the result is .068 wins, or .034 wins per inning

And, with a three-run lead? Reality shows 1 loss in 49 for the aces. 39 for 570 is how the rest of the relievers check in. The ace relievers get a .048 win advantage, or .024 wins per inning. The theoretical model shows an advantage of .043 wins, or .022 wins per inning.

At this point, we see the dangers of small sample size. That two-run lead in the eighth stands out. Clearly, given the choice between the two-run lead or the three-run lead in the eighth, you'd rather have your ace reliever come in with that two-run lead. The actual results imply differently. But, one blown game here and there, and the actual numbers can change drastically (which is why we mentioned the uncertainty levels in those results). This is the reason that theoretical models are very attractive. As long as you can capture some semblance of reality, it's a powerful tool to validate, and sometimes supplant, the things we can infer from data gathered from actual games.

> *The Book* Says:
>
> In terms of leverage, the eighth inning with a one- or two-run lead provides a better opportunity to use your ace reliever than does the ninth inning with a three-run lead.

ENTERING WITH RUNNERS ON BASE

So far, we've only dealt with the situations of having the pitcher enter the game with the bases empty and no outs. But, there are 23 other base/out states the pitcher can face. We can run through the actual data to see what the numbers will show us. So far, sample size has been a thorn in our side. But at the level of detail by base/out states, sample size is certain to kill us. Let's instead go to our theoretical model that has served us so well. For every base/out state in the top of the ninth inning, we will show the expectation of winning for teams with an average reliever (the .500 pitcher) and an ace reliever (the .680 pitcher), and pitching to the end of the inning.

The context for this chart is as follows: the home team has a three-run lead at some point in the top of the ninth inning. (See Table 89.)
- The first four columns show the base/out state at the point the reliever enters the top of the ninth.
- The win % is for the home team: the .500 column is the win % for the home team if they have a league-average reliever pitching; the .680 column is the win % with a great pitcher pitching.
- *Win Gain* is the difference between the two preceding columns.

Table 89.   Chance Of Home Team Winning, By Base/Out State, For Top Of The 9th Inning, With A Three-Run Lead

1B	2B	3B	Outs	.500 (Average)	.680 (Ace)	Win Gain
--	--	--	0	0.965	0.984	0.019
--	--	--	1	0.986	0.994	0.008
--	--	--	2	0.996	0.999	0.003
1B	--	--	0	0.921	0.955	0.034
1B	--	--	1	0.961	0.979	0.018
1B	--	--	2	0.989	0.994	0.005
--	2B	--	0	0.919	0.954	0.035
--	2B	--	1	0.958	0.978	0.020
--	2B	--	2	0.987	0.994	0.007
--	--	3B	0	0.915	0.952	0.037
--	--	3B	1	0.957	0.977	0.020
--	--	3B	2	0.986	0.994	0.008
1B	2B	--	0	0.851	0.900	0.049
1B	2B	--	1	0.918	0.947	0.029
1B	2B	--	2	0.971	0.982	0.011
1B	--	3B	0	0.830	0.887	0.057
1B	--	3B	1	0.907	0.939	0.032
1B	--	3B	2	0.964	0.978	0.014
--	2B	3B	0	0.818	0.876	0.058
--	2B	3B	1	0.891	0.929	0.038
--	2B	3B	2	0.964	0.977	0.013
1B	2B	3B	0	0.739	0.805	0.066
1B	2B	3B	1	0.845	0.889	0.044
1B	2B	3B	2	0.933	0.954	0.021

Let's take a step back for a second. If these pitchers pitched for the entire game, the great pitcher would win 68% of the time, while the average pitcher would win half the time. The win gain for the great pitcher, over nine innings, is .18 wins (.680 - .500). Over one inning, that works out to an average of .02 wins. That number is important to remember. The .02 wins represents the win impact of a great pitcher in a random inning. Sometimes he's worth .05 wins, and sometimes he's worth .01 wins, depending on the game context (inning, score, etc.). On average, it's .02. The more likely the game is on the line, the more crucial the situation, the more there is to leverage. And the result will be a win gain of more than .02 wins.

When you bring in a reliever, you are trying to bring him in when it matters the most (or at least matters *something*). You bring him in to leverage the situation. To leverage a situation, you need to use something valuable at an opportune time. The expected outcome is therefore to earn more than .02 wins per inning. Otherwise, you didn't really leverage anything. As well, earlier in the chapter, we saw that the difference between the ace reliever and other relievers was also .02 wins with a three-run lead in the ninth inning.

What does this chart say about bringing in your best reliever in the top of the ninth, up by three, with the bases empty and no outs? A win gain of .019. That's almost exactly the number we expected if this were a random situation! The conclusion is inescapable: this is not a situation that gives you leverage. You don't bring in your ace reliever here.

When do you bring him in? Ideally, you want to have a leverage of at least double the random situation. This means bringing him in with a situation that has a win gain of at least .040 wins. At the minimum, bring him in with a leverage that is at least 50% higher than random: .030 wins. (We'll discuss these ideal levels of leverage in the next section.) Inspecting this chart (for the three-run lead in the top of the ninth), this means any time that you have at least one runner on base and no outs, you have a situation that can be leveraged to some extent. And with two runners on base and no outs, this is definitely a situation to bring in your ace reliever.

What about the situation where the bases are loaded and there are two outs? The chart says that's only worth .021 wins. It seems like a random situation. However, this is a gain of .021 wins, with only one out to go in the game. The average situation has a win gain of .006 to .007 per out. This fact makes the bases loaded, two outs situation worth triple that of a random situation, and thus it is highly leverageable.

The Book Says:

In terms of leveraging the ninth inning with a three-run lead, you need to have (a) runners on base with zero or one out, or (b) a runner in scoring position with two outs, to make it worthwhile to use your ace reliever.

LEVERAGE AND WASTED OUTINGS

Leverage is the key. When the game is on the line, when one play can be the turning point of the game, we are talking about leverage. The higher the leverage, the more the *chances of winning the game* depend on a good performance. We've already seen how we can identify the leverage of the situation in a couple of cases.

Now, we're going to use that process to determine how well managers actually used their relief aces. The first thing we're going to grant the manager is that he correctly identified the situation in which to bring in a reliever. We don't know if he did, but we'll grant him that benefit of the doubt. We then determine the leverage of the game situation in which each reliever entered the game in the eighth or ninth inning, since these are the innings in which we can conceivably expect our aces to enter. (We're going to set the average leverage as 1.0. A leverage of 2.0 means that the situation has double the impact on winning, compared to some random point in the game.) Finally, for each game, we take the highest of these leverages (which we'll refer to as the *high score*). We would hope that when the manager brought in his relievers, that he gave the highest leveraged outing, the *high score*, to his ace, and the lowest to his worst.

Overall, the average of these *high scores*, over the 140+ games per team that a reliever entered the eighth or ninth inning, was 1.29. This means that if a manager was able to randomly give his ace reliever 60 or 70 of these games, his leverage score would be 1.29. Almost 40% of the games had a high score of at least 1.50, while just under half had a high score of at *most* 0.70. That is, for each team, there was an average of 67 games, in which a reliever was used and was brought into the game in the eighth or ninth, where the highest leverage was less than 0.70. These games are, for all intents and purposes, games reserved for the average to poor relievers. When the leverage is under 0.70, this means that the players have a limited impact in affecting the outcome of the game, regardless of the quality of the pitcher. Our expectation is that the leverage score of the ace reliever be higher than 1.29. After all, that 1.29 includes plenty of games with blowouts. The aces should not see the light of day in these low-leverage games. Did they?

Let's go back to our nine aces, the cream of the crop. These are relievers that should only be used with the game on the line, if at all possible. From 1999–2002, these aces came into games a total of 19% of the time when the leverage of the situation was under 0.70! Almost one-fifth of time, they pitched in a game that should have been reserved for the worst pitchers on the team. Jeff Shaw led the group at 26%, with Billy Wagner at 23%. Six of the remaining seven pitchers were at 16% to 20%. Troy Percival was wasted in only 12% of his games. We realize that an ace reliever must, at times, be used in low-leverage situations, when the manager determines that he needs some work. However, 19% of the time is an awful lot of *tune-up* work.

Not surprisingly, the average leverage of Percival's outing was 2.1, and Jeff Shaw's was only 1.7. Shaw was not used effectively. The other pitchers were all around the 1.9 mark.

How much leverage can be exploited? If we look only at those games with a minimum high score of 1.50, there is an average of 53 games per team. The average leverage in these 53 games is 2.8. There is an average of almost 20 games with a high score of between 0.70 and 1.50 (average leverage of 1.0). If we can give our ace 45 high-leverage games (at a leverage level of 2.8), 10 normal-leverage games (leverage of 1.0), and 5 low-leverage games (leverage of 0.2), this comes out to a leverage of 2.3. This is our target. If a manager can better schedule his relievers, the ace's leverage will go from 1.9 to 2.3. This is a 20% gain! It's like turning someone who can impact his team by winning four more games than an average reliever into winning five more games instead. A 1-win gain is substantial, when dealing with optimization.

The problem lies in those games where the leverage was below 0.70. If we were to list all those games, the managers will surely accept those games as being low-leverage outings, or wasted outings. The sheer high number of wasted games, the 19% of their total appearances, is what reduced our target leverage of 2.3 down to their actual 1.9.

Much too often, a manager lets his relief ace sit on the bench in high-leverage situations in the eighth inning, waiting to use him in the ninth, only to still see him on the bench when the game ends. Eventually, the manager needs to give his ace some work, so he gives him whatever comes up. And this happened in almost one-fifth of the aces' appearances.

The Book Says:

Managers should strive to bring in their aces with a leverage of at least 1.50, even in the eighth inning, and (if at all possible) make sure they don't waste them in games where the pitcher has limited impact on the outcome.

HOW LONG CAN THEY GO?

Here is where you have to start thinking about the usage limits and capabilities of humans, instead of simple computer models. A pitcher needs time to warm up. How much time? This depends on the body of the reliever, but three to four minutes would seem to be the minimum. That works out to needing a two-batter lead time. It's very possible that you can go from a medium-leverage situation to a high-leverage situation to a loss over two batters, at which point you don't need the relief ace any longer. Or it's also possible to be in a medium-leverage situation, have the ace warm up, and the current reliever get two quick outs to end the game. Again, a wasted warm-up for your relief ace. Would Mariano Rivera like to be warmed up 80 times to pitch in 60 games, or would he prefer to warm up and pitch in 65 games? Each of the 60 games may have a win gain of .060 wins, and each of the 65 games may have a win gain of only .055 wins, but either way would work out to 3.6 wins gained for the season.

So, to construct the proper model, you have to be two batters ahead of the curve. You don't want to know when to bring him in, but rather, when to warm him up. And, you have to figure out how much life of the reliever's arm is used up by warming him up, without bringing him into the game. We won't be exploring this question any further, here. Rather, our focus is on full-inning appearances, since there's time to warm up.

Yesteryear

The other question to answer is, how long can a reliever go per outing? Twenty to thirty years ago, relievers threw more often in any given season. However, did this impact their career? Was this a case of burning out your relievers early, with a result of having a shorter career?

Let's construct some time periods based on the birth year of the pitchers: 1932–1941, 1942–1951, 1952–1961, and 1962–1971. Let's take the ten pitchers in each decade with the most pitches thrown, and who had at least 95% of their games in relief. (The estimate of pitches thrown is based roughly on 3.3 pitches thrown per batter faced, plus an extra 1.5 pitches thrown per strikeout, and an extra 2.2 pitches thrown per walk.) Here are those forty pitchers, ordered by the estimated number of pitches thrown. (See Table 90.)

Table 90. **Batters Faced And Estimated Pitch Totals For Full-Time Relievers**

Player	Pitches	PA	GS	G	Pitches per Relief Game	'32-'41	'42-'51	'52-'61	'62-'71
Rich Gossage	28,712	7657	37	1002	26		1951		
Rollie Fingers	25,841	7070	37	944	24		1946		
Tug McGraw	23,749	6444	39	824	25		1944		
Gene Garber	22,987	6439	9	931	24		1947		
Kent Tekulve	21,749	6105	0	1050	21		1947		
Mike Marshall	21,576	5955	24	723	27		1943		
Sparky Lyle	21,417	5944	0	899	24		1944		
Jesse Orosco	21,043	5521	4	1252	17			1957	
Lee Smith	20,830	5487	6	1022	20			1957	
Clay Carroll	20,437	5798	28	731	25	1941			
Bill Campbell	19,553	5322	9	700	27		1948		
John Franco	18,942	5113	0	1036	18			1960	
Tom Burgmeier	18,809	5391	3	745	25		1943		
Ted Abernathy	18,746	5045	34	681	24	1933			
Ron Perranoski	18,383	5089	1	737	25	1936			
Paul Lindblad	18,374	5182	32	655	24	1941			
Mike Jackson	18,056	4802	7	960	18				1964
Greg Minton	17,548	4957	7	710	24		1951		
Jeff Reardon	17,455	4755	0	880	20			1955	
Dan Plesac	17,414	4595	14	1064	15				1962
Darold Knowles	17,391	4762	8	765	22	1941			
Doug Jones	17,328	4787	4	846	20			1957	
Roger McDowell	16,368	4605	2	723	22			1960	
Willie Hernandez	16,267	4435	11	744	21			1954	
Bruce Sutter	15,928	4315	0	661	24			1953	
Larry Andersen	15,449	4229	1	699	22			1953	
Randy Myers	14,640	3808	12	728	19				1962
Dan Quisenberry	14,483	4356	0	674	21			1953	
Bob Wickman	14,072	3810	28	627	19				1969
Mike Stanton	13,968	3756	1	885	16				1967
Jeff Brantley	13,902	3698	18	615	20				1963
Mike Timlin	13,716	3748	4	736	18				1966
Jeff Montgomery	13,700	3687	1	700	19				1962
Roberto Hernandez	13,657	3612	3	762	18				1964
Bob Locker	13,210	3670	0	576	23	1938			
Larry Sherry	13,123	3519	16	416	29	1935			
Jeff Shaw	12,859	3599	19	633	18				1966

Player	Pitches	PA	GS	G	Pitches per Relief Game	'32-'41	'42-'51	'52-'61	'62-'71
Frank Linzy	12,327	3522	2	516	24	1940			
Ron Taylor	11,947	3403	17	491	22	1937			
Jack Baldschun	11,516	3097	0	457	25	1936			

Check out the top of the list. Gossage, Fingers, McGraw, Garber, Tekulve, Marshall, Lyle. The top seven longest-lasting relievers of this 40-year time period were born within eight years of each other, from 1943 to 1951. Note that while the number in the *Pitches* column includes games whether starting or relieving, the pitches per relief game is limited to relief appearances. And these pitchers threw roughly twenty-five pitches in each relief appearance.

And who takes over the bottom half of the list? We find two groups: the pitchers who played in a time when relievers, as a group, were not used much, and the more recent pitchers. While some of those recent pitchers are still active, they won't be moving up the list too high. Here are the averages of the above pitchers for the four decades, while re-membering that this last decade still has active pitchers. (See Table 91.)

Table 91.   Average Pitches Per Game, By Top Relievers, For Each Decade

Decade	Pitches	PA	GS	G	Pitches per Relief Game
'32-'41	15,545	4309	14	603	24
'42-'51	22,194	6128	17	853	25
'52-'61	17,409	4760	3	854	20
'62-'71	14,598	3912	11	771	18

The '42–'51 pitchers threw more pitches than an other group, threw more pitches per game, and have thrown in just as many games as the pitchers in the other decades. The pitchers today may pitch slightly more games per season, but they pitch just as many games throughout their careers. And they throw a lot fewer pitches.

The Book Says:

Relief pitchers of today should be able to handle 25-pitch outings because the pitchers of the recent past were able to do so. Those pitchers had careers, as measured in games or number of pitches thrown, as long or longer than the recent pitchers. Today's relievers are not being used enough.

Aces In The Eighth

OK, we can buy that relievers of past were used more often without impacting their career prospects. But today's pitchers, knowing they will only pitch in one inning, have several advantages. They know they will only go one inning, so they don't need to worry about pacing themselves. They don't have to sit in between innings. Essentially, a relief pitcher can be much more effective if he's in and out in one inning, leaving it all on the mound. Or is he?

Let's once again look at our trusted nine ace relievers (Mo, Hoffman, Percival, et al.). We'll break down their games based on the inning they entered. (See Table 92.)

No surprises here. The ace relievers come in usually in the ninth, and sometimes in the eighth. Let's break it down even further. We're really only interested when the game is still close. Let's look at only those games where the pitcher has at most a three-run lead, or is at worst down by one run. This brings us down to 1,202 close games entering the ninth, and 180 in the eighth.

And, how do they do? Concentrating only on those 1,202 times they pitched in the ninth inning of a close game, their wOBA in that ninth inning is .279. They also faced 3.8 batters per ninth inning. That's a sensational set of performances by nine highly trusted relievers.

Table 92.   Times The Trusted Nine Ace Relievers Enter A Game,
By Inning

Enters Inning	Number of Times
6	3
7	8
8	232
9	1520
10	91
11	28
12	7
13	5
14	3
16	1
19	1

And, how about when they enter the eighth inning? How do they per-form? They entered the eighth 180 times, and in the eighth inning performed at a wOBA of .245, with 1.8 batters in the eighth. That is about as good a performance as you can expect from any pitcher. That's essentially Pedro Martinez at his best. And in the ninth inning of those games? .280, with 3.4 batters faced in the ninth.

Let's recap here. Our ace relievers pitch at .279 or .280 in the ninth innings of close games, regardless of entering in the eighth or ninth inning. However, if they enter in the eighth inning to face one or two batters, they perform at .245 in the eighth inning. It certainly seems like they can really gas it out for one or two batters, sit down, and come back to their normal effective selves. Of course, with such a small sample, this is just speculation. Facing 1.8 batters uses up around seven pitches. The difference between the number of pitches thrown per game by the ace relievers of the past and today is seven pitches.

So far, we can buy that we don't need to bring in our reliever in the ninth inning with a three-run lead, and that we should bring in our reliever with two outs in the eighth inning to face one or two batters. But, how much earlier can we bring him in? Can we bring him in with zero or one out in the eighth inning? Here's what happens when a reliever is brought in, under different circumstances. (See Table 93.)

Table 93.   Performance Of Ace Relievers, By Conditions Of Game When Entered

Enters Inning	With Number of Outs	Games	PA In 8th and 9th	PA/G	Pitches/G	wOBA In 8th and 9th
8	0 or 1	64	370	5.8	22	0.267
8	2	116	574	4.9	19	0.269
9	Any	1202	4548	3.8	14	0.279

The first line says: 64 times our ace relievers came into the eighth inning with zero or one out, and faced 370 batters in the eighth and ninth innings, for an average of 5.8 batters and 22 pitches per game, with a performance level of .267 over the eighth and ninth innings. Across the board, the performance levels are very close. All the apparent advantages that we've studied as far as having our ace reliever enter the game in the ninth inning aren't appearing. Whether we bring in our ace in the eighth or ninth inning, he will perform at his usual high abilities.

The Book Says:

Relief pitchers should be brought in in the eighth inning of close games to face at least one batter. Facing one or two batters in the eighth inning results in no change in performance in the subsequent ninth inning.

Back-To-Back

How about pitching him too often back-to-back, and not having him available because we've used him up too much in the recent past? How often can a reliever go before he loses his effectiveness?

Let's take Ugueth Urbina on July 20, 2001. Four days earlier, on July 16, he faced five batters. Three days earlier, on July 17, he faced six batters. Then another six batters, on July 18. And finally, one day earlier, on July 19, he faced five batters. That's a total of twenty-two batters over four days. You would think that'd be the end of it, right? There's no way he had anything left in the tank on July 20. He was brought in that day and faced three batters. And got them all out.

Of course, this is just one performance by one guy. Let's try to find a few more players. For this study, we will try to identify relievers who had their tanks depleted the most, and were still asked to pitch. We will define another toy, which we'll call *The Tank*. Take the number of batters faced yesterday, plus 75% of the batters faced two days earlier, 50% of the batters three days earlier, and 25% of the batters four days earlier. This will give you the effective number of batters that the pitcher faced. In the Urbina case above, it works out to 13.75 batters.

From 1999–2002, there were 23,240 relief games pitched by our pool of pitchers with at least 800 PA (and excluding any game by the incomparable and unrepresentative Tim Wakefield). Let's look at the 0.1% of pitchers whose tank was the most depleted (twenty-nine pitchers in all, with at least 13.5 batters in The Tank). This is the extreme of all extremes. You have to believe that the manager used these pitchers, even though he knew that their tanks were depleted, simply because he had no other options. And, he's willing to live with a decent chance of a sub-par performance.

Table 94.   Performance Of Mulholland, With Depleted Tank

Date	PA4	PA3	PA2	PA1	PA0	wOBA
30-Jun-00	0	0	34	0	4	0.893
19-Aug-99	0	0	26	0	2	0.000
16-Sep-02	0	28	0	0	11	0.588

The first thing that jumps out is the effect that the emergency relief appearance by a starter had on the study. We'll call this the Mulholland effect. This is what Mulholland's chart looks like, in the three games in which he faced at least seventeen batters (essentially four innings) in any of the prior four days. (See Table 94.)

To read that chart, on June 30, 2000, Mulholland faced four batters, after facing 34 batters two days prior. He had a wOBA of .893 on June 30. Twice he was asked to pitch after starting a game with only one day of rest, and another time with two days of rest. His overall performance in relief under these circumstances was a wOBA of .591. He was brutal.

Since we are really interested in the tank levels of relievers, we'll also remove all such games where a pitcher started a game in any of the prior four days. We are left with twenty performances, including one with Terry Mulholland. (See Table 95.)

Table 95.   Performance Of Relievers, With Most Depleted Tanks

Players	Date	PA4	PA3	PA2	PA1	PA0	wOBA on Date	1999–2002 wOBA
Jason Grimsley	07-Aug-00	0	5	0	16	2	0.375	0.320
Todd Jones	01-Oct-00	0	7	2	12	1	0.000	0.347
Ramiro Mendoza	19-Apr-01	0	5	0	14	1	0.000	0.310
Danny Graves	24-Jul-99	9	0	6	9	1	0.000	0.314
Byung-Hyun Kim	05-May-02	3	8	5	7	3	0.000	0.284
Alan Levine	09-May-00	0	11	0	10	6	0.390	0.333
Terry Mulholland	02-May-01	13	0	0	12	4	0.225	0.365
Bob Wells	24-May-99	0	7	5	8	7	0.510	0.335
Scott Sullivan	01-Jul-02	5	0	5	10	1	0.000	0.324
Byung-Hyun Kim	16-Aug-00	0	7	0	11	1	0.000	0.284
Pat Mahomes	04-Jul-99	0	11	12	0	3	0.000	0.354
Alan Levine	05-Jul-00	8	0	16	0	5	0.000	0.333
Jeff Nelson	17-Apr-00	0	8	0	10	2	0.000	0.287
Ramiro Mendoza	30-Jul-02	12	0	1	10	1	0.000	0.310
Ugueth Urbina	20-Jul-01	5	6	6	5	3	0.000	0.285
Eddie Guardado	27-Jun-00	0	1	12	4	1	0.000	0.294
Jose Mesa	16-Aug-00	4	7	0	9	6	0.793	0.334
Scott Sauerbeck	18-Jul-00	0	9	0	9	4	0.225	0.330
David Weathers	12-Jun-99	0	7	0	10	9	0.511	0.320
Gabe White	31-Jul-99	1	5	5	7	4	0.450	0.310

On average, those twenty pitchers, from four days earlier (PA4) to the prior day (PA0), faced 3-5-4-9 batters. That gives us a Tank value of 15 batters. These pitchers were really used up, but were still asked to come back to pitch. On average, they pitched to three batters on that fifth day (PA0). Some pitched to only one, up to as many as nine (!) batters. Overall, they faced 65 batters (which is of course a tiny sample size), with a wOBA of .302. Given the talent level of these pitchers, we expected a .324 wOBA. That's right, these twenty extreme pitchers, showed an *improvement* after having their tanks depleted. This chart, by itself, is worthless, since anything can happen with 65 PA. But, it does introduce us to the issue.

Could it be that relief pitchers can handle this kind of workload or do we just have too small a sample to draw any conclusions? Let's try to resolve one issue, the small sample size, by looking for a Tank value of at least 10.5. That brings our list of games to 232 (or about 1% of our total pool of games). The wOBA in the date in question is now .327, while the talent level of these pitchers is .322. We see almost no difference.

Let's look at the next 227 most depleted pitchers. How well did they perform after their tanks were depleted? .325. And, what was their overall performance? .325. Exactly the same.

And, how about the next 236 most depleted pitchers? .318. And .321 overall.

If we look at all these pitchers overall, we've got 695 pitchers (3% of all relief games) in our pool. These pitchers are those with their tanks the most depleted. They had a total of 2,893 PA, which is a fairly significant total on which to base our opinions, while maintaining that we are looking at the most extreme of cases. Their wOBA, once their tanks were depleted, was .323. Their performance overall in 1999–2002 was .323.

No effect.

By increasing our sample to the 10% of pitchers with the most depleted tanks, that gives us 2,460 reliever games, with 10,702 PA. We get .319 when the tank is somewhat depleted and .321 overall.

We have to conclude that managers are simply not using relief pitchers enough. Relief pitchers can handle workloads much greater than what they normally get. Once they've been given a very heavy workload (or what passes for a heavy workload in 1999–2002), it appears to have no impact on their performance the next day. We expected at some point that managers must have overworked 1% of their pitchers, and we can't find it.

There's no question that relievers have a point where their tanks are truly depleted. They are human after all. Even Mariano Rivera. But, that point was nowhere close to having been reached in 1999–2002.

The Book Says:

Relief pitchers can handle a much heavier workload than current managers are imposing. Over a five-day period, when relief pitchers are given 16 to 24 batters, their performance is unaffected. Current relief pitchers could probably handle an increase in their workload by 30% to 40%, which is not inconsistent with the workload of relievers in the 1970s.

CHAPTER 9 – TO SACRIFICE OR NOT

Few strategies elicit as much emotion and controversy as the sacrifice bunt. In 1990, Jay Bell of the Pirates had 39 sacrifice hits. He presumably had many more sacrifice *attempts* than that. Some people would argue that he pre-emptively killed a plethora of Pirate rallies, while others might argue that his skill as an accomplished bunter created more runs and more wins for the Pirates than if he had swung away instead. As is often the case in baseball, fans and pundits can argue such things until they are blue in the face, but without a detailed and thorough analysis of the *numbers*, there is simply no way of knowing wherein the truth lies.

Such rhetoric as, "It is a good strategy to put a run on the board as quickly as possible," or, "Late in a close game, getting a single run can be critical," or, in the opposite vein, "Outs are too precious to waste," or, "A sac bunt is a rally killer, period," are just that—rhetoric. They don't enable us to answer the following pertinent questions:

- Is it *ever* correct to sac bunt? In other words, does a sac bunt *ever* increase a team's chances of winning the game, as opposed to swinging away?
- If yes (it is *sometimes* correct), when?
- From what positions in the lineup, by what kinds of batters, with what kinds of hitters following the batter, versus what kind of pitcher, in what park, at what score, and in what inning?

If we can answer all, or even some, of these questions, then perhaps we can put the controversy and the arguments to rest.

Looking at historical data, we see that the sacrifice bunt is a strategy that has dramatically fallen out of favor over the last 25 years or so. In the 1940s, the sacrifice bunt rate in the NL and AL (for non-pitchers) was around 5.5 per 500 PA. By the 1980s, that had dropped to around five, and in 2004, it was only a little over three. Why is the sacrifice bunt not as popular as it once was? As with the stolen base (which has also declined dramatically), many GMs and managers have come to the realization that *small-ball* strategies, like the stolen base and sacrifice bunt, are not as effective in the high run environments prevalent in the modern era of baseball.

As well, conventional *sabermetric* wisdom says that the sacrifice bunt is generally an ineffective and archaic strategy. For example, the three highest-profile sabermetric teams in 2004 in the AL were Oakland, Boston, and Toronto. While the AL average for sacrifice hits per team was almost 39, Boston had only 12, Toronto 10, and Oakland 25, the three lowest totals in the league. The sacrifice bunt appears to be a strategy eschewed by sabermetric teams.

Is sabermetric conventional wisdom correct? (Note that you will not often see the word *sabermetric* juxtaposed with the term *conventional wisdom*, at least not in this book.) You may be surprised at the answer!

Where does the sabermetric notion that a sac bunt is rarely (if ever) productive come from? Well, way back in 1984, Pete Palmer and John Thorn, in their groundbreaking book, *The Hidden Game of Baseball*, said, "The sacrifice bunt . . . is a bad play." They go on to say that, "With the introduction of the lively ball, the sacrifice bunt should have vanished. . . ." They are talking about non-pitcher bunts of course. In fact, unless otherwise noted, throughout the rest of this chapter, when we speak of a sacrifice bunt or just a bunt, we are speaking of a sacrifice bunt or attempted sacrifice bunt by a *non-pitcher*.

Where they derived their conclusions, as outlined in *The Hidden Game*, was from the run expectation and win expectation tables that we have constantly been referring to in this book. Here is a copy of Palmer's original run expectation chart modeled after the 1961–1977 baseball seasons. (See Table 96.)

Table 96.   Palmer And Thorn's 1961 To 1977 Run Expectancies For Each Of The 24 Base/Out States

Number of Outs	0	1	2
Runners			
Xxx	.454	.249	.095
1xx	.783	.478	.209
x2x	1.068	.699	.348
xx3	1.277	.897	.382
12x	1.380	.888	.457
1x3	1.639	1.088	.494
x23	1.946	1.371	.661
123	2.254	1.546	.798

To refresh your memory, here is what those numbers represent. For example, with a runner on first only (1xx), and no outs, the number of runs that an average team scored in an average environment versus an average opponent, was .783. Sometimes they scored no runs, sometimes one run, and sometimes two or more runs, but if we add up the total number of runs scored in that situation (runner on first and one out) in the seventeen-year period between 1961 and 1977, and divide by the number of times that situation occurred, we get exactly .783 runs.

What Palmer and Thorn basically did was look at the run expectancy from this table before and after a *successful sacrifice bunt*, traditionally called a *sacrifice hit*. The *before* number represents the expected number of runs scored (by a league-average batter) without a bunt, or at least including an occasional sac bunt, with a runner on first and no outs; the *after* number represents the run expectancy after a successful sacrifice bunt that results in a runner on second and one out. As you can clearly see from the highlighted areas in this table, a successful bunt starting with a runner on first and no outs *decreases* an average team's run expectancy (RE) by .084 runs. That may not seem like a lot, but it is a fairly large amount as a result of one seemingly innocent strategy still employed by most modern-day managers almost once every two games (it only *seems* more frequent than that). In fact, a .084 run loss would result, on the average, in a .85% reduction in win expectancy (WE) for that game. If a team were to utilize a strategy once every two games that reduced their WE by .85% in each of those games, they would lose an extra .7 games per season (.0085 times 81 games).

Now let's look at the same RE table, based on the higher run-scoring environment of the modern era, in the National League only. (See Table 97.)

Table 97.   Run Expectancies, NL, 2000–2004

Number of Outs	0	1	2
Runners			
xxx	.525	.281	.110
1xx	.906	.541	.238
x2x	1.148	.700	.327
xx3	1.448	.982	.382
12x	1.500	.921	.433
1x3	1.840	1.190	.508
x23	2.073	1.401	.567
123	2.263	1.531	.772

As you can see, the run expectancies are significantly higher, especially with zero and one out. With two outs, the numbers are not very far apart. In other words, in higher run environments, outs become more and more precious and costly. If we now look at the difference between a runner on first with no outs and a runner on second with one out, we see that the reduction in RE is .206 runs, gigantic compared to the .084 runs in the low-scoring era of the 60s and 70s. In fact, .206 runs corresponds to an average reduction in WE of around 2.2%, which is an extra 1.8 losses per season, again assuming that the reduction (via a sacrifice hit) occurs once every two games.

In all fairness to those who advocate the sacrifice bunt, the RE (and WE) from hitting away *by a batter who would actually be called upon to bunt* is substantially lower than the .906 above. The .906 is for *all batters*, including the sluggers who virtually never bunt. The average wOBA for all batters (pitchers included) in the NL from 2000 to 2004 was around .330. For batters (non-pitchers) who actually bunted, it was .319; for batters (again, non-pitchers) who did not bunt (in bunt situations), it was .345. So batters who are called upon to bunt are definitely a weak group of batters, as we would have expected. In fact, rather than an RE of .906 with a runner on first and no outs (based on a league-average .330 hitter), a .319 batter would have an RE of around .875. So a typical reduction in RE after a successful sacrifice by a weak batter (.319 wOBA) is only .175 runs rather than the aforementioned .206 runs (if a league-average batter were to bunt). We arrived at the .875 (the RE of a .319 batter when swinging away with a runner on first and no outs) by using a computer simulation, which we will explain later in the chapter.

Table 98.   Palmer And Thorn's Win Expectancies, Bottom Of The 7th, One-Run Down

Number of Outs	0	1	2
Runners			
xxx	.343	.298	.262
1xx	.413	.348	.289
x2x	.482	.403	.324
xx3	.537	.457	.334
12x	.529	.432	.343
1x3	.594	.483	.353
x23	.654	.546	.393
123	.683	.557	.411

There is one more analysis that Palmer and Thorn did. That is, they recognized that late in a close game, say from the seventh inning on, run expectancy may not be as important as win expectancy. They also surmised that a sacrifice bunt, or other *small-ball* strategies, might increase a team's chances of scoring *at least* one run, at the expense of a big inning, such that it might actually increase a team's chances of winning the game, despite a reduction in RE, or at least not be as bad as the difference in RE suggests. In order to see to what extent this might be true, they looked at a *win expectancy* chart for the bottom of the seventh inning with the batting team down by a run. Again, here is

Palmer and Thorn's original WE table from *The Hidden Game*, based on the 1961 to 1977 run environment. (See Table 98.)

Unfortunately (for those of you who held out hope that a successful sacrifice bunt in the late innings of a close game was a *good* thing), a team's chances of winning the game is still *reduced* after a successful sacrifice bunt, even in the bottom of the seventh inning, down by a run (by an average batter on an average team versus another average team with an average pitcher, etc.). This time a team's winning percentage, or chances of winning the game, is exactly 1% less after a successful bunt. Generalizing the bottom of the seventh inning, down by a run, to *late in a close game*, if a team in the 60s and 70s, when the run environment was comparatively low (as opposed to the current, modern era), were to execute a successful sacrifice bunt late in a close game every fourth day or so, they would win almost a half game *less* per season than if they completely eschewed the bunt. Again, that gap would be reduced if the bunter were a below average hitter.

What about late in a close game in the modern era? (See Table 99.)

Table 99.   Win Expectancies In The Modern Era, National League, Bottom Of The 7th, One Run Down

Number of Outs	0	1	2
Runners			
xxx	.353	.305	.268
1xx	.431	.360	.296
x2x	.487	.399	.322
xx3	.545	.465	.336
12x	.545	.438	.341
1x3	.612	.504	.359
x23	.656	.546	.382
123	.687	.561	.406

In the higher run environment, we see once again that the out is more costly. In fact, a successful sacrifice bunt (by a league-average hitter) in the seventh inning of a one-run game reduces the batting team's chances of winning by more than 3.5%, which is more than three times as costly as in the lower offensive era!

So, it is starting to look like conventional sabermetric wisdom is correct—that the sacrifice bunt is generally *not* an effective strategy (i.e., it *decreases* rather than *increases* a team's chances of winning the game), at least with a runner on first and no outs, a league-average, non-pitcher at the plate (or even a below average hitter), followed by league-average hitters, versus a league-average team, in an average run environment, etc. But, thus far we have only been discussing a *sacrifice hit*, where the batter is out and the runner advances to second. Let's see what actually happens when the batter *attempts* a sacrifice.

THE SACRIFICE ATTEMPT

Anyone who has watched more than a few baseball games is aware of the fact that a sacrifice bunt *attempt* sometimes results in an out and no runner advance, a hit, an error, an occasional walk—in fact, the entire gamut of possible offensive events, even very occasionally, a home run (not a bunt home run, of course; but a regular home run after the batter has failed to bunt the ball in play before accumulating two strikes, and then swings away).

How is it that over the last twenty years, since *The Hidden Game* was published, so few researchers have looked into exactly what happens—how often each offensive event occurs—when a batter attempts a sacrifice bunt? (Tom Tippett won a presentation award at a recent SABR convention, where the topic was the sacrifice bunt, including the various attempt outcomes; in 1963, Lindsey also looked at other results other than a sacrifice hit.) For one thing, the requisite play-by-play data is not widely available. For another, conventional wisdom, especially *sabermetric* conventional wisdom, is often a tough mold to break.

You can well imagine that the value of the sacrifice bunt attempt is explicitly dependent on and very much a function of the *distribution of offensive events* that occurs when a batter attempts a sacrifice. For example, if we told you that when a batter attempts a sacrifice, he gets a bunt single or reaches base on an error (RBOE) one-third of the time (and a successful sacrifice the other two-thirds), it would be a whole new ball game (no pun intended), right? In fact, if a sacrifice attempt resulted in a hit or RBOE (runners on first and second and no outs) 33% of the time and a sacrifice hit (SH) 67% of the time, the RE for a sacrifice attempt would be 1.500 times .33, plus .700 times .67, or .964 runs, substantially higher than the non-sacrifice RE of .906. (These numbers are taken from the modern NL RE table above.)

On the other hand, what if we told you that a sacrifice attempt results in an out and no baserunner advancement one-third of the time and a successful sacrifice (SH) two-thirds of the time? Clearly, the resultant RE or WE would be worse than if the attempt were 100% successful, and a lot worse than hitting away. (These numbers are used for illustration purposes only.)

The bottom line is that unless we can determine how often each offensive event occurs as a result of a sacrifice attempt, we cannot even begin to evaluate if and when a sacrifice is better or worse than hitting away.

Let's start by looking at non-pitcher bunts only. First, we'll get some of the boring data out of the way. From 2000–2004, in the NL and AL combined, 50,426 times a non-pitcher came to bat with a runner on first (and no one on second or third) and no outs. Of those, 5,447 times, or 10.8% of the time, a sacrifice bunt was attempted. As we said earlier in the chapter, you might be surprised at how infrequently a bunt is attempted, even in a sacrifice situation. Of course, most of the time, when a bunt attempt did occur, the score was close, and someone other than a slugger was at the plate. Inning-wise, they tended to occur either in the first inning or late in the game. (See Table 100.) One of the reasons for so many bunts in the first innning is that managers tend to choose number two batters by virtue of their bunting skills, among other things of course. (If managers end up reading our chapter on lineup construction, you will probably see fewer first inning bunts!)

Table 100.   Percentage Of Sacrifice Attempts With A Runner On First And No Outs, By Inning

Inning	Percentage of all sacrifice attempts
1	12.0
2	3.3
3	8.3
4	4.1
5	7.5
6	8.9
7	14.9
8	16.5
9	14.7
10+	10.0

Whether a bunt is attempted in any given inning is influenced by which batters in the order tend to bat in that inning, especially early in a game. Late in a game, who bats in an inning is close to random.

Table 101.   Percentage Of Sacrifice Attempts With A Runner On First And No Outs, By Batting Slot

Batting slot	Percentage of all sacrifice attempts
1	19.6
2	28.5
3	3.2
4	1.1
5	3.8
6	6.0
7	8.8
8	13.7
9	15.4

Since we are looking at the NL and AL, the number nine slot includes pitchers and non-pitchers alike. (See Table 101.) Obviously in the NL, the percentage of bunts from the 9-hole will be much higher than in the AL. As you might expect, most of the bunting is done from the non-power and poor-hitting slots. (See Table 102.)

Table 102.   Percentage Of Sacrifice Attempts With A Runner On First And No Outs, By The Quality Of The Batter As Measured By Their Career wOBA

Quality of Batter	Career wOBA	Opportunities	Attempts	Att/Opp	Percentage of All Sacrifice Attempts
All batters	.343	50,416	5,447	.108	100.0
Weak batters (wOBA < .320)	.297	11,438	2,417	.211	44.4
Strong batters (wOBA > .360)	.375	14,735	654	.044	12.0

As you can see, poor hitters sacrifice about five times as often as good hitters. As well, almost half (44%) of all sacrifice attempts are by the weak hitters. Coincidentally, another 44% of bunt attempts are by the mid-range hitters, and they sacrifice about 10% of the time (of course, a majority are by the low-average batters). The overall league (NL and AL) wOBA for non-pitchers, weighted by number of PA, was .344 from 2000 to 2004. (The .343 in this table is the average wOBA of a batter when there is a runner on first.) The average wOBA of all batters who attempted a sacrifice is .319. Keep in mind that these numbers include all games (close games and blowouts alike). In true sacrifice situations (i.e., close games), players will bunt more frequently.

By the way, a bunt or sacrifice attempt is defined by us as a PA in which at least one pitch was bunted fair or foul plus a small percentage of PA that include only balls and/or called strikes. Unfortunately the data we have does not indicate a bunt and miss or when a batter squares to bunt and takes a pitch for a ball or a called strike. Therefore we are going to incorrectly classify a few PA in which the batter did square to bunt at least once, but did not make contact, or did not square or swing at all. As well, some of our bunt attempt PA are really hybrid PA, in which the batter squared to bunt on at least one pitch and tried to swing away on some other pitch as well. We don't think that these inconsistencies are going to have much of an effect on our overall analysis.

OK, on to the more interesting and pertinent data. Remember, we are trying to determine what the distribution of offensive events looks like when a batter attempts, according to the above definition, a sacrifice bunt—in this case, a non-pitcher, with no outs and a runner on first.

How often do you think that a batter is successful when he attempts to sacrifice? If you first asked, "What is your definition of success?" then you are following this chapter very nicely so far. Let's say that a successful sacrifice bunt attempt is when the runner advances to second or beyond, whether or not the batter made an out, and whether or not the batter actually bunted the ball fair (i.e., it includes when the batter first attempts a bunt and then switches to swinging away, or walks or strikes out while still attempting to bunt). If you answered, "69.3% of the time," you were exactly correct!

So if a typical batter attempting to bunt (including when he switches to swinging away) advances the runner only 69% of the time, what do those successes look like, and what happens the other 31% of the time? Once we answer that, we can figure out the exact run expectancy (RE) and win expectancy (WE) for a typical bunt attempt with no outs and a runner on first, and compare that with the typical RE and WE when not attempting a bunt. Earlier, we merely compared swinging away to an out and a runner advance.

We'll look at the distribution of offensive events after a sac bunt attempt in two ways. First, by the outcome itself, such as a single, a DP, or a home run (remember that our definition of a sacrifice *attempt* includes when the batter switches to swinging away at some point in the PA), and then by the total RE of all the outcomes combined, weighted by their frequency of occurrence. (See Table 103.)

It is not clear from this table if the value of these results *combined* is better or worse than the value of our original assumption—batter out, runner advances to second. If it is worse, then perhaps the traditional sabermetricians *are* right—that the sacrifice bunt *attempt* is rarely if ever correct. If it is better, then . . . well, we'll have to see how much better, and go on from there.

Table 103.   Sacrifice Bunt Attempt, 2000–2004 NL And AL,

Non-Pitchers

Result of sacrifice attempt N=5447	When a bunt is attempted on the last pitch, in percent, N=3835 (70.4%)	When the batter ends up swinging away, in percent, N=1612 (29.6%)	All bunt attempts, in percent
Batter and runner safe on a FC	0.8	0.1	0.6
Batter out, runner advances	65.2	8.4	48.4
Batter out, runner does not advance	6.8	19.9	10.7
Force (same result as above)	7.8	7.6	7.7
DP	1.6	11.3	4.5
BB/HP	1.2	7.6	3.1
K	1.5	22.9	7.8
RBOE	4.2	1.3	3.4
S	10.9	14.8	12.1
D	0.0	4.0	1.2
T	0.0	0.5	0.1
HR	0.0	1.4	0.4

In order to compute the overall value of the above set of potential outcomes, we have to multiply each of the above percentages by the RE (or WE late in a game) after each event. The way we do that is to look at how often each of the base/out states occurs after each of the above outcomes, and then multiply these percentages by the exact RE (plus any runs scored) for each state. If we do that, we get a total RE of .831 runs for a typical bunter. That is the total value of the sacrifice attempt, assuming the above distribution of potential outcomes. (See Table 104.)

Here's how to read this chart: after a sacrifice attempt, the resultant state, *no runners on and no outs*, occurred 0.5% of the time. The RE for that state is .525. Two runs must have scored in order to produce that state. The total value of the resultant state is therefore .525 plus the two runs scored, or 2.525 runs. A runner on second and one out (such as after a sacrifice hit) occurred 48.1% of the time. The RE for that state, and thus its value, is .700 runs.

Table 104.   Base/Out States, RE After A Sacrifice Attempt (NL And AL, 2000–2004, Non-Pitchers Only)

Runners	0 outs Frequency (%)	RE	Runs Scored	1 out Frequency (%)	RE	Runs Scored	2 outs Frequency (%)	RE	Runs Scored
xxx	0.5	0.525	2	0	N/A	N/A	4.5	0.110	0
1xx	0	N/A	N/A	26.1	0.541	0	0	N/A	N/A
x2x	0.6	1.148	1	48.1	0.700	0	0	N/A	N/A
xx3	0.3	1.448	1	0.2	0.982	0	0	N/A	N/A
12x	15.6	1.500	0	0	N/A	N/A	0	N/A	N/A
1x3	2.0	1.840	0	0	N/A	N/A	0	N/A	N/A
x23	2.0	2.073	0	0	N/A	N/A	0	N/A	N/A
123	0	N/A	N/A	0	N/A	N/A	0	N/A	N/A

As you can see, a *sacrifice bunt attempt*, which yields an average run expectancy of .831 (all of the above frequencies times their run values combined), is substantially better than a *sacrifice hit*, where the batter is out and the runner advances to second, which only yields an RE of .700. That is a profound result, if you ask us. The funny thing is that if you were to ask almost any manager whether he would rather advance the runner to second in exchange for an out, or have the batter *attempt* a sacrifice, how do you think he would respond? If you answered, "Take the guaranteed sacrifice," we think that you would be right. What a poor decision that would be. It's not even close.

The Book Says:

If the opposing manager is thinking about attempting a sacrifice (with a runner on first and no outs and a non-pitcher at the plate), tell him that you will gladly give the runner second base in exchange for an out. In fact, tell him that he has that option—in advance—any time there is a runner on first and no outs!

Still, it appears as if conventional sabermetric wisdom is correct. A sacrifice *attempt* (.831 runs), even though a lot better than an out and a baserunner advance (.700 runs), yields fewer runs, on the average, than hitting away (.875—not .906—because as explained earlier, batters who are called on to sacrifice are below average hitters). But what if the run environment were lower, by virtue of a weak overall offense, a good opposing pitcher, weather conducive to a low-scoring game, a pitcher's park, or some combination thereof? We've already told you that small-ball strategies, like the sacrifice bunt, are generally more effective in lower run-scoring contexts. Is it possible that the sacrifice attempt can yield a greater run expectancy than hitting away, in a low run-scoring environment?

Let's use Palmer and Thorn's RE table from the 1960s and 1970s. During this era, the average team scored around four runs per game (RPG) rather than 4.7 RPG in the NL during the last five years. Four RPG would be roughly equivalent to a poor offensive team in Dodger stadium, or an average team versus an excellent pitcher, or an average team on a cold day in Wrigley Field with the wind blowing in. Let's see how many runs a bunt attempt would yield in a 4 RPG environment. Keep in mind that swinging away in the low run environment yields an RE of .783, as opposed to .906 in the modern NL environment.

Applying the 4 RPG RE to the frequencies of the resultant base/out states after a typical sacrifice attempt yields an RE of .782, almost exactly the same as the RE when not sacrificing (.783). So, in a 4 RPG environment, a bunt attempt by a league-average hitter is about as effective as hitting away. What about a below average or above average hitter? Conventional wisdom says that you should bunt a poor hitter more often than a slugger (of course). We will get to the effect of the batter's offensive ability later in the chapter.

Should You Bunt *Early* or *Late* in a Game?

In the above discussion, we were talking about maximizing run expectancy and not necessarily win expectancy. Maximizing RE is generally appropriate early in the game, while maximizing WE is generally appropriate late in the game (technically maximizing WE is *always* the goal, but early in a game, RE and WE are essentially the same thing).

In order to answer the question of whether is it more appropriate to bunt early or late in a game, we need to determine whether or not the distribution of offensive events following a bunt attempt is the same early in a game as it is late in a game. We'll cut to the chase. It's not. Early in a game, with a runner on first and no outs (and a non-pitcher, presumably a non-slugger, at bat), the defense is often agnostic as far as a bunt attempt is concerned. That is, they are prepared for a bunt, but are not particularly expecting one. Late in a close game is a different story. The defense is usually expecting a bunt with a non-power hitter at the plate. How does this affect the bunter's distribution of offensive events? (See Table 105.)

Table 105.   Bunt Attempt Results, Early And Late In The Game

Result after sacrifice attempt	Early (< 7th inning) N=2484 (7.3% of all opportunities)	Late (7th inning or later) N=2963 (17.6% of all opportunities)
Ball bunted in play	64.5	78.3
Batter and runner safe on a FC	0.4	0.9
Batter out, runner advances	41.2	54.3
Batter out, runner does not advance	11.5	10.2
Force (same result as above)	6.7	8.6
DP	5.4	3.9
BB/HP	2.4	3.2
K	7.9	7.5
RBOE	2.7	3.9
S	19.2	6.6
D	1.8	0.6
T	0.2	0.1
HR	0.7	0.3
Total RE	.886	.783

First of all, as you can see, managers elect to bunt quite a bit less often early in a game than late in a game: 7.3% of bunt situations to 17.6%. As well, early in the game, the batter switches to swinging away more often (with less than two strikes *and* with two strikes), and he gets a substantially greater number of singles and fewer sacrifice hits. Late in the game, there are a few more force plays, RBOEs, and safe on a FC, as the defense is more intent on throwing the baserunner out at second, and more rushed in general.

If we again multiply the frequencies of the resultant base/out states based on the above numbers, early in a game, by the RE of those resultant states, using the modern NL RE matrix, and add them all up, we get a total RE of .886! The .831 above was the average across all innings. We are now dangerously close to the RE when not bunting at all (.906), and slightly higher than the RE of .875 that one gets when considering that bunters are typically weak batters. In our opinion, that is another huge revelation. *In the current average NL environment, a sacrifice bunt attempt early in a game, on the average, produces as many runs as hitting away!* Again, this is contrary to traditional sabermetric belief.

What about early in a game, in a low run-scoring environment? If we use the above early-in-the-game frequencies and multiply by the RE in Palmer's 1961–1977 table, we get a total RE from bunting early in a game of .836, which is a lot higher than the original RE (swinging away), with a runner on first and no outs (.783)! Wow! We exceeded our original RE by attempting a sacrifice bunt early in the game—by more than .05 runs. Of course, as the sacrifice bunt becomes more efficacious, as it does in a low run-scoring context, we would also expect the defense to adjust their expectation and their positioning, such that bunting starts to become less effective. This give and take of competing strategies is discussed later in the book in the chapter on *Bluffing In Baseball.*

> *The Book* Says:
>
> Early in the game in a low run-scoring environment, it is correct to often sacrifice bunt with a runner on first and no outs. In an average run-scoring environment, you should occasionally sacrifice to keep the defense honest.

The reason we say *often* and not *always* is two-fold. One, as mentioned above, if you were to always sacrifice bunt with a non-slugger at the plate early in a game, the defense would eventually start playing more aggressively in anticipation of the bunt, taking away some or all of the edge you may have had. Conversely, if you never sacrificed, the defense would always play back and the RE from swinging away would decrease a little. Two, there are several other considerations that a manager can and should use to decide whether to attempt a sacrifice or not.

Now let's take a look at what happens late in a game (say the seventh inning or later), when using WE is more appropriate than using RE. In order to do that, let's switch to the modern National League WE table for the bottom of the seventh inning and down by a run. If we multiply the frequencies of the resultant base/out states after a sacrifice attempt late in a game, by the WEs of those states, we get a total WE of .423. Compare this to an overall WE of .431 with a runner on first and no outs (which presumably includes both bunting and hitting away), and we have virtually the identical situation as we had early in the game—a sacrifice attempt is almost as good as swinging away. (And again, with a below average hitter at the plate, the sacrifice attempt is likely as good as or better than swinging.) If we switch to Palmer and Thorn's lower run-scoring environment, we find that a sacrifice attempt late in a game yields a slightly higher WE than hitting away, .417 to .413. Once again, in a lower run-scoring environment, we might expect the defense to be playing more for the bunt, thus reducing the .417 win expectancy.

The Book Says:

Late in a close game, in a low run-scoring environment, it is cor-rect to often sacrifice bunt with a runner on first and no outs. In an average run-scoring environment, you should sometimes sac-rifice to keep the defense honest.

As you can see, late in a close game, the added benefit of increasing your chances of scoring at least one run makes up for the greater diffi-culty in achieving a successful outcome (because of how the defense is playing). In fact, from now on, rather than doing two separate analyses for every potential sacrifice situation, we are going to use *early in a game* outcomes and run expectancy as a proxy for *late in a game* out-comes and win expectancy. Our assumption, based on the above results, is that what is good or bad for the goose (a bunt attempt early in a game) is also good or bad for the gander (a bunt attempt late in the game). We will, however, address the special circumstance of a tie game in the ninth inning, later in the chapter.

Interestingly, it appears that overall, managers may be sacrificing about as often as they should early in a game, as well as late in a game. As you will also see, however, many managers do not properly take into account other important considerations when deciding whether to bunt or not. Let's take a look at some of these other considerations.

Should Weak-hitting Batters Bunt More Often than Sluggers?

Given the assumption that all batters attempting a sacrifice are equally proficient at bunting and have around the same foot speed (We'll address those issues shortly), is a bunt attempt by a weak batter more efficacious than one by a strong batter? If so, how do we know what the cutoff point is? In other words, given a certain run environment, how do we know how weak the batter must be before it is advisable for him to bunt (with a runner on first and no outs)? A word of caution before we continue: because there are a myriad of considerations that determine whether a sacrifice bunt is correct or not in any one circumstance, not to mention the fact that *game theory* dictates that we constantly mix up our strategies, we cannot state *exactly* what the optimum strategy is at all times.

Assuming a typical bunter (bunting proficiency and speed) and typical baserunner (speed), the RE and WE as a result of a sacrifice attempt changes not only with the run environment, but with the hitting proficiency of the bunter as well. This is a very important point. You would think that the result of a sacrifice bunt attempt would be relatively constant regardless of the hitting prowess of the batter, and that therefore a bunt attempt by a weak hitter would be much more indicated than one by a strong hitter. That is not the case. Here are the RE after a bunt attempt, by quality of hitter. (See Table 106.)

Table 106.   RE After A Bunt Attempt, By Quality Of Hitter, Early In A Game

Type of batter	RE early in a game	Bunt attempts per 100 opportunities
All batters	.894	7.4
Weak (wOBA < .310)	.864	14.8
Average (wOBA .310 to .350)	.890	8.2
Strong (wOBA > .350)	.936	3.3

Wow! That's quite a difference. When a weak batter attempts a bunt, he is not nearly as successful as a stronger one. How can this be? To get a clearer picture of exactly what is going on in a sacrifice situation (with a runner on first and no outs), take a look at this table. (See Table 107.)

If you look closely at the chart, some interesting and telling patterns emerge. First, the result (RE) of a fair bunt is an almost perfect indicator of the defensive alignment or potential defensive alignment (a manager usually has to make his decision before he sees where the defense is going to be playing). Late in a game, regardless of who is bunting, a weak, average, or good hitter, the RE from a sacrifice attempt that results in a fair bunted ball is virtually the same (and quite low). This suggests that late in the game, when a batter is indeed sacrificing, the infield is generally expecting the bunt, regardless of how good a hitter the batter is. On the other hand, when the batter ends up swinging away on the last pitch, after initially sacrificing, the better hitters do substantially better than the weaker ones, as expected. And of course the better hitters produce a higher RE when swinging away from the get-go. By the way, the reason the RE when not bunting are lower later in the game is that the quality of the pitching is about 3% better, on the average (because short relievers are collectively better than starters and middle and long relievers).

Table 107.   RE By Quality Of Hitter, Early And Late In The Game

	All Batters		Weak Batters (<.310 wOBA)		Strong Batters (>.350 wOBA)	
	Early (7.3%)	Late (17.6%)	Early (14.8%)	Late (32.7%)	Early (3.4%)	Late (6.5%)
Fair Bunt less than 2 strikes	.888	.766	.845	.774	.968	.782
All bunt attempts	.894	.783	.864	.775	.936	.838
No bunt attempt	.935	.913	.889	.851	.969	.944

Early in the game, the bunting results of the good and bad hitters are shockingly different. This suggests that early in the game, the defense is not expecting a bunt with a very good hitter at the plate. When they do bunt (only 3% of the time), it is apparently quite a surprise. With a poor hitter at the plate, the defense is generally expecting a bunt, although not nearly so much as late in a game. What is surprising is that the defense appears to be playing more aggressively late in the game with a good hitter at the plate (.782 RE when the ball is bunted fair), than they do early in the game with a poor hitter at the plate (.845 RE with a fair bunt). Given that only 6.5% of the good batters attempt a sacrifice late in a game, while almost 15% of the weak batters attempt to bunt early in a game, this seems rather odd. Perhaps it is obvious to the defense late in the game which good hitters are going to bunt, but it is not so obvious early in the game which of the weaker hitters will sacrifice. It is also possible, however, that managers are not apportioning their bunts properly among their good and bad hitters at the appropriate times during the game. Another likely explanation is that defenses simply aren't as conditioned to expect bunts early in a game as they are late in a close game.

If the RE from a fair bunt is indeed a good proxy for defensive alignment, we can estimate that with the defense playing back (such as early in the game with a good hitter at the plate), the RE from a bunt is around .945; with the defense playing for a possible bunt (such as early in the game with a weak hitter at bat), the RE is around .860; and with the defense playing aggressively for the bunt (late in the game), the RE is only around .775. Again, this is with a runner on first, no outs, and a non-pitcher at the plate. Those are substantial differences that emphasize the importance of the potential defensive alignment when deciding whether to bunt or not. It also emphasizes the importance of anticipating whether or not the batter might be bunting, when deciding what kind of defense to employ.

The Book Says:

When deciding whether to bunt or not, anticipating or observing the position of the infielders is critical. Likewise, when deciding what kind of defense to employ (how aggressively to play for the bunt), it is important to anticipate whether the batter might be bunting or not. Making the correct guess can be worth nearly 0.2 runs!

Because the defensive alignment is different against weak and strong batters early in the game, and because even during a bunt attempt, the batter sometimes ends up swinging away, the RE for a bunt attempt is substantially higher for a good batter than for a weak one, both early and late in the game. What does that tell us? Well, for one thing, it tells us that it is not so obvious that a weak hitter should be bunting just because his RE when swinging away is a lot less than that of a good hitter.

Let's compare a weak hitter's RE from bunting with his expected RE from swinging away from the get-go (no bunt attempt). Remember, his RE from bunting early in a game is .863 (rather than .886 for all batters, and .947 for strong batters). Will his RE from swinging away be better or worse than that, and how can we compute that RE?

Thankfully, we have a computer batting simulator (using Markov chains) that can tell us exactly what the RE is, given any type of hitter, weak or strong, batting within a lineup of average hitters. If we plug into this simulator (*sim*) the component stats for an average modern NL batter with a runner on first and no outs, we get an RE with a runner on first and no outs of .906 (exactly that found in the RE chart). Whew! We're glad the *sim* passed our initial baseline test!

What happens if we plug in the career stats of a light hitting short-stop like Rey Sanchez (a wOBA of .294, 50 points less than the league-average of .344)? (When we simulate hitting away in a sacrifice situation where the defense is presumed to be playing up, we add some "extra" singles per 500 PA to a player's stats.) The computer tells us that San-chez's personal RE with a runner on first and no outs is .866, about the same as if he were to attempt a sacrifice (assuming he is an average bunter).

What about a slightly better hitter like Doug Glanville? His career wOBA is .320. If we plug his stats into the simulator, we get an RE with a runner on first and no outs of .889, quite a bit higher than if he were to sacrifice (.863). Of course, Glanville's RE from a sacrifice attempt is going to be a little higher than Sanchez's, since when Glanville switches to swinging away, he is going to get slightly better results, and the defense might be playing Sanchez a little more aggressively (expecting the bunt more often). So even with an extremely poor hitter like San-chez, a sacrifice attempt appears to be about a break-even strategy; with a below average but not terrible hitter like Glanville, the sacrifice attempt yields an RE less than that from hitting away.

What about a good hitter? We know that his RE from a surprise sacrifice attempt is .947, quite a bit higher than that of a weak hitter. What is a good batter's RE when swinging away early in a game? This time, the presumption is that the defense is not playing up (that's why the RE from bunting is so high), so we are not going to add any hits to the player's career profile.

Let's look at Jeff Kent. His career wOBA is .379, actually a little higher than our average good hitter (.370). When we plug Kent's numbers into the simulator, we get an RE from swinging away of .950. That is a little higher than his estimated RE from a bunt attempt, assuming that the defense is not expecting a bunt.

How about a slightly above average hitter like Brett Boone, whose career wOBA is .344? His RE from swinging away is .910, which is also a little higher that what his RE would be if he attempted a sacrifice, again assuming that the defense were not necessarily expecting a bunt.

The amazing thing is that a bunt from a below average hitter like Glanville is no better than a bunt from an above average hitter like Kent or an average hitter like Boone! The fact that for most types of hitters, weak or strong, the post-bunt-attempt RE are similar to their hit-away RE, suggests that hitters are indeed bunting at around the optimal rates and that the defense is positioned more or less optimally.

The Book Says:

In an average run environment, and not considering the bunting proficiency or speed of the batter, or the speed of the runner on first, if the batter has an expected wOBA of less than .300, 44 points less than the league average, he can attempt a sacrifice bunt, even if the defense is expecting one.

If the batter has an expected wOBA greater than .300, he can sometimes sacrifice if the defense is not playing for the bunt very aggressively. The better the hitter (expected wOBA), the more the defense must be playing back in order for him to bunt. Even an excellent hitter can occasionally bunt as long as it comes as a complete surprise to the defense

Since we know that a lower run-scoring environment (pitcher's park, cold weather, good opposing pitcher, poor-hitting lineup, etc.), is more conducive to the sacrifice bunt, without doing a complete analysis again, we can interpolate our next rule of thumb:

The Book Says:

In a low-scoring environment, and not considering the bunting proficiency or speed of the batter, or the speed of the runner on first (with no outs), almost any batter can attempt a sacrifice bunt, as long as the defense is playing accordingly (the better the hitter, the more the defense must be playing back).

Let's recap five important points discussed so far:

- With a non-pitcher at the plate, and a runner on first and no outs, advancing the runner in exchange for an out is a terrible strategy. It significantly reduces the RE in almost any run environment. It also reduces the WE in almost any run environment, even late in a close game. (This is where the so-called conventional sabermetric wisdom eschewing the sacrifice bunt comes from.)

- A sacrifice bunt *attempt*, again, with a runner on first and no outs, with a typical bunter and typical baserunner, results in enough singles and RBOEs, and other successes (even after accounting for the failures), besides simply advancing the runner in exchange for an out, that the RE and WE from a bunt attempt is significantly higher than the RE and WE from an out and runner advance only. In fact, if a batter is a weak enough hitter, or the run environment is low enough, a bunt attempt yields an RE or WE higher than swinging away. Even with a good hitter at the plate, if the defense is not expecting a bunt, a sacrifice attempt usually yields almost the same RE as swinging away, and sometimes it is higher.

- The higher the run environment, the weaker the batter has to be, after adjusting for the run environment itself, in order to justify a sacrifice attempt. In a low run environment, almost anyone, even a very good or great hitter, can bunt, assuming the defense is playing accordingly.

- Even though advancing the runner in exchange for an out is more advantageous late in a close game (because it is important to score at least one run), this advantage is nullified by the fact that it is more difficult to lay down a successful sacrifice late in the game, when the defense is expecting a bunt. In other words, the WE loss after advancing the runner in exchange for an out is much greater early in the game than late in the game; however, the WE loss or gain early in the game after a sacrifice attempt is almost exactly the same as it is late in the game.

- How the defense is playing (whether they are expecting a bunt or not) in conjunction with the hitting proficiency of the batter are essential factors in deciding whether to sacrifice or not. Because of this, in an average NL run environment, for all but the weakest batters, a sacrifice attempt is almost as good as hitting away. For those extremely poor batters like Sanchez, the bunt is better. Somewhere between Sanchez and an average hitter is the break-even point.

The On-Deck Hitter

Let's discuss some of the other things that a manager should consider in order to decide whether a bunt is warranted or not in any given situation. Many of these factors are the tiebreakers.

Table 108.   **Player A (Tony Womack-Type With More Singles And A Higher BA)**

Offensive Event	Rate per 500 PA
Singles	120
Doubles	20
Triples	5
HR	6
Walks	30

Table 109.   **Player B (An Andres Galarraga With Fewer Singles And More Walks)**

Offensive Event	Rate per 500 PA
Singles	73
Doubles	20
Triples	1
HR	24
Walks	50

In 2004, in an excellent series of articles on the sacrifice bunt by James Click of *Baseball Prospectus*, the author explained (among other things) how the sacrifice bunt is favored more when the following hitters are weak overall, especially in the power department. Actually, the relative value of all hits is virtually unchanged with the runner on second and one out (as compared to a runner on first and no outs). What does change is the value of the walk, which is substantially reduced with a runner on second. As well, the out is not so costly anymore. Therefore, after a successful bunt, you can leverage a low walk, low OBP kind of batter. Let's say we had two players, both of whom had around the same wOBA (i.e., they had the same offensive value in a neutral context), but with vastly different offensive profiles. (See Table 108 and Table 109.)

Both players have around a .358 wOBA, but player A, with a runner on second and two outs, produces an RE of .705, while player B produces an RE of .679.

The Book Says:

All other things being equal, sacrifice more often with a low-walk, low-OBP hitter on deck.

The Speed and Bunting Proficiency of the Batter

Finally, we get to perhaps the two most important, yet often overlooked, factors in determining whether to sacrifice or not. We have hinted at them several times already. They are: the speed and bunting proficiency of the batter/bunter.

Intuitively we know that the bunting proficiency of the man at the plate is, or at least should be, an important factor is deciding whether to bunt or not. How often have we cringed at the sight of someone on our favorite team helplessly flailing away at a pitch he is trying to bunt, while we curse the manager for asking a player to do something that he is clearly not able to do, or at least not able to do *well*?

So far, we've looked at the results of a sacrifice bunt from the perspective of a typical batter (who was asked to bunt). Let's see what the distribution of offensive events looks like when the batter is a proficient bunter and what it looks like when he is not.

How do we determine whether a batter is a proficient bunter? We divided all batters from 2000 to 2004 into three groups, based on their number of bunt *hit* (not sacrifice) attempts per PA. The assumption is that the greater the bunt hit rate, the more proficient they are at bunting (and/or the faster they are). We realize this is not a perfect assumption, but we think that overall, the group of batters with the lowest rate contains the poorest of bunters, and the group with the highest rate contains the best bunters. To be on the safe side (to avoid potential selective sampling issues), for the 2000 sacrifice data we used the 2001 bunt proficiency data, for 2001, we used 2002 data, etc. (for 2004, we used 2003 data).

Table 110.   Sacrifice Attempt Results By The Bunting Proficiency Of The Batter, Early In The Game

Result after sacrifice attempt early in a game	Worst Bunters (Group I) N=660 (3.6%) (.328 wOBA)	Best Bunters (Group III) N=954 (18.0%) (.316 wOBA)	All bunters N=2484 (7.3%)
Ball bunted in play	63.0%	68.0%	64.5%
Batter and runner safe on a FC	0.2	0.4	0.4
Batter out, runner advances	40.9	42.3	41.2
Batter out, runner does not advance	10.8	10.1	11.5
Force (same result as above)	6.8	6.5	6.7
DP	6.1	5.2	5.4
BB/HP	6.7	2.8	2.4
K	8.9	6.3	7.9
RBOE	2.4	3.4	2.7
S	14.7	21.0	19.2
D	1.7	1.8	1.8
T	0.3	0	0.2
HR	0.6	0.2	0.7
Total RE	.867	.907	.886

Here is what the distribution of offensive events looks like for the two extreme groups. (See Table 110.) The last column is for all batters combined. The numbers are for sacrifice attempts early in a game.

As you can clearly see from this chart, the better bunters achieve substantially more singles, a few more RBOEs, and slightly fewer forces and DPs. Also, as as expected, the better bunters bunt the ball in play more often than their poor-bunting counterparts. And of course the better bunters are much more likely to attempt a sacrifice.

In any case, the total RE for the poor, less experienced bunters is .867, lower than the .886 RE for all bunters and substantially lower than the .906 RE for an average batter when swinging away. The good bunters achieve, on the average, a sacrifice attempt RE about the same as that of an average batter swinging away, and substantially higher than their own non-sacrifice RE, given that they have a collective wOBA of only .316, as compared to the league average of .342.

So unless the batter is a pitcher (we'll get to that later), it looks like you *should* cringe when that poor bunter squares to sacrifice! Six hundred sixty, or over 120 per year, are indeed a boatload of bunts given to a group of bad bunters, early in a game no less! Managers are clearly not taking into account the bunting proficiency of the batter nearly as much as they ought to.

What about the foot speed of the batter? If we do the same analysis as above, again dividing all batters into three groups, fast, medium, and slow, based on their triples rate and their number of steal attempts per opportunity, we get around the same results as with the bunting proficiency of the batter. That is true even when we control for bunting proficiency (the proficient bunters and the fast players obviously overlap quite a bit).

The RE for the slow bunters is .847, and for the fast bunters, it is .881. Being slow is a particular detriment to attempting a sacrifice, perhaps even more so than being a bad bunter, yet over 200 slow players were allowed to bunt (again, *early* in a game) over the last five years! In fact, managers probably think very little about the speed of the batter when deciding whether to bunt or not. After all, if the batter gets thrown out and the runner advances, that is considered a resounding success.

Interestingly, for fast batters, the RE when bunting is less than that of medium speed batters. This may be a sample size issue or it may be that the defense expects the faster players to bunt more often, or they are already playing farther in. In any case, as with the poor bunters, slow runners should not be bunting very often, if at all.

Judging from the frequency with which the good bunters bunt early in the game (around the same frequency as all batters late in the game) and their RE after a sacrifice attempt, it appears that the defense is not adjusting their positioning according to the bunting proficiency of the batter nearly as much as they should.

The Book Says:

In an average run environment, almost any batter can bunt as long as he is a good bunter, or a fast runner, preferably both. A poor or slow bunter should rarely be allowed to sacrifice. This trumps our earlier recommendations, which applied to all bunters as a whole, good or bad, fast or slow.

The defense should be particularly aware of the bunting proficiency of the batter and adjust its positioning accordingly. Poor and/or slow bunters do not attempt a sacrifice very often even if they are poor hitters. Good and/or fast bunters bunt a lot, even early in the game.

As always, the recommendations above can and should be adjusted for the run environment. Hopefully, at this point, you can do some of these adjustments by yourself. As we said earlier in the chapter, it is impossible to determine the optimum strategy (bunt or not) at every juncture in the game, given the myriad of factors that affect the decision-making process. However, knowing how each of these factors affects the efficacy of the bunt will enable an astute manager to make the right decision more often than not. As well, when a decision is so close that you literally need a computer in the dugout in order to determine the correct one (as opposed to the rules of thumb herein), it doesn't really matter what you do—you might as well flip a coin (which *game theory* often suggests you do anyway!).

The Speed of the Baserunner

What about the speed of the *baserunner*? One would think that the speed of the baserunner would play a significant role in the success of the sacrifice attempt as well. The total RE early in a game with a slow runner on first is .883. With a fast runner, it is .879. Hmmm. With the faster runner on first, there are, as you would expect, fewer forces and DPs, more singles, and more baserunner advances. The total RE are about the same however. Perhaps the defense is expecting a bunt more often with the faster runner on base, or perhaps we are suffering from small sample size syndrome again. The suggestion is that the speed of the runner is not nearly as important as we might have thought. We think that a manager should keep it in mind, however.

The Book Says:

The speed of the baserunner should probably be considered by the manager when deciding whether to bunt or not, although it is not nearly as important as the speed of the batter.

The Count

Managers will often take the bunt sign off or put it back on one or more times during an AB. Is this wise? As is often the case, it depends. As you have seen, even when a sacrifice bunt is warranted, the decision is often close; there are many factors that can tip the scale one way or the other. Let's say that the batter is sacrificing on the first pitch. He squares and takes the pitch for ball. Should he continue to sacrifice or should he switch to hitting away?

We know that with a 1-0 count, all batters become better offensive players. That is a given. In fact, with a runner on first and no outs, a 1-0 count typically increases a batter's run expectancy by about 5%. Let's see if the RE from a bunt attempt early in a game is increased by a similar amount with a count of one ball and no strikes. (See Table 111.) The PA column gives the number of plate appearances in which a bunt was attempted on the particular count.

Table 111.   RE For Various Starting Counts When Bunting And Swinging Away Early In A Game, NL And AL, 2000–2004, Using The NL RE Matrix

Count	PA	RE when swinging away	RE from a bunt attempt
0-0, all PA	2435	.935	.894
1-0	517	.984	.955
0-0, weak batter, wOBA<.330	1387	.896	.875
1-0, weak batter	314	.944	.902

As you can see from this chart, a bunt attempt by all batters with a 1-0 count increases the RE by about 7%, more than the increase in RE when hitting away. For a weak batter, the RE from a bunt attempt goes up 3%. Because of the small 1-0 count samples, our numbers have a large uncertainty, so our recommendations are to be taken with a grain of salt. With a 1-0 count, a non-pitcher can still bunt.

Table 112.   RE For Various Counts When Bunting And Swinging Away Early In A Game, NL And AL, 2000–2004, Using The NL RE Matrix

Count (PA)	RE when hitting away	RE from a bunt attempt
2-0 (112)	1.090	1.106
2-1 (84)	.997	.985
1-1 (278)	.917	.883
0-1 (558)	.883	.832

Let's look at a few more counts and see how things shake out. (See Table 112.) Because non-pitchers rarely bunt with two strikes, we'll have to wait until we discuss pitcher bunts to see the effect of a two-strike bunt on RE. Even the 2-0 and 2-1 count RE are suspect due to sample size issues. The numbers do however suggest that the count should not change the manager's decision with regard to whether to bunt or not, since the RE from the bunt attempt varies similarly to the RE when swinging away. The changing count does of course give him an opportunity to switch from bunting to hitting away and vice versa, in order to keep the defense on its toes. With a 3-ball count, the paucity of the data does not allow us to do a proper analysis. Because of the likelihood of the walk, and the fact that batters often attempt a bunt when a pitch is not a strike, we assume that most batters should be swinging away when the count goes to three balls (or sometimes "taking," of course, as in a 3-0 or 3-1 count).

The Book Says:

The count does not appear to change the efficacy of the bunt, unless the batter has three balls. With a 3-ball count, a non-pitcher should swing away. At other counts, the batter can sometimes switch tactics to keep the defense on their toes.

Pitcher Bunting

As you have learned, the two basic things that must be determined in order to figure out whether a sacrifice is warranted are: 1) the RE or WE without the sacrifice (hitting away), and 2) the RE or WE when attempting a sacrifice, based on the distribution of offensive events following the bunt attempt.

Let's see how the results of a typical sacrifice attempt by a pitcher compare to that of a non-pitcher, in the NL. We will compare pitcher bunting early in a game to non-pitcher bunting late in a game, since we expect that in both instances the defense is more or less expecting a bunt (at least from certain batters late in a close game). In fact, this time, late in a (close) game will be from the eighth inning on, when the defense is *really* expecting a bunt from a non-slugging, non-pitcher. (See Table 113.)

Table 113.   Results Of A Sacrifice Attempt For Pitchers And Non-Pitchers, NL, 2000–2004

Result after sacrifice attempt	Pitchers, early in a game (87.9%)	Non-pitchers, late in a game (> 7th inning) (20.9%)
Ball bunted in play	88.6%	76.8%
Batter and runner safe on a FC	1.8	1.1
Batter out, runner advances	63.1	54.2
Batter out, runner does not advance	4.3	10.2
Force (same result as above)	8.6	8.5
DP	4.9	4.2
BB/HP	0.8	3.4
K	13.2	7.5
RBOE	2.2	3.6
S	0.9	6.4
D	0.1	0.6
T	0	0.1
HR	0.1	0.4
Total RE	.685	.781

As you can see, pitchers bunt the ball in play far more often than do position players. That is primarily due to the fact that pitchers generally continue bunting with two strikes and non-pitchers do not. In fact, with less than two strikes, pitchers bunt the ball in play only 72.8% of the time, as compared to 75.0% for non-pitchers. If we really want to see how well pitchers bunt as compared to position players, we have to compare them when the ball is actually bunted in play with less than two strikes. (See Table 114.)

Table 114.   Results Of A Sacrifice Attempt For Pitchers And Non-Pitchers, When The Ball Is Bunted In Play With Less Than 2 Strikes

Result after sacrifice attempt	Pitchers, early in a game	Non-pitchers, late in a game
Batter and runner safe on a FC	2.3%	1.3%
Batter out, runner advances	75.9	71.2
Batter out, runner does not advance	4.7	7.2
Force (same result as above)	9.5	8.7
DP	4.5	2.4
BB/HP	0	0
K	0	0
RBOE	2.5	4.5
S	0.7	4.7
D	0	0
T	0	0
HR	0	0
Total RE	.702	.759

Well, we certainly dispelled the notion that pitchers are better bunters than position players! Not only do the non-pitchers bunt the ball in play more often before they get two strikes, but when they do bunt the ball in play, they get substantially better results (by .057 runs in RE). About the only thing that pitchers do better than non-pitchers is bunt the ball on the ground more often (fewer bunt pop outs). They hit into more DPs, and reach base on a single or error substantially less often. Of course, the difference between the pitchers and non-pitchers could be entirely due to foot speed and the position of the defense, so when we say that non-pitchers are better bunters, we really mean they achieve better results.

Anyway, if we go back to Table 113, we see that the RE for a pitcher when bunting early in a game is .685, substantially lower than a non-pitcher bunting early in a game (.866), or even very late in a game (.781). (It is also lower than taking an out and advancing the runner to second, so with the opposing pitcher at the plate, we would *not* make that offer to the opposing manager!)

Most of the difference is probably due to the defense playing more aggressively in anticipation of a bunt. Some of it may also be due to pitchers being poorer bunters and certainly slower runners. (By the way, the RE for pitcher bunting late in the game is about the same as early in the game, suggesting that the defense plays the same with a pitcher at the plate, regardless of the inning.)

So the next question is, what is the RE for a typical pitcher when *hitting away* with a runner on first and no outs? If it is less than .685, which we assume it is, then how good a hitter does a pitcher have to be in order for a bunt to be ill-advised?

Interestingly, 203 times in the NL (12.1% of the time), from 2000 to 2004, across all innings, a pitcher did not bunt with a runner on first and no outs, and the resultant base/out states created an RE of .815 runs, substantially higher than the average .686 RE (.685 was *early* in the game only) after a pitcher bunt attempt. Does this mean that pitchers should rarely if ever sacrifice bunt with a runner on first and no outs? Not so fast!

The .815 RE likely comes from the fact that of these 203 pitcher non-bunts, many of them were by the best hitting pitchers, the run environment was probably high, and the defense was probably surprised. In fact, the average score of the batting team at the time of a pitcher non-bunt was 3.2 runs, as compared to 1.8 when the pitcher was bunting, suggesting a higher run environment (e.g., hot weather, bad opponent pitcher, hitter's park, etc.), or simply a high-scoring game or lopsided score (in favor of the pitcher/batter's team). As well, the non-bunts were indeed by the better hitting pitchers. The average career wOBA of the non-bunting pitchers is .204. For the bunting pitchers it is .187.

So if looking at the actual results of the pitcher non-bunts gives us a deceiving RE, how can we figure out the RE when a typical pitcher hits away, and how can we figure out the break-even point for how good of a hitter a pitcher has to be before he shouldn't be sacrificing?

Enter our old friend the computer simulator! If we plug in a typical .189 wOBA pitcher into an average NL lineup, we get an RE of .686 (that is *without* adding in any extra hits for the defense playing up). Wow! That is right around the same as the RE from bunting! If we throw in the fact that with a runner on first and the infield expecting a bunt, the pitcher should get a few more singles and doubles, the RE from hitting away increases to around .700! No wonder the RE was .815 those 203 times a pitcher actually swung the bat! This is another fascinating revelation, and devastating to conventional wisdom that says a pitcher should *always* sacrifice.

The Book Says:

With a pitcher at the plate with no outs and a runner on first, only a below average hitting pitcher should bunt most of the time. An average hitting pitcher should bunt about half of the time, and a good hitting pitcher should only occasionally bunt. This assumes that the defense is expecting a bunt and positions itself accordingly.

The usual qualifications and considerations apply with a pitcher at the plate: the run environment, the bunting proficiency of the batter/pitcher, the speed of the batter/pitcher, and the speed of the runner on first.

What about with one out, a runner on first, and a pitcher at the plate? You can probably guess the answer to that one! Let's look at the numbers just to make sure.

With a runner on first and one out, when a pitcher attempts a sacrifice, we get a total resultant RE of .326 across all innings, which is right around what it would be if we took the out and advanced the runner (.327). In order to figure the RE when a pitcher swings away, we have to employ our *sim* again.

And the computer says . . .

The RE when an average-hitting pitcher swings away with a runner on first and one out is .354, which is substantially higher than when attempting a sacrifice! That does not include the extra hits you would expect with the infield charging.

If we plug a weak-hitting pitcher (wOBA of .124, or about the bottom 15% of all pitchers) into the simulator, we get an RE of .318. With the infielders charging, that increases to around .325, around the same as a bunt attempt!

The Book Says:

With a pitcher at the plate with one out and a runner on first, only the worst-hitting pitchers should bunt, and even then, only about half the time.

The Two-Strike Count

We told you we would get back to the 2-strike count as soon as we looked at pitcher bunting. Conventional wisdom says that with two strikes, a non-pitcher should almost always switch to hitting away and a pitcher should usually continue bunting. Let's see if that is true.

With a pitcher batting with two strikes, if he puts the ball in play on a bunt, the resultant RE is .650. With a non-pitcher at the plate, it is around .705. What else can happen when the batter continues to bunt after two strikes? He can walk, which rarely occurs, or he can strike out on a foul bunt, a called strike, or a missed bunt. A foul third strike occurs 30.3% of the time when a pitcher continues to bunt after two strikes. We will assume that it is the same for a non-pitcher. Throw in a few called third strikes and missed bunts, and it is around 35%. So 65% of the time, we have an RE of .705 and 35% of the time we have an RE of .541 (runner on first and one out), for a total RE of .648. For a pitcher, it is 65% times .650 plus 35% times .541, or a total RE of .612.

Let's compare that to hitting away with two strikes for both a pitcher and non-pitcher. With an 0-2 count, the RE is reduced by around 12% (it seems like it should be more, but it is not; heck, an *out* only reduces it by 40%). So for a non-pitcher, the RE when swinging away with an 0-2 count with a runner on first and no outs is .88 times .906 or .797, far greater than the estimated RE when bunting with two strikes of .648. So, even a poor hitter should swing away with two strikes. This time, conventional wisdom prevails!

For pitchers, remember that an average-hitting pitcher, when hitting away, generates an RE of .686 with a runner on first and no outs. With an 0-2 count, 88% of that is .603. For a pitcher, the reduction in RE with two strikes is probably more than that. Either way, a bunt RE of .612 is better than swinging away with an 0-2 count, for an average or worse hitting pitcher. A good hitting pitcher can swing away with a 2-strike count. What about other 2-strike counts for a pitcher? A 2-2 count is basically neutral for a non-pitcher. For a pitcher, it is probably a little worse than neutral. With a 2-2 count, an average or better pitcher can swing away. With a 1-2 count, only the better hitting pitchers should swing away. This time conventional wisdom is only partially correct!

The Book Says:

With a 2-strike count, all non-pitchers should swing away. With an 0-2 or 1-2 count, the best hitting pitchers should swing away. With a 2-2 count, an average or better hitting pitcher can swing away; the rest should continue bunting. With a 3-2 count, all pitchers (and non-pitchers of course) should swing away.

Other Baserunner Configurations

Now that you know in excruciating detail how we analyze the sacrifice bunt, we'll briefly look at what happens with a runner on second and runners on first and second. We'll start with non-pitchers only, in the context of the modern NL run environment.

With a runner on second and no outs, the standard NL RE table tells us that an average of 1.148 runs are scored when a batter swings away (actually, when a batter swings away *plus* when he bunts). Let's see what happens when the batter attempts a sacrifice. (See Table 115.)

The results are similar to those with a runner on first. As expected, DPs are reduced, as are outs on the runner trying to advance to third. Even though the overall result (RE) is almost exactly the same early in the game as it is late in the game, there are some differences in the individual outcomes. Late in the game, there are more FCs (with the runner safe) and errors, as the defense desperately tries to cut the runner down at third, and there are fewer singles, as the defense is likely playing closer to the plate and charging the bunt more aggressively.

Right away we can see that the total RE from attempting a bunt with a runner on second and no outs, either early or late in the game, is almost, but not quite, equal to the average RE across all PA (1.148). As with a runner on first, it is also quite a bit greater than the RE after an out and runner advance (.987). Late in the game (bottom of the seventh, down a run), if we use the WE rather than RE tables, we get a total WE after attempting a sacrifice of .482 as compared to a WE of .487 before the PA (swinging away). Also close, but no cigar.

Table 115. Bunt Attempt Results, Runner On Second And No Outs

Result after sacrifice attempt	Early (< 7th inning) N=1605 (13.9%)	Late (7th inning or later) N=2910 (15.6%)	All innings N=2422 (14.4%)
Ball bunted in play	65.1%	71.8%	67.4%
Batter and runner safe on a FC	0.7	2.7	1.4
Batter out, runner advances	51.2	53.6	52.0
Batter out, runner does not advance	14.4	11.6	13.5
Runner out, batter safe	2.4	3.2	2.6
DP	0.6	1.1	0.8
BB/HP	2.0	2.0	2.0
K	8.0	8.4	8.2
RBOE	2.9	4.5	3.5
S	16.1	11.5	14.5
D	1.1	1.0	1.1
T	0.1	0.0	0.1
HR	0.5	0.4	0.5
Total RE (in the modern NL)	1.111	1.099	1.107

The Book Says:

With a runner on second and no outs, give the opposing manager the standing offer of taking an out in exchange for the runner advancing to third, unless you are tied or down by a run in the ninth inning or later.

Let's see how the speed and bunting proficiency of the batter affect the results. (See Table 116.)

Table 116.   Bunt Attempt Results, Runner On Second And No Outs,
By Speed And Bunting Proficiency Of Batter

Result after sacrifice attempt	Slow batter N=259 (8.2%)	Fast batter N=790 (27.2%)	Poor bunter N=736 (7.7%)	Good bunter N=889 (33.0%)
Ball bunted in play	61.8%	67.1%	67.7%	66.9%
Batter and runner safe on a FC	2.3	1.4	1.6	1.0
Batter out, runner advances	50.6	48.2	52.9	48.9
Batter out, runner does not advance	16.6	15.3	12.8	15.6
Runner out, batter safe	1.5	2.4	2.3	3.6
DP	1.5	0.4	1.2	0.6
BB/HP	3.1	1.5	2.4	1.9
K	10.4	8.1	9.0	7.2
RBOE	3.1	3.7	3.9	2.8
S	9.3	17.3	12.1	17.0
D	1.5	1.3	1.0	0.9
T	0	0	0	0
HR	0	0.4	0.8	0.4
Total RE (in the modern NL)	1.051	1.125	1.095	1.109

The speed of the batter appears to once again be a significant factor in the success of the sacrifice attempt with a runner on second and no outs, while his bunting proficiency appears to have only a small impact.

As usual, the run environment and inning/score should be considered as well. Other factors that affect the decision are the count as the PA progresses, and the following batter or batters. If the next hitter is a contact hitter (low K), the bunt is more favorable.

When pitchers attempt a sacrifice bunt with a runner on second, which they do over 82% of the time, once again, their results (as expected) are not nearly as good as when a non-pitcher attempts a bunt. The pitcher RE after a sacrifice attempt is only .919, as opposed to 1.107 for an average non-pitcher, primarily because the pitcher rarely singles when bunting, and the runner gets thrown out at third base three times as often as when a non-pitcher bunts. We chalk this up to the defense playing exclusively for the bunt, safe in the knowledge that the pitcher has a 4-in-5 chance of bunting. When an average-hitting pitcher swings away with a runner on second and no outs, he produces an RE of .935 (not including the extra hits from the defense playing up), according to our computer. In fact, when pitchers did hit away from 2000 to 2004, their teams scored an average of 1.001 runs (again, more than likely they were above average-hitting pitchers, the run environment was high, etc.).

The Book Says:

With a runner on second and no outs, an average-hitting pitcher should sacrifice about half the time, a below average-hitting pitcher should sacrifice most of the time, and an above average-hitting pitcher should sacrifice only occasionally. This is the same as with a runner on first and no outs. Pitchers should never sacrifice with a runner on second and one out.

Let's take a quick look at bunt attempts with runners on first and second, for both pitchers and non-pitchers. (See Table 117.) As with a runner on second only, whether it is early or late in the game does not appear to affect the total RE of the sacrifice attempt with runners on first and second. The RE before a bunt attempt is 1.500 (see the NL RE table), so once again, a bunt attempt yields almost the same RE as hitting away.

Let's see the effect of the batter's speed and bunting prowess. (See Table 118.) The results are similar to that with a runner on first only. The speed and bunting proficiency of the batter significantly affect the RE after a sacrifice attempt.

If we use WE rather than RE late in the game, we get .545 before a bunt attempt (bottom of the seventh inning, down by a run) and .538

after. So once again, a sacrifice attempt late in a game is no more advantageous than early in a game.

With a pitcher at the plate, the RE after a bunt attempt is 1.230, again substantially less than with a non-pitcher at the plate. If we plug an average-hitting pitcher into our *sim,* we get an RE of 1.129 when hitting away. A good-hitting pitcher creates an RE of 1.148.

The Book Says:

With runners on first and second and no outs, all but the very best-hitting pitchers should sacrifice most of the time. The best-hitting pitchers should sacrifice about half the time. Pitchers should never sacrifice with runners on first and second and one out.

Table 117.   Bunt Attempt Results, Runners On First And Second And No Outs, Batter Is A Non-Pitcher

Result after sacrifice attempt	Early (< 7th inning) N=1304 (14.9%)	Late (7th inning or later) N=1003 (23.4%)	All innings N=2307 (17.7%)
Ball bunted in play	72.6%	74.9%	73.6%
Batter and runner safe on a FC	1.2	1.5	1.3
Batter out, runner advances	49.7	53.2	51.2
Batter out, runner does not advance	7.4	9.8	8.5
Runner out, batter safe	8.4	8.7	8.5
DP	4.0	3.5	3.8
BB/HP	1.5	1.3	1.4
K	8.0	7.9	7.9
RBOE	4.5	4.6	4.6
S	13.9	8.4	11.5
D	0.7	0.7	0.7
T	0.3	0.1	0.2
HR	0.3	0.4	0.3
Total RE (in the modern NL)	1.476	1.419	1.451

Table 118.   Bunt Attempt Results, Runners On First And Second And No Outs, By Speed And Bunting Proficiency Of Batter (Non-Pitcher)

Result after sacrifice attempt	Slow batter N=332 (13.5%)	Fast batter N=664 (32.3%)	Poor bunter N=864 (10.9%)	Good bunter N=728 (39.4%)
Ball bunted in play	74.7%	72.6%	72.2%	75.0%
Batter and runner safe on a FC	1.2	0.8	1.7	0.8
Batter out, runner advances	50.9	51.7	50.1	53.0
Batter out, runner does not advance	9.0	6.8	8.4	8.4
Runner out, batter safe	9.0	9.0	9.5	7.7
DP	4.5	3.3	5.0	2.9
BB/HP	0.9	2.1	1.0	1.2
K	8.4	8.6	8.8	7.3
RBOE	5.7	3.8	2.9	4.3
S	9.9	12.7	9.8	13.3
D	0.3	0.6	0.6	0.5
T	0	0.5	0.2	0.1
HR	0	0.3	0.2	0.4
Total RE (in the modern NL)	1.406	1.459	1.410	1.471

In general, it appears that a sacrifice with runners on first and second is more advantageous than a sacrifice with a runner on second only. Even though it is more difficult to sacrifice when the runner on second is forced, that appears to be outweighed by the fact that if one of the baserunners is thrown out, the other baserunner still advances. As well, sacrificing with runners on first and second reduces the number of GDPs, as compared to hitting away.

Speaking of GDPs, all other things being equal, the batter should be more inclined to sacrifice with a runner on first or first and second when he has a high GDP rate (adjusted for the pitcher's groundball rate). For example, if two batters had the exact same stat profile, but one batter hit into 25% more DPs per opportunity, his RE with a runner on first and no outs would be .011 runs worse than the other. The difference between players who ground into the most DPs (like Edgar Martinez) and those who ground into the least (like Tony Womack) is around 50%, or .022 runs in RE. Of course, the batter's speed must also be factored into the equation. If a batter has a high GDP rate because he is a slow runner, his RE from bunting is going to be reduced as well.

The Book Says:

With a runner on first or first and second, and no outs, the batter's GDP rate (adjusted for the pitcher) should be considered in deciding whether to bunt or not.

What happens when we split the batters/bunters into two groups again—weak and strong hitters? The results are similar to that with a runner on first only. With a runner on second only and the infield expecting a bunt, the RE from a bunt attempt is around 1.100 runs. With the infield playing back, it is around 1.150, again a substantial difference. With runners on first and second, the RE with the infield up is around 1.430 and 1.550 with the infield playing back. Once again, with a weak hitter at the plate, the infield appears to be playing up both early and late in the game. With a strong hitter (but still a potential bunter), the infield only plays up late in the game.

How does that inform a manager's bunting strategy? As with a runner on first, a runner on first and second, or second only, the decision to sacrifice or not, all other things being equal, depends on the defensive alignment and the quality of the hitter. With the defense playing up, anticipating a bunt early in the game, only the poorest hitters should bunt. With the defense playing back, almost any batter can bunt. Late in the game, with the defense almost surely anticipating a bunt, all but the best hitters can still bunt (a good hitter can bunt if the defense is playing back). As we said, with a runner on first and second, the batter should be more likely to bunt than with a runner on second only, even though it is easier to force the runner at third.

The Book Says:

With a runner on first or first and second, and no outs, late in the game, with the infield playing up, all but the best hitters can bunt. Early in the game, if the infield is expecting a bunt, only the weakest hitters should bunt; if the infield is not expecting a bunt, any batter can bunt. The speed and bunting proficiency of the batter should be considered. Slow/poor bunters should rarely bunt and fast/good bunters can bunt more often.

Finally, we'll take a brief look at runners on first and third. With a non-pitcher at the plate, managers elected to sacrifice with runners on first and third and no outs only 42 times in the last five years, or less than 1% of the time. Some of those may have been suicide or even safety squeezes, although conventional wisdom eschews the suicide squeeze with no outs, and you rarely see the safety squeeze anymore in professional baseball. In any case, when they did attempt a bunt, the resultant RE was 1.697, substantially less than an average RE when swinging away (1.840). Suffice it to say that a bunt attempt by a non-pitcher in this situation is rarely advised and, thankfully, rarely used.

What about pitchers? The RE after a bunt attempt by a pitcher with runners on first and third and no outs was 1.409. They sacrificed 69.4% of the time. Of the 31% of the time that a pitcher did not bunt with runners on first and third and no outs, an average of 1.512 runs actually scored.

What does the computer tell us? The theoretical RE from swinging away with a pitcher at the plate and no outs is 1.493, a little higher than after a sacrifice attempt, and a little less than what actually occurred. This appears to be about a break-even situation.

What about with runners on first and third and *one* out? How often do pitchers attempt a sacrifice bunt (not a squeeze) in this situation? If you guessed 51.8% of the time, you were right again! Let's see if that is too much, too little, or just about right.

The RE after a sacrifice bunt attempt by a pitcher with runners on first and third and one out is .731. The 48% of the time that the pitcher did not bunt, an average of .962 runs were scored, much better than when sacrificing. Once again, these non-bunts were probably by the better hitting pitchers, and the defense was probably somewhat taken by surprise. Still, that is an awfully large difference. Turning to our trusty computer, let's see what the theoretical RE looks like when an average-hitting pitcher swings away in this situation. The RE from an average-hitting pitcher swinging away is 1.15 runs! That is over .4 runs better than a sacrifice attempt. Apparently managers are bunting way too frequently in this situation. In fact, this is one of the worst (most costly) strategies a manager can employ—having the pitcher sacrifice with runners on first and third and one out.

The Book Says:

With a runner on first and third and one out, rarely (if ever) sacrifice with a pitcher at the plate! With no outs, an average-hitting pitcher can sacrifice about half the time, a poor-hitting pitcher can sacrifice most of the time, and a good-hitting pitcher should rarely sacrifice. Again, the groundball tendencies (GDP rate) of the batter and opposing pitcher can be taken into consideration.

Close Games in the Ninth Inning

So far, with one exception, when we were talking about late in the game, we were talking about the seventh inning or later. In fact, we were using the WE tables for the bottom of the seventh inning down by a run in order to analyze and determine proper late-inning strategy. What about later in the game than that? What about, for example, the ninth inning of a tie game? Conventional wisdom says that a sacrifice by anyone other than a real slugger is almost mandatory in that situation. In fact, between 2000 and 2004, in the ninth inning or later of a tie game, teams attempted a sacrifice 54.1% of the time with a runner on first and no outs. Of course, the pool of players who come to bat in this situation includes players like Barry Bonds, Frank Thomas, and Manny Ramirez, among others, who virtually never bunt. If we eliminate all players with a wOBA over .340 from the equation, that 54.1% jumps to 81.5%. Even then, the 18.5% who did not sacrifice had an average wOBA of .325 while the 81.5% who bunted had a combined wOBA of .298. So, virtually all of the weaker batters and most of the non-sluggers were called on to bunt. With a runner on second or first and second, and a .340 or worse batter at the plate, teams sacrificed 71.1% of the time (bunters' wOBA was .294; non-bunters' was .319).

Since we *know* that it only takes one run to win in the bottom of the ninth (or later) of a tied game, is it in fact correct to bunt almost everyone who has a wOBA of less than .340? The problem, as you might expect, is that it is extremely difficult to sacrifice in the ninth inning of a tied game, with the defense breathing down your neck. In addition, with the opposing team expecting almost nothing *but* a bunt, hitting away becomes that much more productive. Let's compare the results of a bunt attempt early in a game, in the seventh and eighth innings, and in the ninth inning of a tied game, with a runner on first and no outs. (See Table 119.)

As you can see, bunting is indeed more difficult in the ninth inning of a tied game than in the seventh or eighth inning (even though the runner advances on an out more often) and exceedingly more difficult than early in the game, as you would expect. The net result is that an average batter who bunts (a slightly worse hitter than a league-average batter) achieves a greater WE from hitting away than from attempting a sacrifice, even in the bottom of the ninth inning of a tied game. Without going through the numbers, the results are similar with a runner on second or on first and second.

Finally, although pitchers rarely come to the plate in the ninth inning or later, all but the best hitting pitchers should bunt.

Table 119.   Bunt Attempt Results, Runner On First And No Outs, By Inning And Score

Result after sacrifice attempt	Less than 7th inning, any score (6.9%)	7th or 8th inning, any score (13.9%)	9th inning, tied game (54.1%)
Ball bunted in play	64.5%	76.9%	80.4%
Batter and runner safe on a FC	0.4	0.8	0.9
Batter out, runner advances	42.9	54.7	59.7
Batter out, no runner advance	11.2	10.2	7.9
Runner out, batter safe	6.7	9.3	9.4
DP	5.3	4.0	3.8
BB/HP	1.2	1.2	2.3
K	7.6	7.1	8.1
RBOE	2.8	4.3	3.3
S	19.5	7.5	4.0
D	1.7	0.6	0.5
T	0.2	0.1	0
HR	0.6	0.2	0.3
Total RE (in the modern NL)	.876	.763	.743
Total WE (bottom of the ninth, tied)	.716	.701	.696

WE in the bottom of the ninth, tied game, runner on first and no outs (hitting away) = .715

The Book Says:

In the ninth inning of a close game, below average hitters should bunt most of the time, given typical speed and bunting ability. Average hitters should bunt about half the time. Above average hitters should rarely bunt. The speed of the lead runner appears to be a significant factor in the success or failure of the sacrifice attempt in the ninth inning, and as always, the speed and bunting proficiency of the batter should be strongly considered.

SUMMARY

If you were expecting a nice, tidy set of rules, such as, "It is rarely correct to sacrifice bunt in this day and age," or, "A bunt is only warranted in the late innings of a close game," you are probably disappointed. Unfortunately, or fortunately, depending upon your point of view, analyzing the efficacy of the sacrifice bunt in the various situations is so complex and difficult and the results are often so close, that we can offer only a few clear-cut rules of thumb and a myriad of recommendations built on somewhat shaky foundations.

We do hope, however, that you now have a clearer understanding of what factors should be considered when a manager makes a decision to sacrifice or not. Of course, it's not like a manager has more than an instant or two to make that decision, so we would hope that you might cut your favorite or not-so-favorite manager some slack when his speedy, good-bunting number-two hitter sacrifices in the first inning. Of course, the next time you see Woody Williams or Livan Hernandez (good-hitting pitchers) square to bunt with a runner on first and one out, or you see a batter on your favorite team continue to sacrifice with a 3-0 count, shake your head, and hope for the best.

CHAPTER 10 – BOOTS WERE MADE FOR WALKING

Of all of the statistics that Barry Bonds has piled up in the last few seasons, perhaps the most impressive is the number 120—the number of times he was intentionally walked in 2004. For comparison, the largest number of intentional walks awarded in a season to anyone else was 45 to Willie McCovey in 1969 (at least since the statistic began being tracked in 1955); even Bonds had been intentionally walked at most 68 times in a season prior to 2004 (including 35 intentional walks in his home run record-breaking 2001 season). The reason we find this to be so impressive is that the other stats show Bonds's skills—what happens if a pitcher challenges him—but the number of intentional walks shows just how much he has changed the way that managers approach the game of baseball. In effect, Bonds forced teams to rewrite *The Book*.

We actually feel that the recent changes to *The Book* on intentional walks have done us a favor. There isn't a lot in the way of age-old conventional wisdom on this topic (or, more correctly, the conventional wisdom is conflicting), but instead, the fact that managers have been changing their criteria for issuing intentional walks means that there is some openness to some new analysis. So let's have a look.

Before we plow you under with numbers, let's remind ourselves of the reasons a manager might call for an intentional walk. With less than two outs, a man on second or third, and first base open, a walk will set up a double play (and potentially a force on the lead runner). An intentional walk can also let you pick the hitter you pitch to—either to avoid pitching to a very good hitter, or to skip the #8 hitter in a NL lineup to get to the pitcher. Naturally, combining these makes the walk even more attractive—for example, with one out, a man on second, and Bonds at the plate, walking Bonds would set up a potential double play, set up a force at third, and avoid letting Bonds bat.

Of course, each of these arguments has its counter. In the first case, a walk will force your pitcher to throw the ball over the plate to the next batter to avoid a subsequent (unintentional) walk, which may result in a higher probability of the next batter hitting well. If you're walking an outstanding hitter, you're still adding a baserunner (and thus setting up a more dangerous situation), and you are also making it likely that he will come up sooner the next time through the batting order. Likewise by walking the #8 hitter, you're putting a guy on base that probably would have gotten out anyway and missing the chance of having the pitcher lead off the next inning.

For the sake of simplicity, we'll first examine situations in which all batters in a lineup are equal, in order to see if there are any game situations in which a walk is generally beneficial to the pitching team. After that, we'll examine more realistic situations in which we're contemplating walking a better hitter to get to a worse one.

INTENTIONAL WALK SITUATIONS

We first turn our attention to situations in which the score, outs, inning, baserunners, etc., call for an intentional walk if the opposing lineup contains nine identical players. Specifically, in what base/out situations would you want to walk the current batter and pitch to an equivalent one? The answers are pretty straightforward. It should be obvious that you would never want to advance the lead runner, which eliminates half of the base states (bases empty, man on first, men on first and second, and bases loaded). As an aside, we note that this isn't *exactly* the same as first base being open. One could issue a walk with men on first and third and not advance the lead runner; likewise issuing a walk with the bases empty would advance the lead runner (in this case, the batter).

The main situational reasons for walking a batter (i.e., reasons unrelated to avoiding a better hitter) would be to set up a double play or a force on the lead runner. Neither of these reasons makes sense when there are two outs—the double play is impossible, and only the force out at first is needed—so we can probably focus merely on the zero- and one-out states.

Now let's test our intuition against the numbers. You will recall that the *Toolshed* chapter contains the number of runs a team can expect to score from any base/out state. Since we know the result of a walk—for example, bases empty becomes a man on first—we can fairly easily calculate the change in run expectancy as the result of a walk. Here is the table for all 24 base/out states. (See Table 120.)

Table 120.   Runs Gained From Walk

Bases Occupied	0 Outs	1 Out	2 Outs
2B, 3B	0.362	0.217	0.175
2B	0.393	0.263	0.119
Empty	0.397	0.273	0.129
3B	0.424	0.251	0.154
1B, 3B	0.570	0.422	0.260
1B	0.633	0.417	0.217
1B, 2B	0.853	0.686	0.339
1B, 2B, 3B	1.000	1.000	1.000

The first item of note is that every value in the table is positive. This means that the walk is *always* beneficial to the batting team (again, assuming average batters and pitchers) if we're just focusing on run expectancy. The second item of note is that the swings are biggest with no outs and smallest with two outs. This doesn't mean you should walk batters with two outs; it merely reflects the fact that run expectancy swings are smaller with two outs since the next batter is always more likely than not to make an out, ending the inning.

Now let's take a look at the numbers. It should come as no surprise that walking in a run costs your team exactly one run, and thus bases loaded is the worst situation in which to issue an intentional walk (or even an unintentional one). Next worst is when there are men on first and second, and the walk advances both of them. In general, we see that the batting team picks up the most runs from the walk when there is a man on first base, giving support to the philosophy of only issuing the walk when first is open.

This still leaves us with the "first base open" situations. However, even in these cases, the best a walk can do is give away .119 runs, so why are we even going over this? The answer is simple. Baseball is about wins and losses, not number of runs scored. Naturally, scoring runs helps you win, but if you've got a lead in the ninth, what matters is the probability of preserving the lead, not the expected number of runs allowed. Or if you're tied in the bottom of the ninth, the only statistic of significance is the probability of escaping the inning without allowing a run.

Once again, we refer you to the *Toolshed* chapter, where our discussion of Markov chains included a table listing the probability of scoring 0, 1, 2, 3, 4, or 5+ runs from any of the 24 base/out states. From that table, we see that if there are men on second and third and one out, there is a 30.2% chance of not scoring, a 28.5% chance of scoring one run, a 22.4% chance of scoring twice, and an 18.9% chance of scoring three or more runs. By issuing a walk to load the bases, these numbers turn into 31.8%, 25.3%, 15.5%, and 27.4%, respectively. In other words, we increase the chance of escaping the inning scoreless by 1.6%, but also greatly enhance the odds of giving up a big inning. Thus the expected number of runs allowed will go up—but if it's a tied game in the bottom of the ninth, all that matters is the fact that you're also increasing the likelihood of preserving the tie. Assuming that you have a 50-50 chance of winning a game in extra innings, the increase of 1.6% in the odds of making it into extra innings gives a 0.8% increased chance of winning the game.

Actually, we could have calculated the 0.8% number more easily, by looking at the win probability tables. In a tied game in the bottom of the ninth, a batting team with runners on second and third and one out has an 84.9% chance of winning. Walk the batter to load the bases, and this *drops* to 84.1%, an improvement of 0.8% for the pitching team. Unfortunately, only about once in 275 games does one find it tied in the bottom of the ninth with runners on second and third and one out. And with the increased odds of 0.8% of the fielding team winning, a manager would need to manage 34,000 home games—and presumably 68,000 total games—for this piece of knowledge to win one extra game!

There is only one other situation in which the pitching team's win probability will increase as a result of the walk (all batters being equal). Again with one out, but this time with a man on third only, the batting team's win probability is 83.5%. After the walk, it's 83.2%, an improvement of 0.3% for the pitching team. As you might guess, having a baserunner only on third is not all that common, and happens with one out in the bottom of the ninth in a tied game about once every 260 games. Thus you would have to manage something like 86,000 home games (172,000 total games) to win one extra game using this tactic.

OK, so as a situational coaching tool (i.e., with all batters equal and just looking for game situations in which a walk is profitable), intentional walks aren't terribly useful. If you use the "optimal strategy" of issuing intentional walks *only* with a man on third, possibly on second, and first base open with one out in a tied game in the bottom of the ninth, you will win one extra game every 49,000 or so games you manage. Now we're all for playing the odds, but unless you're planning on having a 300-year career, you might as well just forget about intentional walks as a situational tool in this scenario. There are probably more useful things for you to spend your time worrying about.

The Book Says:

If all batters have equal ability, intentionally walking a batter to set up a double play, force, or other situation is at best a break-even move (or insignificantly better than a break-even move). Doing so early in a game is counterproductive, since it increases the odds of a big inning more than it increases the odds of a scoreless inning.

ANATOMY OF A WALK

Reading the last section, you may be wondering how some of these "truths" can be correct. For example, back to our simplest possible situation—a tied game in the bottom of the ninth. The pitching team's only goal is to escape without allowing any runs; so if the lead runner is on third, what does it matter who is behind him? If anything, additional baserunners merely give additional chances to get someone out, and possibly set up a double play and/or force at home plate.

The numbers say otherwise. From the run probability tables (again from the *Toolshed* chapter), here are the odds of getting out of an inning without issuing a run for each base/out state. (See Table 121.)

Table 121.   Odds Of Scoreless Inning

Bases Occupied	0 Outs	1 Out	2 Outs
Empty	.703	.824	.922
1B	.557	.713	.865
2B	.367	.586	.774
1B, 2B	.353	.566	.767
3B	.141	.330	.732
1B, 3B	.125	.336	.709
2B, 3B	.133	.302	.721
1B, 2B, 3B	.125	.318	.670

What is intriguing is that, regardless of the number of outs, you're better off with a runner on second than with runners on first and second. Likewise, you're better off with a runner only on third than with runners on third and other bases.

Once again, this might be counterintuitive since the lead runner is the winning run; so it really shouldn't matter what happens behind him, right? And, even better, filling the bases behind him gives the possibility of a force and/or double play—meaning that we should be *better off* with the bases filled up behind the lead runner. Let's take a look at MLB average batting statistics when the bases are loaded with two outs, compared with when runners are on first and third with two outs. (See Table 122.)

Table 122.   Average Batting Stats (Normalized To 600 Non-IBB PA)

Situation	PA	1B	2B	3B	HR	NIBB	HBP	RBOE	SO	Other Outs
Loaded	56466	92	24	5	14	45	4	7	94	315
1B, 3B	77733	97	24	4	13	49	4	7	86	316

What's noteworthy in this table is that the two stat lines aren't all that different. Specifically, pitchers are almost as likely to issue unintentional walks with the bases loaded as they are when runners are on first and third. This is the reason that these two situations are not equivalent, in terms of scoring the lead runner—a walk with men on first and third loads the bases, while a walk with the bases loaded will score a run.

In short, putting yourself in a situation in which even a *subsequent* walk would advance the lead runner is a bad idea. The fact that these are exactly the same situations in which the lead runner can be forced out explains why setting up a force on the lead runner is generally unwise.

The Book Says:

Walking a batter to set up a force on the lead runner is dangerous. While it does allow the possibility of the force, it also means that the lead runner would advance on a subsequent (presumably un-intentional) walk.

WALKING GREAT HITTERS

In reality, of course, intentional walks are generally issued when the on-deck hitter is worse than the current batter. The most notable case is Barry Bonds, who of course is much better than the on-deck hitter, regardless of who that may be. But let's explore the more general question. How good does a player have to be to warrant an intentional walk—or at least how much better than his teammates (specifically, the on-deck hitter) must he be?

Before we start looking at the numbers, let's clarify what will and will not be considered in this section. For now, let's assume that all of the batter's teammates are average hitters with a wOBA of .335, and that the pitcher, defense, ballpark, and all other factors are average. We will discuss these factors later. We also note that matchup-specific effects such as platoon ratios, groundball vs. flyball hitters and pitchers, etc., must have already been taken into account. In other words, when we are discussing a .400 hitter, what we mean is a hitter who is expected to have a wOBA of .400 in the present at-bat rather than someone who is expected to have a wOBA of .400 over the course of a season.

Initially, let's examine the simplest possible situation, in which a player has eight teammates, all of whom are exactly league-average players. In other words, following the player's at-bat, the team can be expected to score like an average team. How does this affect our tables above? In this table, we give the change in run expectancy (RE) following a walk as a function of the batter's wOBA and the current base/out state. (See Table 123.)

We computed these values for three possible wOBA values of the batter, again with all eight teammates assigned a wOBA of .335. The first set of values (wOBA=.400) corresponds to a very good player, such as Berkman, Glaus, Helton, Chipper Jones, followed by average hitters. This is the sort of situation one might come across rather frequently. The second chart corresponds to an elite, unprotected hitter, such as Pujols. (We will use the term "unprotected" to mean "followed by average hitters.") Given the small number of such hitters and the low odds that such a hitter would not be protected, it seems unlikely that this chart would be useful. The third set of numbers represents an extreme case that one is unlikely to ever face. It would be equivalent to Barry Bonds in his best-ever season, again with no protection.

Table 123.   Effect Of Walk On Run Expectancy

Bases Occupied	Outs	.400 wOBA	.465 wOBA	.530 wOBA
Empty	0	.349	.300	.251
1B	0	.553	.473	.393
2B	0	.329	.264	.200
1B, 2B	0	.750	.647	.554
3B	0	.361	.298	.235
1B, 3B	0	.473	.377	.280
2B, 3B	0	.278	.193	.109
1B, 2B, 3B	0	.873	.745	.618
Empty	1	.238	.203	.169
1B	1	.349	.281	.213
2B	1	.197	.131	.065
1B, 2B	1	.579	.472	.365
3B	1	.187	.123	.059
1B, 3B	1	.324	.226	.128
2B, 3B	1	.138	.059	-.020
1B, 2B, 3B	1	.857	.714	.571
Empty	2	.107	.085	.062
1B	2	.170	.124	.078
2B	2	.059	-.004	-.065
1B, 2B	2	.251	.163	.075
3B	2	.086	.019	-.048
1B, 3B	2	.162	.063	-.035
2B, 3B	2	.071	-.033	-.137
1B, 2B, 3B	2	.850	.699	.548

From the change in run expectancy, it is fairly clear to see that intentional walks should be reserved for very special circumstances. In situations an opposing team is likely to see frequently (wOBA=.400), issuing the walk always increases the expected number of runs. Even in the case of facing an elite hitter (wOBA=.465) with no protection, one would need two outs, a man on second, and first base open. For the least likely (and thus largely irrelevant) case—the Bonds case—one can issue the walk any time there are two outs and the walk would not advance the lead runner, or with one out and men on second and third.

Let's compare this to what managers actually did. This table gives the percentage of plate appearances in which the batter was intentionally walked in 2000–2004, not counting #8 hitters or ninth inning or later at-bats. (See Table 124.)

Table 124.   Fraction Of Plate Appearances That Were IBB

Runners	No Outs	1 Out	2 Outs
Empty	0.0%	0.0%	0.0%
1B	0.0	0.0	0.0
2B	0.3	2.9	4.7
1B, 2B	0.0	0.0	0.1
3B	0.2	3.2	2.8
1B, 3B	0.0	0.1	0.2
2B, 3B	3.1	15.8	8.5
1B, 2B, 3B	0.0	0.0	0.0

The chart shows some good news and some bad news, in terms of evaluating managers. First the good news: the most common situation for intentional walks (one out, runners on second and third) is indeed one of the four situations in which intentional walks can be a good idea if the batter is significantly better than the following hitters. And the other three (two outs, runners on second and/or third) are also situations in which managers issue the walk a non-negligible fraction of the time.

We also find that, for the most part, managers walk the right hitters. For example, with men on second and third and two outs, we estimate that the wOBA of the current batter needs to be at least 14% higher than that of the following hitters to justify the walk. And indeed, when the current batter is that good, he is walked 26% of the time, compared with just 7% when he isn't significantly better than the following hitters.

Unfortunately, we also see that managers are relatively comfortable issuing walks with no outs and men on second and third, one out and a man on second, and one out and a man on third. In none of these situations is a walk *ever* recommended early in the game—even in the extreme case with Bonds at his best at the plate, and league-average hitters behind him.

The Book Says:

Issuing an intentional walk to an outstanding hitter will almost always increase the opposing team's run production. The only base/out situation in which a walk reduces the run expectancy is when there are men on second and third, two outs, and an unprotected elite (Pujols-like) hitter at the plate.

BOTTOM OF THE NINTH

Now let's take a look at the bottom of the ninth inning, when all that matters is giving up fewer than a specific number of runs. For example, if you have a one-run lead and give up two runs, you might as well give up four runs since you lose either way. To account for this, we now list the effect of a walk on the odds of scoring one or more, two or more, or three or more runs. (See Table 125.)

From this table, we see that if a scoreless inning is the primary concern, there are many more opportunities to profitably issue walks. Even for our "common" case of an unprotected hitter with wOBA of .400, we see that it is generally OK to issue the intentional walk any time that doing so will not advance the lead runner.

Table 125.   Effect Of Walk On Scoring Probabilities

Bases	Outs	.400 wOBA			.465 wOBA			.530 wOBA		
		1+	2+	3+	1+	2+	3+	1+	2+	3+
Empty	0	.124	.111	.059	.100	.098	.052	.077	.085	.046
1B	0	.171	.139	.120	.141	.116	.107	.111	.092	.093
2B	0	-.007	.115	.108	-.028	.095	.096	-.049	.074	.084
1B, 2B	0	.201	.171	.131	.174	.142	.109	.146	.113	.087
3B	0	.006	.123	.113	-.006	.100	.099	-.018	.076	.085
1B, 3B	0	-.011	.140	.115	-.021	.108	.090	-.032	.076	.064
2B, 3B	0	-.003	-.008	.088	-.013	-.034	.066	-.024	-.060	.044
1B, 2B, 3B	0	.112	.217	.177	.099	.186	.145	.086	.154	.114
Empty	1	.093	.082	.036	.074	.073	.032	.055	.064	.028
1B	1	.116	.089	.082	.086	.069	.072	.055	.049	.062
2B	1	-.010	.076	.074	-.041	.058	.064	-.072	.039	.055
1B, 2B	1	.206	.128	.093	.165	.098	.074	.124	.068	.054
3B	1	-.031	.083	.075	-.057	.063	.065	-.083	.043	.055
1B, 3B	1	-.011	.107	.086	-.040	.076	.065	-.068	.044	.044
2B, 3B	1	-.036	-.014	.068	-.054	-.043	.051	-.073	-.072	.035
1B, 2B, 3B	1	.286	.210	.124	.254	.168	.093	.222	.126	.062
Empty	2	.043	.043	.014	.028	.038	.012	.013	.033	.010
1B	2	.072	.038	.041	.046	.024	.036	.020	.010	.032
2B	2	-.033	.036	.037	-.074	.022	.032	-.115	.009	.028
1B, 2B	2	.052	.087	.047	.008	.063	.034	-.036	.039	.021
3B	2	-.024	.048	.041	-.071	.034	.036	-.117	.021	.032
1B, 3B	2	-.010	.071	.040	-.061	.045	.026	-.112	.019	.012
2B, 3B	2	.006	-.027	.038	-.039	-.067	.026	-.085	-.106	.013
1B, 2B, 3B	2	.609	.049	.083	.549	.004	.058	.488	.041	.033

If you have a one-run lead, the question becomes that of giving up (preferably) zero runs, and definitely no more than one run. In other words, if you give up zero runs, you win. If you give up one run, you go into extra innings (and have a 50% chance of winning). And if you give up two or more runs, you lose. So the change in win expectancy is related to the average of the "1+" and "2+" columns above. In this situation, walks can be safely issued when there are men on second and third (regardless of the number of outs) for any of the three batter wOBA cases in this table. With two outs, one can also issue the walk to an unprotected, elite batter when doing so does not advance the lead runner.

With a two-run lead, the only viable intentional walk situation exists with men on second and third, two outs, and an unprotected, elite hitter.

The Book Says:

When tied in the bottom of the ninth, a team can issue an intentional walk to any unprotected star hitter, provided that doing so does not advance the lead runner. With a one-run lead, an unprotected star hitter can be walked whenever there are men on second and third (with any number of outs).

OTHER LATE INNINGS

So far, we've taken care of the two "easy" cases—early in a game, when run expectancy is equivalent to winning probability, and in the bottom of the ninth, when you know exactly how many runs you can afford to give up. What about other late-inning situations?

Unfortunately (for those who love intentional walks), the effect of a walk in *any* late inning other than the bottom of the ninth is similar to early-game situations. The reason is that your team will always have at least one chance to score, and if you do score, you're most likely to score one run, second-most likely to score two runs, and so on. In other words, the more runs you give up, the lower your chance of winning, and thus, for the most part, we revert to caring primarily about run expectancy.

However, the "for the most part" of the last sentence hides a few special cases. From the bottom of the sixth inning onwards, a walk can be safely issued when the pitching team is trailing or tied, there is one out, men on second and third, and an unprotected star hitter (wOBA=.400) is at the plate. The threshold for how good this hitter must be decreases slowly, so that by the bottom of the eighth and top of the ninth he needs to have a wOBA of only .370.

The second special case is that, in the bottom of the eighth and top of the ninth, an unprotected hitter whose wOBA is .390 or higher can be walked with two outs, a man on second, and when the pitching team is trailing or tied.

Other walk situations are available for unprotected hitters with wOBA values of .450 or higher, but this situation is sufficiently rare that we will not describe these in detail at the moment.

The Book Says:

In general, intentional walk decisions before the bottom of the ninth are similar to those early in the game, since minimizing runs allowed is more important than giving up fewer than a specific number of runs. However, some situations do give good opportunities for intentional walks. The most profitable is when there is one out, men on second and third, and the pitching team is trailing or tied.

RUN-SCORING ENVIRONMENT

All of the above calculations assume that the run-scoring environment is typical of major league averages in the last few seasons. In other words, based on the opposing pitcher, fielders, ballpark, weather, etc., average hitters would expect to score an average number of runs.

We have redone the calculations above for several run environments, ranging from unrealistically low (1.25 runs per game) to unrealistically high (14 runs per game). While we do find that intentional walks are favored more in high-scoring environments and less favored in low-scoring environments, this doesn't change the rules we've laid out thus far. The key factor for determining whether or not to walk a batter is how good that batter is, relative to his teammates. We examine the effect of teammates in the following section.

The Book Says:

The decision to walk or not is almost completely unaffected by the quality of the pitcher and defense, ballpark effects, or other aspects of the run-scoring environment.

ON-DECK AND LATER HITTERS

In our above calculations, we assumed that all eight of the batter's teammates are league-average hitters. Naturally this is not true. And if the batter being considered for an intentional walk is the best on his team, he has likely been given some "protection" in the form of an above-average hitter behind him in the lineup. As well, good hitters tend to be *bunched up* in a typical lineup.

The idea of protection is that, if the on-deck hitter is a poor hitter, the opposing team will be happy to walk the batter and pitch to the on-deck hitter, even though there is an extra man on base. However, if the on-deck hitter is sufficiently good that he is more dangerous with an extra runner than the batter is in the current game situation, the pitcher will have to pitch to the current batter. (Naturally, this need not be in the form of an intentional walk; generally an unprotected hitter will be pitched around, and thus given fewer hittable pitches and more unintentional walks. We discuss "pitching around" hitters at the end of the chapter.)

To calculate this effect, we have recomputed the above table, but with the on-deck hitter midway between the batter's wOBA and the league-average wOBA. In other words, the .400 hitter is protected by a .367 hitter, the .465 hitter is protected by a .400 hitter, etc.

We find that, when there are zero or one outs, the on-deck hitter's skill matters very little. It may make a particular IBB situation less attractive, but will rarely turn an IBB situation into a non-IBB situation. This should not come as a huge surprise, given that with less than two outs, at least one or two subsequent hitters are expected to come to the plate anyway, whether you walk the current batter or not (barring a double play of course). In other words, what matters with one out is probably something like the average of the next two hitters, and with no outs it is probably something like the average of the next three.

When there are two outs, the on-deck hitter is likely to be the final out of the inning, and thus his batting skill matters a great deal when deciding on the intentional walk or not. Let's see how this affects our "tie game, bottom of the ninth" walk rules. For the level of protection we are assuming, we find that a star (wOBA of .400) hitter protected by a .367 hitter should be walked in all of the situations recommended above except when there are two outs and men on first and third. For this particular situation, the protection changes the 1.0% *decrease* in scoring probability into a 1.6% *increase*. Similarly, an elite (wOBA of .465) hitter protected by a .400 hitter can be walked in all of the situations previously recommended, except when there are two outs and men on second and third.

What about for other skill levels of the on-deck hitter, or what if there are fewer than two outs? One can easily see this getting ugly, especially with the no-out case. Instead of just worrying about how much better the current batter is than the on-deck hitter, one has to worry about how much better he is than the next *three*, whether or not the on-deck hitter is better or worse than the one behind him, if the third hitter is perhaps the best of the bunch, and so on.

Fortunately, we can make an approximation here and merely calculate the net effect of the next few batters rather than the individual effects of each of the subsequent batters. We call this the *teammate wOBA*. Based on what we said above, you will probably guess that when there are two outs, this value is pretty much equal to the on-deck hitter's wOBA. And when there are zero or one outs, this value is mostly a weighted average of the next three or two batters' wOBA, respectively. Here is how these *teammate wOBA* numbers are calculated exactly:

no outs : $.30 \times \text{wOBA1} + .29 \times \text{wOBA2} + .29 \times \text{wOBA3} + .12 \times \text{wOBA4}$

one out : $.44 \times \text{wOBA1} + .44 \times \text{wOBA2} + .12 \times \text{wOBA3}$

two outs : $.85 \times \text{wOBA1} + .15 \times \text{wOBA2}$

In the above equations, wOBA1 is the wOBA of the on-deck hitter; while wOBA2, wOBA3, and wOBA4 are the wOBA of the three following hitters. In all three cases, the *teammate wOBA* is mostly an average of the minimum number of batters we expect to see (double plays notwithstanding), plus a small amount of the following hitter.

The Book Says:

With no outs, the following three batters will probably all bat following a walk, and thus the abilities of all three should be considered equally when deciding whether or not to issue a walk. With one out, the following two batters should be considered equally. Only when there are two outs is the decision to walk the current batter primarily a function of the skill difference between the batter and on-deck hitter.

The beauty of defining *teammate wOBA* is that, in determining the usefulness of an intentional walk, we can boil everything down to a single value: the current batter's wOBA divided by the *teammate wOBA*. The columns in the previously-presented tables ("Effect of Walk on . . .") correspond to ratios of 1.19, 1.39, and 1.58, respectively. In the following table, we provide the minimum ratio of batter wOBA to *teammate wOBA* that justifies an intentional walk. (See Table 126.) If a particular game situation either is not listed or has no value showing, an intentional walk should never be issued. Note that "behind" and "ahead" refer to the pitching team.

This table summarizes all of the results we have presented thus far in this chapter. We see, for example, that intentional walks should probably never be issued with no outs (except for the special case of the bottom of the ninth), as it is only recommended with runners on second and third, late in the game, and with an elite hitter at the plate without protection.

With one out, walks should never be issued when doing so would advance the lead runner (the bases are empty, there is a man on first, men on first and second, or bases loaded). The only *really* good walk situation with one out (and not in the bottom of the ninth) is when there are men on second and third (you may notice this situation is a recurring theme in this chapter). In this situation, being in the later innings of a game or having a better hitter at the plate makes the walk a better option, to the extent that a team trailing or tied in the top of the ninth only needs to have a wOBA ratio of around 1.08 to justify the walk.

With two outs, once again we see that walks are never justified when the lead runner would be advanced. One should generally be cautious about issuing a walk with men on first and third, but the other three possible baserunner combinations (second, third, and second and third) give ample opportunities for issuing walks when the wOBA ratio exceeds 1.2 and your team is trailing, tied, or leading by a run or two. A final feature of this table worth noting is that intentional walks are generally more valuable when the pitching team is behind than when they are ahead. (Managers already know this—from 2000 through 2004, 57% of intentional walks came when the pitching team trailed and 33% came in tied games.)

Table 126.   Minimum wOBA Ratio For Intentional Walks

			Runs Behind					Tie	Runs Ahead				
Inning	Bases	Outs	5	4	3	2	1	Tie	1	2	3	4	5
Top 1	-23	1	1.30	1.32	1.34	1.37	1.40	-	-	-	-	-	-
Top 1	-2-	2	1.28	1.29	1.30	1.32	1.34	1.36	1.39	-	-	-	-
Top 1	--3	2	1.35	1.36	1.37	1.39	-	-	-	-	-	-	-
Top 1	-23	2	1.26	1.26	1.27	1.28	1.29	1.30	1.32	1.34	1.36	1.38	-
Btm 1	-23	1	1.28	1.29	1.32	1.34	1.37	-	-	-	-	-	-
Btm 1	-2-	2	1.27	1.28	1.29	1.31	1.32	1.34	1.37	-	-	-	-
Btm 1	--3	2	1.33	1.34	1.36	1.37	1.39	-	-	-	-	-	-
Btm 1	-23	2	1.25	1.26	1.26	1.27	1.28	1.29	1.31	1.33	1.35	1.37	1.40
Top 2	-23	1	1.28	1.30	1.32	1.35	1.38	-	-	-	-	-	-
Top 2	-2-	2	1.27	1.28	1.29	1.31	1.33	1.35	1.38	-	-	-	-
Top 2	--3	2	1.34	1.35	1.36	1.38	1.40	-	-	-	-	-	-
Top 2	-23	2	1.26	1.26	1.27	1.27	1.28	1.29	1.31	1.33	1.36	1.39	-
Btm 2	-23	1	1.26	1.27	1.29	1.32	1.35	1.39	-	-	-	-	-
Btm 2	-2-	2	1.26	1.27	1.28	1.29	1.31	1.33	1.36	-	-	-	-
Btm 2	--3	2	1.33	1.34	1.35	1.36	1.38	-	-	-	-	-	-
Btm 2	1-3	2	1.39	-	-	-	-	-	-	-	-	-	-
Btm 2	-23	2	1.25	1.25	1.26	1.27	1.27	1.28	1.30	1.32	1.35	1.38	-
Top 3	-23	1	1.26	1.28	1.30	1.33	1.36	-	-	-	-	-	-
Top 3	-2-	2	1.26	1.27	1.29	1.30	1.32	1.35	1.39	-	-	-	-
Top 3	--3	2	1.33	1.34	1.35	1.37	1.39	-	-	-	-	-	-
Top 3	1-3	2	1.40	-	-	-	-	-	-	-	-	-	-
Top 3	-23	2	1.25	1.26	1.26	1.27	1.28	1.29	1.31	1.34	1.37	-	-
Btm 3	-23	1	1.24	1.25	1.27	1.30	1.33	1.37	-	-	-	-	-
Btm 3	-2-	2	1.25	1.26	1.27	1.28	1.30	1.33	1.36	-	-	-	-
Btm 3	--3	2	1.31	1.32	1.34	1.35	1.37	1.39	-	-	-	-	-
Btm 3	1-3	2	1.38	1.39	-	-	-	-	-	-	-	-	-
Btm 3	-23	2	1.24	1.25	1.25	1.26	1.27	1.28	1.30	1.32	1.36	1.39	-
Top 4	-23	1	1.24	1.25	1.28	1.30	1.33	1.38	-	-	-	-	-
Top 4	-2-	2	1.25	1.26	1.27	1.28	1.30	1.33	1.37	-	-	-	-
Top 4	--3	2	1.31	1.32	1.33	1.35	1.37	1.40	-	-	-	-	-
Top 4	1-3	2	1.38	1.39	-	-	-	-	-	-	-	-	-
Top 4	-23	2	1.24	1.25	1.25	1.26	1.27	1.28	1.30	1.33	1.37	-	-

Inning	Bases	Outs	Runs Behind						Runs Ahead				
			5	4	3	2	1	Tie	1	2	3	4	5
Btm 4	-23	1	1.21	1.22	1.24	1.27	1.30	1.33	1.39	-	-	-	-
Btm 4	-2-	2	1.23	1.24	1.25	1.27	1.28	1.30	1.35	-	-	-	-
Btm 4	--3	2	1.30	1.31	1.32	1.33	1.35	1.37	-	-	-	-	-
Btm 4	1-3	2	1.37	1.38	1.39	1.40	-	-	-	-	-	-	-
Btm 4	-23	2	1.24	1.24	1.25	1.25	1.26	1.27	1.28	1.31	1.36	-	-
Top 5	-23	1	1.22	1.23	1.25	1.28	1.31	1.35	-	-	-	-	-
Top 5	-2-	2	1.24	1.25	1.26	1.28	1.30	1.32	1.38	-	-	-	-
Top 5	--3	2	1.31	1.32	1.33	1.34	1.36	1.39	-	-	-	-	-
Top 5	1-3	2	1.38	1.39	1.40	-	-	-	-	-	-	-	-
Top 5	-23	2	1.24	1.25	1.25	1.26	1.26	1.27	1.29	1.34	1.40	-	-
Btm 5	-23	1	1.18	1.20	1.22	1.24	1.26	1.30	1.36	-	-	-	-
Btm 5	-2-	2	1.23	1.23	1.24	1.25	1.27	1.29	1.35	-	-	-	-
Btm 5	--3	2	1.29	1.30	1.31	1.32	1.34	1.36	-	-	-	-	-
Btm 5	1-3	2	1.36	1.37	1.38	1.39	-	-	-	-	-	-	-
Btm 5	-23	2	1.24	1.24	1.24	1.25	1.25	1.26	1.27	1.32	1.38	-	-
Top 6	-23	1	1.18	1.20	1.22	1.24	1.27	1.30	1.38	-	-	-	-
Top 6	-2-	2	1.22	1.22	1.23	1.24	1.26	1.28	1.35	-	-	-	-
Top 6	--3	2	1.28	1.29	1.30	1.31	1.33	1.35	-	-	-	-	-
Top 6	1-3	2	1.35	1.36	1.37	1.38	1.39	-	-	-	-	-	-
Top 6	-23	2	1.23	1.23	1.24	1.24	1.25	1.25	1.27	1.33	-	-	-
Btm 6	-23	1	1.15	1.16	1.18	1.19	1.22	1.24	1.31	-	-	-	-
Btm 6	-2-	2	1.20	1.20	1.21	1.22	1.23	1.24	1.31	-	-	-	-
Btm 6	--3	2	1.26	1.27	1.28	1.29	1.30	1.31	1.38	-	-	-	-
Btm 6	1-3	2	1.33	1.34	1.35	1.36	1.37	1.38	-	-	-	-	-
Btm 6	-23	2	1.22	1.23	1.23	1.23	1.23	1.24	1.25	1.30	1.40	-	-
Top 7	-23	1	1.16	1.17	1.18	1.20	1.23	1.25	1.33	-	-	-	-
Top 7	-2-	2	1.21	1.22	1.23	1.24	1.25	1.26	1.36	-	-	-	-
Top 7	--3	2	1.28	1.29	1.29	1.31	1.32	1.33	-	-	-	-	-
Top 7	1-3	2	1.35	1.36	1.36	1.37	1.39	1.40	-	-	-	-	-
Top 7	-23	2	1.23	1.23	1.24	1.24	1.25	1.25	1.26	1.33	-	-	-
Btm 7	-23	0	1.38	1.39	-	-	-	-	-	-	-	-	-
Btm 7	--3	1	1.37	1.38	1.40	-	-	-	-	-	-	-	-
Btm 7	-23	1	1.12	1.13	1.14	1.15	1.17	1.16	1.24	-	-	-	-
Btm 7	-2-	2	1.19	1.20	1.20	1.21	1.22	1.21	1.31	-	-	-	-
Btm 7	--3	2	1.26	1.26	1.27	1.28	1.29	1.27	1.38	-	-	-	-
Btm 7	1-3	2	1.33	1.33	1.34	1.35	1.36	1.34	-	-	-	-	-
Btm 7	-23	2	1.23	1.23	1.23	1.23	1.23	1.24	1.23	1.30	-	-	-

			Runs Behind						Runs Ahead				
Inning	Bases	Outs	5	4	3	2	1	Tie	1	2	3	4	5
Top 8	-23	0	1.39	1.40	-	-	-	-	-	-	-	-	-
Top 8	--3	1	1.37	1.38	1.39	-	-	1.40	-	-	-	-	-
Top 8	-23	1	1.12	1.13	1.14	1.15	1.17	1.16	1.25	-	-	-	-
Top 8	-2-	2	1.18	1.19	1.19	1.20	1.21	1.19	1.31	-	-	-	-
Top 8	--3	2	1.24	1.25	1.26	1.26	1.27	1.26	1.37	-	-	-	-
Top 8	1-3	2	1.32	1.32	1.33	1.34	1.34	1.33	-	-	-	-	-
Top 8	-23	2	1.22	1.22	1.22	1.22	1.23	1.23	1.22	1.32	-	-	-
Btm 8	-23	0	1.33	1.34	1.35	1.36	1.37	1.33	1.34	-	-	-	-
Btm 8	-2-	1	1.39	1.39	-	-	-	1.33	-	-	-	-	-
Btm 8	--3	1	1.31	1.32	1.33	1.34	1.35	1.23	-	-	-	-	-
Btm 8	1-3	1	-	-	-	-	-	1.38	-	-	-	-	-
Btm 8	-23	1	1.07	1.07	1.08	1.09	1.10	1.04	1.13	-	-	-	-
Btm 8	-2-	2	1.16	1.16	1.17	1.17	1.17	1.13	1.24	-	-	-	-
Btm 8	--3	2	1.22	1.22	1.23	1.23	1.24	1.19	1.31	-	-	-	-
Btm 8	1-3	2	1.29	1.30	1.30	1.31	1.31	1.26	1.37	-	-	-	-
Btm 8	-23	2	1.21	1.21	1.21	1.21	1.22	1.22	1.19	1.27	-	-	-
Top 9	-23	0	1.33	1.34	1.35	1.36	1.37	1.33	1.33	-	-	-	-
Top 9	-2-	1	1.38	1.39	1.40	-	-	1.32	-	-	-	-	-
Top 9	--3	1	1.31	1.32	1.33	1.34	1.35	1.22	-	-	-	-	-
Top 9	1-3	1	-	-	-	-	-	1.37	-	-	-	-	-
Top 9	-23	1	1.07	1.08	1.08	1.10	1.10	1.03	1.14	-	-	-	-
Top 9	-2-	2	1.15	1.16	1.16	1.17	1.17	1.12	1.27	-	-	-	-
Top 9	--3	2	1.22	1.22	1.23	1.23	1.23	1.18	1.34	-	-	-	-
Top 9	1-3	2	1.29	1.29	1.30	1.30	1.31	1.25	-	-	-	-	-
Top 9	-23	2	1.21	1.21	1.21	1.21	1.21	1.22	1.18	1.31	-	-	-
Btm 9	-2-	0	-	-	-	-	-	1.13	-	-	-	-	-
Btm 9	--3	0	-	-	-	-	-	1.29	-	-	-	-	-
Btm 9	1-3	0	-	-	-	-	-	0.99	-	-	-	-	-
Btm 9	-23	0	-	-	-	-	-	1.14	1.14	-	-	-	-
Btm 9	-2-	1	-	-	-	-	-	1.14	-	-	-	-	-
Btm 9	--3	1	-	-	-	-	-	0.96	-	-	-	-	-
Btm 9	1-3	1	-	-	-	-	-	1.12	-	-	-	-	-
Btm 9	-23	1	-	-	-	-	-	0.83	1.00	-	-	-	-
Btm 9	-2-	2	-	-	-	-	-	1.04	1.20	-	-	-	-
Btm 9	--3	2	-	-	-	-	-	1.10	1.27	-	-	-	-
Btm 9	1-3	2	-	-	-	-	-	1.16	1.34	-	-	-	-
Btm 9	-23	2	-	-	-	-	-	1.23	1.15	1.23	-	-	-

The Book Says:

The usefulness of issuing a walk to a good hitter can be determined by comparing the ratio of his wOBA to his *teammate wOBA* with the values in the table above. If the ratio exceeds the number in the table, a walk can be issued. If the value in the table is higher or no value is given, the batter should not be walked.

A caveat to all of these calculations is that, to compute this table, we have assumed that all of a player's batting stats scale equally. Thus a player with a wOBA 10% higher than average has 10% more singles, 10% more doubles, and so on, *including 10% more walks* than an average hitter. In reality, the player's tendency to draw unintentional walks is totally irrelevant to the question of whether or not to intentionally walk him, seeing as any type of walk has the same impact on the game. So, in terms of pitching to the hitter vs. walking him, we are trying to balance the potential positive (a strikeout or out on a batted ball) with the potential negative (a hit or error). So if we really want to get this right, we should remove walks (and hit by pitch) from consideration and compute the batter's wOBA for his other plate appearances. Multiplying this non-walk wOBA by 1.12 will scale it to the normal wOBA scale, and from there we can divide it by the *teammate wOBA* to compute the ratios used in the above tables.

The Book Says:

To get a more accurate evaluation of the benefit of walking a batter, one should omit walks and hit batsmen from the batter's wOBA and multiply the result by 1.12.

A second caveat deals with the double play rate of the on-deck hitter. The calculations above assume that the ratio of double plays to other outs is the same for all hitters; in reality, groundball hitters, groundball pitchers, and slow runners all create higher double play rates. While this obviously has no effect on two-out situations (which constitute the majority of intentional walk situations), it can have a large effect when there is zero or one out.

For example, if the on-deck hitter has a double play rate that is twice the league-average, the wOBA ratio threshold for one out and men on second and third drops to about 1.0 early in the game when tied or trailing, and by the top of the ninth is a very low 0.6 when tied or trailing. The other situation in which intentional walks become extremely attractive (again, with a high GDP batter coming up) is with one out and a man on third only. In this case, the wOBA ratio threshold drops to 1.0 when tied or trailing in the bottom of the seventh, and by the top of the ninth is about 0.9. A third situation is one out and men on first and third; in this case the ratio reaches about 1.0 in the bottom of the eighth (again only if tied or trailing).

Naturally, all one-out and no-out states become better intentional walk situations, but none as dramatically as these three.

The Book Says:

If the on-deck hitter grounds into a lot of double plays, the criteria for walking the batter when first base is open can be reduced. An on-deck hitter who is prone to double plays can be best exploited if there is one out, a runner on third, and possibly one other runner on base.

PITCHERS

So far, our discussion has been focused on whether or not to walk a very good hitter to face whomever is behind him, most likely an average hitter. However, a second common situation for issuing an intentional walk is when the #8 batter is at the plate and the pitcher is on-deck. (In NL games, the #8 hitter is walked about one-third of the time when there are two outs, first base is open, and there is a man on second and/or third. These account for about one-third of all intentional walks issued in NL parks.) Once again, the choice is between pitching to the current hitter, or putting an extra man on base and pitching to an inferior hitter.

Unlike the above situations, however, there are a few additional complications we need to consider. First, the lineup returns to the top of the order after the pitcher completes his time at bat, meaning that the advantage of facing inferior hitters lasts for only one plate appearance. Should the inning not end with the pitcher getting out (for example, if there are fewer than two outs), you will have to face the opposing team's best players, who are almost certainly better than the #8 batter you walked.

The second complication is due to the fact that the eighth hitter in the lineup is generally a weak hitter as well. Would you rather pitch to the #8 hitter (and probably get him out) and have the pitcher lead off the next inning with a likely out, or would you rather have the leadoff batter start the next inning? More often than not, the first option is better overall, so the walk should be reserved for a situation in which the potential for a big inning exists should the current (#8) hitter get a base hit (i.e., if there are runners on second and third).

Finally, it goes without saying that one can only employ this strategy if one is confident that the opposing manager will not pinch-hit for his pitcher. Thus, we can focus exclusively on early-game situations, which, for the purposes of analysis, have the advantage that we need only concern ourselves with changes in run expectancy. For an average eighth hitter (wOBA=.300) and pitcher (wOBA=.165), we calculate the following changes in run expectancy from a walk to be as follows. (See Table 127.)

Table 127.   Runs Gained Walking #8 Hitter

Bases Occupied	0 Outs	1 Out	2 Outs
Empty	0.346	0.216	0.069
1B	0.579	0.317	0.087
2B	0.344	0.204	-0.005
1B, 2B	0.818	0.583	0.081
3B	0.373	0.190	0.012
1B, 3B	0.491	0.283	0.013
2B, 3B	0.284	0.131	-0.054
1B, 2B, 3B	1.021	0.963	0.768

We first note that, as expected, a zero-out or one-out walk is counterproductive. With two outs, once again we see that advancing the lead runner is always a bad idea. For the other four situations, the only one in which the run expectancy drops significantly is when there are runners on second and third, while the other three leave the run expectancy largely unchanged. However, this ignores the run expectancy of the *next* inning, which is also affected by the decision to walk or not. (To repeat what we said above, if you issue the walk, the leadoff hitter probably leads off the next inning; if you pitch to the #8 hitter, the pitcher probably leads off the inning.) So, taking into account the total effect of the walk decision, the *only* situation in which one should walk the eighth hitter is when runners are on second and third, with two outs.

For a pitcher who hits well (wOBA=.220), even this situation is no longer worth the walk. Just pitch to the #8 hitter. On the other hand, if the pitcher is a bad hitter (wOBA=.115), one can also issue the walk with men on first and third. Likewise, the quality of the #8 hitter also matters—if he is worse than a .300 hitter, he should be pitched to.

So, what do managers actually do? In the case of two outs with men on second and third, they do the right thing, walking the #8 hitter about half the time. "About half" is optimal because a particularly good-hitting pitcher or poor-hitting #8 hitter negates this walk situation. However, when there is a runner on second or third (but not both), the intentional walk is still issued about half the time. These are situations that *never* call for the walk. On the other hand, a walk with runners on first and third is not issued enough (only 2% of the time). We also find that managers walk the #3 hitter about 20% of the time when there are men on second and third but just one out, another clear mistake.

As with the case of walking good hitters (from the previous section), the walk calculations can be made even more accurate by omitting walks and hit batsmen from the wOBA calculations and multiplying the resulting non-walk wOBA by 1.12.

The Book Says:

The eighth hitter should be walked to get to an average-hitting pitcher only when there are two outs and men on second and third. For a weak-hitting pitcher, one can also walk the #8 hitter if there are two outs and men on first and third. For a strong-hitting pitcher or particularly weak #8 hitter the walk is never a good option.

PITCH COUNT

So far, we have only discussed how to proceed from the start of a plate appearance, when the count is 0-0. What about other counts? If the count gets to 3-0, perhaps you might as well limit the damage by issuing the fourth ball rather than risking the hitter teeing off on a hanging curve?

At first glance, this looks like the obvious answer for all but the worst hitters. From 2000–2004, the average wOBA at a 0-0 count was

.337, while the average at 3-0 was .578—an increase of 72%. Even accounting for the fact that hitters facing 3-0 counts tend to be better than average (and pitchers at 3-0 tend to be worse than average), we find that an average hitter facing an average pitcher at 3-0 will expect to have a wOBA of .569, an increase of 69% from the 0-0 count. One would be tempted to therefore multiply the batter's wOBA by 1.69 when the count is 3-0 and consult our "Minimum wOBA Ratio for Intentional Walks" table to determine whether or not the player should be intentionally walked. Given the huge increase in the player's wOBA, you should nearly always issue the walk, right?

Not so fast. As we noted above, the decision-making process should ignore unintentional walks and hit batsmen, as these outcomes have exactly the same impact as intentionally walking the hitter. And the reason an average hitter with a 3-0 count has a wOBA of .569 is that he has a high probability of being walked (60%, to be precise). So the question isn't how much the count affects the player's *overall* wOBA, but rather how the count affects his non-walk wOBA.

As it turns out, most of the impact of count on wOBA is due to the change in probability of a walk or strikeout. When the count is a pitcher's count, the batter is more likely to strike out, and thus the wOBA goes down. In a hitter's count, the walk is more likely, increasing the wOBA. So if we're omitting walks from our wOBA calculations, it stands to reason that the huge increases one sees in hitters' counts will be significantly reduced. And indeed, this is the case. (See Table 128.) This table lists normal and non-walk wOBA by pitch count, as well as the ratio of the non-walk wOBA to the average of .337, adjusting for the quality of the average batter and pitcher at each count. (As usual, we multiply non-walk wOBA values by 1.12 so that they are comparable to the normal wOBA values.)

From this table, we see that non-walk wOBA values in hitters' counts don't change as much due to pitch count as do the normal ("total") wOBA values. So while the batter at 3-0 has his wOBA increased by 69% relative to average, the non-walk wOBA is increased by only 14%. So no, in terms of intentional walk calculations, a 3-0 count doesn't turn Rey Ordonez into Barry Bonds.

Table 128.   Total And Non-Walk wOBA By Count (2000–2004)

Count	Total wOBA	Non-walk wOBA	Count Multiplier
0-0	.337	.337	1.00
1-0	.374	.357	1.06
2-0	.442	.378	1.12
3-0	.569	.386	1.14
0-1	.290	.295	0.88
1-1	.320	.313	0.93
2-1	.376	.339	1.01
3-1	.492	.372	1.10
0-2	.222	.222	0.66
1-2	.245	.238	0.71
2-2	.292	.261	0.77
3-2	.401	.295	0.88

So to account properly for the pitch count, one ought to multiply the wOBA ratio (the player's non-walk wOBA) by the Count Multiplier in the preceding table. This adjusted wOBA ratio can then be checked on the "Minimum wOBA Ratio" table from earlier in the chapter to decide if the batter should be intentionally walked.

Looking over the count multipliers, you are probably not surprised. With a strong hitter's count (3-0, 2-0, or 3-1), the batter has the luxury of waiting for a hittable pitch, and therefore has a higher than normal wOBA—even after excluding walks. Therefore, even if the current batter wasn't good enough to warrant an intentional walk at 0-0, it may be a good time to reconsider. Moderate hitter's counts (1-0 and 2-1) make the batter a little bit more dangerous, so if the decision not to walk him at 0-0 was a close call, it might be better to walk him now. And of course, at a neutral or pitcher's count, if it didn't make sense to walk him at 0-0, you don't want to start now.

The Book Says:

The pitch count has a moderate affect on intentional walk decisions. When the batter has a good hitter's count, one should consider intentionally walking him. For example, a batter with wOBA of .340 and 3-0 count should be considered equivalent to a batter with wOBA of .388 and 0-0 count—thus, if you would have walked a .388 hitter from the start of his at-bat, you should just toss the fourth ball to the .340 hitter and move on.

PITCHING AROUND THE BATTER

So far, we have examined only the questions with "yes/no" answers about whether or not a batter should be pitched to. In reality, there are intermediate answers as well, as a pitcher need not throw pitches down the middle of the strike zone, or for that matter within the strike zone at all. In other words, the pitcher can pitch in such a way that the odds of a non-intentional walk are higher, while the odds of a well-hit ball (should the batter not be walked) are lower. While we'd love to be able to conduct a thorough analysis of this, the available data do not include accurate pitch locations.

Instead, we will have to use certain situations as a proxy for what we think a pitcher is likely to do in a given situation. In other words, if the situation allows for an intentional walk (good hitter at the plate, poor hitter on deck, one or two outs, batting team leading or tied, and first base is open) but the pitcher opts to pitch, then we would guess that the pitcher is probably at least being a bit more careful than he would otherwise be. On the other hand, if the situation were identical but a good hitter was on deck, we assume the pitcher is pitching normally. If our theory were correct, in the first situation we would see more walks and fewer well-hit balls; in the latter we would see the reverse. Is this what we actually find?

From 2000–2004, there were over 800,000 plate appearances in which the batter had over 200 PA during the five-year span and in which the next hitter was not a pinch hitter. In these plate appearances, an intentional walk was issued 0.7% of the time. We next define a "likely intentional walk situation" as one in which there are one or two outs, the game is tied or the pitching team is trailing, first base is open, and there is a man on second or third. And indeed, 84% of intentional walks occur in these situations, at a rate of one intentional walk in every twelve plate appearances.

Now let's see how well good hitters perform in these situations when they have protection and when they don't. We define "protected" in this instance as having an established good hitter on deck, and "unprotected" as having an established poor hitter on deck. (See Table 129.) This table lists the average stats of these good hitters when protected and when not protected, with both stat lines scaled to 600 plate appearances. For comparison, we also computed the average stats when the pitching team is ahead by at least two runs (again with a good hitter at the plate), a situation that is never an intentional walk situation.

Table 129.   Batting Stats For Good Hitters, In Likely IBB Situations

Status	wOBA	1B	2B	3B	HR	NIBB	HBP	RBOE	SO	Other Out
Unprotected	.380	83	32	3	16	91	10	6	108	251
Protected	.376	83	31	3	18	83	10	6	104	262
Leading	.382	92	31	3	21	72	7	7	97	270

So, no surprises. With the weak hitter on deck, we get considerably more walks and a few more strikeouts, both of which we expect to see if the pitcher is pitching around the corners. Specifically the walk rate goes from 13.8% with protection to 15.2% without protection, while the strikeout rate increases from 17.3% to 18.0%. And, regardless of the on-deck hitter, the pitcher is avoiding the batter more than he would in a poor walk situation—when ahead, the walk rate is 12.0% and the strikeout rate is 16.1%. So, we can reasonably conclude that we are measuring what we expected—that pitchers throw more balls when a walk isn't such a bad prospect, thus dramatically increasing the number of walks and also somewhat increasing the number of strikeouts.

However, not everything in this table makes sense. The entire point of protecting a batter is to improve his offensive output (wOBA) by forcing the opposing pitcher to pitch to him. And indeed, we saw above that opposing pitchers pitch to protected hitters, something that is evidenced by the fewer walks. However, when the ball is put into play, we see no significant difference between how the two sets of hitters perform. The unprotected hitters have a wOBA of .395 (counting only balls that are hit), compared with .391 for protected hitters. The difference of .004 is not statistically significant. For comparison, the good hitters in the "leading" situation have a "contact" wOBA of .404, which is a somewhat statistically significant deviation from the other values.

In short, protecting a star hitter appears to accomplish very little. He indeed gets fewer walks; however, there is no evidence that he gets more hittable pitches, since the pitcher *always* avoids pitching to a good hitter when the situation would call for an intentional walk.

Table 130. Batting Stats In Potential IBB And Non-Walk Situations, Scaled To 600 PA

Status	wOBA	1B	2B	3B	HR	NIBB	HBP	RBOE	SO	Other Out
potential IBB	.352	85	28	3	15	75	8	6	105	275
non-walk	.340	91	26	3	15	63	7	6	100	289

Where we do find a significant difference in the pitcher's approach is in situations in which a walk would or would not be considered. (See Table 130.) The table contains the average statistics (again, from 2000–2004) of all hitters, split between situations in which an intentional walk would be considered and those in which one would not be considered. Because defensive positioning adjustments due to baserunners can change the batter's wOBA (as we discuss in the chapter on baserunning), we consider only at-bats in which first base is open and second and/or third are occupied. If the pitching team is ahead or there are no outs, we call it a non-walk situation; otherwise we classify it as a potential IBB situation.

While before, we were trying to draw conclusions from a few thousand PA, we now have over 20,000 to produce more accurate results. So not surprisingly, we find once again that, in situations in which a walk is a good option, the pitchers indeed walk the batter more frequently. Also, by pitching around the corners, the batters occasionally will swing and strike out, leading to more strikeouts.

However, what we hoped to find was that, when pitchers pitch around the corners, batters tend to make worse contact (if they make contact at all). And we don't see this. Instead, we again find that, if walks are ignored, the two types of hitters perform equivalently in wOBA. (The slight increase in strikeouts is compensated by a slight increase in the fraction of balls hit well when contact is made.) In short, we simply cannot find any evidence to suggest that the pitcher's approach has any significant impact on the batter's stats, aside from the obvious changes in walks and strikeouts.

In terms of an alternative to intentional walks, pitching around a hitter accomplishes very little, as it merely increases the ratio of walks to non-walks without significantly affecting how well the hitter performs if he isn't actually walked. In other words, if you'd rather have a walk than whatever the hitter normally does if he doesn't walk, then you should walk him. If you'd rather have what he normally does, you should pitch to him normally.

The Book Says:

If a pitcher is trying to avoid pitching to a hitter, the hitter is significantly more likely to draw a walk, and moderately more likely to strike out. Specifically, a good, unprotected hitter in a good intentional walk situation is about 25% more likely to walk than the same hitter in a bad intentional walk situation, as well as about 10% more likely to strike out. Even an average hitter, with an average hitter on deck, is 20% more likely to draw the walk if the situation is a common one for intentional walks, and about 5% more likely to strike out.

However, if the ball is hit into play, the pitcher's approach (pitching to him, versus pitching around him) has no significant effect on the hitter's statistics.

SUMMARY

The intentional walk is an inherently attractive strategy for a manager, as it allows risk management—taking a known bad result rather than risking a possibly disastrous one. It also allows the manager to obey the adage of not permitting the opponent's best player to beat you. In this day and age, when managers are fired at the drop of a hat, these issues are not necessarily unimportant. (On the other hand, this makes it all the more important that general managers understand how to play the percentages, leaving the managers free to make the moves that maximize their teams' chances of winning rather than being judged based on their adherence to "conventional wisdom.")

Ultimately, baseball teams are measured by wins and losses. And, in terms of effects on the game outcome, we find that the negative from putting an extra runner on base usually outweighs the positive from facing a weaker batter. The only situation in which we can generally recommend an intentional walk is when there are two outs and men on second and third. Even then, it requires either an elite hitter at the plate with average hitters behind him, or a pitcher on deck.

Intentionally walking an average batter just to set up a force on the lead runner is a very bad move, as any benefit is negated (actually more than negated) by the risk of advancing the lead runner on a subsequent walk. However, walking the batter to set up a double play situation (one out, man on third, first base open) will improve your odds of escaping the inning without allowing any runs to score. If the game is tied in the bottom of the ninth, this move is recommended unless the batter is worse than the following hitters. (Doing so earlier in the game is not recommended, however, since it increases the odds of a big inning.)

In the bottom of the ninth, you know exactly how many runs you can afford to give up, and thus the rules for issuing walks change somewhat. For example, when tied, any unprotected star hitter can be walked, provided that the lead runner does not advance as a result of the walk. With a one-run lead, the unprotected star hitter can be walked any time there are runners on second and third.

Because the decision to walk or not involves so many factors, we have provided an extensive table listing the minimum ratio of the batter's wOBA to the following batters' composite wOBA for which a walk improves your team's odds of winning. To make this calculation as accurate as possible, we recommend the following three steps:

- Instead of using the batter's plain wOBA, calculate it while ignoring walks and hit batsmen. The resulting value will be lower than his normal wOBA, so multiply by 1.12 to return it to the same scale.
- The batter's wOBA should be multiplied by the appropriate pitch count multiple: 1.14 at 3-0, 1.12 at 2-0, 1.10 at 3-1, and 1.06 at 1-0.
- The "following batters' composite wOBA" is a weighted average of the wOBA of the next two to four batters, with the number of batters averaged depending on the number of outs.

For realistic game situations (i.e., not 20 runs per game), the run-scoring environment does not affect the intentional walk considerations. However, the on-deck hitter's double play rate does affect this calculation, and teams should be more aggressive intentionally walking when there is one out, a man on third (and possibly first or second), and a double play-prone hitter on deck.

When playing in a NL park, it is advisable to intentionally walk a typical (wOBA of .300) #8 hitter to get to a typical (wOBA of .165) pitcher only when there are two outs and men on second and third. While other situations may also seem attractive for the intentional walk, any advantage in terms of getting out of the current inning by walking the #8 hitter to face the pitcher are more than negated by missing the chance to start the subsequent inning with the pitcher leading off. If the pitcher is a particularly weak hitter (by pitcher standards), the #8 hitter can also be walked if there are men on first and third. A weaker #8 hitter should never be walked, nor should the walk be used if the pitcher is an above-average hitter (again, by pitcher standards).

Finally, we examined the less-drastic step of pitching around a hitter—throwing at the edges of the strike zone. While this indeed increases the rate at which the hitter draws walks, it does not significantly affect how well he performs when he doesn't walk. Thus, if you'd rather have the walk than his normal non-walk outcome, you should walk him; if not, you should pitch to him normally.

CHAPTER 11 – RUNNING WILD

A runner finds himself on first base. What's the first thing the announcer says, especially if he's a particularly fast runner? "That guy can really disrupt the defense."

As in everything, you change a situation, and everyone is affected somehow. With a runner on first base, the pitcher gives him an extra look and he pitches from the stretch. The first baseman is on the bag. If the runner moves, one of the middle infielders is moving toward second base. The infield is playing at double play depth with less than two outs. So, yes, the defense is disrupted. "How *much* is the defense disrupted?" is the real question. And, what about the batter? Why would he be immune to the antics of the defense and the runner? He's thinking of moving the runner over, taking advantage of the hole on the right side, taking a pitch to protect the runner. So, yes, the hitter is disrupted too. Again, the real question is, "How *much* is the hitter disrupted?" Let's find out.

Going through the 1999–2002 games, we'll concentrate on all batters with at least 800 plate appearances (excluding intentional walks and bunts). From those batters, we'll select all plate appearances where he has a runner on first base, and the other bases are empty. This gives us over 100,000 plate appearances. The overall wOBA of these batters (based on all of their PA), weighted by how often they found themselves with a runner on first base, is .358. This is essentially the talent level of our sample of hitters. In the particular situation of a man on first base, and the runner staying put, the wOBA of these batters is .366. Ah-ha, our first evidence that the defense has been disrupted. We expected our batters to hit .358, since this is the overall average for 1999–2002 for these particular hitters. But, they actually hit .366. Let's break this one down even further. With two outs, the defense isn't as concerned with the runner on first base. With two outs, our batters hit .355, or 3 points less than their overall average. With zero or one out, they hit .372, or 14 points above their overall average!

The batting approach with two outs is much different than with zero or one out. Comparing these situations with a runner on first, batters walk and strikeout more with two outs, and hit HR at the same rate. The biggest difference is on balls hit in the field of play: .319 with zero and one out, compared to .299 with two outs. We explain this as a result of the defense playing at double play depth, or possibly playing in expecting the bunt, with less than two outs, but at normal depth with two outs. When we talk about a disrupted defense, we don't necessarily mean that they are *distracted*.

The Book Says:

A runner on first with less than two outs is an enormous disruption on the defense. The batter gains 14 points to his wOBA.

Batter Splits

Do certain families of batters have a particular advantage in the situation of runner on first and less than two outs, compared to their overall wOBA in any situation?

We broke up the batters into power/neutral/punchless, and there was no difference. They each gained 13 to 15 points. We then tried aggressive/neutral/patient, and once again no difference: they also each gained 13 to 15 points.

When we broke the hitters into flyball/neutral/groundball, we did have a slight deviation. Groundball hitters only had an 8-point advantage, while the others had 12 to 16 points. This is a strange result, since we expected the groundball hitters to have an advantage: the middle infielders are playing in, so groundballs are more likely to go through the infield. A possible explanation is that pitchers try to throw pitches that induce groundballs. As we learned in an earlier chapter, groundball hitters do not fare well against groundball pitchers.

Next we broke up the batters based on their speed (fast, neutral, slow). The slow runners had an 18-point advantage, the neutral runners 15 points, and the fast runners only 5 points. It seems that with the infield in, it's more likely that the batter's speed isn't as effective. While he may have been used to getting his infield hits with the infield playing back, he's not as fortunate with the infield in.

How about lefties and righties? Left-handed batters have a 20-point advantage, while righties have a 10-point advantage. In this case, it's easy enough to understand: the hole on the right side is there for the taking, and lefties are able to take advantage of that more than righties.

Does experience matter? We broke up the hitters into young (under 25), old (over 35), and the rest, which we call middle-aged. The middle-aged batters had a 16-point advantage, the old batters had a 10-point advantage, and the young batters had a 1-point advantage! This is a very interesting result. What we have here is a situation where the defense has been greatly disrupted, but that the young batters are giving that entire advantage back, as they've been disrupted by the runner just as much!

The Book Says:

The type of batter most disrupted by having a runner on first base, with less than two outs, is the young, fast, and/or ground-ball hitter. Left-handed batters are the most likely to take advantage of the defense with a runner on first and less than two outs.

Runner Speed

Now let's turn our attention to the speed of the runner on first base, with less than two outs. We broke up the runners into: slow, normal, fast-non-disruptive, and fast-and-disruptive. For those last two categories, we're trying to differentiate between fast runners who usually stay on first base from the aggressive ones who attempt a lot of steals. A fast runner who is not aggressive won't have the batter take a pitch as often, and won't have the defense moving around as much, etc. Andruw Jones and Torii Hunter are examples of fast runners who are non-disruptive.

Our calculation of the *speed* of the runner was based on how many extra bases he takes, compared to an average runner. For every runner, we counted the number of times they were on first with no outs followed by a single, and how often they ended up at second, third, home, or were thrown out. We compared that to the league average, and came up with a differential. We repeated this for one out and two outs. This process was repeated with the runner on second followed by a single, the runner on first followed by a double, and the runner on first followed by a ground-ball out. We also looked at the propensity for a player to ground into a double play. We did similar calculations for SB and CS compared to opportunities. The higher the total differential of all these calculations (per opportunity), the faster the runner. The classification of *disruption* was based on the rate of stolen base attempts per opportunity. The careful reader will note that these measures have some selective sampling. However, we believe the effect to be small enough that it should not impact the results.

Focusing on the slow, normal, and fast-non-disruptive runners, we find the advantage to the batter is 12 to 16 points. Since these classes of runners are all non-disruptive, it seems that the speed of the runner is not an influence here. The defense plays the same way, and the batter reacts the same way.

But, what about with a fast and disruptive runner? The advantage to the batter is two points. That's right, just two.

Here are the twenty runners identified as fast and disruptive. (See Table 131.) The *Actual wOBA* is the wOBA of the batters when those runners are on first base. The *Overall wOBA* is the wOBA of those same batters, over all of their PA.

Table 131.   Batter/Pitcher Performance, With 20 Fastest & Most Disruptive Runners On First

Runner	Overall wOBA	Actual wOBA	Difference
Reggie Sanders	0.357	0.453	0.096
Carlos Beltran	0.369	0.419	0.050
Brian Lee Hunter	0.361	0.401	0.040
Roger Cedeno	0.345	0.381	0.036
Rafael Furcal	0.380	0.401	0.021
Johnny Damon	0.359	0.376	0.018
Tom Goodwin	0.345	0.360	0.014
Jimmy Rollins	0.364	0.377	0.014
Juan Encarnacion	0.351	0.364	0.013
Juan Pierre	0.351	0.348	-0.003
Mike Cameron	0.358	0.352	-0.006
Eric Young	0.351	0.335	-0.016
Raul Mondesi	0.379	0.362	-0.017
Tony Womack	0.370	0.351	-0.018
Luis Castillo	0.333	0.310	-0.023
Rickey Henderson	0.366	0.340	-0.026
Quilvio Veras	0.360	0.328	-0.032
Dave Roberts	0.349	0.313	-0.037
Eric Owens	0.359	0.321	-0.038
Alfonso Soriano	0.377	0.317	-0.060

To read the first line: when Reggie Sanders is the runner on first base, the quality of batter at the plate has an overall wOBA of .357. But, that batter's actual wOBA with Sanders on base is .453. For every Reggie Sanders and Carlos Beltran, with whom their batters perform far better, you have an Alfonso Soriano and Eric Owens, with whom their batters perform far worse. Remember, the typical batter has a 12 to 16 point advantage with a non-disruptive runner. Only five of the above runners see their batters improve their wOBA by more than that amount. Eleven of these runners see the overall performance of their batters decline. The sample size for any one individual is too small to say if these particular runners are more disruptive to the defense or to the hitter, but overall, the group sample is pretty damning.

A young batter at the plate or a disruptive runner on first base each have exactly the same effect. Both the young batter and the disruptive runner completely remove the advantage of the disrupted defense.

The Book Says:

The disruptive runner has an enormously negative influence on the batter, enough to almost completely offset the disruption caused to the defense.

Disruptive Events

The focus so far has been on the situation where the runner is not going. Now, let's turn our attention to the rest of the situations—the ones where a disruptive event has happened. We're talking steals, pickoffs, wild pitches, everything. Anytime something happened regarding the runner while the batter was at the plate, we're calling that a disruptive event. How did this affect the batter? When a disruptive event happened, the batter ended up with a wOBA of .355, or three points below his overall wOBA for 1999–2002. So, it seems that disruptive events, on the whole, don't affect the batter too much. However, we have different types of disruptive events. We have events that are elected by the runner, and others that are initiated by the defense. Here's the full chart. (See Table 132.)

With a wild pitch (WP) and passed ball (PB), the batter usually gets an extra ball in the count (though some batters do swing at such poor pitches). The net effect is an 18-point advantage. (Of course, the average ball increases a batter's wOBA by 74 points, so even these 18 points are less than one might expect.) The pickoff (PK) and balk (BK) are plays that don't involve the hitter, and we see a slight overall positive effect for the batter. The defensive indifference (DI) has a large negative effect on the batter. The sample size is small, and there may be other variables at play here, like facing a predominant number of good relievers. In all these cases, given the sample size, the numbers are not very significant.

Table 132. Batter/Pitcher Performance, By Disruptive Event, With Runner On First

Disruptive Event	PA	Overall wOBA	Actual wOBA	Difference
WP	1872	0.362	0.383	0.020
PK	940	0.355	0.368	0.012
PB	409	0.363	0.368	0.005
CS	1536	0.352	0.348	-0.004
SB	6934	0.358	0.349	-0.008
BK	284	0.355	0.343	-0.012
DI	463	0.358	0.334	-0.024

But, when it comes to the runner-elective disruptive play, the stolen base attempt, the batter pays the price. Overall, a steal attempt results in an 8-point loss to the batter. (It's an 8.5% loss on a successful steal, and a 4.1% loss on a caught stealing. The overall average is 7.7%.) However, it's actually worse than this. Remember that, if the runner just stays put, the batter gets a 14-point advantage. If the runner takes off for second, the batter gets an 8-point disadvantage. That is a swing of 22 points!

The Book Says:

The stolen base attempt reduces the wOBA of the batter by 22 points, compared to the situation if the runner elected not to attempt to steal.

While most disruptive events result in the runner being out or advancing one base, the stolen base and pickoffs are a little different. A pickoff results in an out only 75% of the time; 17% of the time, the runner finds himself on second base, and 8% of the time, he'll end up with multiple bases.

With a stolen base, the runner will find himself on third base or scoring 8% of the time. Breaking it down by the speed of the baserunner, and the numbers range from 5% for the slow runner to 9% for the fast-and-disruptive runners.

What influences the success rate of the stolen base attempt? We are all well aware that the talent levels of the runner, pitcher, and catcher play primary roles, so we don't need to consider those. Among the secondary influences, there's the pitcher's handedness, the turf, and possibly even the batter's handedness. Let's look at each influence, one or two at a time.

We will start with an easy one. We know that it's harder to steal second with a lefty on the mound, than with a righty. And, if we look at our data, we see that runners are successful 71.8% of the time against righties and . . . uhh . . . 76.9% against lefties?!? How in the world does that make sense?

Let us present the data first. (See Table 133.)

Table 133.   Batter/Pitcher Performance, By Pitcher Handedness, With Runner On First

Pitch Hand	Disruptions	SB	CS	PK	BK	WP	PB	DI
Left	126	52	16	25	5	20	4	3
Right	149	76	30	10	3	19	5	6

Those numbers are "per 1,280 times on first base, with no one else on base." The average per team per season is 1,280. Disruptions are the sum of all the numbers to the right (SB, CS, PK, etc.). If the numbers don't add up, it's because of rounding. As you can see, the number of disruptions when a righty is on the mound is about 20% more compared to a lefty. In other words, runners are already accounting for the difficulty of stealing against a lefty by stealing less frequently.

There should be one thing that jumps out at you: with a lefty on the mound, there are only 16 CS, but 25 pickoffs. With a righty, it's 30 CS and only 10 pickoffs. If you were to focus only on the SB and CS numbers, you'd think that runners had a field day with lefties. But, a pickoff is essentially a CS. From this point forward, we're going to include the pickoff as a failed stolen base attempt. At the same time, a balk can also be considered a successful stolen base attempt. The net result is the same, and the condition in which a balk takes place is the same as a pickoff. Using our new definition for the successful steal, the success rate against righties is 66.4%, and 58.7% against lefties. Ah, that makes a lot more sense. That's an enormous 8% advantage that lefty pitchers have against righties.

The Book Says:

It is much harder to steal against a lefty than a righty. The lefty advantage is 8 percentage points compared to the righty.

What if we throw in the handedness of the batter? A lefty batter may prevent the catcher from picking off the runner at first. As well, catchers typically throw with their right hand, and may be hindered by a lefty batter, as they come up to throw. Anyway, that's the theory. Here are the numbers, with a righty pitcher on the mound. (See Table 134.)

Table 134.   Batter/Pitcher Performance, With Right-Handed Pitcher And Runner On First

Pitch Hand	Bat Hand	Disruptions	SB	CS	PK	BK	WP	PB	DI	SB%
Right	Left	145	73	29	9	2	19	5	7	66.4%
Right	Right	151	78	31	10	3	20	4	4	66.4%

The percentage is 66.4%, whether a lefty or righty batter. All the numbers pretty much look like a perfect match.

And here are the numbers with a lefty pitcher on the mound. (See Table 135.)

Table 135.   Batter/Pitcher Performance, With Left-Handed Pitcher And Runner On First

Pitch Hand	Bat Hand	Disruptions	SB	CS	PK	BK	WP	PB	DI	SB%
Left	Left	129	56	15	24	4	21	4	4	60.4%
Left	Right	125	51	16	25	6	20	3	2	58.1%

So we indeed measure a slightly lower success rate for the runner with a righty batter than with a lefty. This is what we thought should happen. The lefty batter hinders the catcher, and the runner ends up doing better. But, why do we see this effect with a lefty pitcher, but not a righty? Most likely, this is just a sample size issue, as the lefty/lefty situation is based on only 1,047 disruptions and thus the difference can be explained by random statistical variations alone.

The Book Says:

The batter's handedness is likely not a factor in the stolen base success rate of the runners.

Let's also look at the running surface: artificial turf and grass. Fast-and-disruptive runners are successful 76% of the time on artificial turf, while they are safe only 71% of the time on grass. Fast-non-disruptive runners have only a 1 percentage point advantage on turf. With average runners, the gain is 4 percentage points. But it is with slow runners that the gain is the most. A 53% success rate on grass, and a 63% rate on artificial turf.

The Book Says:

Artificial turf gives a 3 percentage point advantage to the runner. It is especially advantageous to the slow runner, who gains 10 points with the turf.

BASES, RUNS, AND WINS

Let's now focus on the gain in bases, runs, and wins.

As we learned, some successful steals (as well as some pickoffs) find the runner advancing two bases. So, rather than look at it in terms of safe and out, let's look at it in terms of number of bases gained per movement. The stolen base attempt (and remember we are including SB, CS, PK, and BK) adds .737 bases per movement. The average run value of a base is about .153 runs. The runner also accumulates .322 outs per movement, and the run value of the out is about -.426 runs.

How did we figure all of that out? Let's look at part of our run expectancy (RE) chart. (See Table 136.)

Table 136.   Run Expectancy, By Base/Out State (Subset Of An Earlier Chart)

1B	2B	3B	0 Outs	1 Out	2 Outs
--	--	--	0.555	0.297	0.117
1B	--	--	0.953	0.573	0.251
--	2B	--	1.189	0.725	0.344
--	--	3B	1.482	0.983	0.387

With a man on first, and no one else on, the team is expected to score .953 runs with no outs. If the runner gets to second, and all other things are equal, that run expectancy is now 1.189, or a positive change of .236 runs. A two-base gain would be a change of .529 runs. Concentrating only on these two outcomes, the one-base gain occurs 91.5% of the time, and the two-base gain occurs 8.5% of the time. Our weighted average here is .261 runs per event. Each event has a gain of 1.085 bases, making the run value of each base worth .241 runs. (Whether it's clearer to think of the gain in terms of bases or opportunity, the reader is invited to choose.) Repeating this process for one (.174 runs per base) and two (.097 runs per base) outs, we can then weight our numbers by how often the stolen base is attempted by out. Those weights would be 26% for no outs, 33% for one out, and 40% for two outs. The weighted average comes in at .153 runs per base, or .166 runs per stolen base event.

An out would turn the .953 run situation into a .297 run situation, or a net loss of .656 runs. Continuing the process for one and two outs, and the run value of the out is a loss of .426 runs.

So, what is the net change in runs? The average runner gained .737 bases × .153 runs per base minus .322 outs × .426 runs per out = −.025 runs. So, on average, the stolen base attempt, just from the perspective of trying to get into scoring position, is a net negative. Throw in the negative influence on the batter following an attempt, and it's a big negative.

Breaking it up by the speed of the runner, and the fast-and-disruptive runner gains .015 runs per attempt, while the fast-non-disruptive runner loses .015 runs. That gives the disruptive runner a .030 run gain. However, with the incredible negative influence that the disruptive runner has on the batter, much of that advantage is wiped away. Concentrating on the fast-non-disruptive runner, even though he gains .76 bases per movement, and is out 31% of the time, he is still a net negative. He is trying to steal too often.

The average runner loses .038 runs per movement, while the slow runner loses .072 runs per movement. Why in the world do slow runners move so often? It's possible that the hit and run has an influence here, as a failed hit and run will often lead to a caught stealing.

What is the break-even point, at which the steal attempt has zero overall influence? Ignoring the disruptive effect on the batter, if the runner succeeds 72% of the time, while gaining .78 bases per movement, he will add as many runs as his outs will remove.

$$.78 \times .153 = (1 - .72) \times .426$$

This break-even point is far higher than the league average of 67.8%.

How about close and late situations? Surely the break-even point changes under those conditions? Surely.

Let's look at a tied game in the top of the seventh, with two outs. How successful does the runner need to be to steal? In that situation, and assuming both teams are equals throughout the game, the batting team has a 45% (.450) chance of winning. If the runner finds himself on second base, that goes up to .471. And .480 if he finds himself on third base. Since we know that about 8.5% of the time he'll find himself on third base if he is safe, that makes our expectation .472 if the runner is safe. If the runner is out, the inning is over, and his team now has a .408 chance of winning.

Let's recap: if safe, you gain .022 wins, by going from .450 to .472. If out, you lose .042 wins, by going from .450 to .408. Essentially, it's almost twice as damaging to be out than to be safe. The break-even point becomes 65.6%.

$$.656 \times .022 = (1 - .656) \times .042$$

This is interesting. In a random situation, we know that the break-even point is 72%. In the real world, we know that runners are safe 67.8% of the time, making us think that they are not smart basestealers. But, in this situation, the break-even point is only 65.6% of the time. Could it be that since runners can pick and choose their spots, that they choose these types of game situations? That is, they purposely choose a game situation where the impact of scoring the next run is felt more powerfully than if they simply selected a random situation to steal in?

We went through every stolen base event with a man on first only, and assigned a win probability for that particular game state. In the above example of top of the seventh and two outs, the win probabability for the team at bat was .450. Adding up the nearly 13,600 times that a stolen base event occurred, the average win probability was .580. What does this tell us? That a stolen base is usually attempted by the team that is leading. Specifically, we find that 42% of steal attempts happen when the batting team is leading, 25% happen when they are trailing, and the remaining 33% when the score is tied.

Here's a handy chart. (See Table 137.)

Table 137.   Change In Probability Of Winning, By Score, When Runner Stealing Is Safe Or Out

Bat Score	% of times	Start Win Probability	Win if Safe	Win if Out	Break-even
-3	3%	0.178	0.013	(0.041)	0.754
-2	6%	0.276	0.018	(0.053)	0.739
-1	12%	0.371	0.028	(0.064)	0.700
0	33%	0.530	0.025	(0.051)	0.680
1	14%	0.682	0.018	(0.036)	0.673
2	11%	0.792	0.012	(0.025)	0.667
3	8%	0.877	0.008	(0.016)	0.669
Average	100%	0.580	0.019	(0.040)	0.687

The last line tells us that of all times that a stolen base event happened, the win probability was 58.0%. When the runner is safe, it adds .019 wins to the game situation, and when the runner is out, he removes .040 wins. The break-even point is a 68.7% success rate.

Remember how we said the league-average success rate is 67.8%? Well, we have just determined that the true break-even point is 68.7%, which is pretty close! However, if the break-even point is 68.7%, teams should only be trying to steal when the chance of success is *at least* 68.7%. The true average should be higher than 70%.

When the batting team is ahead, the break-even point is around 67%. The further behind the batting team is, the higher the break-even point. Why is that? Because the cost of the out is greater than the cost of the base. Compare the *up by one* and *down by two* data. In either case, the average safe play will add .018 wins. But, look at what happens if the runner is out. Up by one, and the out costs .036 wins. Down by two, and the out costs .053 wins. The out is 50% more damaging when down by two than when up by one.

The caught stealing prevents a big inning from happening, while a stolen base adds insurance to an already existing lead. Teams seem to have grasped this already. Six percent of stolen base events occurred when the batting team was down by two runs. But up by two runs, and that number is 11%. Down by three, it's 3%. Up by three, and it's 8%.

If we include the inning, the break-even points become even more polarizing. If down by two in the seventh or later innings, the break-even point is at least 75% in all instances. In the ninth inning, the break-even point hovers around 90%! And, what did teams actually do? In the seventh or later innings, and down by at least two runs, there were 419 stolen base events from 1999–2002. That's 419 times when the odds were stacked highly against the batting team and they decided to go for it anyway. It is only three or four times per team per year. But, why throw away those chances? Those teams, at the point they took their crazy chance, had only an 8.9% chance of winning. They ended up winning 7.4% of the time. When we look at each of these stolen base events, one at a time, we find that the successful steal would have added .009 wins to a team's chance of winning, while the out would have removed .041 wins, making the break-even point almost 82%! Managers were faced with a high risk/low reward scenario, and they went for it. Even more amazingly, they were successful over 80% of the time! Undoubtedly, since very few basestealers are successful 80% of the time, many of these events were recorded as SB, when they should have been marked as DI. If you assume that one-fourth of these events were actually defensive indifference plays, then each team took two or three crazy chances per year. The sharp-eyed reader will notice that in these horrible conditions, the cost of the caught stealing (.041) is very close to the cost of the caught stealing at a random point in the game (.040, as noted in the chart on the previous page). However, the gain on the successful steal in these scenarios (.009) was half that of the random successful steal (.019).

When down by one, the break-even point hovers around 70% throughout the game. And, teams' stealing patterns were consistent with this knowledge. They stole around the same number of times on an inning-by-inning basis, when down by one run. Their overall success rate, however, was only 68%.

With a tied game, the break-even point hovers at 69% in the early to mid-game innings, as it begins its rapid descent. In the seventh inning, it drops to around 66%. In the eighth inning, it's around 63%. In the ninth and later innings of tied games, the break-even point is down to 60%. And what actually happened? In the eighth and later innings of tied games, when the break-even point is 61%, runners were safe 70% of the time! Remember, since the average runner is safe 68% of the time, this must mean that it's mostly the good runners who are stealing in these situations. But, with the risk/reward balance shifted heavily toward the mediocre runners, teams should definitely try to be as aggressive as possible in these late inning situations.

The *up by one* situations mirror the tied-game situations through the first seven innings. In the eighth and later innings, the break-even point hovers around 65%. And in these innings, teams were actually successful 69% of the time. Since we want the runners to only steal when they think they'll be successful *at least* 65% of the time, the average should probably come in at around 68 or 69%. So, teams ran wisely in these situations.

The *up by two runs* situations have the break-even point at an almost perfect match to the up by one situations. And, in reality, teams' successes also matched those when up by 1: 69%.

When up by three or more runs, the break-even point is around 67% throughout the game. Teams were successful 71% of the time in the late innings.

The number of outs also plays a role in determining when to steal. Focusing only on the eighth and later innings of very close games (tied, or one team is ahead by one run), the break-even point when there are no outs is about two percentage points lower than with one or two outs.

It is also worth remembering that these break-even points assume that the batter was not affected by the stolen base event. Since we know that batters are affected following a stolen base event, the break-even point would need to rise a few percentage points to compensate for taking the bat out of the hitter's hands.

The Book Says:

The break-even point for the stolen base is highly dependent on the inning and score. The most desirable situations are tied games in the later innings or ones in which the batting team is ahead. The least desirable situations are down by at least two runs in the later innings.

CHAPTER 12 – BLUFFING IN BASEBALL

GAME THEORY

Game theory is a complex topic combining mathematics and social psychology. Simply speaking, it is the analysis of decision-making in a game or conflict involving two or more participants. Game theory is implicated in many different contexts, such as the stock and bond markets, the economy in general, poker, gin, backgammon, and of course, professional sports. We'll elucidate some of the central concepts of game theory by first discussing one aspect of a popular parlor and gambling game—bluffing in poker.

As almost anyone who plays poker knows, the proper use of the bluff is an important weapon in the poker player's arsenal. In the interest of simplicity, we'll restrict the discussion to the strategy of bluffing against one opponent on the last bet in a typical poker game like Texas Hold'em or Seven-Card Stud. Suppose that after all the cards have been dealt, it's your turn to bet, and you are 100% sure that you can't win in a show-down (you are positive that your opponent has a better hand than you do). This means that the only way you can win is by betting and having your opponent fold his hand (a bluff). What should you do? Well, that's where game theory comes into play.

If your opponent never folds a hand in the face of a possible bluff, then clearly it is correct for you to *never* bluff. You would be throwing your money away. You simply check and fold, if your opponent bets, or you check and show down the hand if your opponent checks also. Of course, either way you lose, but at least it doesn't cost you an additional bet.

What about if your opponent always folds unless he has a strong hand—in other words, he never tries to *pick off* a bluff? In this case it would be correct for you to always try a bluff when your hand is too weak to win in a showdown. Even if your opponent sometimes calls your bet with a strong hand, he'll have enough weak hands, which he'll throw away, to make a bluff profitable for you in the long run (assuming there is enough money in the pot, which there usually will be).

Most opponents, however, fall somewhere in between these two extremes. That is, they sometimes fold their hand in the face of a potential bluff and they sometimes call with a weak hand, knowing that they can only beat a bluff. In this case, what do you do? It turns out that, if your opponent will call a potential bluff too often, as compared to what the game theory *equilibrium point* (we'll get to that in a minute) dictates— even a smidgen too often—it is correct for you to *never* bluff; if he folds his hand too often—again, even just a smidgen too often—in the face of a potential bluff, then it is correct for you to *always* bluff. Of course, if your opponent is observant and smart, eventually he will realize that you are always or never bluffing, and adjust his calling frequency accordingly. In fact, if your opponent figures out that you are bluffing too little or too much, it becomes correct for him to start calling or folding *all the time*. In that case, of course, *you* would then have to re-adjust your strategy. As you can see, this give and take, or constant re-adjusting of strategies, can go on and on *ad infinitum*.

What if you don't know your opponent's strategy with respect to calling potential bluffs, and you can't estimate it, or you suspect that your opponent is an expert player? Or what if your opponent is an expert player and he is trying to figure out how often to call and how often to fold against you? As it turns out, the mathematical solution to both of these problems, how often to bluff or call a potential bluff, is determined by the amount of money already in the pot, how often you bet (or check) your legitimate hands, how often those hands win, and the size of the last bet.

Let's take the specific case where there is one card to go in a Texas Hold'em game, you have a 15% chance of ending up with the winning hand, and an 85% of ending up with nothing. There is $80 already in the pot, and the last bet is $20. How often should you bet, knowing that you stand an 85% chance of losing should your opponent call, and knowing or suspecting that your opponent is an expert strategist himself? We'll skip the math, but as a potential bluffer, you want the ratio of your legitimate (and winning) bets to your bluffs to equal exactly the *pot odds* that your opponent is getting when he is faced with the decision of whether to call or not. (In poker, the term *pot odds* is the ratio of the amount of money already in the pot to the amount of your bet, usually expressed as *something-to-one*. For example, if there is $70 in the pot and you are faced with a $20 call or a $20 bet, your pot odds are 70-to-20, or 3.5-to-1.) Back to our example.

Since there is $100 in the pot and your bet is going to be $20, your opponent will be getting 5-to-1 odds on calling a potential bluff (the $100 now in the pot versus his $20 to call your bet). Therefore, the ratio of your winning hands to bluffs should be 5-to-1 as well. Since you are going to bet a winning hand 15% of the time, you must bluff another 3% of the time, which is actually 2.55% of the time that you miss your hand (3% of 85% equals 2.55%). Of course, the other 82.45% of the time, you will check and lose, either in a showdown if your opponent checks, or when you fold in the face of a bet. Using this strategy, no matter how often your opponent calls or folds, both you and he will win or lose exactly the same amount of money in the long run.

The optimal calling frequency (assuming that your opponent is using optimum bluffing frequency as described above) is simply calculated. If your opponent may be bluffing, and he is getting 4-to-1 odds on a bluff (like betting $20 to win $80, as in the above example), then you want the odds against you folding to be 4-to-1 as well; therefore, you will call 80% of the time and fold 20%, in a random fashion. If you do that, there is nothing your opponent can do to increase (or decrease) his or your expectancy in the game. No matter how often he bluffs, you will both win or lose the same amount of money in the long run.

When all players in a contest have arrived at their respective optimum frequencies, in terms of how often a particular strategy should or shouldn't be used, such that neither player can take advantage of their opponent's strategy, the game is said to be in a state of *equilibrium*. Of course, in reality in poker, things are rarely that straightforward, even if both players are expert strategists. For example, when you bet a legitimate hand you are usually not 100% certain that you are going to win if your opponent calls (you may even get raised), there are often certain "river" cards (in Texas Hold'em) that suggest either a bluff or a value bet, and player "tells" can influence both players' decisions. Let's get back to baseball.

THE SACRIFICE BUNT

A similar dynamic to bluffing in poker occurs in many facets of a baseball game. We briefly discussed the concept of game theory in the chapter on sacrifice bunting. Remember that the run or win expectancy of the sacrifice bunt is largely dependent on where the defense is playing—in other words, how much they are anticipating the bunt. Playing up in expectation of a bunt is like calling a potential bluff in poker, and playing back is like folding a weak hand when your opponent bets after the last card is dealt.

So what does this mean in terms of baseball and game theory? As we saw in the chapter on sacrifice bunting, not only is the result of the sacrifice attempt very much a function of where the defense is playing, but at almost all points in the game and with almost every kind of batter (weak or strong), the run expectancy (RE) or win expectancy (WE) from attempting the sacrifice is very close to that when swinging away. This is a profound result, perhaps a little surprising, but one that is *fully expected* according to the tenets of game theory!

Let's imagine for a second that the Earl Weavers and the sabermetricians are right and that bunting costs a team a small amount of run expectancy (assuming that the infield is playing for the possibility of a bunt), say .01 runs, and therefore no one should ever attempt a sacrifice. And let's imagine that teams heeded this advice and stopped bunting. Obviously, if that were the case, the defense would not need to play for the bunt; the third baseman could comfortably play back, the first baseman would not need to charge or even "cheat in" a little after the pitch is thrown, and the second baseman would not need to cheat toward first (to cover first base on a bunt). They could play exactly as they do now with *one* out and a non-pitcher at the plate.

We told you in the chapter on sac bunting that when the defense is playing *somewhat* for the bunt early in the game (with non-sluggers at the plate of course), the batter, when swinging away, gets a few extra hits that sneak through the "out of position" infield. In fact, early in the game, a batter gets around three extra singles and one extra double or triple per 500 PA when the infield is anticipating a possible bunt and he swings away. That corresponds to more than a .01 run improvement in the expected outcome. However, if batters never bunted and the infield adjusted accordingly (by always playing back), the RE from swinging away would be reduced by more than .01 runs, more than negating the advantage gained by eschewing the bunt. All of a sudden *not* bunting becomes incorrect!

So if bunting were *not* correct given where the infield currently plays—up a little in anticipation of a possible bunt—but the infield would play back if the batting team never bunted, thus making it worthwhile again for the batting team to bunt, what is a manager to do? It seems like he's damned if he does and damned if he doesn't! In comes game theory to the rescue. In order to create a situation where the defense cannot take advantage of a predictable decision by the batting team, the batting team must sometimes bunt and sometimes swing away, and the defense *must* play somewhere in between "back" and "up." That is *exactly* what we see in traditional baseball!

The Book Says:

Even if bunting is not *technically* correct (the RE or WE is less than that from swinging away), given that the infield is anticipating a possible bunt, if it is at all close, which it often is (see the chapter on sac bunting), the batting team must sometimes attempt a sacrifice to keep the defense from playing all the way back. How often depends, among other things, on the difference between the RE or WE when bunting and when swinging away, given the circumstances of the game and the personnel (batter, pitcher, etc.) involved.

From the defense's perspective, in order to keep the batting team from bunting or not bunting *all the time*, they must usually play somewhat "agnostically" (not too far in and not too far back) in a potential bunting situation. As with the batting team's optimum frequency for bunting, how much they play for the bunt depends upon the difference in RE or WE between bunting and swinging away, given the circumstances of the game. Game theory dictates that an equilibrium point is reached, as in the poker bluffing example above, when each side operates such that their opponent cannot take advantage of their strategy no matter what they do. The fact that the RE from bunting and swinging away is so close in so many different scenarios in baseball, as we saw in the chapter on sac bunting, suggests that managers are electing to sac bunt a near perfect percentage of the time and that defenses are playing up or back in a near perfect configuration, depending on the game situation.

Now, what percentage of time a manager attempts a sacrifice in any given situation (the score, inning, run environment, the batter's hitting ability, bunting ability, and speed, the subsequent batters, etc.), and where the infield should "set up" (the equivalent of how often they should play back and how often they should play up), as we said, depends on the relative values of the swinging away RE (or WE) and bunting RE (or WE), given an "in-between" (agnostic) defensive positioning. The further apart they are, the further from .500 the swing away/bunt ratio should be and the farther up or back the defense should play. There is a point, of course, where the differences in RE or WE between bunting and swinging away are so great that the batter should never bunt (or never swing away) and the defense should not anticipate the bunt at all (or be breathing down the batter's neck). Those situations are usually fairly obvious.

Just because we find that managers are positioning their defense and bunting in a near-optimum manner *overall*, according to game theory, this does not mean that they are doing so in every possible situation. In fact, in our sac bunting chapter we identified several scenarios in which managers bunted too little or too much (mostly the latter), and although it is difficult for us to identify (our data do not tell us where the defense is playing), there are no doubt instances in which the defense is playing too far up or back. It is also true that, as we explained in the poker example at the beginning of this chapter, one player's optimum strategy would change if his opponent were not optimizing his strategy according to game theory. At that point, the equilibrium point would not be met, and one player would be able to take advantage of the other. Remember we said that if a poker player bluffs too often, even by a little bit, the correct "response" is to *always* call a potential bluff. How long that out-of-balance situation remains depends on the awareness and skill of the opponent who is not initially optimizing his strategy.

What happens in reality in poker when an opponent bluffs too often is that an expert player will still throw away his hand every once in a while, in order to induce him to continue to bluff too frequently. If he simply called him all the time (which would be the "technically" correct thing to do), his opponent, unless he was a compete idiot, would eventually start to bluff less often or even stop bluffing altogether.

In baseball, we have shown that managers at times tend to bunt too often, for example, with poor bunters or slow runners at the plate. Given that, it is correct for the defense to play a little more "in" than the "equilibrium point" would otherwise dictate (assuming that the batting team were bunting optimally). However, if they were to play *too* far in, it would give the batting team's manager reason to start bunting less, which would encourage him to manage more optimally (since he is bunting too much in the first place).

In poker, an important axiom for the expert player is to *not encourage his opponent to play more optimally, if he is playing sub-optimally in the first place.* That's why the expert player occasionally throws away his hand (and often "advertises" it) against an inferior opponent who bluffs too frequently. He wants to make sure he *continues* to bluff too frequently. The same thing holds true in baseball. If your opponent manager calls for a bunt too often in any given situation, play a little farther back on defense than game theory would dictate (given that your opponent is bunting too much) in order to encourage him to *continue* bunting too frequently.

The Book Says:

When you know or suspect that an opponent manager is calling for the bunt too little or too much, according to game theory, or that they are not positioning their defense (in the face of a potential sacrifice) in an optimal manner, you should alter your strategy (from the equilibrium point), but not too much that you force your opponent to start managing significantly more optimally himself.

We've also shown in the sac bunt chapter that managers tend to bunt too frequently with pitchers at the plate, depending upon the game situation and the hitting prowess of the batter-pitcher. In fact, that is probably the most egregious of the sacrifice bunt "errors" (and ironically, the one that you don't often hear people, even sabermetricians, criticize). What does that mean in terms of game theory? It depends on whether you are the batting team or the defense. If you are the defense and you recognize that opposing pitchers are bunting too much, you play in as far as you can without encouraging them to bunt a whole lot less. How far in you play depends on how stubborn the opposing manager is. Anyone who watches a lot of games can easily see that managers are quite stubborn when it comes to pitchers bunting. No matter how aggressively the defense appears to play up, most managers have their pitchers bunting a high percentage of the time, at least with a runner on first and no outs, and usually with one out as well. This strategy is akin to the expert player *always* calling a potential bluff against an opponent who bluffs too much (rarely, if ever, "throwing him a bone"), because that opponent stubbornly refuses to alter his sub-optimal bluffing frequency.

From an offensive perspective, with your pitcher at the plate in a potential sacrifice situation, the defense, as we just said, will usually be playing quite aggressively in anticipation of the bunt—and correctly so, given that most managers elect to have their pitchers bunt most of the time. If you are an astute manager, however (or at least one who has read this book), it is correct for you to substantially decrease your bunting percentage, at least until the defense starts to "catch on" and plays a little less aggressively. At that point you can bunt a little more. This "back and forth" of competing strategies may go on either in practice or in theory until either the equilibrium point is reached, or until one party refuses to budge from its sub-optimal strategy (like the amateur poker player who continues to bluff too much) and the other party responds accordingly (the expert player who calls potential bluffs most of the time, but occasionally throws his over-bluffing opponent "a bone").

There are many other specific situations in which game theory comes into play vis-à-vis the sacrifice bunt. The important point to remember is that against a manager whom you know or suspect is an expert strategist, either by design or by accident (it doesn't matter which), you must "play your cards" optimally according to game theory. If you don't think that the opposing team's manager is an astute strategist, then you must tailor your strategies to his strategies and responses (and potential responses), making sure that you don't accidentally encourage him to move *too much* in an optimum direction.

THE PITCHOUT

While sacrifice bunting is not generally though of as a "cat and mouse" (vernacular for having game theory implications) type of strategy (even though, as we have shown, it should be), the pitchout generally is. It is well-known that the idea of the pitchout is not only to "pick-off" a potential stolen base, hit and run, or suicide squeeze, but to plant the idea of a *possible* pitchout in the opposing manager's mind such that it reduces the chances of him calling for a steal, hit and run, or squeeze, presumably when it is in his team's best interest to do so (you wouldn't want to discourage an opponent from doing something that was *not* in his best interest, would you?).

Let's start by examining the cost of the pitchout. As we saw in the sac bunt chapter, the addition of a ball to the count on a pitchout, whether the manager guesses right or not (unless of course, the batter swings anyway), costs the defensive team a certain amount of run or win expectancy. The cost depends upon the count when the pitchout is called. A pitchout at 0-2 is not nearly as costly as one at 2-0 or 2-1. Of course, the batting team's manager is more likely to steal, hit and run, or squeeze at a count in which the opposing manager is less likely to pitch out, which would make the pitching team manager *want to* pitch out more often at an unfavorable count (like 2-1). In other words, we find the usual "give-and-take" dictated by game theory.

How much does a pitchout cost? As we just said, it depends on the count. At 0-2, a pitchout is not all that costly. An average batter with an 0-2 count has an expected wOBA of .222. At 1-2, the expected wOBA becomes .245. The cost of the pitchout, therefore, at an 0-2 count, is only 23 points of wOBA. With a runner on first and no outs, this change in wOBA corresponds to around a .03 run difference in RE. With two outs, it is around .02 runs.

In contrast, a pitchout on a 2-1 count costs a whopping 116 points in wOBA. With one out and a runner on first, that corresponds to .11 runs in RE. With no outs, it is even worse, .15 runs, and with two outs, it is .07 runs. Clearly, it is not generally wise to call a pitchout with a 2-1 count, unless you are pretty certain that the opposing manager is putting on whatever play you are trying to "pick-off" or discourage. How certain do you have to be?

Let's assume that the baserunner is attempting a steal for sure, with one out. We start with an RE of around .612 (a runner on first, one out, and a 2-1 count on the batter, a typical leadoff hitter). (We get that from our computer simulator.) On average, when a baserunner is attempting to steal on a pitchout, he is going to be out 52.7% of the time. So if the runner is going and we pitch out, 52.7% of the time we are left with two outs, no runner on base, and a 3-1 count on the batter. The RE for that state and that count is around .155 runs (again, according to our sim). The other 47.3% of the time, the runner is safe (even with the pitchout), and we are left with a runner on second, still one out, and a 3-1 count on the batter. That corresponds to an RE of around .871.

Let's see what the weighted average is.

.155 times .527 (52.7%) plus .871 times .473 (47.3%) equals .494, which is in fact a significant improvement over not pitching out at all (remember our original starting RE with a runner on first, one out, and a 2-1 count on the batter, was .612), assuming that without the pitchout, the baserunner is going to be caught stealing around 30% of the time (the average break-even point for a stolen base attempt). Of course, if the baserunner is really good, he will be safe more often than that with no pitchout, and the RE without the pitchout is going to be greater than .612, making the pitchout an even *more* effective play. However, if the baserunner had better than a 70% success rate in the first place, the 52.7% CS rate on the pitchout would probably decrease as well, thus making the pitchout a *less* effective play. So the baserunner's stolen base success rate is probably only marginally important at best.

Remember that the above numbers were predicated on the baserunner going 100% of the time when the pitchout was executed. That is not usually the case. In 2001, in the NL and AL combined, when a manager pitched out, the baserunner or baserunners (as in a double steal) were running only 23% of the time. Interestingly, in 2001, most managers were "right" around 20 to 27% of the time, whether they called the pitchout ten times during the season or 70 or more times. It appears, at least from that one-year sample, that no one manager is much better at "guessing right" than another, but that some of them prefer the pitchout much more than others. For example, Jimy Williams called for a pitchout an astounding 106 times in 118 games in 2001, with a 27.4% success rate (the runner was going 27.4% of the time), while Narron, Tracy, and Torborg called for one only 28 times in 405 total games, with a combined success rate of 28.6%, not significantly different than Williams's 27.4%.

Back to our original question. How sure does a manager have to be that the runner is going (assuming a runner on first only) before he calls a pitchout on a 2-1 count and one out? We already saw that if he is 100% certain, then the pitchout is always warranted. It turns out that the break-even point is around 54.3%. If a manager thinks that the runner is going to attempt a steal at least 54.3% of the time with a 2-1 count on the batter and one out, it is correct for him to pitch out. Since overall, managers only "guess right" around 23% of the time, he has to be especially sure that the runner is going on a 2-1 count. Of course, many steals (and hit and runs) occur on the 2-1 count, so maybe that 54.3% expectation, given the right situation, the right baserunner, etc., is not so unreasonable.

What about with an 0-2 count, which is the best time to execute the pitchout, at least in terms of the cost? As we said above, the cost of the 0-2 pitchout is only 23 wOBA points, which is around .025 runs with one out. How often does a manager have to "be right" in order to pitch out on an 0-2 count with one out? If we do the same calculations as above, we find that the break-even point is only around 18%. So because of the relatively small cost of an 0-2 pitchout (with one out), a manager can safely do so when there is only an 18% or greater chance of the runner going on the pitch. Keep in mind that unless the success rate of the baserunner is above the break-even point (70% or so, depending upon a whole slew of factors), the defense does not need to ever pitch out unless the offense ends up running too frequently (with a "negative expectancy"), which is unlikely to occur. It is only when there is a "positive expectancy" to the stolen base attempt in the first place, that the defense need concern itself with occasionally pitching out to discourage the offense from attempting a steal 100% of the time.

Not surprisingly, the stolen base attempt occurs least frequently with an 0-2 count than at any other count, other than at 2-0, 3-1, and (of course) 3-0. Here are the relative frequencies with which stolen bases are attempted at each count. (See Table 138.) Keep in mind that this data does not include when the baserunner is running on the pitch and the batter puts the ball in play, so that the actual numbers may be slightly different than indicated.

Table 138. **Stolen Base Attempts When The Batter Does Not Put The Ball In Play, 2002–2004, NL And AL**

	Number of attempts				Fraction of all attempts	Success rate (including pitchouts)			
Count	0 outs	1 out	2 outs	Overall		0 outs	1 out	2 outs	Overall
0-0	635	1017	1199	2851	.250	.710	.703	.723	.713
0-1	279	485	513	1277	.112	.656	.666	.741	.694
0-2	85	166	293	544	.048	.729	.807	.734	.756
1-0	337	547	481	1365	.119	.685	.665	.740	.697
1-1	296	481	526	1303	.114	.632	.640	.730	.675
1-2	178	326	453	957	.084	.747	.788	.740	.758
2-0	92	123	133	348	.030	.793	.740	.812	.782
2-1	196	276	275	747	.065	.643	.659	.742	.685
2-2	195	353	257	805	.070	.728	.694	.798	.735
3-0	14	18	15	47	.004	.786	.944	.933	.894
3-1	64	98	77	239	.021	.563	.429	.545	.502
3-2	289	636	18	943	.083	.478	.531	.722	.519
All counts	2660	4526	4240	11426	1.000	.667	.666	.737	.692

Note: At a 3-2 count, most of the "attempts" (when the runner is going on the pitch) are not recorded. The only time a 3-2 count stolen base attempt is recorded is when the batter strikes out and the inning is not over. Remember that when the batter puts the ball in play, walks, or strikes out to end the inning, "attempts" are not recorded for any of the counts.

Now let's look at a similar table for pitchouts. (See Table 139.)

Table 139.   Pitchouts By Count, 2004–2005, NL And AL

Count	Number of pitchouts				Fraction of all pitchouts	How often runner goes	How often runner out when going
	0 outs	1 out	2 outs	Overall			
0-0	149	269	188	606	.451	.160	.443
0-1	92	100	88	280	.208	.143	.600
0-2	25	26	90	141	.105	.142	.550
1-0	19	46	11	76	.057	.250	.632
1-1	60	60	27	147	.109	.163	.542
1-2	8	17	42	67	.050	.254	.588
2-0	0	3	0	3	.002	.000	.000
2-1	3	9	2	14	.010	.286	.500
2-2	2	4	3	9	.007	.444	.500
3-0	0	1	0	1	.001	.000	.000
3-1	0	1	0	1	.001	.000	.000
3-2	0	0	0	0	.000	.000	.000
All counts	358	536	451	1345	1.000	.167	.520

As you can see from the first table, the overwhelming plurality of stolen base attempts occurs at an 0-0 count. Not surprisingly, most pitchouts (45.1%) occur at that count as well. Game theory would suggest that this is correct, as the optimum frequency of both the stolen base attempt and the pitchout depend upon two things—one, the relative cost of the strategy if it fails, and two, the frequency at which the opponent uses its countervailing strategy. The analogy in poker is one, the pot odds that are given (how much money is already in the pot compared to the amount of the last bet) and two, how often each opponent bluffs or calls a potential bluff. Once again, there exists an equilibrium point in terms of the stolen base attempt and the pitchout; each manager executes his strategy a certain percentage of time such that his opponent cannot take advantage of that strategy. No matter what that opponent does (steal or not steal, pitch out or not pitch out), his expectancy is the same. That equilibrium point depends upon the game situation, the personnel involved, and as we can see from the discussion and charts above, the count on the batter.

As with the sacrifice bunt, the pitchout is a viable strategy even if it may not be "technically" correct in any particular situation, in that it forces the opposing team to attempt a steal that much less frequently. In other words, the chance of a baserunner stealing does not have to be higher than the technical break-even point in order for a pitchout to be correct. Of course, as we pointed out earlier, in order for the occasional pitchout to be indicated at all, the value of the stolen base attempt (without the pitchout) must be positive (for the offensive team) in the first place. That means that it makes no sense to pitch out, even occasionally, with a baserunner who is not expected to have a stolen base success rate above the break-even point, unless of course he is going to steal on any particular count an inordinate percentage of the time. In practice, we rarely see a pitchout unless there is a very good basestealer in a situation where he is likely to run.

The other side of the coin is that even if a stolen base attempt does not have a positive expectation, *after taking into consideration the likelihood of a pitchout*, the offensive team still must occasionally attempt a steal in order to force their opponent to occasionally pitch out. What we find fascinating is that much of the analyses done by even the most astute sabermetricians, especially when it comes to strategies like the stolen base, sacrifice bunt, and the hit and run, do *not* include elements of game theory, and therefore, their conclusions are often incorrect.

As with the sacrifice bunt and other strategies that involve game theory, if the opponent manager is not acting optimally, then his opponent's strategy must change from the equilibrium point as well. As we told you, managers are very different when it comes to how often they pitch out. Consequently, their opponents must adjust their strategies accordingly. Against managers like Dierker, Torborg, and Tracy, who hardly ever pitch out, or at least they didn't in 2001, teams should attempt the stolen base, hit and run, and the suicide squeeze more often than versus the league as a whole, and certainly more often than versus managers like Hargrove, Cox, Jimy Williams, and Valentine, who pitch out a lot. Against these "pitchout happy" managers (remember their success rates are not any higher than any other manager's, so it is not like they are the best "guessers"), those strategies should almost never be used.

We don't think that teams adjust their basestealing, hit and run, and squeeze frequencies nearly as much as they should, based upon their opposing managers' tendencies, and we certainly don't think that enough managers are using the pitchout strategy optimally. If they were, all of them should have about the same pitchout frequency (the equilibrium point). Clearly that is not the case.

The Book Says:

Managers should use the pitchout on occasion and according to game theory, based on the relative cost of its failure and success and the relative basestealing frequencies of their opponents. A manager does not want to pitch out so little that he encourages his opponents to "run amok" against him, unless of course the baserunner has a less than break-even stolen base success rate (without the pitchout), given the game situation and the pitcher/catcher combination. He also does not want to pitch out so much that his opponents rarely run against him (remember that every pitchout costs a team runs). Pitching out around once every three to four games versus an average team over the course of a season appears to be around the optimal (equilibrium point) frequency.

The Book Also Says:

The same is true of basestealing. A manager cannot call for an attempted steal so often and so predictably (even if that is technically correct in certain situations and with certain personnel) that it becomes correct for his opponent manager to always or at least frequently call for a pitchout. He also cannot call for a steal so infrequently (unless all of his baserunners are so incompetent and/or slow) that his opponent never has to pitch out. He must occasionally have his players steal even with a negative expectancy (including the pitchout) in order to force his opponent to occasionally pitch out.

The Book Also Says:

Managers should pay particular attention to their opponents' tendencies to pitch out, steal bases, hit and run, and squeeze. They should respond accordingly, however, they must be careful that they don't stray too far from the equilibrium point (if the opponent is not at the equilibrium point), lest they encourage their opponents to play more optimally. For example, against a "pitchout happy" manager like Jimy Williams, it may be correct to never hit and run or attempt a steal. If you do that, however, Williams will eventually stop pitching out, or at least will pitch out less often. You must "throw him a bone" every once in a while to encourage him to continue pitching out too frequently.

As we have alluded to several times already, the suicide squeeze is also a strategy that very much implicates game theory. Without delving into its nuances, suffice it to say that if the squeeze is anywhere near a viable strategy, it cannot be executed very much at all, because of the high cost of failure, and the ease with which it can be thwarted (via the pitchout). Because the squeeze should be and is in fact executed so infrequently, the pitchout should be used sparingly as well. While managers should generally squeeze and pitch out to thwart a possible squeeze as often as the equilibrium point dictates, as with the sacrifice bunt, and the pitchout/basestealing/hit and run, they should adjust their strategy according to the tendencies of their less astute managerial opponents (those who do *not* use game theory to dictate their tendencies).

PITCH SELECTION AND GAME THEORY

Probably the most important aspect of *game theory* and baseball involves the pitcher/batter confrontation. For example, as most baseball fans know, pitchers are generally taught to "get the first pitch over for a strike" (easier said than done for some pitchers, right?). At the same time, many batters, and in fact batters in general, do not like to offer at the first pitch, even if they perceive it as a strike, or even better, a hittable pitch. Some batters, like Vladimir Guerrero, are notorious first ball hitters. How often do batters in general take (not swing at) the first pitch? (See Table 140.)

As you can see, the average batter takes the first pitch 71% of the time. Compare that to only 56% for the second pitch. When the first pitch is taken, over 40% of the time it is a strike. On the second pitch, when the ball is taken, it is a strike only 30% of the time. Clearly batters in general do not particularly like swinging at the first pitch whether it is a ball or a strike. It's no wonder that pitchers are instructed to "get the first pitch over for a strike." Even when a pitcher throws a first pitch strike, it appears from the above data (we say *appears* because we don't know what percentage of first-pitches swung at were actually strikes), that batters only swing at them around 40% of the time. It also appears that pitchers throw about 50% first strikes.

Table 140.   First-Pitch Results, 2002–2004, NL And AL (Hit By A First Pitch And Intentional Balls Not Included)

First-Pitch Result	Rate
Pitches taken (per pitch)	0.711
Pitches swung or bunted at (per pitch)	0.289
Balls Taken (per pitch taken)	0.578
Strikes Taken (per pitch taken)	0.422
Swing or bunt and miss (per pitch not taken)	0.194
Foul (per pitch not taken)	0.366
Put in play (per pitch not taken)	0.440

So what is happening here? If batters don't often swing at first pitches, even strikes, and pitchers are instructed to "get the first pitch over," why do they only throw about 50% first strikes? Is that the best they can do? Are they trying with all their heart and soul to throw a strike 100% of the time on the first pitch and the best they can do is 50%?

To get an idea of the "best a pitcher can do" in terms of throwing strikes, we looked at all pitches following a 3-0 count, with no outs and no one on base, and a pitcher at the plate. We figured that if that isn't when a pitcher is *really* trying to throw a strike, well, he probably doesn't belong in the major leagues. Keep in mind though that our pool of pitchers with 3-0 counts are going to be the "wilder" ones in the first place, such that whatever strike percentage we come up with on the next pitch is going to be less than what we would expect from an average pitcher who happens to find himself in a 3-0 situation. Anyway, with a pitcher at the plate and a 3-0 count (and no outs and no one on base), pitchers throw 70.1% strikes. Heck, even with a weak (less than a .333 career wOBA) non-pitcher at the plate (and no outs, no runners on), pitchers (at least the wilder ones who find themselves in 3-0 counts) still throw 66% strikes. So the average pitcher appears to be able to throw at least 70% strikes if he really wants to.

So, then, why do they only throw 50% first-pitch strikes? If you've been following this chapter even a little, you know the answer. If they threw more first-pitch strikes, batters would presumably swing more often and get more hits (increasing their ensuing run expectancy) than they would otherwise. There must be an equilibrium point reached among pitchers and batters, such that pitchers only throw about 50% strikes on the first pitch and batters only swing about 30% of the time. It would take some complicated analysis to prove that this is indeed the correct equilibrium point according to game theory—such an analysis would be the subject of another day, or perhaps our next book.

The Book Says:

Even though pitchers are instructed to "get the first pitch over," and the average batter does not particularly like to swing at the first pitch, even first-pitch strikes, pitchers must throw first-pitch strikes less often than they are capable of (by not throwing right down the middle and mixing in an occasional off-speed pitch) in order to prevent the batter from swinging at a higher percentage of first pitches.

What about the fact that some hitters simply prefer to take the first pitch more often than others, and some pitchers simply cannot throw as many first-pitch strikes as they would otherwise like to, *or* some pitchers prefer to throw more or fewer first-pitch strikes than the average pitcher? If a pitcher throws a high percentage of first-pitch strikes for whatever reason, then it might actually be correct for a batter to swing almost every time he perceives the pitch a strike, at least one that is in the "fat" part of the strike zone. However (and again, you already know this if you have been paying attention to this chapter), if he swings at *too* many pitches, he is going to encourage that pitcher to start throwing fewer and fewer first-pitch strikes. Once again, we have the typical give and take of game theory.

Similarly, if a batter is known to be *very* selective on the first pitch, like a Wade Boggs or Kevin Youkilis (the most patient first-pitch hitters "take" an astounding 85–90% of the time), the pitcher might as well throw that 70% or more first strike that he is capable of, right? Again, no! If he did that, these batters are smart enough to eventually start swinging more. So a new equilibrium point must be reached such that the pitcher *is* going to throw more first-pitch strikes versus these guys, but not so much that he forces then to significantly alter their first-pitch approach. The same is true of the impatient first-pitch hitters, like Guerrero (45% take), Alou (52%) or Dmitri Young (52%). Why would you throw these guys a first-pitch strike in the first place? For one thing, they don't swing at *too* many pitches *out of the strike zone*. Many of those 50% or so first-pitch swings are when a strike is actually thrown. More importantly, if you rarely threw them a first-pitch strike, they would stop being so aggressive.

The Book Says:

There is a wide variance in "first-pitch preference" among batters (from around 50% to 90% in "percentage of first-pitches taken"). Against patient first-pitch hitters, pitchers should throw mostly strikes, probably in the 60% range. Against the impatient ones, they should try and throw to the corners more and mix in more off-speed pitches. Their first-pitch strike frequency against these batters should be around 35 to 40%. Batters need to adjust their first-pitch tendencies as well, depending upon the tendencies of the pitcher. Batters and pitchers (and catchers) should know the first-pitch tendencies of their opponents.

After the first pitch is thrown, things get complicated. What pitch to throw depends on the pitcher's repertoire, his control, the batter's strengths and weaknesses, the count, the baserunners, the score, the inning, the subsequent batters—in short, all the usual stuff. One thing that is often overlooked, however, in discussing pitch selection, is the role of *game theory* (what a surprise, right?). By that, we mean how much should a pitcher *randomly* mix up his pitch selection, in any given situation, in order to confuse the batter, or more precisely, to prevent him from taking advantage of a predictable strategy, which is really what game theory is all about?

Let's say that there is a runner on third and one out in a close game in the late innings, the count is 0-2 on the batter, and the pitcher has a very good curve ball, which he often uses as his "out" or strikeout pitch. Conventional wisdom says that he should throw that curve ball out of the zone and hope that the batter chases it for the strikeout (assuming that he has confidence in his catcher's pitch blocking ability). Well, if that is conventional wisdom, and the pitcher and catcher know that he is supposed to throw that pitch, then surely the batter knows it as well? And if the batter knows that he is going to get a curve ball in the dirt, surely he can lay off the pitch—in fact, he can simply decide beforehand not to swing at all.

Against an astute batter who has some pitch recognition ability and is not simply compelled to swing at any 0-2 pitch in the dirt, then yes, the decision to throw that pitch 100% of the time is not a good one. It will simply be a wasted pitch (for a ball) most of the time. Of course, with the 0-2 count and two bases open, the cost of the ball is not all that great, especially in contrast to the gain if the batter does somehow swing at the pitch and strike himself out. The pitcher also has the added benefit of occasionally missing his location *a little* such that he accidentally throws a perfect pitcher's pitch, a curve ball right on the black or just off the plate!

In any case, game theory dictates that in most instances in which the cost of failure (in this case, mainly a ball) versus the benefit of success (the strikeout) is not so disparate, the pitcher must not throw any one pitch 100% of the time, in order to keep the batter from knowing exactly what is coming, and thus acting accordingly (in this case, not swinging, unless the pitcher accidentally throws a strike).

Once again, the optimal percentages are dictated by a number of things, among them the cost/benefit ratio of success or failure, and the anticipated response of the batter (how likely he is to swing at that curve ball in the dirt, even if he suspects that it is coming). And, as we have already explained, if we can't reliably anticipate the response of the batter, or we suspect that he is a game theory expert, the optimal percentages are equal to the equilibrium point.

What we find in practice is that the more extreme the count and the situation, the more the percentages move away from 50/50. In the above example, the pitcher might want to throw that curve ball in the dirt 80% or even 90% of the time (depending on the batter, his control, etc.), but he must also throw other pitches, occasionally even a strike, in order to keep the batter "honest" (prevent him from taking advantage of a predictable strategy, which is easy for an astute batter to do).

Similarly, with a 3-0 count, in a situation where the pitcher does not necessarily want to walk the batter (like, with no outs and no one on), he cannot throw a fastball right down the middle 100% of the time (well, maybe he can versus another pitcher or a similarly weak batter— sometimes the optimal percentage for a particular alternative is zero or 100). It must be 90/10 or even 80/20, depending upon the tendency of the batter (how often he swings at 3-0 pitches) and his overall batting prowess (which affects the cost/benefit ratio).

At less extreme counts and situations (where the cost/benefit ratio is not that high), the proper percentages are closer to 50/50. For example, with a 2-2 or 1-1 count in a low-leverage situation, a pitcher can and should randomly throw almost any type of pitch (and to different locations). Again, the types of pitches and percentages are always affected by the batter's tendencies, the pitcher's repertoire, and the game situation. The important thing to remember is that in baseball, it is rare for the "correct" pitch in any given situation, even an extreme or high-leverage one, as in the example above (0-2, runner on third), to be one that is thrown 100% of the time. There should almost always be an alternative or several alternatives, in order to keep the batter "honest."

The Book Says:

Pitchers should rarely (if ever) plan on throwing only one particular pitch in any given situation to any given hitter. They should throw a certain pitch a certain percentage of the time, and another, different pitch (or location) another percentage of the time, etc. That way, the batter cannot guess precisely what is coming.

What these percentages are depend upon the usual things—the count, the game situation, the batter's tendencies, and the pitcher's abilities. In general, the more astute the batter is, and the greater his pitch recognition abilities and "self-control," the more the pitcher has to randomly mix up his pitches and strategies.

Pitchers and their catchers should be particularly aware of how often batters respond correctly (or not) to the most likely pitch, given the count and game situation. Armed with this information, they should adjust their strategies (frequencies of the various pitches and locations) accordingly.

There are many other situations in baseball that implicate game theory. Just about anything where there are two competing strategies will qualify—pickoff attempts at first base, especially by a left-handed pitcher, or even something as subtle as the number and pattern of looks to second by a pitcher when there is a runner on second base. We have tried to present to you some of the more salient and interesting situations in which game theory is used, abused, and sometimes ignored in baseball. The next time you wince (or scream bloody murder) when the pitcher on your favorite team throws an 0-2 fastball right down the middle and gives up the game-winning home run, remember that he may have simply been pitching according to game theory, and he was planning on throwing that pitch only 1% of the time.

APPENDIX – DON'T TRY THIS AT HOME

THE GORY DETAILS

If what follows reads like a mathematics text, well, to some extent it is. Our goal is to explain all (or at least most) of the mathematical principles used herein, rather than peppering the main text of the book with occasional lessons in math. If you want to understand the details of our calculations, feel free to read on. If not, you can just take our word that we're doing our calculations correctly. We emphasize that the math in this section is included for the sake of showing our work; if you wish to skip over some parts where the math gets too intense, feel free to do so.

Measuring Average, Standard Deviation, and Variance

We begin by defining some mathematical terms frequently seen throughout the book. We'll begin with the concept of "average" (which is the same as the "mean"). Most of you are probably familiar with this term. Given a series of values, their average equals their sum divided by the number of values in the series. For example, if you wish to average 0, 0, 2, 3, and 5, you divide their sum (0+0+2+3+5=10) by 5 to get 2. In mathematical terms, you calculate the average using the following expression:

$$\bar{x} = \frac{1}{N}\sum_{i=1}^{N} x_i, \tag{1}$$

where $\bar{x}$ is the mean (2), N is the number of data points (5), and x_i is the ith data value (0, 0, 2, 3, or 5). Because we will be using this and other equations later, we will number this one as "equation 1." (The Σ symbolizes that a sum is being taken; in this case, a sum over all values of x_i.) An alternative definition of the mean is:

$$\bar{x} = \sum_x xP(x) \equiv \langle x \rangle, \tag{2}$$

where $P(x)$ is the probability of drawing a particular value x. In the above example, $P(0)$ is 0.4 to denote the 40% chance (2 zeroes out of 5 numbers, or 2 divided by 5) that the drawn value is zero; $P(1)$, $P(4)$, and $P(5)$ are 0.2 to denote the 20% chance (1 in 5) of drawing any of these three values, and all other values of $P(x)$ are zero. Note that the total of the probability values always equals *exactly* one:

$P(0)+P(1)+P(2)+P(3)+P(4)+P(5)=1$.

The symbol $\langle x \rangle$ denotes the *expectation value* of x, which we will use as shorthand for the probability-weighted sum. It is exactly equal to, and the same as, the mean.

Standard deviation and variance are a bit more complex. Some of you may be familiar with these terms as well. Put simply, standard deviation is the typical difference between numbers in your series and the average, and variance is the square of the standard deviation. Variance (σ^2) is calculated using:

$$\sigma^2 = \frac{1}{N-1}\sum_{i=1}^{N}(x_i - \bar{x})^2, \tag{3}$$

or

$$\sigma^2 = \left(\sum_x x^2 P(x)\right) - \bar{x}^2 = \langle x^2 \rangle - \langle x \rangle^2. \tag{4}$$

As with $\langle x \rangle$, the symbol $\langle x^2 \rangle$ denotes the expectation value of x^2. For the above series of points, the variance is calculated using the first of the two equations, and equals

$$\sigma^2 = \frac{1}{5-1}\left[(0-2)^2 + (0-2)^2 + (2-2)^2 + (3-2)^2 + (5-2)^2\right]$$
$$= (4+4+0+1+9)/4 = 4.5$$

The standard deviation is the square root of the variance (4.5), which is 2.12. In other words, from our set of five values, we estimate that they are drawn from a distribution centered on 2.00 with a typical spread of 2.12 from the central value. If this distribution is a bell curve (Gaussian, in mathematical parlance), 68% of points will fall within one standard deviation of the mean, and 95% of points will fall within two standard deviations of the mean.

In general, we will be dealing with distributions that are not strictly Gaussian, since, for example, it is clearly impossible to have an OBP that is less than zero or greater than one, and Gaussian curves extend to infinity at both ends. Fortunately, unless the mean is less than three standard deviations from zero or one, the Gaussian approximation is adequate; thus, throughout this book, we will be able to treat our distributions as if they were in fact Gaussian.

Uncertainty

From the above example, it's clear that we're ignoring one giant issue—how well we know the average and standard deviation. In the above example, we calculate that the average is *exactly* 2. But how confident are we that the *real* average (what we would get if we averaged a million measurements rather than just the five) is 2.000, and not 2.001? Likewise, there is a limit to the accuracy we are willing to claim we know as the real variance and standard deviation. How does one calculate this?

As noted in the previous section, we will use a Gaussian (bell curve) for our probability distributions. Mathematically, this means that the probability of a measurement giving a value of x is calculated using the following equation:

$$P(x) = \frac{1}{\sqrt{2\pi\sigma^2}} e^{-\frac{(x-\bar{x})^2}{2\sigma^2}}.$$

As always, $\bar{x}$ is the mean of the distribution and σ is the standard deviation. For the less mathematically inclined (who have survived this far), the symbol e^x denotes the value e (approximately 2.8) to the xth power. For example, 4^3, or 4 to the third power (also, 4 "cubed"), equals $4 \times 4 \times 4$, or 64; likewise 3^4, or 3 to the 4th power, equals $3 \times 3 \times 3 \times 3$, or 81. The symbol $\sqrt{\ }$ denotes that a square root is being taken of whatever is inside the symbol (in this case, $2\pi\sigma^2$).

Now we have some fun with the math. We know from above that $P(x)$ is the probability of measuring a point whose value is x. Flipping this around, the same function also gives the probability of a particular mean value being correct, given that a point whose value is x was observed. In other words, given one point x and a measurement uncertainty (standard deviation) of σ, we can write that the mean value $\bar{x}$ is constrained by the following probability distribution:

$$P(\bar{x}) = \frac{1}{\sqrt{2\pi\sigma^2}} e^{-\frac{(\bar{x}-x)^2}{2\sigma^2}} = Ce^{-\frac{\bar{x}^2 - 2\bar{x}x}{2\sigma^2}},$$

where C is a constant (not a function of $\bar{x}$) whose value is unimportant for our purposes (it ensures that the total probability is one).

If there is more than one data point, we multiply the probability of drawing each point from the distribution, which gives us:

$$P(\bar{x}) = \prod_{i=1}^{N} Ce^{-\frac{\bar{x}^2 - 2\bar{x}x_i}{2\sigma^2}} = Ce^{-\frac{N\bar{x}^2 - 2\bar{x}\sum x_i}{2\sigma^2}} = Ce^{-\frac{\bar{x}^2 - 2\bar{x}\sum \frac{x_i}{N}}{2\sigma^2/N}}.$$

Note the similarities between the final forms of the preceding two equations. Essentially two things have changed. First, instead of the lone value x used for the estimate of $\bar{x}$, we now have the mean ($\sum x_i / N$). That the values are averaged to estimate $\bar{x}$ is self-evident of course, but it is good to see it come out of our calculation. The other change is more important; we see that the variance in our estimate of $\bar{x}$ is now σ^2/N instead of merely σ^2. The uncertainty is the square root of this, or $\sigma/\sqrt{N}$.

Applying this to the example above, we can now state that the mean is 2.00±0.95—in other words, there is a 68% chance that the mean of the distribution is between 1.05 and 2.95.

OK, what about the variance? The math here gets even more intense (it involves computing the variance of the variance), so we will spare you the gory details and simply cut to the chase. The uncertainty in the variance equals $\sigma^2 \sqrt{2/N}$, while the uncertainty in the standard deviation equals $\sigma/\sqrt{2N}$. Thus, for our five-point illustration, we also can state that the variance equals 4.50±2.85, and that the standard deviation is 2.12±0.67.

What is probably most important to draw from this section is that uncertainties go down as the square root of the number of points. In other words, if you want to make twice as accurate a measurement, you need *four times* as much data. This is the reason why, even with a full season's worth of baseball data, you can conclude surprisingly little about a player's skills.

In addition to telling us how accurately we have measured something, uncertainties serve a second purpose when we need to combine two estimates of the same value. Suppose that, in addition to our mean of 2.00±0.95, a second estimate of that mean (say from another sample of data from the same population) is 3.10±0.50. Which is right? We could simply pick the more precise measurement (3.10±0.50), but in doing so we are totally throwing out the information that resulted in the first estimate. Surely there must be a better way to do this, and indeed there is. The solution is to make a weighted average of all estimates of a value, with each value weighted by the inverse of the square of the uncertainty. So, in this example, we weight our first estimate of 2.00 by $1/0.95^2$ (1.11) and our second estimate of 3.10 by 0.50^2 (4.00). Thus, our final estimate of this value is

$$\bar{x} = \frac{2.00/0.95^2 + 3.10/0.50^2}{1/0.95^2 + 1/0.50^2} = \frac{14.62}{5.11} = 2.86.$$

As one would expect, the combined estimate is significantly closer to the more accurate measurement, but it still uses all of the known information. The uncertainty in this value is given by:

$$\sigma(\bar{x}) = \frac{1}{\sqrt{1/0.95^2 + 1/0.50^2}} = \frac{1}{\sqrt{5.11}} = 0.44.$$

Again as one would probably expect, the final uncertainty is a bit smaller than the smaller of the two uncertainties. For the general case, in which one is averaging a large number of measurements with uncertainties, the average and uncertainty are calculated by:

$$\bar{x} = \frac{\sum x_i / \sigma_i^2}{\sum 1/\sigma_i^2} \tag{5}$$

and

$$\sigma(\bar{x}) = \frac{1}{\sqrt{\sum 1/\sigma_i^2}}. \tag{6}$$

Random Variation in Binomials

With our introduction to basic statistical terms and uncertainties, we now look into one of the most important concepts in this book: random variation. Let's begin with the simplest case, the *binomial*, in which there are two possible outcomes. If you flip a coin, you know there is about a 50-50 probability that it will land on either side. If you flip it twice, it follows that there are four possible outcomes: heads-heads, heads-tails, tails-heads, and tails-tails, each with a 1/4 probability of occurring. Or, if you are just tallying the number of heads, there is a 25% chance that you will have gotten heads twice, a 50% chance of getting heads once, and a 25% chance of getting heads zero times. For any number of flips, N, the probability of getting exactly x heads equals

$$P(x) = \frac{N!}{x!(N-x)!} 0.5^N,$$

where the "!" symbol denotes the factorial (i.e., $4! = 1 \times 2 \times 3 \times 4 = 24$) and $0!$ is defined as 1. We can easily verify the 25%, 50%, 25% probabilities above:

$$P(0) = \frac{2!}{0!2!} 0.5^2 = \frac{2}{1 \times 2} 0.25 = 0.25,$$

$$P(1) = \frac{2!}{1!1!} 0.5^2 = \frac{2}{1 \times 1} 0.25 = 0.5,$$

$$P(2) = \frac{2!}{2!0!} 0.5^2 = \frac{2}{2 \times 1} 0.25 = 0.25.$$

In baseball, the most common use of binomial statistics is on-base percentage (OBP). Of course, in this case, we can't assume that all players have exactly a 50% chance of reaching base, so we must generalize the above equation:

$$P(x) = \frac{N!}{x!(N-x)!} r^x (1-r)^{N-x},$$

where $P(x)$ is the probability of reaching base x times, N is the number of plate appearances, and r is the odds of reaching base (i.e., the player's expected OBP).

After one plate appearance, the player's actual on-base percentage is either zero (if he gets out) or one (if he reaches base). The odds of it being zero are $(1-r)$, while the odds of it being one are r. Thus, we can write the expectation values as follows:

$$\langle x \rangle = \sum_{x=0}^{1} x P(x) = 0P(0) + 1P(1) = r$$

and

$$\langle x^2 \rangle = \sum_{x=0}^{1} x^2 P(x) = 0P(0) + 1P(1) = r.$$

OK, so you're probably not going to be shocked to find out that the expected player's on-base percentage equals his probability of reaching base. What we're after is the variance in this value, which from the preceding sections equals:

$$\sigma^2 = \langle x^2 \rangle - \langle x \rangle^2 = r - r^2 = r(1-r).$$

We're almost there. Recalling the relation between the variance of a single measurement and the uncertainty of the mean, we calculate the uncertainty in a player's measured OBP (or any other binomial statistic) to be

$$\sigma(\bar{x}) = \sqrt{r(1-r)/N} = \sqrt{\frac{OBP(1-OBP)}{N}},$$

using the fact that r is the player's real OBP; N is again the number of plate appearances. An average player (OBP of around .330) will have a random uncertainty in OBP of $.47/\sqrt{N}$.

We emphasize that this uncertainty is due to random fluctuation alone. For example, there is a small but non-zero chance of flipping "heads" five times in a row with an unbiased coin (to be precise, a 1-in-32 chance). Likewise, there is a non-zero chance that a player who always has a 35% chance of reaching base of having an OBP of .250 in any number of plate appearances. (Looked at the other way around, there is a non-zero chance that a player has an "observed" or "measured" OBP of .250, yet is legitimately a .350 OBP hitter.) To avoid confusion, we will refer to "OBP skill" as the player's probability of reaching base (i.e., how good he really is), and "measured OBP" as the fraction of times he has actually reached base (how well he has performed).

Random Variation in Multinomials

As you see throughout the book, our preferred average is not on-base percentage, but rather wOBA—a weighted combination of outcomes that is scaled to typical OBP values. This statistic is not a two-outcome binomial, but rather a multiple-outcome statistic called a *multinomial.*

In general, if the probability of each possible outcome is r_i, the probability of measuring x_i occurrences of each outcome in a total of N chances is given by:

$$P = N! \prod_i \frac{r_i^{x_i}}{x_i!}.$$

You can verify that the binomial is merely a simple case of this, as $r_1 = 1 - r_o$ and $x_1 = N - x_o$.

Fortunately, the equations for mean, variance, and uncertainties all remain valid; we need only to recompute the expectation values. For a general multinomial, these values are as follows:

$$\langle x \rangle = \sum_i w_i r_i$$

and

$$\langle x^2 \rangle = \sum_i w_i^2 r_i,$$

where w_i is the weight associated with each outcome. For the case of wOBA, these equations become:

$$\langle x \rangle = .72r(\text{NIBB}) + .75r(\text{HBP}) + .90r(1\text{B}) + .92r(\text{ROE}) + 1.24r(2\text{B}) + 1.56r(3\text{B}) + 1.95r(\text{HR})$$

and

$$\langle x^2 \rangle = .52r(\text{NIBB}) + .56r(\text{HBP}) + .81r(1\text{B}) + .85r(\text{ROE}) + 1.54r(2\text{B}) + 2.43r(3\text{B}) + 3.80r(\text{HR})$$

The first formula, of course, is just the expected wOBA. We note that the weights in the second formula are similar to a scaled slugging average (0.8–0.9 times the number of bases); thus, it is the power hitters who will suffer the most from random variation in their wOBA, while singles hitters will be much more consistent.

For the more complex work we will show, we actually will have to compute this correctly by using the expectation values of wOBA and the second equation with the weights squared. However, a reasonable approximation for players with average profiles (i.e., HR/H and BB/H ratios) is:

$$\langle x^2 \rangle = 1.1 \langle x \rangle;$$

therefore we can approximate the variance in wOBA after N plate appearances as

$$\sigma^2 = \frac{\text{wOBA}(1.1 - \text{wOBA})}{N},$$

and the uncertainty in the measured wOBA as

$$\sigma(\bar{x}) = \sqrt{\frac{\text{wOBA}(1.1 - \text{wOBA})}{N}}.$$

Using this approximation, we calculate that the uncertainty in wOBA equals $.50/\sqrt{N}$ for a typical player (wOBA=.33), an increase of 7% in the uncertainty, compared with regular OBP.

Measuring Population Variations

Several times in this book, we will need to measure the inherent player-to-player variation in a particular skill (in other words, differences in the underlying skill levels of players). We don't mean the standard deviation of the measured stats, as measured stats include effects of random fluctuations—which we have already shown can be quite large (even for a significant number of plate appearances). Rather, what we are after is the standard deviation of the underlying skill levels.

In order to calculate this, we rely on the fact that the total observed variance equals the variance from random fluctuation plus the variance from differences in the players' skill levels. Or, to put it another way, the variance in underlying skills equals the total observed variance *minus* the random variance. For example, suppose you are trying to calculate the standard deviation of player skill levels for OBP. Let's say you have a set of players with 500 plate appearances each, and that the standard deviation of their OBP is .033. From the chart in our binomial variance section, you know that random variation contributes .021 to this. Thus we estimate the variance in the underlying skill level to be $.033^2-.021^2=.00065$, corresponding to a standard deviation of .025. In other words, the standard deviation of the player skill levels is .025, meaning that (assuming the mean is .330) 68% of players in the sample have true skill levels between .305 and .355, and 95% are between .280 and .380.

Unfortunately, the cases we will be dealing with are not this simple. Specifically, players won't always have uncertainties in the observed OBP of $.47/\sqrt{N}$ because they don't have the same true skill levels (and thus our approximation of .47 isn't always correct), nor will everyone have exactly the same number of plate appearances. In short, the uncertainty in the observed OBP will vary from player to player, making this more challenging. We get around this by computing the variance in OBP on a player-by-player basis; on average, the square of the difference between a player's OBP and the average OBP (i.e., the total observed OBP variance) should equal the expected random variance plus the variance in OBP skill levels:

$$\left(OBP_i - \overline{OBP}\right)^2 = \frac{OBP_i(1-OBP_i)}{N_i} + \sigma^2_{OBP,i},$$

where OBP_i is player i's measured OBP, $\overline{OBP}$ is the league-average OBP, N_i is player i's number of plate appearances, and $\sigma_{OBP,i}$ is the standard deviation of player OBP skills. Actually, it's a bit more complicated than this, since $\overline{OBP}$ is calculated using all player OBP, including that of the player being examined. Naturally the inclusion of the player's OBP in the league-average decreases the expected variance from random fluctuations, so that the equation above becomes:

$$\left(OBP_i - \overline{OBP}\right)^2 = \frac{OBP_i(1-OBP_i)}{N_i}\left(1 - \frac{N_i}{N_{tot}}\right) + \sigma^2_{OBP,i}$$

$$= \frac{w_i OBP_i(1-OBP_i)}{N_i} + \sigma^2_{OBP,i}$$

where N_{tot} equals the total number of plate appearance used to calculate the league-average OBP, and w_i is shorthand for the $(1-N_i/N_{tot})$ factor. Rewriting this to solve for $\sigma_{OBP,i}$, we get:

$$\sigma^2_{OBP,i} = \left(OBP_i - \overline{OBP}\right)^2 - \frac{w_i OBP_i(1-OBP_i)}{N_i}.$$

Recalling that the uncertainty in the variance equals the total variance times the square root of two, we can write this mathematically as:

$$\sigma(\sigma^2_{OBP,i}) = \sqrt{2}\left[\frac{OBP_i(1-OBP_i)}{N_i} + \sigma^2_{OBP,i}\right].$$

So, with these equations, we now have a measurement (with uncertainty) of the variance of player-to-player OBP skills for each player in our sample. Using the earlier equations for combining multiple measurements to produce a single value, we can calculate σ_{OBP} (the variation in OBP skills) using:

$$\sigma^2_{OBP} = \frac{\displaystyle\sum_i \frac{\left(OBP_i - \overline{OBP}\right)^2 - w_i OBP_i(1-OBP_i)/N_i}{2\left[OBP_i(1-OBP_i)/N_i + \sigma^2_{OBP}\right]^2}}{\displaystyle\sum_i \frac{1}{2\left[OBP_i(1-OBP_i)/N_i + \sigma^2_{OBP}\right]^2}}.$$

For the sake of completeness, we also compute the uncertainty in σ_{OBP} with

$$\sigma(\sigma^2_{OBP}) = \frac{1}{\sqrt{\displaystyle\sum_i \frac{1}{2\left[OBP_i(1-OBP_i)/N_i + \sigma^2_{OBP}\right]^2}}}.$$

We acknowledge that this is somewhat circular, as σ_{OBP} is used in the equation to measure itself, but it is a sufficiently small term that the solution can be iterated—i.e., you solve it once with σ_{OBP} set to an initial guess, solve it a second time with σ_{OBP} set to the measured value from the first solution, and so on, until a consistent solution is obtained.

Calculations using these principles in somewhat different scenarios are also needed. For example, if we are looking for player-to-player variation in platoon splits, we are comparing a batter's performance against left-handed pitching with the same batter's performance against right-handed pitching.

$$\left(\text{OBP}_{\text{LHP},i} - \text{OBP}_{\text{RHP},i}\right)^2$$
$$= \frac{\text{OBP}_{\text{LHP},i}(1 - \text{OBP}_{\text{LHP},i})}{N_{\text{LHP},i}} + \frac{\text{OBP}_{\text{RHP},i}(1 - \text{OBP}_{\text{RHP},i})}{N_{\text{RHP},i}} + \sigma^2_{\text{platoon},i}.$$

Of course, if we are discussing right-handed batters, they ought to perform better against lefties than against righties. In other words, we *expect* that OBP_{LHP} will exceed OBP_{RHP}; what we care about is whether some players have greater or lesser platoon splits than average. In this case, we choose to characterize the average platoon split as a multiple, defining m as the average ratio of OBP_{RHP} to OBP_{LHP}. Including this factor, the above equation becomes:

$$\left(m\text{OBP}_{\text{LHP},i} - \text{OBP}_{\text{RHP},i}\right)^2$$
$$= m^2 \frac{w_i\text{OBP}_{\text{LHP},i}(1 - \text{OBP}_{\text{LHP},i})}{N_{\text{LHP},i}} + \frac{w_i\text{OBP}_{\text{RHP},i}(1 - \text{OBP}_{\text{RHP},i})}{N_{\text{RHP},i}} + \sigma^2_{\text{platoon},i}.$$

Note that the weight term w_i returns in this equation, as the average platoon ratio was presumably calculated using all available data (including this player's plate appearances). From here, we repeat the above math steps to estimate the player-to-player variance in platoon ratio skills.

Likewise, we can measure population variations in wOBA values by replacing the $r(1-r)/N$ variances with the appropriate wOBA variances.

Estimating Skills using Regression Toward the Mean

Suppose that you flipped a coin three times and came up heads all three times. Does this mean that you found a coin that comes up only heads? Or did you just get lucky? Chances are, it is the latter. After all, you stand a 1-in-4 chance of getting the same result on three straight coin flips (if the coin is "fair"), while the likelihood of this being a magic ("unfair") coin that only comes up one way or the other is quite small.

Still, there is some non-zero chance that your coin is off balance to the extent that the "heads" probability could be greater than 50%, and thus we have to take this into account if we're estimating the likelihood of a future coin flip coming up heads. So how exactly does one go about estimating the probability of a future coin flip, balancing the knowledge that coins tend to be adequately balanced with the knowledge that this particular coin gave you three straight heads? We'll consider two examples.

In the first example, we make no assumption regarding the fraction of coins that are "unfair." In other words, we think it is as likely that a coin would always come up heads as it is that a coin would come up heads half the time (or, for that matter, never). So our "population" of coins consists of coins that flip to heads anywhere from never (0%) to always (100%), with any percentage being just as likely as any other. Mathematically, we can write that the coin population is characterized with an average of 50% and standard deviation of 29%. This means that, before a coin has been flipped, we estimate that its probability of flipping to heads is .50±.29 (as usual, we write the uncertainty as one standard deviation).

After making three coin flips, all of which come up as heads, we now have additional information about this coin. Namely, in these three coin flips, the fraction of the time we got heads is 100%, and the expected random fluctuation in three coin flips is 25%. Thus, our measurement of the rate at which this particular coin comes up as heads is 1.00±.25.

So, putting this together, we have two estimates of the coin's probability of flipping to heads. One, based on the characteristics of the population of all coins, is .50±.29. The second, based on data from this particular coin, is 1.00±.25. As we have mentioned already, to combine these two estimates, we weight them by the inverse of the square of the uncertainties. Using equation 5, the estimated probability of this coin flipping to heads the next time equals:

$$f = \frac{.50/.29^2 + 1.00/.29^2}{1/.29^2 + 1/.29^2} = 0.81.$$

The uncertainty in this estimate (from equation 6) is:

$$\sigma_f = \sqrt{\frac{1}{1/.29^2 + 1/.25^2}} = .19.$$

In other words, combining everything we know about this coin—that it is a coin, and how it flips, we estimate an 81% probability that it will flip to heads the next time, but still have a rather large (19%) uncertainty in this estimate. Put into baseball terms, someone who knows nothing about baseball and observes only three plate appearances will not have much of an idea how likely a player is to get on base.

In our second example, let's take a more realistic coin population. For example, let's suppose that 98% of coins are perfectly balanced, 1% always come up heads, and the other 1% always come up tails. Once again, an average coin will flip to heads half the time. We calculate this using equation 2, and defining f as the fraction of times that a coin flips to heads:

$$\langle f \rangle = \sum_f f \times P(f) = (0.00 \times 0.01) + (0.50 \times 0.98) + (1.00 \times 0.01) = 0.50.$$

To calculate the standard deviation in this population, we use equation 4:

$$\sigma_f^2 = \left(\sum_f f^2 \times P(f) \right) - \langle f \rangle^2 ,$$
$$= \left[(0.00 \times 0.01) + (0.25 \times 0.98) + (1.00 \times 0.01) \right] - 0.50^2 = .005$$

or

$$\sigma_f = 0.07.$$

Thus, before our coin has been flipped, we estimate the probability of it coming up heads to be .50±.07.

As with the first example, our measurement (and measurement uncertainty) is that the coin's probability of coming up heads is 1.00±.25. Combining our knowledge of the characteristics of coins in general with the performance of this particular coin, we again use equations 5 and 6 to calculate our expectation of the coin's future flips:

$$f = \frac{.50/.07^2 + 1.00/.25^2}{1/.07^2 + 1/.25^2} = 0.54.$$

The uncertainty in this estimate (from equation 6) is:

$$\sigma_f = \sqrt{\frac{1}{1/.07^2 + 1/.25^2}} = .07.$$

This result (that we estimate a 54% chance that the coin will flip heads the next time) is about what one might figure intuitively. Even with a perfectly unbiased coin, three consecutive flips will come up heads 1/8 of the time, so having three consecutive flips as heads is not all that unusual. However, a coin that comes up only heads would be extremely unusual, and thus we are more likely to believe that this is an unbiased coin that happened to come up heads three times than we are to think that this is a biased coin.

Since this is a baseball book, we'll switch to a baseball illustration. Suppose that the league-average OBP is .330, and we've established (using the techniques from the previous section) that the standard deviation of player OBP skills is .025. So in the absence of all information, we estimate that any particular player's OBP skill is .330±.025. Now suppose that we have a player who has an OBP of .450 in 100 plate appearances, which gives us a measured OBP of .450 and uncertainty in this measurement of .050. As we have mentioned already, to combine these two estimates, we weight them by the inverse of the square of the uncertainties (equation 5, for those counting). Thus the estimated OBP skill of this player equals:

$$\text{skill} = \frac{.330/.025^2 + .450/.050^2}{1/.025^2 + 1/.050^2} = .354.$$

Put simply, because the variation in players' skills is smaller than the accuracy in this player's measured OBP, we estimate that the player's OBP skill is closer to the league-average than to his measured value. On the other hand, had his .450 OBP been in 400 plate appearances, both uncertainties would be .025, which would change the calculation to:

$$\text{skill} = \frac{.330/.025^2 + .450/.025^2}{1/.025^2 + 1/.025^2} = .390.$$

So for this player, 400 plate appearances is the break-even point in which our estimate of his OBP skill is half based on his performance and half based on the league-average.

The fact that one must consider the standard deviation of the population skills is what is referred to as *regression toward the mean*. Simply put, if the standard deviation of the population is quite small, one assumes that deviations from this are probably due to random deviation and thus one estimates player abilities very close to the overall averages. On the other hand, if the standard deviation of the population is large, the reverse is true.

We conclude this section with a few approximations that are used throughout this book, and should give you a good feeling for how much one has to regress toward the mean. If we use the estimate of uncertainty in OBP ($.47/\sqrt{N}$), one estimates a player's OBP skill as:

$$\text{skill} = \overline{\text{OBP}} + \frac{N/.22}{N/.22 + 1/\sigma^2}(\text{OBP} - \overline{\text{OBP}})$$

$$= \overline{\text{OBP}} + \frac{N}{N + .22/\sigma^2}(\text{OBP} - \overline{\text{OBP}})$$

Back to our example, if the standard deviation of the population skill level is .025, a player would need $.22/.025^2 = 350$ plate appearances for his estimated OBP skill to be based half on his performance and half on the population average.

Likewise, using our estimate of uncertainty in wOBA ($.50/\sqrt{N}$), one would estimate a player's wOBA skill as:

$$\text{skill} = \overline{\text{wOBA}} + \frac{N/.25}{N/.25 + 1/\sigma^2}(\text{wOBA} - \overline{\text{wOBA}})$$

$$= \overline{\text{wOBA}} + \frac{N}{N + .25/\sigma^2}(\text{wOBA} - \overline{\text{wOBA}})$$

Thus if the standard deviation of the population wOBA skill level is also .025, a player would need $.25/.025^2 = 400$ plate appearances for his estimated wOBA skill to be based half on performance and half on the average. The reason for the increased number of plate appearances for a player to prove himself is that the wOBA statistic is more susceptible to random fluctuation, and thus measurements of wOBA can't be trusted as much as measurements of OBP.

What is worth noting is the amount that one must regress toward the mean is related to the variance of the player skill levels and the number of trials (in this case, the number of plate appearances). Thus, if a particular skill had a variance of .018 rather than .025, players would have to post 700 or 800 plate appearances for their estimated skill levels to be half based on performance. And, of course, if a particular skill has zero variation whatsoever (all ballplayers have exactly the same skill level), one will always regress all the way to the mean, regardless of how many plate appearances one has.

You may be wondering why we bother going through all of this work to calculate how much something needs to be regressed. After all, why not just use year-to-year correlations to estimate all of this? The answer is that some skills are too small to be measured using year-to-year correlations; solving things the hard way is a lot more work but provides a more precise result (i.e., one with smaller uncertainties). A good illustration comes from our platooning study, where we measured a platoon skill variation of .014±.002 for right-handed hitters. Using the equation above to calculate the regression amount, we find that to estimate a player's platoon split, one would use:

$$\text{skill} = \overline{\text{split}} + \frac{N_{e\!f\!f}}{N_{e\!f\!f} + (1130 \pm 360)}(\text{split} - \overline{\text{split}}),$$

where $N_{e\!f\!f}$ is the effective number of plate appearances, and is defined as

$$\frac{1}{N_{e\!f\!f}} = \frac{1}{N_{\text{LHP}}} + \frac{1}{N_{\text{RHP}}}.$$

For a typical player-season in our 2000–2004 data, a player will have 350 appearances against righties and 150 against lefties, giving an $N_{e\!f\!f}$=105, and a regression equation of:

$$\overline{\text{skill}} = \overline{\text{split}} + \frac{105}{1235 \pm 360}(\text{split} - \overline{\text{split}})$$
$$= \overline{\text{split}} + (.085 \pm .025)(\text{split} - \overline{\text{split}})\ .$$

In plain English, the typical full-time player will retain 8.5±2.5% of his platoon split (relative to league-average) once regressed, which means that we expect a correlation slope of .085±.025 between platoon splits in consecutive seasons.

Now, trying to calculate the correlation from direct observations, we consider consecutive seasons in which a right-handed batter had at least 300 appearances against righties and 100 against lefties. Using the 2000–2004 data, 321 such pairs of seasons exist, and the slope of the measured correlation equals .034±.056—consistent (within the uncertainties) with our more complicated measurement but also consistent with zero correlation.

Clearly the "hard" way is the superior approach, as it provides smaller uncertainties and thus allows us to search for smaller effects.

One important caveat, however, is that the population variation we are measuring this way includes *everything* that is different. For example, in measuring variations in hitters' OBP skills, we are including variations in ballpark effects, average quality of opposing pitchers, usage in platoon situations, and so on. In other words, rather than the measured variance equaling the population variance plus the random variance, the measured variance equals the population variance plus the random variance plus the variance from pitcher quality plus the variance from ballparks, etc. Thus, if we are attempting to measure one specific effect, such as platoon ratios for right-handed hitters, it is critical to restrict the data sample such that the only difference between the two samples (OBP vs. LHP and OBP vs. RHP) is the handedness of the opposing pitcher.

INDEX

THE AUTHORS

Tom Tango runs the Tango on Baseball website and has consulted for major league baseball teams. He lives in New Jersey.

Mitchel Lichtman has been doing sabermetric research for over seventeen years and was the senior analyst for a major league baseball team. He lives in New York.

Andrew Dolphin has been working on sports statistics for over ten years; some of his work is posted on the Dolphin computer rankings website and he works as a consultant for a major league baseball team. He has a B.S. from Harvey Mudd College and a Ph.D. from the University of Washington. He lives in Tucson, Arizona.